Designing Systems
for
Internet Commerce
Second Edition

Designing Systems
for
Internet Commerce
Second Edition

G. Winfield Treese
Lawrence C. Stewart

✦✦ Addison-Wesley

Boston • San Francisco • New York • Toronto • Montreal
London • Munich • Paris • Madrid
Capetown • Sydney • Tokyo • Singapore • Mexico City

The publisher offers discounts on this book when ordered in quantity for bulk purchases and special sales. For more information, please contact:

> U.S. Corporate and Government Sales
> (800) 382-3419
> corpsales@pearsontechgroup.com

For sales outside of the U.S., please contact:

> International Sales
> (317) 581-3793
> international@pearsontechgroup.com

Visit Addison-Wesley on the Web: www.awprofessional.com

Library of Congress Cataloging-in-Publication Data

Treese, G. Winfield.
   Designing systems for Internet commerce / G. Winfield Treese, Lawrence C. Stewart.—
  2nd ed.
    p. cm.
  Includes bibliographical references and index.
  ISBN 0-201-76035-5 (pbk. : alk. paper)
   1. System design. 2. Electronic commerce. I. Stewart, Lawrence C. II. Title.

QA76.9.S88 T74 2003
658.8'00285'4678—dc21

200074788

ISBN: 0-201-76035-5
Text printed on recycled paper
1 2 3 4 5 6 7 8 9 10—CRS—0605040302
First printing, September 2002

For Nina and Alexander

Contents

Part Two   The Technology of Internet Commerce

CHAPTER 8   *The Internet and the World Wide Web*   123

CHAPTER 9   *Building Blocks for Internet Commerce*   141

Preface

In 1994, _The Economist_ ranked the Internet between the telephone and the printing press in its long-term impact on the world. Just as those inventions transformed society, so the Internet has already begun a transformation—one that is happening much faster than the earlier revolutions. Commerce, of course, is one arena already feeling the effects of the Internet. In the past few years, we have seen dramatic changes in some businesses, the creation of new businesses, and significant effects on others.

When the first edition of this book was published in 1998, Internet commerce was still a relatively new idea and was not yet part of the mainstream thinking of businesses around the world. Today, that situation has clearly changed. Many companies now have long experience with Internet commerce, and some sellers, such as Amazon.com, have become household names. Indeed, since 1998 we have seen an enormous rise and fall of Internet commerce excitement, as the so-called dot-com companies have grabbed investment and attention but precious little revenue. Many people have concluded that Internet commerce was simply a quickly passing fad, all hype and no reality.

We think that the opposite is true. The Internet continues to revolutionize business in many ways, and one of those ways—which is the focus of this book—is the selling of goods and services directly to buyers over the Internet. The truth today is that many companies are doing it, and doing it profitably. This book is about creating the kinds of computer systems that can be used for that kind of business.

So what went wrong with the dot-coms? It is easy to find many problems, including some that seem laughably obvious in hindsight. A common and fundamental problem, however, was that the companies failed to focus on the use of Internet technology to deliver value to customers. What we attempt to do in this book is to explore precisely how to do that. The business strategy is, of course, a critical aspect of success in Internet commerce. Sometimes that strategy is essentially a traditional one that can now take advantage of the Internet as a new channel, whereas at other times the technology provides entirely new ways of bringing value to customers. We explore both of these paths.

In a sense, Internet commerce is no longer a cutting-edge idea. Rather, it has become one of the standard ways of doing business, even if not quite everyone is doing it yet. Such a shift in business practice has many implications, and one of the most important is that the computer systems have to get it right. In the early days of Internet commerce, losing an order wasn't a fatal mistake. The systems were not always robust. That situation has clearly changed. Today's customers have much higher standards and expectations, and they can easily find a competitor who can do a better job if one company fails to satisfy them. Sadly, many companies have not yet learned this lesson. As we were writing the last few pages of the manuscript for this book, there were reports of a well-known merchant system that allowed customers to change the prices at will. Such problems today are not just curiosities; they are significant risks to a company's continuing business.

The audience for this book is what we call the *Internet commerce team*. This team includes people responsible for business and those responsible for technology. It includes those who develop the strategic vision for a company and those who put the strategy into action. In other words, the Internet commerce team is the group of people who work to make Internet commerce happen, from vision to implementation.

Throughout the book, we emphasize both *practice* and *principles*—the what and the why. Practices are the actions—the specific ideas for specific circumstances. Principles are the general rules—the elements on which practices are built. As technology changes (or, for that matter, as business models change), the practices will need to change. The principles, in contrast, change more slowly and can be applied in a wide variety of circumstances. When a team understands the principles underlying what they do, they can adapt to changing circumstances and develop new practices. Without that understanding, they can become incapacitated when the situation changes and different practices are required.

What the technology brings is a combination of new opportunities, changing cost structures, new customers, and shorter response times. The technological opportunities must be combined with and tempered by the business goals. This book is about that combination—designing computer systems for doing business on open networks.

When we say this book is about design, we mean that it is intended to help with the design process. It doesn't give all the answers; the actual design for your business requirements is likely to be very different from someone else's. Nonetheless, we can explore some of the common issues and critical questions to ask when planning any system for Internet commerce. In the process, we look at some of the key technologies of today and apply those technologies in several examples.

A word of warning: at times it may seem that we are overly concerned with potential problems—the things that can go wrong. These are not reasons to avoid Internet commerce. Rather, we think it is important to approach Internet commerce as you would any other business proposition, understanding the downside as well as the upside, the risks as well as the benefits. On balance, using the Internet for commerce can be a tremendous asset for businesses. Doing everything possible to maximize the chances for success is merely good business.

We have created a Web site for this book at http://www.serissa.com/Commerce/.

Changes in the Second Edition

Most of the changes in this edition reflect one of two things: first, the experience that has been gained with Internet commerce systems over the past four years, and second, some new technologies that have emerged during that period. The new technologies include widespread use of XML, the growing use of Web services, evolution in content management systems, the importance of integration with other enterprise information systems, and the growth of mobile and wireless systems.

Some things have not changed. As before, our focus remains primarily on the use of the available technology to deliver value to customers and on the importance of system architecture in achieving that end. We hope this will help you create Internet commerce systems that will result in successful businesses.

We wrote the first edition of this book while employed at Open Market, Inc., where we began developing systems for Internet commerce in 1994. Open Market was acquired by divine, Inc., in October 2001. Although many of Open Market's Internet commerce products are no longer available, we have continued to use some of the architectural approaches developed there as useful examples in this edition.

Acknowledgments

This book is an attempt to write down what we have learned about Internet commerce so far. Much of our experience in this area is drawn from our associations with Open Market and Serissa Research, but we have applied many of the lessons learned about the Internet and about systems design during our earlier careers at Xerox, Digital Equipment, and MIT, as well as from our academic associations with MIT, Harvard, and Stanford University.

We are indebted to our colleagues at the former Open Market for their work in building real systems for Internet commerce. We especially thank Shikhar Ghosh for his thoughts on Internet business strategy. We learned much from Open Market's customers as well.

The editorial team at Addison-Wesley has been outstanding, with our editor Karen Gettman, assistant editor Emily Frey, production coordinator Genevieve Rajewski, copy editor Craig Kirkpatrick, proofreader Marcy Lischke, and the editor who inspired this work, Carol Long. We would also like to thank Mary Hart and Jacquelyn Doucette again for their help with the first edition.

We have been fortunate to have many insightful reviewers for this edition. Our thanks to Paul Baier, Mike Carifio, Gary Eichhorn, Sigmund Handelman, Keith Lietzke, Russell Nelson, and the anonymous reviewers. The first edition benefited from review by Russell Nelson, Nathaniel Borenstein, Marcus Ranum, Richard Smith, Dave Crocker, Brian Reistad, Ray Kaplan, Bruce Schneier, John Adams, John Romkey, Fred Avolio, Kurt Friedrich, Alex Mehlman, Paul Baier, Ian Reid, Jeff Bussgang, and Kevin Kuechler.

We would also like to thank Professor Lee McKnight and the faculty, staff, and students of the Edward R. Murrow Center in the Fletcher School of Law and Diplomacy at Tufts University for providing Win Treese with a congenial environment for writing as well as many helpful discussions.

Writing a book is a challenge not only for the authors, but for their families as well. We thank our wives, Marie Briasco and Cathy Briasco, and our children for their patience and understanding while we disappeared to "work on the book."

Win Treese
Wayland, Massachusetts
treese@serissa.com

Larry Stewart
Wayland, Massachusetts
stewart@serissa.com

CHAPTER 1

Introduction

For I dipped into the future, far as human eye could see,
Saw the Vision of the world, and all the wonders that would be;
Saw the heavens fill with commerce, argosies of magic sails,
Pilots of the purple twilight dropping down with costly bales;

—Alfred, Lord Tennyson[1]

Internet commerce has become the new frontier for businesses around the world. Although what is now the Internet began more than 30 years ago, only in the past few years have we seen significant use of the Internet for commerce. The explosive growth of the Internet has been accompanied by claims of business revolution, ways to "make money fast working out of your home," and even the end of the nation-state. In the late 1990s, many overhyped startups spent huge amounts of venture capital, promised to change the rules of their industries, and then went bankrupt on failed business models.

Despite the collapse of many so-called dot-com companies, we believe that the convergence of the global Internet with commerce will fundamentally change the way business is done. This book is about how to create the systems that will make Internet commerce successful. Internet commerce brings new technologies and new capabilities to business, but the fundamental business problems are those that merchants have faced for hundreds or even thousands of years: you must have something to sell, make

---

1. Alfred, Lord Tennyson, *Locksley Hall* (1842).

it known to potential buyers, accept payment, deliver the goods or services, and provide appropriate service after the sale. Most of the time, you want to build a relationship with the customer that will bring repeat business.

Why the Internet and Why Now?

In the short term, there are two reasons for a company to get involved in Internet commerce.[2]

1. The top line: the ability to reach new customers and create more intimate relationships with all customers

   On the Internet, every business has a global presence. Even small and medium-sized companies can now easily reach customers around the world. The technology of computing and communications enables a business to know more about its customers, share more of its information with customers, and apply that information to improving relationships and creating sales.

2. The bottom line: dramatic cost reductions for distribution and customer service

   The Internet dramatically lowers the distribution costs for information and dramatically improves the ability to keep information current. Today's customers are demanding more information about the products and services they purchase, and the ability to deliver that information (and do it cheaply) becomes an important part of making the sale. Furthermore, on the Internet, information may *be* the product.

Over the long term, the Internet may well change the structure of the competitive landscape. Instant communications has already started to transform the relationship between businesses and their customers, and the conversion from physical to digital will change the sources of business value. In many cases we are still learning the nature of these changes. For example, will the network lead to great consolidation of suppliers or to a flowering of thousands of small merchants, each newly capable of global distribution? There are powerful arguments for both scenarios, and the past few years have seen successful examples of both. Even more fundamentally, businesses will face competition from companies that started in completely different industries, requiring fundamental reassessment of their value propositions for the customer.

These considerations follow almost naturally from the technical and economic nature of the Internet. Following are some of the key properties of the Internet.

- The Internet is interoperable.

  Almost by definition, a computer is connected to the Internet if it can communicate with any other computer connected to the Internet. There are two factors that make this possible: the use of standard protocols and the availability of universal

---

2. An alternative view is that the two reasons for a company to get involved in Internet commerce are the same as those for many areas of business: fear and greed.

naming, addressing, and routing. The standards of the Internet make this communication possible, without requiring prearranged agreements about how computers will communicate.

- The Internet is global.

Because the Internet structure is based on standardized and universal connectivity, it has rapidly become a global network. Because the network itself is used to distribute software, there is a readily available worldwide base of users with a common set of software, forming a foundation for business systems with a broad base of potential users.

- The Web makes it easy.

The World Wide Web[3] has made highly functional multimedia content easily available to users worldwide. People with little or no computer experience can get connected to the Internet and use Web browsers very successfully.

- The costs of the network are shared across multiple applications and borne by the end users.

Most businesses and consumers connected to the Internet pay for their own connections, and they are then free to use the network for any number of purposes. In consequence, a provider of information does not need to pay for a distribution system, other than its own connection to the network. The users of the service pay for the distribution. Because the network is shared among many users, the cost of this essential infrastructure is amortized across a wide variety of applications.

Access to a Global Market

Globalization is a common word these days, as advances in communication and transportation make it possible for businesses to operate worldwide. Suppliers and customers may be located anywhere. In many cases, countries are lowering or removing barriers to trade, encouraging more and more international commerce.

The Internet is accelerating this trend. By providing worldwide, high-bandwidth communications, the Internet makes it possible to work more effectively with customers, partners, and suppliers around the world—but it does more than that. Because the cost of the communication is essentially the same whether the parties are down the street or halfway around the world, the Internet makes such collaboration and commerce much more efficient.

In effect, everyone on the Internet can have a global presence. More to the point, everyone on the Internet actually does have a global presence, whether he or she thinks

---

3. Like many technologies, the Internet comes in layers. The base layer of the Internet includes the fundamental naming, addressing, routing, and communications machinery. Above that, the World Wide Web is a particular, extremely popular application that uses the Internet for communications. In turn, business applications can run layered on top of Web technologies. We explore the details more fully in Chapter 8.

of it that way or not. Anyone on the Internet can view your Web page, for example, and you don't have to do anything special to enable him or her to do so.

This is not to say that the Internet makes international trade easy. As we shall see, there are still issues of language, payment, currencies, taxation, and shipping, as well as differing national, regional, and local regulations. For many businesses, however, the experience may well be like those of any number of small bookstores who put up Web sites and suddenly received orders from Indonesia or Nepal. That the Internet is already making the world smaller is not an overstatement—it's the daily experience of millions of Internet users.

Dramatic Reduction in Distribution Costs

In the United States, sending a printed brochure or catalog in bulk through the postal service can cost several dollars for each recipient. Sending the equivalent in electronic mail, or simply providing the same *brochureware* on a Web site, requires some up-front investment to be on the network, but the per-recipient cost is nearly zero.

One of the most intriguing possibilities of the low distribution costs is the ability to provide even more information at lower cost and to have that information be always accurate, up-to-date, and searchable. Customers of all kinds are demanding more, and more accurate, information about what they buy. Electronics engineers are interested in detailed specifications, sample schematics, and design notes for components that they might use for a new product. Consumers want to know how the product works, how it compares with others, even its environmental impact. The low cost of providing such information over the Internet makes it possible to do so: any other way would be prohibitively expensive.

Of course, the same ideas hold for selling information products online. These "digital goods" can be delivered over the network cheaply and efficiently. For some products, this can mean eliminating expensive packaging, such as CD-ROMs and packing materials. For others, it is a new distribution channel that complements those already in place. The cost, low to begin with, is the same for customers all over the world.

Strategic Issues

We believe the advent of the Internet brings with it two strategic issues: concentration versus empowerment, and new competitive challenges.

Concentration Versus Empowerment

The Internet permits direct access from creators of value to consumers and greatly reduces the costs associated with distribution. This could lead to a great concentration of suppliers or to the opposite—the creation of tens of thousands of small and medium sized suppliers to global niche markets. It seems likely that both will happen. On the one hand, there may be a handful of music supersites combining excellent prices, great customer service, and worldwide distribution, but there won't be hundreds. On the other hand, easy access to a global community can enable marginal niche markets to reach a critical size capable of supporting a profitable business. For example, an electronic store serving the global market for antique buggy whips could be a viable business.

New Competitive Challenges

The Internet short-circuits traditional distribution chains in a way that can change the nature of competition. The most obvious are changes in geography and cost structure. Because it is not necessary to create an expensive distribution channel to enter a new territory, the Internet can bring formerly disjoint enterprises into direct competition. For the consumer, these lowered barriers of entry can create advantages, but for the producer, costs and efficiencies must become competitive worldwide.

More interesting things start to happen when previously separate industries begin to compete. Consider the example of selling financial instruments. Traditionally, banks and brokerages have provided trading services, whereas publishers have provided comparative information. On the Internet, these lines become blurred and may disappear entirely. Because content can be linked directly to transactions, a user who links to a financial information site could place an order on the spot. Is the publisher in the trading business, or is the brokerage now a publisher? Sometimes the situation defies analysis, but thinking through who owns the customer relationship is a good place to start. As always, keep a very clear view of the value provided by your business to your customers.

What Do We Mean by "Internet Commerce"?

So far, we have used the term *Internet commerce* generally, without being specific about what it means. Because it means different things to different people, we want to be precise about what it means in this book. By *Internet commerce*, we mean the use of the global Internet for purchase and sale of goods and services, including service and support after the sale. The Internet may be an efficient mechanism for advertising and distributing product information (sometimes called *brochureware* in the trade), but our focus is on enabling complete business transactions.

Other Types of Electronic Commerce

Internet commerce is but one type of the more general electronic commerce. Electronic commerce has a much longer history, although much of it was behind the scenes, typically linking suppliers to large manufacturers or service organizations.

Speaking broadly, electronic commerce includes the use of computing and communication technologies in the financial business, online airline reservation systems, order processing, inventory management, and so on.

Historically speaking, the best-known idea in electronic commerce has been Electronic Data Interchange (EDI). Originally created for linking together the participants in the transportation industry, EDI has become a common tool for many organizations working with their suppliers and partners. *EDI* is really an umbrella term for many different kinds of activities, each specialized for a particular trading relationship. Creating an EDI relationship is often a long process, requiring detailed negotiation over message types and data formats (unless, of course, one party is powerful enough to dictate the terms to the other). EDI has been tremendously useful for many organizations that have created EDI systems and that could afford to invest in them.

It is worth noting that EDI and the Internet do not exclude one another. Indeed, EDI, which specifies certain kinds of messages, can be used with the Internet, which is a way of moving data. Many companies are already using the Internet as the communications substrate for EDI applications, and there are specialized products on the market for creating EDI-Internet applications.

Internet commerce, in contrast, transcends many of the restrictions of EDI. Companies can communicate over a shared public network, rather than building specialized networks or contracting for expensive Value-Added Network (VAN) services. EDI formats themselves are being replaced by Extensible Markup Language (XML) formats that are more general, more extensible, and easier to use. More importantly, the Web allows spontaneous business transactions between buyers and sellers with no prior relationships. That first step may be the beginning of a long-term relationship, and in some cases it will make sense for the trading partners to negotiate specialized messages, EDI or otherwise, to enable them to work together more effectively.

Business Issues in Internet Commerce

First and foremost, Internet commerce is about business: using the network effectively to achieve business goals. Current technology, including changes in both computing and communication, provides many tools that can be used in reaching those goals. If we do not have a clear idea of our business goals in using the network, then technology cannot help us achieve them.

This is not to say that business goals cannot be changed to take advantage of current technology. Often the technology allows new kinds of operations that were previously too expensive. It is entirely appropriate, for example, to choose a new focus on closer customer relationships using the Internet to communicate with customers. Without the network, such a goal might have been too expensive or difficult to achieve. The Internet might enable a company to achieve that goal in a way that it could not have achieved it before. However, the business goal, including how to measure success, is the key, not just an idea such as, "Hey, we could send e-mail to our customers!" Indeed, a common problem with simplistic ideas such as this has been "What happens when they send back?"

Business issues for Internet commerce cross the entire range of business activities, from attracting customers to fulfilling their orders, and from sales to accounting. They include questions that businesses ask about any new idea.

- How does it fit with our strategy? Should we change our strategy?
- What does this mean to our competitive situation?
- Do we expect return in the short term, or is this a long-term investment?
- How much will it cost? What do we expect to accomplish?
- How will we measure the success?
- How does this affect our sales channels, our partners, our suppliers?

Every company has many other questions used in evaluating new activities, and the Internet should not be exempted from such thinking.

One thing to watch for in Internet commerce is that although the costs of getting started may seem very low, a project may grow to significant size over time. There is always something new to add—some new technology twist to throw in or a seemingly small extension to a Web site to incorporate. Setting up a Web site used to seem easy: a few HTML pages, hosting on a local Internet service provider (ISP), and maybe handling of some electronic mail. Contrast such a system with one that allows real-time catalog updates, keeps and uses customer profiles, takes payment in various ways, links to inventory and fulfillment systems, and provides customer support. One approach is to allow such functions to accrete willy-nilly onto an initial Web site over time; a second approach is to plan an evolving site, learning from each step and modifying the plan as appropriate. Although a company might succeed with the first approach, it probably will not have an accurate idea of what it cost, and it may not have any way to figure out whether or not it has succeeded. The second approach may not provide the instant gratification of getting a Web site running as soon as possible (although delivering a site quickly might be a goal of the more careful process), but it does allow a company to focus on what it is doing and what it is getting for its investment. We don't recommend a third alternative of designing and building the perfect system all at once. That takes a long time, and whatever is done will need to be changed as circumstances and technologies change, as they inevitably will.

In large part, this book is about the issues involved in following the second approach (that is, the evolving Web site). Different companies will, of course, have different business issues and goals. In this book, we have set out to explore many that are common across businesses. Even when the issues are not directly on target for a particular business, we hope they will inspire other questions that are, leading to a successful plan for Internet commerce.

Technology Issues in Internet Commerce

Technology is, of course, what makes Internet commerce possible. The invention and subsequent spread of the World Wide Web, in particular, provided the technical foundation for many different applications, including those for business. Since its introduction, the Web has changed rapidly, with both rapid growth in usage and dramatic evolution in protocols, systems, and applications. For commerce systems, there are two key technology issues: which technology to use, and how to deal with the fast pace of technological change.

This book is mostly about the first issue: how to apply Internet technology to business problems. Commerce applications bring together many technology components: the Web, databases, high-speed networking, cryptographic algorithms, multimedia, and others. Putting them together to form a secure, high-performance, integrated system can be challenging, but the principles and ideas presented here should provide some useful guidance. The earliest Internet commerce systems were custom software. Over the past few years, it has become possible to assemble a commerce system by using toolkits to integrate software modules and applications from different suppliers. Mature packaged application software for Internet commerce is available as well, in which a complete or nearly complete system is available from a single supplier, perhaps needing integration only to connect it to existing business systems.

The second technology issue, the pace of change, is a fact of life on the Internet today, and there is no end in sight. To be successful, therefore, any commerce system must be prepared to accommodate and incorporate new technologies as they become available. The key to such adaptability is a coherent system architecture that lays out what is to be accomplished and why. By focusing on the ends and the fundamental principles, we can adopt new technologies that help us achieve those ends, while avoiding new technologies that may seem exciting but in reality do not fit in with our goals or the system. The rise of toolkits, modules, and application software help a great deal in coping with technological change, because the costs of adapting and using new technologies can be amortized over many customers.

Who Owns Internet Commerce in an Organization?

Who owns Internet commerce in an organization? Who operates the system? Is it sales and marketing, or the information technology (IT) group, or, if transactions are involved, the accounts receivable department? At first glance, this may seem an odd question to ask, especially because for any particular group the answer may appear obvious. In fact, the experiences of many companies suggest that a clear understanding of the answer is a critical factor in success. The problem is that it is far too easy to have more than one group think that it is driving Internet commerce for an organization, leading to confusion within the organization, as well as for customers. To compound the problem, fragmented attempts at Internet commerce will often result in money being spent on the same or similar basics: hardware, core software components, network connections, and so on. Such fragmentation can also confuse customers, who tend to think of a company as a single coherent entity, not a collection of divisions or business units that reflect internal organization.

In reality, successful Internet commerce is almost always a combined effort, drawing on the strengths of many different groups within a company: sales and marketing for effectively presenting products or services on the Net, IT for operating or outsourcing the round-the-clock commerce systems, links to the accounting systems for transactions, and so on. In the past, many companies have begun their Internet presence as a fringe operation—often appropriately so, thereby avoiding the slowness and stodginess of a corporate bureaucracy. Today, however, using the Internet is not a luxury or an experiment for most businesses. Effective Internet commerce is an extension of a company's business, and so should draw on the resources of the company. Internal bickering over ownership can easily lead a project (or projects) to failure, leaving a company unable to move quickly enough to adapt to the rapid pace of change in commerce applications. In our experience, successful Internet commerce demands the attention of senior management.

Structure of the Book

This book is divided into three parts. In the first part, we analyze the business requirements for Internet commerce and identify several fundamental design issues for commerce systems in business-to-business applications, retail, and the information industry. In the second part, we describe some of the fundamental technologies used for Internet commerce. We pay special attention to Internet and Web technologies, system design, cryptography and security, payment systems, and transaction processing. Finally, in the third part, we "put it all together" into hypothetical examples that show a complete system, and conclude with an assessment of the challenges ahead.

Part One: The Business of Internet Commerce

Chapter 2 examines the commerce value chain. Part of the design of any business system is to develop a clear and accurate view of all the elements necessary for the system to be successful. An engine does not make an automobile, and an entire car is useless without roads, gas stations, and passengers. The commerce value chain helps us identify all the elements necessary for success.

Chapter 3 is devoted to Internet business strategy. The degree of change that the Internet makes in the economic landscape has not been seen since the development of the railroads 150 years ago. The consequent changes in economies of scale and scope require new strategic thinking.

In Chapter 4, we introduce business requirements and issues for Internet commerce systems by looking at examples aimed at consumer retail, business-to-business cataloging, and the publishing and sale of information goods. A successful commerce system requires alignment among many constituencies, including consumers, merchants, financial processors, governments, and technologists. These groups have different priorities, and social, legal, and technological constraints can affect the viability of the business. Chapter 5 examines some of these issues in the context of Internet commerce. Many of the difficulties and problems with Internet commerce arise when these different groups are (or appear to be) in conflict. Successful businesses must navigate these shoals in working effectively with customers, partners, and suppliers.

In Chapter 6, we discuss the components and roles of, and architectural approaches to, Internet commerce, and we introduce the concept of decomposition of functions and the notion of trust models. Approaching the design of a system using a high-level architecture can allow the creation of a system that evolves and adapts over the long term as technologies and business requirements change.

There are many ways to design, develop, install, and operate information technology systems, from in-house development to packaged software operated by a service bureau. Chapter 7 addresses the planning and project management issues that go far beyond the features and functionality of software.

Part Two: The Technology of Internet Commerce

The second part of the book focuses on technology issues, with an eye toward understanding the key ideas underlying the technology.

As an introduction, Chapter 8 surveys the technological underpinnings of the Internet and the World Wide Web. In Chapter 9, we go beyond the basics to look at how the technology can be applied to systems for Internet commerce.

In Chapter 10, we discuss a philosophy of design, architectural principles, and the making of design decisions. These decisions are often independent of implementation technology, which enables an implementation to swap in new technological components as they are developed.

The Extensible Markup Language (XML) was just emerging when the first edition of this book was published. Chapter 11 examines XML in detail, and discusses how XML can be used in many different ways for e-commerce systems. In particular, XML is a core technology of the emerging area of Web services.

Chapter 12 discusses the creation and management of content for Internet commerce. Loosely speaking, content is whatever people look at, or listen to, on the Net, including documents, video, music, and so on. We survey the means of creation, management, and commerce-enabling of content.

One of the biggest issues for Internet commerce systems is security. Modern cryptography is the foundation of security systems for commerce, and Chapter 13 provides a quick overview of the field. Simply using cryptography (in some unspecified way) rarely creates a secure system, so we discuss how to think about the use of cryptography in applications. In Chapter 14, we go beyond the foundation of cryptography to the design of secure systems. We advocate a systemic design approach to the security of Internet commerce systems. Proper use of cryptography is a key factor, but careful design of security policies, mechanisms, characteristics of the application, and containment procedures all play important roles.

Payment systems have often been touted as the core of Internet commerce systems, and they clearly play an important role. In Chapter 15, we discuss a variety of payment systems and their application to Internet commerce. Beyond the technical aspects of payment systems, we discuss their trust models and cost structures.

In the early days of Internet commerce, shopping carts were relatively simple. This is no longer the case, and we examine shopping carts and order management in detail in Chapter 16.

Commerce is an exchange of goods for value received. Transaction processing is the part of the system that ensures that a business transaction is completed once the parties agree to it. In computer systems, especially those distributed across a network, this is often not as easy as it seems, especially when something goes wrong. Chapter 17 introduces this complex topic, including a discussion of issues such as scaling, performance, reliability, and business record keeping.

Enterprises require complete business solutions, and Chapter 18 examines the challenges of integrating Internet commerce systems with other enterprise computer systems. It also details some of the auxiliary systems necessary for dealing with taxes, shipping, and inventory.

As Internet commerce has grown in importance, so has the importance of building systems for high performance and high reliability. In Chapter 19, we look at some of the architectural approaches for building large-scale e-commerce systems.

The final chapter on Internet commerce technology, Chapter 20, looks at the emerging area of mobile and wireless systems and the role they play in e-commerce systems.

Part Three: Systems for Internet Commerce

Now that we have created a plan and surveyed available technology components, how can we assemble a working system? Chapter 21 describes hypothetical examples of comprehensive systems for Internet commerce, tying together many of the technologies and design issues explored in the previous chapters. The examples cover business-to-business, business-to-consumer, and information commerce systems.

Over time, Internet commerce will change rapidly. Once your system is up and running, how do you keep up-to-date in this rapidly changing world? We discuss how to stay on track when buffeted by the evolution of technology, and Chapter 22 lays out some paths for the future.

Part One

The Business of Internet Commerce

CHAPTER 2

The Commerce Value Chain

He chose to include the things
That in each other are included, the whole,
The complicate, the amassing harmony.
—Wallace Stevens[1]

Introducing the Commerce Value Chain

When a consumer buys a manufactured item in a store, it is merely one step in a complex process that began with the raw materials used in creating the item. At each step in that process, something of value was added. That value might have been refining the raw materials, molding them into a useful shape, transporting them for further processing, or selling the item to the final consumer. We sometimes refer to this as the *value chain* for a product—the chain of adding value in creating and delivering a product.

Even though this idea of a value chain is most clearly exemplified by a manufactured product, we can use it to describe many kinds of business activities, including more focused components of the very broad chain just described. For example, we can look at the value chain of a retail store, which includes selecting products that will be sold, purchasing them from a wholesaler or manufacturer, arranging attractive displays, advertising to attract customers, assisting customers with their selections, taking payments for the products, and delivering the products to customers. Each of these links

---

1. Wallace Stevens, "It Must Give Pleasure," *Notes Toward a Supreme Fiction* (1947).

in the chain is important to the business, and if any one of them breaks down, the entire business is affected.

Similarly, we can look at the development of a system for Internet commerce in terms of the value chain needed by the business. In part, the value chain will be related to that of the underlying business (for example, selling books). Another part comes from looking at the value chain required by doing business online. Understanding these two pieces and how they fit together is an important part of creating a successful business in Internet commerce. We will discuss the value chain from a third perspective—in terms of all the customer-facing activities of a business.

In this chapter, we look at a very general value chain for Internet commerce, as shown in Figure 2-1. This value chain is focused on the interactions of a business with its customers. The details will certainly be different for different businesses (and for some different business models), but we have found this general approach to be very effective in organizing an approach to business online. The components of this general value chain are as follows.

1. Attract customers.

   Marketing—get and keep customer interest.

2. Interact with customers.

   Sales—turn interest into orders (generally *content*).

3. Act on customer instructions.

   Order management—order capture, payment, fulfillment.

4. React to customer requests.

   Customer service, technical support.

We look at these components in more detail in the next section.

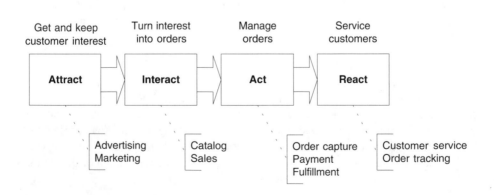

FIGURE 2-1. **The Commerce Value Chain**

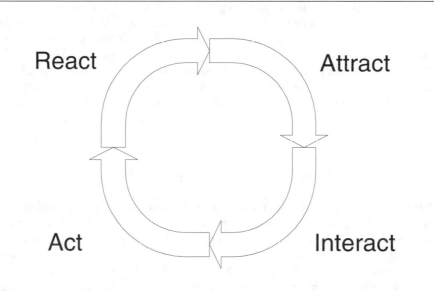

FIGURE 2-2. **The Commerce Value Cycle**

Another way to look at the value chain is as a cycle of continuing interactions with customers, as shown in Figure 2-2. After the current transaction is completed, there is an opportunity for repeat business, and the business should take advantage of all it has learned through the cycle. We look at some ways to analyze and profit from such information in Chapter 6.

Looking at the value chain for a business helps to define areas of focus—what the business is best at, or where the most emphasis should be placed. Even in businesses that may appear to be very similar, differences in emphasis can have major effects, both for Internet commerce and for more traditional forms.

For example, consider two bookstores: one that emphasizes large selection and one that emphasizes personal service. In the physical world, such a difference is reflected in many decisions, such as where to locate the store, the size of the store, the kinds of employees who should be hired, and the kinds of computer systems needed to support the business. Similarly, on the Internet such bookstores would develop their businesses quite differently. A focus on large selection might require a comprehensive database and tools for searching for books in different ways (by title, author, publisher, ISBN, and so on), whereas a focus on personalized service might result in forums for discussions among customers, interaction between customers and employees, and other kinds of services.

Thinking carefully about the value chain can help one select the most important ideas from a long list of possible activities in Internet commerce. The large bookstore, for example, may want to provide all of the services of the smaller one, but if it does not focus first on its core abilities—providing easy access to a large number of books—it is much less likely to succeed. When moving a business onto the Internet, it is tempting to try to do everything, because it seems easy, because competitors are doing it, or simply because it seems possible. Rather, it is important to use the Internet to reinforce the core strategy of the business. It is necessary to have an explicit strategy for each part of the value chain, not merely for those in which your business is differentiated. On the other hand, it is not necessary to do everything yourself. Many companies work with partners to fill out the value chain, so that each link is strong.

Components of the Commerce Value Chain

The key components of the value chain can be very different for different industries, and even among different businesses within a particular industry, such as in the following example. In this section, we look at a generic value chain for Internet commerce. In part, it serves as an example of how one might break down a value chain to analyze it more closely, and in part it exemplifies some of the most important components for business on the Internet. Throughout this section, we use catalogs for consumer retail purchases as examples. In the next chapter, we look at several different kinds of businesses and how the commerce value chain applies to them.

Attract Customers

The first component of the generic Internet commerce value chain is *attract*. By this we mean whatever steps are taken to draw customers into the primary site, whether by paid advertising on other Web sites, electronic mail, television, print, or other forms of advertising and marketing. The point of this phase is to make an impression on customers and draw them into the detailed catalog or other information about products and services for sale.[2]

Interact with Customers

The second component is *interact*. By this we mean turning customer interest into orders. This phase is generally content-oriented and includes the catalog, publications, or other information available to the customer over the Internet. The content may be distributed by many different mechanisms, such as the World Wide Web or electronic mail. In some cases, there may be links between Internet commerce and content distributed by other media, such as CD-ROMs.

Editorially, content may change infrequently or frequently. Technically, content may be *static* or *dynamic*. Static content typically consists of prepared pages, such as those

---

2. With the advent of active advertisements with built-in transactional capability, the lines between the phases of the value chain are becoming blurred.

from a catalog, that are sent to a client on request. These pages must be re-created whenever the information on them changes. Dynamic content, on the other hand, is generated at the time of the request, drawing on one or more information sources to produce an appropriate page of information for the client. Some sources of information for dynamic content include databases, such as a parts database with pricing information; the capabilities of client software, such as the graphic formats that can be used; or even who the clients are or what organizations they represent. Dynamic content is often used when the editorial content changes frequently, or when the natural storage medium for the information is a database, or when the information is used for multiple purposes.

We discuss the creation and presentation of content in more detail in Chapter 12.

Act on Customer Instructions

The next component in the commerce value chain is *act*. Once a buyer has searched through a catalog and wants to make a purchase, there must be ways to capture the order, to process payment, to handle fulfillment, and to perform other aspects of order management.

Order Processing

Often a buyer wants to purchase several items at the same time, so order processing must include the ability to group items together for later purchase. This capability, sometimes called a *shopping cart* in the case of retail transactions, usually includes the ability to modify the contents of the shopping cart at any time. Thus, the buyer is able to discard items, add new ones, change the quantities, and so on. When the buyer is ready to complete the purchase, it is often necessary to compute additional charges, such as sales tax and shipping costs. The order processing system then presents the buyer with an itemized order form, including all charges, so the buyer can pay for the items.

Shopping carts and order management are discussed in more detail in Chapter 16.

Payment

Depending on the terms of the order, the buyer may pay for it (or provide payment instructions) as part of the order capture. Once an order is final, the buyer can pay for it. As in the real world, there may be many ways to pay for an item. Some of the methods may be online analogs of those found in the real world: credit cards, purchase orders, and so on. Other methods of payment may exist only for Internet commerce, using new technologies developed especially for a networked system. For example, in an online publishing system, it may be feasible to charge a small amount for a single magazine article, rather than requiring the customer to purchase the entire magazine.

The single most important property of an online payment system is that the seller can use it to collect payment from the buyer. That is, no matter which payment mechanisms each one may be capable of, there must be at least one on which they can agree. This property has several implications. First, the seller's system must be able to handle the kinds of payment that are important to the seller's business. For example, credit cards are commonly used for consumer retail transactions, but businesses often buy from each other using purchase orders. There may also be nontechnical constraints on which payment methods can be used. To accept credit cards, a merchant must have an account with an acquiring bank that handles the transactions. Without such an account, creating the technical infrastructure to allow for credit card payment is useless.

Second, the seller must be careful about imposing requirements on the buyer's system. If the buyer must have a particular software package to handle a particular kind of payment system, the universe of possible buyers is likely to be much smaller than it would be otherwise. In some cases, of course, all of the desired customers will have such software, or be willing to obtain it. Again, the key point is to keep the customer and the business in mind when selecting the technology.

Note also that completing this stage does not necessarily mean that funds have been transferred into the seller's bank account. Some payment instruments, including both credit cards and purchase orders, extend credit to the buyer, who will make the actual payment later. In such cases, it is common for the seller's system to authorize the transaction, whether by requesting such authorization from a third party (such as the bank that issued a credit card) or in accordance with its own internal rules (such as whether or not a purchase order relationship has been established). As we shall see later, final settlement of a transaction may not take place until the item has been shipped.

We discuss payment systems and how they can be used in Chapter 15.

Fulfillment

Once the order has been placed and the payment (or at least a satisfactory promise of payment) has been made, the next step is fulfilling the order. How this is done depends on the type of product or service being purchased. If the item ordered is a *physical good* (sometimes called a *hard good*) that will be delivered to the buyer, then the order is usually forwarded to a traditional order processing system, with the result that someone picks up the object, packs it, and ships it. In this case, the online commerce system must have a method for forwarding orders. This step could be as simple as printing out or faxing an order form for a person to handle, or it might use a more complicated interface, such as EDI, to another computer system. The precise mechanism, of course, depends on how orders are handled by the rest of the business.

A second kind of order is a request for a service to be performed in the real world. For example, one might order a singing telegram online. Although the fulfillment happens in the physical world, this is a service, not a physical good. For our purposes, however, we can think of services as being handled as though they were physical goods. The order is passed to a system or a person, who causes it to be fulfilled.

The third kind of order is closely tied to the Internet. We call this category *digital goods*.[3] Digital goods include a wide variety of online delivery, including software that is delivered online, news articles, reports, access to a database for a period of time, and so on. Delivering digital goods can be quite complex, as we shall see. We discuss the integration of systems for fulfillment of physical goods in Chapter 18 and fulfillment of digital goods under Information Commerce, which begins on page 61.

React to Customer Inquiries

Finally, after a sale has been completed, the customer may have some questions or difficulties that require service. Although many questions must be answered by a person, others can be answered with the appropriate information system. For example, a transaction system that keeps track of all of a customer's purchases can generate a statement summarizing them. Customers who are wondering whether or not their orders have been shipped might check back with the system. A more complicated example is how the system handles a failure when delivering a digital good.

Suppose that a customer buys a software package online. While the software is being downloaded to the customer's computer, an error in the network causes the download to fail. What can the customer do? Clearly the item should not be repurchased, so the customer needs some *proof of purchase*—such as a receipt—that the fulfillment server will accept in order to allow the customer to attempt another download.

Using people to answer customer service calls can be very expensive, so it is worth investing in systems that answer questions that do not require the capabilities of a person. As noted previously, these systems often provide routine (or even exceptional) information in response to simple queries. But at least as important is designing the system to remove the need for the customer to ask the question. In the preceding software example, the use of the receipt allows the customer to solve the problem easily, without having to call anyone for assistance.

Who Is the Customer?

One of the most important questions for any business is "Who is the customer?" This may seem to be an obvious question, but often businesses (or other organizations) do not have a clear understanding of the answer, and sometimes the answer is more subtle

---

3. Digital goods are sometimes called *soft goods* to differentiate them from *hard goods*. This can cause confusion with the traditional meaning of *soft goods* (apparel), so we prefer the term *digital goods*.

than it first appears. For example, consider a company that sells electronic components used in personal computers. In one sense, the customer is the organization that assembles the computers, which buys components in large quantities. It is the organization that places the orders, negotiates terms, takes delivery, and pays for the components. But perhaps a more important group of customers are the specifying engineers—the people who decide which parts go into the computers. Once that decision has been made, much of the rest follows more or less automatically, as long as a satisfactory contract can be negotiated, and as long as the supplier can provide the correct items on time and with good quality.

To sell effectively to these two types of customers, the company would probably adopt very different strategies. Similarly, in designing online commerce systems to work with these customers, the company would create very different systems. The specifying engineers, for example, must be able to find the parts they need in the catalog quickly. They must also have access to detailed information, specifications, and sample schematics illustrating how parts can be used, and a way to order sample parts for building prototypes.

Customers of the other kind—organizations that manufacture computers using the parts—have a very different set of problems to solve. They order parts in large quantities, and they need to ensure timely delivery and to arrange payment based on a complex contract. Although both kinds of customers can benefit from using the Internet, it would be impossible to create a successful system without understanding in detail who the customers are and what problems they have to solve.

Developing Customer Relationships with Internet Commerce

Good relationships with customers are often one sign of a successful business. Customers with good relationships tend to buy from the same vendors again and again, and it is almost always easier to keep a customer than to find a new one. As with the question "Who is the customer?" this may seem obvious, but it is frequently treated as a secondary concern. From the perspective of Internet commerce, we can look at two particular aspects of customer relationships: improving the existing service for customers and finding ways to apply new technologies to deliver better or different service.

One of the best ways to build strong relationships is through communication. Customers want to know where a vendor is going, what it can do, why there is a problem, whether or not there are problems on the horizon, and so on. They also want this communication to be efficient and to be focused on their interests. Any particular customer of AT&T, for example, is probably not interested in knowing about everything that AT&T does. Some customers are interested in how to lower their personal long-distance bills, whereas others want to know how to create a global telecommunications infrastructure.

The Internet enables vendors to communicate with customers in ways that are efficient for both parties. It is efficient for vendors because the incremental costs of communicating are small, and because the messages can be specific to individual customers or groups of customers. It is efficient for customers precisely because it can be focused directly on their needs and interests. Conversely, if the vendor does not make efficient use of the communication, customers may object and the relationship may be soured.

This communications capability can also be used to provide new services, particularly up-to-date status information about an order or service. For example, many logistics companies (such as Federal Express and United Parcel Service) have created ways to check on the status of a delivery. The Internet makes it possible to connect these companies with their customers more closely, thereby improving their customer relationships.

Marketing on the Internet

Many people are attracted to Internet commerce because the Internet offers a new way of marketing. Although this book is not about marketing on the Internet, this section describes a few of the relevant concepts and issues. Over the past few years, the hype about marketing on the Internet has swung between two extremes: the Internet is a completely new and different medium for marketing, or it's just another medium like print or television. Another aspect of marketing on the Internet is the combination of communications with other recent applications of technology to marketing, such as the use of very large databases with extensive information about demographics and transactions.

The Internet Is Different from Other Media

One of the most important properties of the Internet is that everyone can be a publisher, reaching the same worldwide audiences that giant media conglomerates reach. More than anything else, this property defines how the Internet is different from other media. The telephone allows one to call one person at a time, limiting (in time) the number of people one can reach. Using a telephone also requires both people to be available to talk at the same time. Traditional mass media, such as dnewspapers, dmagazines, and television, reach large audiences, but the ability to do so is limited, either by the availability of scarce resources such as available television channels, or simply by the investment required to create and distribute the medium.

These limitations do not apply to the Internet. For most communications, using tools such as electronic mail or the Web, the sender and receiver do not need to be present at the same time to communicate with each other (as long as their computers can do so, of course). On the Internet, there is very little that distinguishes the computer system of a single person from the many systems of a large corporation. There may be differences in available bandwidth and server capacity, but not in the possibility of reaching a large audience.

What are the implications of these differences? One is obvious: small merchants can reach customers on the Internet very effectively. A second implication is that the communications technology, combined with databases of customer information, preferences, and so on, makes it easier to reach customers as individuals. These properties can be the basis of new marketing campaigns that build on the core capabilities of the network.

The Internet Is the Same as Other Media

Faced with the differences of the Internet as a marketing medium, many people thought, "This is so different that I don't need to know anything about traditional marketing." Few of the businesses begun on that principle in 1994 are still around, but this reaction remains common as more people discover the Internet.

As with some of the other topics we have discussed, the classic business and marketing questions are still relevant.

- Who is the customer?
- What does the customer need?
- What does the customer want?
- What message do you want the customer to remember?
- How can information be presented to the customer most effectively?

Technology is no substitute for a good understanding of the basic principles of marketing and knowledge of the customer. What it can provide is the ability to reach the customer in more interesting and sophisticated ways.

Understanding the Demographics

Of course, one of the key questions in marketing is the demographics of the universe of possible customers. As the Internet has grown, the demographics have changed substantially. The network began in the research community, then grew to widespread use in academia. Technology companies were attracted, followed by other businesses, and now a large number of consumers. Because of this rapid change, which continues to occur, we do not discuss the details of Internet demographics here. Rather, we believe that there are a few important principles to remember for including Internet demographics in a marketing plan.

1. The demographics are changing rapidly. What is true today might not be true tomorrow, so it is important to watch the trends and how they might affect the marketing plan. Increasingly it is true that *everyone* is on the Internet.

2. Focus on the demographics of target customers, rather than searching Internet demographics for interesting potential customers. Then look for ways to take advantage of their Internet use to reach them, whether this is done with the Web, electronic mail, or another application.

One-to-One Marketing

A current hot topic in marketing of all kinds is *one-to-one marketing*.[4] Rather than targeting a mass audience, one can make a very direct pitch to individual customers by tailoring the messages to their known interests, likes, dislikes, and buying histories. This requires the collection and processing of large amounts of information about customers, their buying habits, and other relevant demographic information. In many cases, the market is a small group of similar customers. One-to-one marketing is being used in such areas as direct mail, carefully focused television advertising, and provision of selected coupons to individuals at point-of-sale terminals.

The Internet is an ideal medium for one-to-one marketing, because the communication technology immediately provides the direct channel. A Web site can identify customers before they browse a catalog and then use those identities to customize the presentation. This customization can take many forms, such as selecting which items to display, providing targeted special offers, or inserting advertisements of likely interest. Even when customers are anonymous, their behavior may provide some clues that are useful in tailoring a message. A search engine, for example, may select advertisements to display based on the customer's apparent area of interest.

As another example, an airline may have special fares to advertise. In general, customers are interested only in flights originating from their home cities, so most information in a mass advertisement would be irrelevant to most customers. Simply by keeping track of a customer's home city, the airline can send an electronic mail notice of special fares that is almost certainly of more interest to the customer than a complete listing of specials.

Advertising

Advertising on the Internet takes many forms. One of the simplest is a Web site describing products or services for sale. Of course, just having a Web site is no guarantee that potential customers will visit, so ads are placed in many other locations. Many companies purchase ad space on other Web sites, hoping to lure customers who visit those sites. Internet search engines are a common location for ads, because of the volume they attract, but any popular site may be a good location. Keeping in mind issues of demographics, a good site for advertising need only be popular with potential cus-

---

4. For example, see Don Peppers, *The One to One Future: Building Relationships One Customer at a Time* (Doubleday, 1993).

tomers, not necessarily popular with the Internet at large. Increasingly, advertisements in print or on radio and television quote Uniform Resource Locators (URLs) to link those media to the Internet.

Another form of advertising is placing links to a Web site in places that potential customers may visit. Such sites may include search engines, general or specialized directories, reference materials describing the kinds of products or services being sold, and so on.

Advertising on the Internet should be done with care, however. Because the network began in an academic and research setting, there is considerable resentment toward intrusive advertising. Sending unsolicited advertising to Internet mailing lists (a practice sometimes called *spamming*) is widely disliked, as well as being inappropriate for most lists.

Doing Business Internationally

One of the most revolutionary things about the Internet is the way it brings people and organizations together around the world. For someone in Cambridge, Massachusetts, there is very little apparent difference between communicating with someone in New York City and with someone in Bombay, India, except possibly the available network bandwidth and a slight difference in latency. This ability gives any online business the potential to reach customers around the world and to become a true international business.

International business issues, however, are not so simple. From the relatively straightforward problems of currency conversion, to the problems of presenting one's message in several languages, to the complexities of import/export laws and tariffs, there are a host of new problems to address.

In this section and the next, we discuss some of the most important issues in creating an effective international online business. Many of these issues concern reaching customers effectively, such as using local languages. Others are concerned with legal and regulatory questions that must be addressed before a business is permitted to operate at all.

International Software

The most important aspect of software for use in different countries is that the presentation, such as the user interface, can be adapted to local conventions. In many cases, this means translating all of the displayed information into local languages. To do this, the software must be able to display whatever character set is required (a stringent requirement, because some languages require multibyte characters whereas most software stores each character in a single byte). The software must also be capable of using the translated messages, which is not always the case.

In addition, the software must be able to handle the local currency (and, for some locales, multiple currencies at the same time).

International Content

Internet commerce may be the first exposure a business has to the complexities of the international environment. Beyond mere translation of text, true internationalization of content requires extensive work. Here we list just a few issues.

- References to local geographies, people, and news events do not translate well.
- Humor doesn't translate well.
- Sometimes words, particularly product names, have very different interpretations in different countries.
- Trademarks work differently in different countries.
- Colors, particularly as used in corporate color schemes and logos, make different impressions in different cultures.

These sorts of issues are well understood by multinational companies but represent serious problems for smaller companies wanting a global presence.

Privacy

Many countries, especially in Europe, have strict laws governing the collection and use of personal information about consumers. Although the details of such laws are beyond the scope of this book, any online business operating in such countries must be sure that its systems comply with local law.

In any case, it is good business practice to inform customers of what kinds of data are being collected and how this data is being used (for one-to-one marketing by the same business, sold to others for marketing purposes, and so on). Most consumers on the Internet know very little about issues of privacy online, so they may have unrealistic expectations. By explaining the relevant privacy issues up front, a business can avoid later problems if customers feel their privacy has been compromised.

The Legal Environment

The rapid development of computer and communications technology has presented many challenges for legal systems around the world. For example, the ability to gather, correlate, and search large volumes of information about individuals and organizations raises questions of privacy that simply did not arise before the technology was developed. These challenges are magnified by the pace of technology's evolution, which moves much more quickly than the legal system. Some experts and other observers are calling for wholesale changes in the law to adjust to a technology revolution.

In this book, we take a practical view of the legal situation for Internet commerce. Business operates in a legal environment, and many business practices are codified or enforced by the legal system. Contracts, for example, are governed by law, but this law arose out of the needs of businesses. Legal systems will not change overnight, but they may certainly adapt to new business practices and requirements that arise from Internet commerce. Many of the key questions that arise for online businesses are not settled, and new laws and court decisions will change the rules. The important point is that the legal environment is an integral part of the world that Internet commerce systems live in, and we must be sure to take it into account in developing strategies for Internet commerce.

This section outlines many of the important legal issues and problems to consider in planning systems for Internet commerce. The authors are not lawyers, and our discussion is not intended to replace the advice of a competent attorney. We do suggest that it would be wise to consult an attorney who understands and appreciates the effects technology is having on business and the law.

Taxation

One of the most immediate legal questions that arises is taxation, especially sales tax. Since businesses are legally obligated to pay taxes, it is important for software systems to compute taxes where appropriate and to keep the records necessary to prove that the business is complying with the law. Unfortunately, computing taxes can be very complicated, depending on many factors, such as the type of good or service for sale, the parties involved, the location(s) at which the seller does business, and the location of the buyer. In the United States, sales taxes are imposed by states, counties, and municipalities, so the tax rules are different for many different jurisdictions. It is beyond the scope of this book to explore these issues in depth, but anyone doing business online should be sure to understand the obligations regarding taxation and to implement a system capable of complying with the law.

Of course, the rules for taxation differ from country to country, so any system that will be selling products or services on an international basis may need to take these differences into account.

Many governments, both national and regional, have considered imposing new taxes for online businesses. Many feel strongly that such taxes will hamper the development and adoption of Internet commerce systems. The U.S. government, for example, has imposed a moratorium on new Internet-based taxes while the sector grows and evolves. In any case, it is important for online businesses to be alert for changes that may affect their operations.

Digital Signatures

In the real world, personal handwritten signatures are used on many business documents to indicate that the business agrees to the statements in the document or to authorize the actions described. We generally assume that a signature is unique to an individual and that it is not forged. Electronic documents cannot be signed by hand, but cryptography has given us a tool to accomplish the same purpose: digital signatures. We discuss the technology of digital signatures in Chapter 13. For the moment, it is sufficient to understand that a digital signature on an electronic document can be used in many respects just as a signature is used. An electronic contract, for example, might be digitally signed by the parties to it, just as paper contracts are signed by hand.

Several countries, including the United States, have passed legislation that recognizes electronic signatures of various kinds as legally binding under certain circumstances. Cryptographically strong digital signatures are just one type of possible electronic signature. The actual implementation of these laws is still new, so it is important to take care in understanding the legal issues and requirements. In addition, there is by no means any international consensus on digital signatures, so international businesses must be especially careful in using them.

Regulation of Cryptography

The use of cryptography is fundamental to providing the security required for Internet commerce. Cryptography encompasses encrypting data for privacy, providing reliable means of verifying identities, recording digital signatures, and ensuring that there has been no tampering with messages and other documents. The technical details of cryptography are described in Chapter 13.

Governments have long taken an interest in cryptography because of its role in protecting information. In some cases, the use or sale of cryptographic technology is regulated (and, of course, the regulations differ from country to country). In the past, for example, the United States has restricted the export of strong cryptography in mass-market software. Today, such applications must be licensed for export. Going through the licensing process requires an understanding of the bureaucratic procedures, which remain cumbersome. While the United States currently has no restrictions on the use of cryptography by its citizens within the country, other countries may regulate the import and use of cryptographic systems.

For online businesses in the United States, these issues are usually not relevant, unless the business is creating and selling software for encryption. However, such regulations affect the security of Internet commerce systems around the world, and they may specifically affect transactions between foreign customers and U.S. businesses. If the customer's system has weak security, then the overall security of the transaction is also weak. In addition, the lack of uniformity means that it is much harder to build confidence in the security of the global Internet commerce infrastructure.

Denied Parties

In the United States, the commerce department maintains a list of countries and individuals suspected of terrorism or the support of terrorism. Commerce with people or places on the list is forbidden.

The Problem of Uncertainty

A significant risk for online commerce is that so many legal questions remain unanswered. In the United States, it is clear that the legal system must evolve, at least somewhat, to meet these challenges. Some of that evolution will happen in Congress and in state legislatures, but many of the most important changes will come from the courts as they apply existing laws and precedents to cases involving online businesses. Because many of the technology questions are complex, it is difficult to predict how the courts will rule in many situations.

We believe that the benefits of Internet commerce more than justify taking the risk. But as companies proceed, they should be mindful of the legal issues involved and be careful to ensure that they understand the implications and risks inherent in their actions.

Summary

The commerce value chain gives us a useful way to think about Internet commerce projects. By focusing on the value delivered to the customer, rather than on the technology, we can more readily understand what pieces we need to assemble for the application. Then, with an idea of the customer value firmly in mind, we can develop the business strategy, which is the subject of the next chapter.

CHAPTER 3

Internet Business Strategy

The best ideas are common property.

—Lucius Annaeus Seneca[1]

Commerce and Technology Revolutions

It may seem odd to have a chapter on broad-brush business strategy in a book about the design of systems for Internet commerce. We think it makes sense, because the Internet changes so many of the facts underlying the basic assumptions of business. Jeff Bezos of Amazon.com has noted that changes in technology or infrastructure affect commerce in two phases, or waves. In the first wave, companies use the new technology to improve old processes and business models. In the second, more important wave, companies use the new technology for complete reinvention of their businesses. As we will see, the last time something as important as the Internet happened to business was in the middle of the nineteenth century when the railroad changed the world. That transition took 50 years. The Internet transition is happening much faster.

Because of the speed and scope of the changes introduced by the Internet, designers of Internet commerce systems cannot focus merely on the technology, but must also understand their companies' fundamental business strategies. Business leaders must also appreciate the technology enough to think through their strategies in terms of both new competitive opportunities and new competitive threats.

---

1. Lucius Annaeus Seneca (c. 4 B.C. – A.D. 65), *Epistles.*

Before the Railroad	After the Railroad
Travel between New York and Boston in four days	Travel between New York and Boston in less than one day
Transportation depends on weather and location of waterways	Transportation depends on the ability to lay rails
Dispersed work force (92 percent of population in 1830 is rural)	Concentrated work force (50 percent of population in 1920 is urban)
8,000 U.S. time zones	Four U.S. time zones
Vacation (if at all) near home	Vacation away from home
Transport a ton of goods for 5–15 cents per mile (by wagon or steamboat in 1825)	Transport a ton of goods for 1 cent per mile (by rail in 1884)

TABLE 3-1. **Changes Wrought by Rail Transportation**

Some companies will find that the Internet is not very close to their core strategies. A manufacturer of high-value products, where distribution costs are not a large part of the cost structure, may find its business strategy little changed. However, even these sorts of enterprises may find Internet technology a better way to work with suppliers and customers than previous methods, and its use may produce substantial savings.

Other companies, who add relatively less value to their products, or for whom distribution costs are high, or whose competitive environment is limited by geographic or informational barriers to entry, may indeed have to rethink their core business strategies.

Amazon.com and eBay notwithstanding, there is evidence that companies in a strong pre-Internet position can retain that position through a "bricks and clicks" strategy, by embracing the Internet as a central part of their traditional business. Nevertheless, in previous technology-driven business revolutions, new leaders have emerged.

A Historical Analogy

Few innovations have the capability of changing the entire competitive business environment. During our lifetimes, only the Internet has the potential to affect commerce as much as the nineteenth-century railroad did. "The impact of the rail network was like nothing the United States had ever seen before or indeed has seen since."[2] To understand the long-term business potential of the Internet, it is first helpful to understand the railroad.

---

2. Alfred D. Chandler and Richard S. Tedlow, *The Coming of Managerial Capitalism: A Casebook on the History of American Economic Institutions* (Richard D. Irwin, 1985).

	Railroad (1825–1890)	Internet (1969–Present)
New infrastructure	First water-independent transportation infrastructure	First global public information infrastructure
Original purpose (not commerce)	Passenger traffic; military	Military and civil defense; research
Importance of standards	Width of tracks (gauge)	Network and communications protocols (TCP/IP)
New security challenges	Railway police hired to manage new crimes	Security protocols and standards
Source of innovation	Steel production, accounting, logistics	Software, networking, fiber optics
Accelerate fundamental economic trends	Industrial age (key enabler: steam engine)	Information age (key enabler: computer)

TABLE 3-2. Comparison of Railroad and Internet Infrastructures

The railroad was first introduced in 1825 and became the dominant mode of transportation in the United States by 1890. Consider some of the changes wrought during this period, as shown in Table 3-1.

Today's Internet is remarkably similar to the nineteenth century's railroad infrastructure development, except that the Internet is developing much faster. Consider some of the factors listed in Table 3-2. The last entry in the table is particularly important—both the railroad and the Internet accelerated a fundamental economic change that was already underway. In the case of the railroad, cheap transportation accelerated the industrial revolution, whose key enabler was the steam engine. In the case of the Internet, cheap communication is accelerating the information age, whose key enabler is the computer. Bob Metcalfe, one of the inventors of the Ethernet computer network, explains this effect through Metcalfe's Law: *The utility of a network increases as the square of the number of nodes connected.* The ability to route goods by rail between arbitrary factories accelerated the industrial revolution. Likewise, the ability to route information between arbitrary computers is accelerating the information age.

In terms of their impact on commerce, today's Internet is also remarkably similar to the nineteenth century's railroad. Consider the following factors.

- Economies of scale

  Railroads made large mining and agricultural operations practical. The Internet makes it possible to offer an enormous number of titles in one store such as Amazon.com or CDNow.

- Source of competitive advantage

  Transportation enabled a regional competitive advantage, such as that employed by the vineyards of France to dominate the wine market. The Internet can enable a single site, such as Travelocity, to offer full services.

- Inventory needs

  Just-in-time delivery of coal enabled factories to run with little energy inventory. Because the Internet can deliver perfect copies of information goods immediately, digital goods commerce sites may need no inventory at all.

- Variety, choice, and availability

  Rapid transportation made perishable goods such as fish and fruit more widely available. The Internet can eliminate distribution bottlenecks that limit the market for information.

- New opportunities

  By capitalizing on the economies of scale, the railroads, in effect, created large-scale corporations. Indeed, some of the earliest large corporations of the industrial age were themselves railroads. Similarly, the opportunities of the Internet enabled eBay, CNet, and Yahoo to grow to substantial size very rapidly.

The Internet Value Proposition

Internet commerce must start with a strategy, and the analysis of strategy starts with value. What are the sources of Internet value? We believe the ability of the Internet to change the landscape of commerce comes from two key ideas: the Internet can be used to transform customer relationships, and it can displace or alter traditional sources of business value. These two ideas lead in turn to four basic strategies for a business to consider both in exploiting the Internet and in defending itself against competitors.[3]

Transforming Customer Relationships

By exploiting the Internet, many aspects of traditional commerce can evolve from being supplier-centered to being customer-centered, as shown in Table 3-3. This idea leads to two business strategies: a customer-centered business organized around a product or organized around meeting all the needs of a particular group of customers. We call the first approach the *channel master* strategy and the second the *customer magnet* strategy.

Displacing the Sources of Value

The Internet, by moving commerce from the physical world to the information world, enables commerce to shift from dealing with atoms to dealing with bits. The effect of this conversion is shown in Table 3-4. A focus on the supply chain leads to the strategy we call the *value chain pirate*; a focus on distribution—reaching the customer—leads to the strategy we call the *digital distributor*.

---

3. These ideas are largely attributable to Shikhar Ghosh and were described in "Making Business Sense of the Internet" in *Harvard Business Review* (March–April 1998).

Supplier-Centered	Customer-Centered
Supplier chooses hours of operation	Supplier always available, customer chooses hours
Supplier chooses locations of service	Service delivered at customer location
Supplier delivers services	Customer serves himself
Focus on supply chain	Focus on customer needs
One-to-many	One-to-one

TABLE 3-3. Transforming Customer Relationships

Physical World	Information World
Atoms	Bits
Physical value	Digital value
Economies of scale	Economies of scope
Mass-produced	Mass-customized
Information value	Knowledge value
Distribution as a constraint	Distribution as an enabler
Local	Global

TABLE 3-4. Displacing the Sources of Value

Four Strategies

The two key ideas, using the Internet to transform customer relationships and to displace traditional sources of value, lead to our four Internet business strategies: channel master, customer magnet, value chain pirate, and digital distributor. In many situations, mixed strategies may also be useful.

Channel Master

The channel master strategy works by using the Internet to build deeper relationships with customers in order to sell one's traditional goods and services. The channel master is organized around products, concentrating on the best possible delivery of those products and their related services. A company using the channel master strategy reengineers all of its customer-facing activities—channel masters must integrate the commerce value chain with their existing operations.

Example: Cisco Systems

Cisco Systems is an $18 billion provider of Internet software, hardware, and services. Cisco uses its Web site as its primary sales channel to its customers and partners. By the fall of 2001, its Internet channel was operating at a $12 billion annual run rate.

- Attract—get and keep customer interest.

  Cisco offers a full online catalog and demonstration of its ordering process. Customers are notified of pricing changes for prespecified products.

- Interact—turn interest into orders.

  The online catalog enables searching, browsing, and configuration of purchases. Intelligent agents suggest alternatives (such as software upgrades) and identify errors.

- Act—coordinate order fulfillment.

  Orders link to procurement and order management databases. Customers can monitor or receive notifications about order status and check lead times.

- React—provide after-sales service.

  Customers can access comprehensive documentation and self-help intelligent agents. A Bug Alert mechanism automatically notifies customers of bugs.

The results for Cisco have been spectacular: 70 percent of all product support is delivered through the Internet, and a very large fraction of orders now arrive through the Internet channel.

Customer Magnet

The customer magnet strategy works by using the Internet to attract a customer group by meeting their broadly shared needs with a knowledge-sharing environment and aggregated supplier access. The customer magnet is organized around a group of customers, delivering a broad range of products and services to those customers. A company using the customer magnet strategy seeks to be the destination of choice for a whole category of customers. Customer magnets must integrate the value chains of multiple suppliers into one customer-facing whole.

Example: Yahoo

Although it started as a directory of Web sites, Yahoo tries to be the first place people visit when they go online and tries to get them to linger on Yahoo rather than go elsewhere. In addition to providing information, Yahoo offers free services such as e-mail, instant messenger, and Web sites (via GeoCities).

- Attract—get and keep customer interest.

  Yahoo offers a tremendous amount of free information and links to other sites through its directory. Members participate in discussion groups and real-time conferences on many topics and can set up new ones via Yahoo Clubs.

- Interact—turn interest into orders.

  Yahoo operates Yahoo Shopping, which offers retail shopping, warehouse shopping, auctions, and classified ads.

- Act   coordinate order fulfillment.

  Yahoo shops offer the usual array of delivery options. Yahoo also offers the ability to set up and operate a new shop within Yahoo Shopping.

- React—provide after-sales service.

  Even though many Yahoo shops are operated by other businesses, Yahoo has chosen to offer a uniform level of after-sales service through a buyer protection program that covers all Yahoo shops.

According to Nielsen Netrating, over 60,000,000 unique users visited Yahoo during March 2002. On average, each user spent well over an hour at various Yahoo sites.

Value Chain Pirate

The value chain pirate strategy works by capturing someone else's margins by displacing them from their value chains. The value chain pirate is organized around the value chain, seeking to leapfrog both upstream and downstream providers in an effort to connect suppliers with customers more directly. A business using the value chain pirate strategy seeks the positions on the value chain that offer the greatest leverage. Value chain pirates must use the commerce value chain to support new relationships directly between suppliers and buyers.

Example: Autoweb

Autoweb displaces part of the value chain of car dealerships by selling cars directly to consumers (with the actual delivery handled by a traditional dealer).

- Attract—get and keep customer interest.

  Autoweb offers a no-haggle service backed by extensive online information about cars and options.

- Interact—turn interest into orders.

  Autoweb has complete information about cars, options, and colors available so that prospective customers can accurately request a quote for the vehicle of their choice.

- Act—coordinate order fulfillment.

  Autoweb uses traditional dealerships for delivery and service and has partnerships with other companies to provide insurance and financing.

- React—provide after-sales service.

  Autoweb provides extensive information on warranty issues, recalls, insurance, repairs, and maintenance.

Autoweb was acquired by Autobytel in 2001.

Digital Distributor

The digital distributor strategy works by eating away at traditional value propositions by focusing on pieces of the value that can be delivered better through the Internet. A company using the digital distributor strategy is organized around disaggregating traditional bundles of products and reaggregating products and services that can be efficiently delivered through the Internet. Digital distributors must create a new customer value chain from scratch.

Example: Monster.com

Monster.com began by offering online employment advertising for high-technology jobs. This was a natural entry at the time, because high-technology workers were very likely to be connected to the Internet. As the Internet has become a cross section of global society, Monster.com has added job listings spanning all industries and has built a global network of national services. In addition, Monster.com has aggregated other services related to career management, such as resume listings, moving, real estate, education, and finance.

- Attract—get and keep customer interest.

  Monster.com offers free services to individuals both to build traffic for advertising revenue and for its paid services, and to attract employers, who pay for their listings.

- Interact—turn interest into transactions.

  Monster.com offers automatic Job Search Agents, which send e-mail to customers to alert them about new postings matching the profile of their desired jobs.

- Act—coordinate fulfillment.

  For employers, Monster.com offers a variety of tools, such as resume screening. For employees, Monster.com facilitates closing a new job through such capabilities as cover letter management.

- React—provide after-transaction service.

  Monster.com offers a variety of services, such as an apartment finder and moving services, to assist individuals who have found new jobs.

In April 2002, Monster.com was listing 800,000 jobs.

New Competitive Threats

Each of the four Internet business strategies can be used alone or in combination by competitors, and each forms a different kind of threat to a business.

1. Channel master

   Can competitors create superior channels to your customers? Your customers could be attracted, by better prices, better service, and more convenience, to a competitor who takes a holistic view of the channel.

2. Customer magnet

   Can competitors attract your customers and sell them your products? You could lose your customer base to someone offering a broader range of services, and be forced to survive as a commodity wholesale supplier to your competitor.

3. Value chain pirate

   Can competitors hijack your position in the value chain? Your supplier could leapfrog your position in the value chain and sell directly to your customers. Your distributor could obtain parts directly from your suppliers.

4. Digital distributor

   Can competitors disaggregate your value proposition? If your value proposition is based on an aggregation of goods and services, it is possible for a niche competitor to excel at some part of the overall offering.

These questions can be answered only in the context of a concrete business situation, but an example may be instructive. Consider what happened, or what might have happened, to traditional full-service investment brokerage firms in the late 1990s. The value proposition of the full-service investment brokerage is one-stop shopping for the sale of analysis and trading services. Over the past few years, they have faced competitive threats from new and unexpected directions. What happened when competitors adopted each of the four Internet business strategies?

1. Channel master

   Other brokerage firms went online with retail brokerage services, providing customers with a more convenient and full-featured channel to essentially the same products and services. Many customers started to switch brokers simply because they could use the Internet.

2. Customer magnet

   Investment sites such as the Motley Fool formed communities of avid investors, who used the site as their primary (if not exclusive) source of investment research and information. Although it was not common, such a site could potentially offer commoditized brokerage services under their brand, undercutting the traditional broker.

3. Value chain pirate

   New online discount brokers, such as E*Trade, arose to bump traditional brokers out of the value chain, even though they focused on only a part of the range of services (namely, trading) provided by full-service firms.

4. Digital distributor

Wall Street City has built a business selling research, analysis, and investor education from their Web site without also providing trading.

New Competitive Opportunities

The dualism of competitive threats is that they are also new competitive opportunities. Again, each of our four business strategies must be analyzed for its applicability to your business.

1. Channel master

Can you improve your customers' buying experience by improving your cost, convenience, or ability to customize?

2. Customer magnet

Do your customers share broad needs that lend themselves to new bundles of products and services?

3. Value chain pirate

Can you jump over your direct suppliers or customers and capture their margins? Can you afford to alienate your distribution chain if you do so?

4. Digital distributor

What parts of other companies' value propositions could you improve by offering them on the Internet? What offerings could be added to your own package to make it more attractive?

Disintermediation and Reintermediation

In the early days of Internet commerce, many people predicted that the Internet would disintermediate the middlemen in the complete value chain of bringing physical and digital goods and services to customers. By this, they meant that customers could go directly to the sources of value, such as manufacturers or publishers (or even authors). In fact, such disintermediation has not been common, for several reasons. First, when the revenue volume of Internet commerce is small, it makes little sense to risk alienating a distribution channel that provides much more revenue. Second, the required business focus and operational capabilities are different at different points in the ultimate value chain, and many producers are simply not very good at direct interaction with the customer. Indeed, some so-called middlemen distributors have grown stronger as they have taken advantage of the Internet and other information technologies to provide better service to their direct customers.

Instead, what we have seen is the beginning of a wave of *reintermediation,* in which the old distribution chains to the end customer are disrupted and reconstructed to make more effective use of information technology, including the Internet. In this reconstruction, middlemen who provide little value beyond moving and storing physical goods are probably at greatest risk of being cut out. Indeed, one can argue that a good measure of importance in the distribution chain is the information value added at each point.

Summary

We advocate a three-step approach to selecting and implementing a business strategy for the Internet: select a strategy, design the commerce value chain, and implement an evolving solution.

In the first phase, think through the overall strategy from the points of view both of potential competitive opportunity and potential competitive threats from others. Will you be a channel master, a customer magnet, a value chain pirate, or a digital distributor? Or is a combination the correct strategy? This process should lead to your *virtual value proposition.*

Next, consider each stage of the commerce value chain and your preferred approach to attracting customers, interacting with them, acting on orders, and reacting to customer service requests. We suggest an "outside-in" approach, focused on the relationship of customers to each aspect of the business.

Finally, plan an iterative implementation, so as not to be caught by surprise by a technology shift or a change in market conditions.

CHAPTER 4

Business Models—Some Case Studies

From things that differ comes the fairest attunement.
—Heraclitus[1]

Introduction to Business Segments

There are many different kinds of businesses on the Internet, and each kind has specialized requirements for an e-commerce system. For this book, we have selected the following three kinds of businesses for detailed consideration of system requirements and design options.

1. Consumer retail

   Businesses selling physical goods directly to individual end consumers. We will further separate retail businesses into large businesses with complex requirements and small and medium-sized enterprises with more basic needs (and smaller budgets) for Internet commerce.

2. Business-to-business cataloging

   Businesses with online catalogs selling products to other businesses. We focus on MRO (maintenance, repair, and operations) goods rather than COGS (cost of goods and services) ordering. COGS generally implies large production orders for manufacturing, and although online systems and technologies such as EDI (Electronic Data Interchange) are used for this category of commerce, by the time a

---

1. Heraclitus (c. 540 – c. 480 B.C.), *On the Universe.*

product is in production, catalogs of components are not the issue. We do specifically include the use of online catalogs for designers wanting to select components for later use in products.

3. Information commerce

This is a broad category, but we include businesses that plan to distribute digital goods (information products and services) online with fulfillment right over the network. Publishers of online magazines and the online distribution of software, although quite different businesses, would both be included. The essential feature is online fulfillment.

In a marketing sense, a business segment is a collection of companies in the same business area, such as passenger car manufacturers or newspaper publishers, who would have similar requirements for products and services. We are doing something slightly different; we are using the word *segment* to describe collections of businesses with similar requirements for Internet commerce, whether or not they are in the same business area.

Note, however, that Internet businesses learn from many other kinds of Internet businesses, especially in regard to tools and techniques on how to use the Internet effectively. Thus, many business-to-business sites have learned how to build effective customer experiences by examining what is done by leaders such as Amazon.com and eBay.

Segment Granularity, Market Size, and Timing

Segmentation can occur at any level of granularity. For example, newspaper publishers might be further segmented into chains, large market dailies, and community weeklies. For Internet commerce, a segment such as information commerce would break down into publishing, software distribution, and information services. Information services might break down into information search and retrieval, reservations, and financial services.

There are many reasons for segmenting a market or an area of technology, but they largely boil down to focus. *Focus* means concentrating on exactly those elements that are essential to the application or market, and not diverting effort toward those elements that are either not needed or not appreciated by the customer.

Segment granularity is a difficult issue. If the segment is too broad, then development resources may not stretch across all the necessary features. If the segment is too narrow, the market may not be large enough to support the business.

Segment Similarities and Differences

There are great similarities in the requirements of our three chosen segments. All have the need to attract customers, present products, assemble orders, do transactions, accomplish fulfillment, and deliver customer service. We will focus on these common elements but also describe the areas in which the segments have very different requirements. As an illustration, the retail segment has a great need for merchandising capability, whereas business-to-business applications may have requirements for payment by purchase order and for approval workflow.

The information commerce segment may be the most distinct of the three, because information businesses may not need physical delivery of products and the corresponding customer service mechanisms but will have very complex requirements for online fulfillment.

Commerce Value Chain

In keeping with the structure of the preceding chapter, we will examine our chosen segments using the structure of the commerce value chain shown in Figure 2-1 on page 16.

- Attract—advertising and marketing
- Interact—content
- Act—order processing, payment, fulfillment
- React—customer service

In keeping with the systems design structure of this book, we break up the transaction processing phase of the value chain into separate sections: order processing, payment, and fulfillment.

Consumer Retail

This section discusses the commerce value chain for businesses selling goods directly to individual end consumers.

Value Proposition

The consumer retail segment has probably the least certain value proposition of the three. There are several ways to look at it, but the ability to deliver a precise message to a worldwide audience inexpensively creates several opportunities.

- Ability to reach a global market

  Because the Internet reaches consumers worldwide, a small local or regional business can suddenly reach a global audience. This can result in increased sales with minimal costs for distribution. An alternative view is that the worldwide audience can enable a niche market to gain a critical mass of customers, which may create a whole new class of retailers.

- Reduced marketing and selling expenses

  The creation and distribution of catalogs for direct marketing represent a substantial cost of sales. Although content creation costs for an online catalog may be higher than for a traditional catalog, the Internet greatly reduces printing and mailing costs.[2]

- Increased efficiency of operation

  In traditional catalog order businesses, orders are processed over the telephone or by mail. These are labor-intensive processes. On the Internet, the consumer does much more of the work of creating a complete order, which can then be automatically entered into the order processing system. In addition, the network can be used for customer self-service and inquiries that would otherwise tie up operators.

- Ability to target consumers more precisely

  Online and interactive sites permit marketing narrowcasting to target customers. With paper catalogs, it is costly to print different catalogs for different customers, but on the Internet, such *one-to-one* marketing is entirely possible and increasingly easy to implement.

- Ability to convey more accurate and timely product and availability information

  Because the content of an online catalog of goods is easily changed in comparison with printed materials, it can be both accurate and timely. The catalog can accurately reflect inventory and can also be used to sell small lots of products whose available quantities would not justify space in a printed catalog.

System Functionality

Retail business occurs on many scales, from small shop to large multinational company. The larger enterprise will naturally have more complex requirements for Internet commerce than the smaller.

- Small shop

  A small ongoing business may have a relatively static catalog and simple requirements for record keeping, payment, and order entry. Advanced features such as real-time inventory checks would not be available. The store catalog would be created using a commerce-enabled desktop publishing application and would be oper-

---

2. Technically, the Internet removes printing and mailing costs, but these savings are somewhat offset by the cost of providing the Internet service itself.

ated by an outsourcing company offering Web site hosting services. Orders would be collected by a commerce service provider[3] and sent to the shop by fax. Online payment would be by credit card or not required at all. Customer service would be most easily handled by telephone or unstructured e-mail. Typical merchandising techniques would be coupons or occasional sales.

- Medium-sized direct marketing

  Depending on the number of items (SKUs, or *stock keeping units*) in the catalog, the online catalog would be produced either by a product database together with display templates to generate catalog pages on the fly, or by a desktop catalog authoring system generating product pages. Online orders would require shopping cart features, tax and shipping charge calculation, and credit card payment, and would be delivered to the store electronically. Given sufficient size, a customer registration database and online customer service would be included. Merchandising techniques would include coupons, promotions, sales, and perhaps membership discounts.

- Large retailer

  The most demanding retailer would require a highly dynamic Web site with the capability of handling frequent product and pricing changes. Product display would be linked to inventory on hand. Order taking could include both private label and traditional credit cards, as well as on-account purchasing. Orders would be routed electronically to the retailer's ERP (*enterprise resource planning*[4]) system. Merchandising techniques could be highly complex, including one-to-one marketing and cross selling (suggesting accessory or complementary products, electronic coupons, and other special offers). For international sales, support of multiple languages and currencies would be important. For retailers with Web sites and existing physical stores—so-called bricks and clicks—there are additional opportunities for linkage between the Web and physical stores, such as store pickup of merchandise.

With these general outlines of functionality in mind, let's take a more detailed look at the various parts of these systems.

Attract—Advertising and Marketing

Attracting customers includes such diverse activities as advertising, coupons, promotions, sales, frequent buyer programs, and similar mechanisms. We call these activities *merchandising*. They are intended to build brand awareness, attract customers,

---

3. A commerce service provider is a company offering Internet transaction services on an outsourced basis.
4. *Enterprise resource planning system* is a general term encompassing accounting systems, manufacturing planning, and other mission-critical business applications. We discuss integration with ERP systems in Chapter 18.

and make customers more likely to buy. To some extent, these activities fall into multiple elements of the commerce value chain. For example, one may receive a coupon as the result of making a purchase.

- Advertising

    Advertising puts the merchant or product in front of the consumer's eyes, either in store, such as "visit our housewares department," or out of store, such as on the side of a bus. On the Internet, advertising takes many forms, including banners on popular sites, e-mail newsletters, or simply listings on widely used search engines. Advertising is typically an expense for a retailer, but advertising can be revenue to a vendor in the information commerce segment.

- Coupons

    Possession of a retailer's coupon typically confers a lower price for the consumer. A coupon may appear as part of an advertisement or may be given out at the checkout stand, triggered by purchasing activity. Coupons are used to build awareness of a product and to induce consumers to try a new brand, with the hope that they will switch. Internet-based digital coupons may directly link to a transaction service.

- Sales

    A *sale* means special prices for products for a limited period, perhaps with limits on the number of units available to any individual buyer. Sales are used as general promotions to build a customer base and increase awareness (in conjunction with advertising), and also as a way to clear built-up inventory, such as after a major holiday.

- Promotions

    Sales and coupons are examples of promotions, but a promotion can be quite complex. For example, a promotion might include a special price on a bundle of products even from different retailers, such as tuxedos, cake, and honeymoon arrangements as a complete wedding package.

- Frequent buyer programs

    Frequent buyer and other types of customer loyalty programs offer promotions to frequent customers. For example, purchases create frequent buyer points, which can be redeemed for goods and services. Since points are not useful at all retailers, the consumer has an incentive to concentrate purchases with one or a few retailers.

- One-to-one marketing

    Retailers try to learn as much about their customers as possible. When products that are more or less the same are available from a number of sources, retailers compete on the basis of convenience, price, and quality of service. The Internet removes the geographic basis of convenience, and price is always a difficult basis for competition, leaving quality of service. Knowing a lot about a customer can help a retailer provide high-quality service. *One-to-one marketing* generally means the customization of a system to the level of the individual consumer. It includes such things as the creation of individual customer profiles and the generation of content specific to the user.

The goal of all of these approaches is to draw customers to the e-commerce site. Each approach should also be measured for its effectiveness—not just in getting prospective customers to the site, but also in converting them to buyers.

Interact—Content

The simplest way to view retail Internet commerce content is to view it as the online equivalent of a direct marketing catalog. This is probably accurate for the broad middle of the market, but the Internet is a platform that can offer commerce services to the millions of small merchants around the world. For these organizations, simple desktop publishing of commerce-enabled catalogs may be appropriate. For stores with up to a few hundred items, the catalog could be created or modified by marketing personnel or anyone familiar with desktop publishing.

Further upscale, frequent price changes and product changes make a simple desktop publishing model untenable. In this segment, a desktop database coupled to an authoring tool or an online database creating Web content on the fly would be used.

At the most complex end of the market, dynamic catalogs, perhaps driven by real-time inventory information, would be used. The complexity of the technology would require ongoing information systems support.

Act—Order Processing

Order processing functions appropriate for retail purchases include the following kinds of activities.

- Shopping cart or order aggregation function

  On the Internet, a shopping cart is not a physical cart, but a logical database of items being considered for purchase. The shopping cart may include the capability of the buyer to change the quantity or other attributes of an item, and can contain hypertext links back to the catalog page from which the item originated. An electronic shopping cart may also be able to accumulate coupons and contain items from multiple vendors to facilitate comparison shopping.

- Order validation

  It might be appropriate to validate an order based on a variety of business rules. A simple rule might be that a coupon must apply to an item in the shopping cart. As more complex examples, a PAL television receiver would not work in North America, and a collection of computer system components might not be complete without a necessary cable. A merchant might not forbid such a suspect order from going through, but calling the matter to the buyer's attention could reduce downstream returns and customer service costs.

- Application of coupons or other discounts

  Coupons and other forms of merchandising such as affinity programs and quantity discounts are logically applied to the entire order. The order aggregation function in principle could recognize sets of items that together have a package price, whether the items are selected together or separately.

- Cross selling

  It might be appropriate to offer the buyer additional merchandise, depending on the current contents of the shopping cart or the buyer's previous shopping and purchasing behavior. (The latter capabilities are relevant only if the identity of the buyer is known, because a shopping cart might be anonymous or registered.) For example, a purchase of a flashlight might trigger an offer of batteries.

- Calculation of sales and other taxes

  Sales taxes require complex rule sets involving the tax classification of the product, the location and tax status of the buyer, and the location and tax status of the seller. In the United States, there are more than 6,000 tax jurisdictions at the city, county, and state government levels. Elsewhere, Canada has provincial sales taxes (PST) and a national goods and services tax (GST), and Europe has a complex set of value-added taxes (VAT). An Internet commerce system must correctly handle this complexity.

- Calculation of shipping and delivery charges

  In the case of physical goods ordered online, most orders will be delivered rather than picked up. Shipping charges may be bundled into the price, but frequently they are extra. Several different forms of delivery may be available (overnight, two-day, ground), and the charges may depend on the quantity of items, their weight, and their value. Note that more and more traditional retailers are allowing items ordered on the Internet to be picked up at their stores. While this avoids shipping costs, it requires an extra level of integration for the seller's systems to ensure that the order is fulfilled properly.

- Presentation of the rolled-up order to the buyer

  It is important for the buyer to know what is being purchased at what prices. This can help build consumer acceptance of a new medium as well as reduce downstream customer service, returns, and disputed handling costs.

Once a final validated order is available, the buyer will select a payment mechanism. It may happen that the price depends on the payment mechanism, such as a discount for a particular scheme. In that case, the selection of the mechanism should be viewed as part of order processing.

The details of several of these steps are discussed in Chapter 16.

Act—Payment

In real-world retail settings, the majority of payments occur by cash, credit, check, or payment card. Payment cards may be further divided into credit cards, charge cards, and debit cards. As we will discuss in Chapter 15, each of these types of payment has an electronic analog; but for our present purposes, we are interested in a quick outline of the business properties of these mechanisms.

Cash

- Cash is a bearer instrument.

  The seller does not need to trust the buyer when cash is used—assuming that counterfeiting is not a problem. The value is inherent in the instrument and is transferred immediately from buyer to seller. The buyer, on the other hand, has to trust the seller to deliver the product once cash has been delivered.

- Cash is anonymous.

  The seller does not have to know the identity of the buyer in order to accept cash. Cash is also suitable for transactions of which the buyer does not require a transaction record. On the Internet, other means of tracing buyers, including the shipping address for physical delivery, may limit the utility of this property of cash.

- Cash is suitable for small-value transactions.

  Because cash can have very small transaction costs, it is suitable for small-value purchases. The total system costs of handling cash, including counting, storage, security, mistakes, theft, and so forth, can be quite high, however, so this property of cash should be analyzed carefully.

Credit

It was once common for retail establishments to extend credit to their customers. This is still common for services (electricity, telephone), but rather less so for retail businesses. Many companies have branded credit cards, but these are considered elsewhere. Credit may have a larger role on the Internet as a means of efficiently handling small-value transactions, but this will be considered in the section on Information Commerce.

Check

A check is an instruction from the buyer to the buyer's bank to pay the seller a certain amount of money. The redemption of a check is not really ensured until the check is deposited and cleared through the banking system and its value is actually moved from the buyer's account to the seller's account. Funds may not be available to back the check, or the buyer may stop payment.

Checks also require authentication. A seller does not know for sure that the buyer has the authority to write a check on a given account. In addition to the risks of nonpayment due to the lack of a guarantee, a check may be invalid if it is forged. Another way to say this is that there is no obvious connection between the check and the person writing it. This is why sellers ask for other forms of identification and why check guarantee services exist.

A check is also a contract. Even if payment of a check is halted, a signed check may represent a contract between buyer and seller and therefore be capable of collection. In accepting checks, the seller accepts a certain amount of risk of nonpayment. On the other hand, the seller is not paying someone else to assume the risk.

Debit Cards

A debit card is a kind of payment card that directly transfers funds from the buyer's bank account to the seller. These cards are widely used in Europe and the Far East, and less widely used in North America. Debit cards benefit the seller, because payment is guaranteed and immediate, and transaction costs are lower than for credit cards. Debit cards may be less advantageous to the buyer because they have contractual terms that are different from those of credit cards and (in the United States) do not provide the consumer protections of the Consumer Credit Protection Act.

Credit and Charge Cards

Credit cards are so ubiquitous that few people appreciate their complexity. Incidentally, a charge card is a purchasing card that does not extend credit; the full amount of the charges are due when the monthly bill arrives. The operating framework for credit cards is provided by the card association regulations (Visa, MasterCard, American Express, and so on) and, in the United States, by the Consumer Credit Protection Act.

From the seller's perspective, the salient facts about credit cards are as follows.

- Credit cards may or may not guarantee payment.

  When a credit card is presented in person, and the retail clerk complies with all the steps of the process, such as requiring and checking the cardholder's signature and obtaining a real-time authorization, then the card association will guarantee payment. In other situations, such as mail or telephone order (MOTO) or other card-not-present transactions, the merchant may have to assume more risk of nonpayment.

- Credit cards have substantial transaction fees.

  The seller typically pays a fee of several percent of the transaction value for a credit card purchase. The fee is generally composed of two parts: a flat fee to the various parties who handle the mechanics of authorization messages and so forth, and a percentage to the acquirer (typically the seller's bank) and the issuer (typically the buyer's bank) for assuming various risks. The overall rate might be something like 25 cents plus 2 percent. This fee structure means that the effective percentage fee grows as the transaction value shrinks, so that using a credit card for a 25-cent purchase would result in a net loss to the seller. With typical transaction values in the physical world, this is not usually a problem because the average Visa transaction is something like $70.

From the consumer's perspective, credit cards provide several protections. First, they provide protections against theft or misuse. The Consumer Credit Protection Act (in the United States) provides that a cardholder is not liable for any unauthorized charges once the issuer has been notified of loss or theft, and in any event, the cardholder is not liable for more than $50 of unauthorized charges. The principle in effect here is that the issuers and credit card system operators should be responsible for ensuring adequate system security. Some card issuers are now promoting Internet commerce by reducing this liability limit to $0.

Second, merchants are validated. Consumers have some assurance of the bona fides of the seller by virtue of the seller's acceptance of the card. The card issuers hold the buyer harmless if it turns out that the merchant is fraudulent. This is a substantial benefit for commerce over the Internet, where the buyer does not have access to traditional means of inquiry about the status of a merchant.

Third, the card issuer provides some customer service. Generally speaking, if a consumer buys something with a credit card, the card issuer offers a single point of contact for disputes. In cases of nonperformance by the seller, or even of poor-quality goods, the buyer can dispute the resulting charge with the benefit of substantial clout. Some cards extend consumer warranties and offer various kinds of insurance.

Summary

In practice, credit cards are by far the primary form of payment for retail transactions on the Internet. As we shall see in Chapter 15, there have been many proposals for Internet analogs of these payment mechanisms, but only credit cards are nearly universal.

Act—Fulfillment

Fulfillment refers to the process of delivering the goods ordered to their destination, and includes the following steps.

1. Transmitting order information from point of sale to warehouse
2. Packing and assembling the order for shipment
3. Shipping and delivery

For physical goods, except for the first step, Internet commerce has the same fulfillment issues as other sorts of remote retail commerce. The main difference for Internet commerce is how the order information is transmitted. Order entry, however, may occur in various ways within Internet commerce.

A small business might maintain its Web presence at a hosting service located separately from the business itself. As orders come in, they must be conveyed back to the company's fulfillment function. This might be accomplished by fax, by regular or encrypted e-mail, or by polling an online list of pending orders.

A midsized company, particularly one already equipped for mail-order business, may want to integrate orders originating on the Internet with others. This integration can be manual or automatic, depending on the volume of orders expected.

Finally, a large business engaging in Internet commerce will most certainly want to integrate the order stream originating on the Net with other order streams. This integration may take the form of a direct link between the Internet transaction machinery and its existing order management or ERP system.

Relationship Between Payment and Fulfillment

Generally, payment is not due until the seller is ready to deliver goods. When a credit card is used for payment, the card association rules generally require that although authorization can occur at the point and time of sale, settlement, which actually transfers funds, can occur only upon shipment. This implies either that there must be notification from the fulfillment service back to the payment function or that the settlement part of payment can be handled by the fulfillment service.

React—Customer Service

The Internet presents many opportunities for either improving the value of customer service delivered or reducing its cost. The key observation is that in most settings, customer service representatives are acting essentially as human modems. For example, in telephone customer service, the operator listens to information coming in by telephone and keys it into a customer service application terminal. Then the operator reads some amount of information off the screen back into the telephone. Because the Internet puts a screen right in front of the customer, there is an opportunity for customer self-service and a reduced cost structure.

Opportunities for Improved Service

- Greater service capacity

  With Internet service, the system is available 24 hours a day, 7 days a week with no need to schedule a flexible work force according to peak hours and seasons. With communications routed over a global network, *follow the sun* support can switch from one support center to another as daylight hours move around the globe.

- Reduced error rates

  Errors associated with the human-modem functions can be eliminated, and the screens seen by the customer can be backed by immediate feedback and automatic step-by-step validation of input. With online forms, users can check choice boxes to indicate their intentions, and calculations can be done immediately by computer, further reducing errors.

- Richer information available

  There is no need to restrict the information available to voice, so tables, text, images, and graphics can all be used.

- Self-help or community help

  Frequently Asked Questions is a great format for customer self-help. In customer service the same questions arise all the time. These questions can be addressed in a searchable knowledge base.

- Direct linkage to status information

  Inquiries about order status can be directly linked over the network to sites maintained by all the parties involved, such as shipping and delivery companies.

- Proactive information delivery

  Information about product features, shipping delays, and recalls can be "pushed" to customers by e-mail or posted to their online personalized statement pages.

- Multiple-language support

  Separate sets of Web pages can be maintained for all languages used by the customer base.

Opportunities for Reduced Costs

There are obvious economies for electronic customer self-service. Since customers have direct access to relevant information, an organization may need fewer customer service representatives, or it may reallocate their time to other tasks. Consequently, the physical plant costs are also reduced, with savings on real estate, buildings, equipment, and operating costs. Finally, telecommunications costs are reduced, because each "call" has much lower overhead and is multiplexed on a shared network.

Business-to-Business Models

In this section, we discuss catalogs for maintenance, repair, and operations (MRO) goods and for component sourcing for products. MRO goods are such things as office supplies, physical plant repair parts, and consumables such as cleaning supplies. These areas of commerce are characterized by high-volume, low-value purchases, repeat business from the same customers, and high order processing costs for both buyers and sellers.

Value Proposition

The key benefits of putting a business-to-business catalog online are immediate cost savings and an ability to provide better service.

- Reduced cost of selling

  In addition to the cost benefit of an online catalog over the printing and distribution expenses of paper, many business applications require a depth of information that is difficult to represent on paper. For example, engineers use catalogs to select components for new product designs. Once a part has been selected, other services such as faxback are often used to obtain detailed drawings and schematics. These functions are largely information-based and can be conducted online.

- Reduced order processing costs

  MRO purchasing tends to involve large numbers of low-value orders. As such, the order processing costs can be significant. By automating the ordering process flow, these costs can be substantially reduced. (Handling a purchase order costs between $50 and $300, split between buyer and seller.)

- Improved service levels for low-volume customers

  Business-to-business catalog companies frequently provide special services for their largest customers. These services, such as custom catalogs, special negotiated prices, and order aggregation, have traditionally been economical only for large customers. The Internet can bring these value-added features within reach of smaller-volume customers.

- Higher-quality information for customers

  The electronic medium of an online catalog permits it to be searchable and to contain a much greater depth of product information than would be possible on paper. Searching makes the catalog easier to use and can be a competitive advantage simply because it is faster. Depth of information is possible because the hypertext capabilities of the World Wide Web permit the user to click through a catalog item to reach detailed product information and application information *underneath*.

- Accurate information

  Unlike paper catalogs, an online catalog can always be up-to-date, with accurate product information, availability, and prices updated in real time.

Differences in Relation to Consumer Retail

With substantial background from the consumer retail segment in mind, this section discusses business requirements for business-to-business cataloging in terms of the differences in relation to consumer retail.

Attract—Advertising and Marketing

Many of the merchandising techniques of retail also apply to business-to-business commerce. The key problems for a seller are to attract the attention of a recommender on the buyer side and to become a qualified, or ideally a preferred, vendor.

Interact—Content

Our model for the use of Internet commerce for selling MRO products is an online catalog. At a high level, business catalogs are very much like consumer catalogs, but there are a number of differences.

Searching Is Essential

Business catalogs can be very large; it is not uncommon for a catalog to contain 50,000 or 100,000 different parts. For this reason, searching capability is essential. For industrial parts, the searching mechanism should not have a predefined hierarchy. If the customer is looking for 2-inch, 90-degree brass pipe fittings, there is no obvious reason to search for these attributes in any particular order. One solution to this problem is a technique known as *parametric search*.

In this example, the requisitioner may be faced with a catalog of thousands of pipe fittings. After selecting *brass*, the catalog might inform the requisitioner that there are 3,200 types of brass fittings. Selecting *90-degree elbow* might reduce the number to 300; selecting *2 inch* might further reduce the number to 10, representing various couplings. Once the number of hits has been sufficiently reduced, it makes sense to scroll through an exhaustive list of the 10 possible parts.

Custom Catalogs

Businesses that do repeat business with other businesses often evolve special agreements and special pricing, and even design special components not available to other customers.

- Special part numbers

  The electronic nature of an Internet catalog makes it feasible to publish a different version for each significant customer. The part numbers displayed can be the customer's part numbers instead of, or in addition to, the supplier's part numbers.

- Special pricing

  Pricing by special agreement or according to volume schedules can be reflected directly in an online catalog.

- Security requirements

  In order to keep one customer's activity secret from another, business-to-business catalogs have higher authentication and security requirements than is typical for retail. For example, if the catalog shows special pricing by corporate agreement with a specific customer, only employees of that customer should be allowed to access the catalog.

Act—Order Processing

Business-to-business order processing can be substantially more complex than retail order processing. On the seller's side, real-time checks of inventory availability and order consistency are likely, as are the order processing components of business-oriented payment mechanisms. On the buyer side, the order processing can be much more complex.

Approvals and Workflow

In business ordering, there are a variety of roles.

- Requisitioner—individual who wants something purchased
- Approver—individual who authorizes the funding for the purchase
- Purchaser—individual who does the purchasing

In consumer purchasing, these roles are usually held by a single individual, whereas in business they may be separate and never in the same place at the same time. To the extent that a purchasing agent has a clerical role, the automation of Internet commerce may reduce the need for that role, permitting it to be combined with that of the requisitioner.

The major order processing function essential for business-to-business applications is an approval workflow mechanism that permits an order, once composed, to be routed through the appropriate process. Additional issues include requirements for line-item-level detail, cost allocation, and fine-grained control over shipping and delivery.

Delegation

An important capability in systems intended for business-to-business use is the ability for an authorized user to delegate authority to another user. In the consumer model, parents may have some control over the online purchasing abilities of their children, but the requirements are much more complex in the business context.

- A department administrator delegates authority to department members to log in to and search supplier catalogs.
- A manager delegates authority to a subordinate to approve purchases while the manager is on vacation.

Act—Payment

Several additional means of payment are appropriate for business-to-business commerce.

Purchase Orders

A purchase order is not really a payment mechanism itself but rather a means of creating billing records for later settlement by a direct payment instrument. At the point of sale, the purchase order connects the order, typically via a reference number, to the order tracking system of the buying organization.

In Internet commerce, a purchase order is an acceptable means of payment only if the buying organization has arranged credit with the seller and the buyer is appropriately authenticated and authorized by the buying organization to make purchases.

Procurement Cards

Procurement cards work the same way as credit cards but have several features specialized for business commerce. The idea of procurement cards is to delegate purchasing authority to the lowest levels possible within an organization, but to provide high-quality reporting to enable proper financial controls.

- Goods category restriction

  When a procurement card is used to make a purchase, the authorization decision is based not only on the remaining credit available but also on the Selected Industry Code of the store, the purchasing history of the buyer, and perhaps information about the product being sold (if the authorization system has such information available). The buying organization sets up a proper profile for each buyer, which might permit the purchase of $100 per month of office supplies but not hardware or food. Procurement card support in an Internet commerce system requires that the system transmit detailed information on purchases to the card authorization network, in addition to amounts.

- Reporting

  Standard credit cards provide information on purchasing in the form of items on the paper monthly bill. Procurement cards provide detailed purchase reports to the buying organization, often in near real time, in an electronic form.

Electronic Funds Transfers

Electronic funds transfers are somewhat akin to checks in that they are instructions to transfer funds from one account to another. Like checks, EFT has a fixed overhead cost unrelated to the amount of the transfer, and also like checks, the funds transfer networks do not assume liabilities for customer service. Unlike other payment mechanisms, electronic funds transfers are fast—overnight or immediate—and provide both parties with immediate acknowledgment of their execution.

In the United States, there are really two EFT networks: the Automated Clearinghouse (ACH) network, which is used for automatic payroll deposits, investment funds transfers, and bill payment; and the various AutomatedTeller Machine (ATM) networks, which are used for obtaining cash and for using debit cards at gas stations and grocery stores.[5] The ACH network typically works overnight, whereas the ATM networks work in real time.

For Internet commerce, EFT payments offer more immediate effect and a reduced requirement for trust between parties compared with checks, and a lower cost structure than credit or procurement cards. However, the ACH network was intended for transactions such as automated payroll deposit, and it has fairly complex technical and administrative procedures for setting up a transfer; the ATM networks work for individual payments but usually require a complex infrastructure to handle PIN numbers securely.

Act—Fulfillment

Business-to-business needs add some additional requirements for fulfillment systems.

- Predefined ship-to addresses

  When requisitioners can order small to medium-sized items without review, and when the volume of orders makes any after-the-fact review unlikely, fulfillment systems can provide some additional protection against abuse of the system by permitting only predefined ship-to addresses to be used. This capability will typically be part of the order management phase, but linked to fulfillment. When business purchasing is set up, a set of predetermined legitimate shipping addresses are loaded. Requisitioners can select from them, but not alter them.

- Order aggregation

  When a business sends a large volume of small orders to a supplier, aggregating the orders in a single shipment on a daily or weekly basis can save shipping and overhead costs. Traditionally, this order aggregation is done by hand, but electronic systems make it easier. Even if orders are entered by individual requisitioners, the fulfillment stage of the commerce system can recognize a common buying organization and shipping address, and combine orders.

- Multiple ship-to addresses, scheduled deliveries

  In business, it frequently happens that a central purchasing organization buys a large quantity of supplies for the benefit of multiple locations. In this case, the fulfillment system has to handle multiple shipping addresses, perhaps on a line-item basis. When orders are aggregated, even for a single location, then the fulfillment system must designate the final destination of each part of the order.

---

5. There are also institutional large-dollar-transaction networks such as CHIPS and Fedwire.

React—Customer Service

For business-to-business commerce, we broaden the definition of *customer service* to include all services delivered after the point of sale—training, technical support, and software maintenance, for example, in addition to traditional customer service.

- Training

  For many products, online training may be an effective means of customer education. Unlike paper training manuals, but like computer-based training, Internet-based training can be highly interactive. Not only can the training system include simulations or access to the real product (for software products, anyway), but instructors can communicate with students online.

- Software maintenance

  Software maintenance refers to the practice of delivering patches and version upgrades to a software product for a fixed annual fee—in effect, a subscription—following the purchase of an initial version. The Internet is a nearly ideal channel for distribution of software, and it is equally suited to the delivery of upgrades. With a software purchase, a vendor might supply a subscription enabling the customer to download new versions as they are released.

- Technical support

  After the sale, many companies sell technical support, which includes answering questions about the product and its application and assisting with working around bugs and other sorts of product problems. For high-technology equipment and software, the network can be used for remote diagnosis and even repair. One additional opportunity for vendors is to set up an electronic community for their customers. Online forums and files of frequently asked questions can be effective means of customer self-help.

Information Commerce

In this section we discuss the use of the Internet for commerce in *digital goods*, which can be fulfilled right over the network.

Value Proposition

The essential features of online information commerce are the collapse of the traditional distribution chain and the ability to explore new business models.

- Collapse of the distribution chain

  On the Internet, information providers have direct access to information consumers, without an intervening distribution channel. For the first time, the marginal cost of delivering a product to an incremental consumer is very near zero. In addition, there are no limitations on shelf space or channel bandwidth to boost distribution costs artificially.

- Business models

  Because the medium is ultimately flexible, information providers, be they publishers or authors of software, can easily experiment with new business models such as software rental, pay-per-view documents, and microtransactions, as well as traditional models such as advertising and subscriptions. In effect, the efficiency of the medium and the reduction of transaction costs enable the unit of information commerce to be much smaller.

Business Models

One of the challenges of information commerce is how one makes money. We review some of the revenue models for information commerce.

Advertiser Support

A content provider can generate revenue through advertising. Advertisers pay for impressions, a set of eyes looking at their advertisement. A site that has interesting and compelling content attracts lots of visitors, and the advertisers will pay for that. If the site can also collect registration information from visitors that includes demographic information such as age, sex, or zip code, then advertisers will pay more.

On the World Wide Web, there is also the technical opportunity to gauge the effectiveness of an advertisement by the numbers of users who click it.

Subscription Services

Subscriptions are a traditional model for print and can also work online. In a subscription model, the consumer pays a recurring fee for ongoing access to information.

Bundling Arrangements

In order to achieve a sufficient critical mass of information to attract visitors, content owners may sell access rights to each other's constituencies, or a service provider who is not directly in the content business may license access to content for their users.

Document Sales

This is a broad category, encompassing, for example, the sale of research reports or individual articles, or the online sale and delivery of software.

Usage-Based Charging

In this business model, users pay according to usage. Usage can include many attributes, such as connect time, search queries, or number of pages viewed. Both information products, such as online newspapers, and information services, such as search engines or online games, are amenable to usage-based charging.

Information Marketplace

Because the Internet greatly reduces transaction costs, it could lead to a world in which the ultimate providers of information sell directly to the ultimate consumers in a vast information marketplace. Perhaps the most intriguing set of questions is what roles there will be for middlemen, distributors, and aggregators of information.

For an information marketplace to evolve, the following components are necessary.

- Rights management

  For authors and publishers to distribute their information online, they must be able to specify the permitted uses of the information in a standard format.

- Containers

  A *container* is an envelope that protects information in transit and before sale. Containers can be freely distributed on the network, on a CD-ROM, or via broadcast. When the contents of a container are purchased, the container unlocks to reveal the content. Frequently, different fees apply for viewing, printing, and other forms of access. Containers can also be used to prevent an authorized user of information from distributing it to unauthorized users.

- Superdistribution

  The concept of superdistribution encompasses the encoding of distribution rights along with information in a secure container. An information aggregator can purchase rights to redistribute the content in a container and pass a modified container along. When the end user eventually pays for access, part of the fee goes to the distribution chain and part to the original author.

- Clearinghouses

  Clearinghouses both for copyright management and for payment are necessary components for the information marketplace. Clearinghouses collect fees from end users and distribute them according to the rules in the secure containers.

Differences in Relation to Consumer Retail and Business-to-Business Cataloging

This section discusses the business requirements for information commerce in terms of the differences between it and consumer retail and business-to-business cataloging.

Requirements for Customer Systems

The segments discussed previously might have quite complex requirements for the purchaser, but in terms of Web browser capabilities or platform capabilities to run client applets, information commerce might put more stringent requirements on the buyer simply to handle the information content itself.

Interact—Content

In information commerce, the content is itself the product. We will discuss some of the problems of online delivery under Act—Fulfillment. In this section we discuss the varieties of online products and services being sold.

- Software

  The Internet is a natural medium for online distribution of software. Except for printed manuals and recording media, software consists entirely of information. Online software distribution includes selling the right to download a distribution kit, accepting payment for shareware, free downloading of distribution kits combined with sale of a license key, and subscriptions to software for network computers.

- Searchable databases

  Content providers can charge for access to databases, including search facilities. The information in such a database can be of high value, and sometimes the value is really in the organization of the information. Charging can be usage-based or subscription-oriented.

- Dynamic information

  The Internet is a great medium for distribution of newsfeeds, financial quotes, sports news, and other rapidly changing information. So-called push distribution can deliver dynamic information directly to the desktop.

- Online magazines and newspapers

  This sort of content is essentially the same as the content delivered on paper, but is made more valuable by timeliness and an ability to search. Online magazines can also be personalized to the individual and even composed from a variety of sources.

- Reports and documents

  Online repositories of reports and documents save a great deal of duplicate effort in comparison with paper. With paper, manual filing is very expensive and adds little value. Electronic filing makes sure documents are never lost or misfiled, multiple copies are available for checkout, and searching and indexing make the content accessible.

- Multimedia objects

  Given adequate bandwidth (wait a few years), it is perfectly feasible to deliver full-fidelity movies and television on the network. Images, audio, and low-fidelity video are already widely used on the Web.

- Interactive services

  Online forums, chat rooms, telephone calls, virtual worlds (multiuser dungeons), and games can all be delivered online.

- Information services

  Stock brokerages, banks, travel agencies, and ticket agencies are all examples of information services in which no physical objects need change hands. All these sorts of businesses can be carried out online.

Act—Order Processing

The primary differences between order processing for information commerce and for the other segments are that the user experience may need to be much simpler and authentication plays a more central role. Because information commerce may be carried out in microtransactions, individual purchase events should be very fast and should not intrude on the user's experience.

Authentication is especially relevant because of the need for online fulfillment. For example, in the case of an ongoing subscription, the system needs to authenticate (identify) the user at the time of purchase, and make appropriate database entries, so that the same user can be authenticated and authorized at the time of information delivery. Alternatively, the transaction must result in some sort of digital receipt or capability that confers access to the fulfillment server.

Act—Payment

Several additional payment systems seem appropriate for information commerce. Naturally, heavyweight payment systems such as purchase orders and credit cards are completely appropriate for large-value purchases such as long-term subscriptions or downloaded software.

Sometimes the choice of a payment system is made for business reasons, such as the approval process or risk management, and sometimes for economic reasons. When economics is important, the size of the transaction is the key factor. Each payment mechanism has a typical transaction cost, ranging from $0.25 for a credit card transaction to perhaps $50 to $100 for processing a purchase order. Obviously a purchase order is uneconomical for a $10 purchase, but what happens when the purchase is $0.10 or less? The necessary answer is to use a payment mechanism with an appropriately small transaction cost.

Electronic Cash

Electronic cash systems have several cash-like properties, such as anonymity, but the relevant characteristic for us is a typically low transaction cost. An electronic cash transaction may be viable in the five-to-ten-cent range. Systems that require a real-time link to a clearinghouse will have higher transaction costs than systems that work in disconnected environments.

Microtransactions and Tokens

Microtransactions are very similar in structure to electronic cash but have transaction costs that can make them useful for transactions of fractions of a penny. Token systems are those in which large amounts of money are traded for tokens or credits (a private currency, really) that can be used only at a particular service. Several microtransaction systems have been proposed; the basic idea is to modify the basic client-server protocol of the World Wide Web so that individual interactions debit the buyer and credit the seller. Tokens can be implemented more simply—by keeping the user's credit balance at the server.

Transaction Aggregation

Without extra technology, the seller has the option of collecting multiple billable events and charging for them by the batch. This process can amortize the transaction overhead over a large number of transactions, hopefully bringing the exchange of value into an economical range for the given payment system. Aggregation can be either of two types.

1. Taxi meter, or charge up

   In this system, the meter accumulates usage charges, and the buyer pays for them all at a later date. The difficulty is that the seller is extending credit to the buyer, which may be problematic when the buyer is unknown or anonymous. With credit cards, it is possible to obtain an authorization (guarantee of credit availability) in advance of settlement (funds transfer) so that the credit risk can be transferred to the card issuer.

2. Parking meter, or pay down

   In this system, the buyer prepays a lump sum, perhaps $10, and then uses the credit balance during the course of some time period. The difficulty here is the seller's stance toward refunds (typically none) and the seller's responsibility not to lose credit balance records.

In both models of transaction aggregation, there are many technical details and questions of business policy. For example, should the necessary authorizations be immediate or can they be deferred?

Act—Fulfillment

For Internet commerce in physical goods, fulfillment is carried out through traditional channels.[6] For digital goods managed by information commerce, fulfillment is carried out online. For different kinds of content, different mechanisms for fulfillment are appropriate.

Downloading

The simplest forms of digital goods are those downloaded to the client computer once. Online purchases of software and reports fit this category. Typical mechanisms include charging for the download itself, charging for access rights to the download area, and charging for a license key. The differences are subtle but important: what happens when the download fails? Disks can fill up, modems can be cut off, or the power can fail. For these reasons, it is prudent to plan for download failures and to recover from them automatically.

- Charging for download

  This method is appropriate for small downloads, which are unlikely to fail. If the download does fail, either the user will pay again or a customer service call will result, with a request for a refund. Charging for download may be the best choice for microtransactions, where the theory is "optimize the common case." Most downloads will succeed, so they should proceed with no user intervention. The user will not worry about the occasional double charge for retrying a failed connection attempt, because they are so inexpensive anyway.

- Charging for license key

  Charging for the license key to unlock the download permits the download area to be publicly accessible, because the download is useless without the key. If the locking technology is such that a given key works only on a particular computer, then once created, the key can be distributed freely as well, because it is useless anywhere else than its intended destination. Delivering the key and content separately is complex and perhaps suitable only for higher-value purchases (unless the whole procedure is automated).

- Charging for access

  Charging for access to the download area is an interesting hybrid design. In this case, access to the fulfillment area is granted for a reasonable period of time, deemed sufficient for all users to successfully download the product. For example, download access might be granted for eight hours—long enough for several attempts to download the product.

---

6. At least until the advent of the matter restorer PC peripheral, which will create the physical object given its description. For example, see Neal Stephenson, *The Diamond Age* (Bantam Books 1996) or George O. Smith, *The Complete Venus Equilateral* (Ballantine 1976).

Subscriptions

We distinguish a subscription from a download by the notion that a subscription carries with it some sort of ongoing access to a service, which essentially means that the user who bought the subscription must be able to authenticate herself to the service and that the service grant authorization for access going forward. There has to be a subscription database that says who is to be granted access (authorization), and there has to be a way for a user to prove that she is who she claims to be (authentication).

There are several ways to solve these problems, but any solution must allow for such complexities as renewals, grace periods, refunds, access to multiple fulfillment servers, and user access from multiple computers.

Push Content

Fulfillment of push content, which is actively delivered by the content service rather than downloaded by the user, is managed either by creating a database record at the server to enable delivery (point-to-point delivery) or by delivering credentials to the end user that permit the content to be tuned in and decoded (broadcast delivery).

React—Customer Service

The key customer service issues for information commerce are the same as for other segments.

- I didn't buy that (or I don't remember buying that).
- I didn't receive the delivery (or it arrived here broken).
- I didn't like what I received.
- I was charged the wrong amount.

The difference is that in information commerce there is every possibility of using technology to ensure delivery, to the point that "I didn't receive the delivery" is a very rare complaint.

Copy Protection and Rights Management

One other problem with digital content is that it can be copied. The difference between information delivered physically (books, magazines) and information delivered online is not that copying is impossible offline but that copying is incredibly cheap online. The content owner has several choices.

- Don't worry about it.

   Doing nothing about rights management may be the best choice. If the information is already available for free at the library, for example, there is not much point in spending money or causing customer inconvenience to prevent occasional copying. In this case, however, there is some value in helping to set the social context that copying without paying is wrong, and in managing one's exposure. Similarly, it may be appropriate to do nothing if the content itself is not what is valuable about the online service. For example, if the ability to search is what is valuable, there may be minimal value in preventing copying.

- Make copying very difficult.

  If the information sold is of very high value, then there is benefit in making it difficult to copy. Container technology or license keys for software can be appropriate mechanisms.

- Make tracing the thief easy.

  This is analogous to dye packets in the teller's drawer. The dye doesn't make the bank hard to rob, but it makes it pretty easy to locate the thief. In information commerce, it is possible to watermark or fingerprint each distributed copy of content so that each copy is distinct and registered. If copies of a watermarked document come to light, they are easily traceable to the original customer.

- Make paying for copies easy.

  If there is an easy-to-use, always available way to pay for copies, the majority of honest customers will use it. If no one knows whom to pay or how to pay, then copying will flourish. This approach works especially well for information intended for professional customers. Such customers expect to pay for value received, and often pass along information charges to their customers anyway.

Summary

In this chapter we have discussed business models and business issues for three business segments that benefit from Internet commerce: consumer retail, business-to-business cataloging, and information commerce. There are obviously many other business segments—government and health care are but two examples—that stand to benefit from applying Internet technology, but we hope our three choices cast a broad enough net to engage the reader into thinking carefully about the opportunities presented by the Internet and into analyzing carefully the complete customer value chain.

Within any business segment, whether related to the Internet or not, different participants have different goals. At a high level, for example, customers want the best products at the lowest prices, and vendors want to make as much money as possible. Understanding these differences and how to reconcile them in successful sales is a key part of any business strategy. Internet technology, in general, and Internet commerce, in particular, bring some thorny issues to the fore. In the next chapter, we look at some examples of these issues and discuss ways to analyze and address them in commerce systems.

CHAPTER 5 _____ *Conflicting Goals and Requirements*

It is a very hard undertaking to seek to please everybody.
—Publilius Syrus[1]

The first rule in business is *know your customer*. If you know what your customer wants, and you deliver it better than anyone else, you can be successful. Often, however, problems arise because systems must serve many kinds of customers who have conflicting requirements. Sometimes the customers do not know what they want, especially in an entirely new area. This chapter surveys some of the rough ground of Internet commerce: those areas in which the participants have different goals, needs, and priorities.

Goals of the Participants

Systems for Internet commerce have many masters. This section illustrates some of the resulting complexity of the goals and interests of some of the key constituencies.

Buyers

In the context of this section, *buyer* means customer. It seems obvious that commerce systems must meet the needs of customers, but different kinds of buyers want different things, and their interests are sometimes at cross-purposes with those of sellers.

---

1. Publilius Syrus (1st century B.C.), *Maxims.*

Retail Customers

By *retail customers*, we mean buyers using systems for business-to-consumer commerce.

- Convenience

  The Internet is an alternative to driving to a store and browsing, and to bulky and out-of-date paper catalogs. If using the network is not easier than the alternatives, few people will bother.

- Price

  Retail consumers are frequently very price-sensitive, especially for products that are commodities or products for which there are several alternatives.

- Selection

  Consumers are interested in choosing from the broadest possible selection within their area of interest. This can be for two reasons. A buyer may be looking for the best set of features and functionality among a broadly used product. Or a buyer may be looking for a rare or unusual product. In the former case, selection is for the purposes of comparison, whereas in the latter case, the consumer feels it more likely to find the niche product from a seller who has a broad selection. The Internet offers another alternative for the buyer of unusual items: because the network can reach a worldwide audience, even niche markets may be large enough to support a specialized retailer.

- Privacy

  Many consumers are very reluctant to part with personal information for fear of being the target of junk mail or advertising, or simply because they feel their private lives are no one else's business. These consumers are likely to be offended to learn that their network browsing and buying habits are being carefully monitored.

- Service

  Some consumers are not price-sensitive, but service-sensitive. They patronize merchants who greet them by name, who keep them informed of new products, and who run establishments in which the customer is always right.

- Security

  Consumers want to be assured that their credit card numbers and other sensitive information are adequately protected.

Business Customers

Business customers are buyers who use Internet commerce systems in the course of their daily jobs (for example, an administrator reordering office supplies, or an engineer specifying components for a new product design).

- Personalization

  Sellers would like their retail customers to be repeat buyers, but it is essential that business customers be repeat buyers. Much of the business world runs on purchasing contracts, special pricing, volume discounts, and the like. These aspects of commerce will also be reflected on the Internet. In a world with alternative suppliers and intense competition, sellers will work hard to personalize their services and to offer the best possible service, both to entice new customers and to raise disincentives for current customers to switch.

- Ease of use

  Since business customers are almost by definition repeat customers, ease of use is vital. For the office supplies customer, the seller will make it easy to call up and reuse previous orders. For the specifying engineer, the seller will make it easy to search for and locate components. In both cases, speed is essential, because browsing and purchasing are not the end goals of activity but rather nuisances that take time away from the buyer's primary responsibilities.

- Security

  The security concerns of business customers are not so much about the security of credit cards as about keeping their competitors from finding out what they are doing, and ensuring the integrity of business records in company computer systems.

Sellers

In the context of this section, *sellers* include merchants engaged in business-to-business or business-to-consumer commerce and publishers and content providers engaged in information commerce.

- Reaching new markets

  Sellers are interested in exploiting the potential of the Internet for reaching new markets.

- Creating and strengthening customer relationships

  It is the rare seller who has a unique product that is not available from an alternative supplier. Consequently, sellers are interested in moving up the value chain and offering products that are less commoditized or in other ways creating barriers to exit for their customers. Part of building customer relationships is learning about one's customers, which frequently includes gathering as much customer information as possible.

- Cost-effectiveness

  Internet commerce systems can greatly reduce distribution costs and customer service costs.

- Security

  Sellers are extremely interested in the integrity of their marketing presence, their prices, their customer records, and their business records.

Conflicts can easily arise within a business planning an entry into Internet commerce.

- Management information system (MIS) and information technology (IT) departments may feel they should own and operate any Internet commerce system because it necessarily involves computing.

- Conversely, MIS departments may be very reluctant to deploy an Internet commerce system because it is new and different.

- Sales departments may feel threatened by the ability of the Internet to collapse distribution channels.

Financial Processors

The financial processor operates the part of the credit card processing system that accepts transactions from merchants and forwards them to the merchants' banks. More broadly, we include financial authorization and settlement services independent of payment mechanism, credit card or otherwise.

- Security

  Transaction security is paramount for a financial processor. Security includes the privacy and accuracy of records as well as the authenticity and integrity of requests.

- Transaction volume

  Processors make money either as a flat fee per transaction or as a percentage of the transaction amount. Consequently, they are keenly interested in raising transaction volume—either the number of transactions or their monetary total.

- Cost structure

  Processors are not paid on the basis of their costs, but on the work they do. The Internet as a communications infrastructure raises some intriguing possibilities for reducing telecommunications costs or even transferring the costs to other parties.

- Added services

  Financial services are commodities. Like other suppliers of commodities, processors are interested in adding additional services to increase their ties to their customers.

- Risk management

  Much of the complexity of the financial network connecting buyers, sellers, and financial institutions is concerned with allocating risk and responsibility for losses to the various involved parties. The processor is interested both in requiring the use of systems that minimize risk and, to the greatest extent possible, in transferring risk to other parties.

Government

- Security

  Government interest in security generally refers to national security. This area in-cludes government controls on imports, exports, and the use of cryptography and controls on money transfers and sales to blacklisted people and organizations.

- Legal controls

  Governments are interested in ensuring business and consumer compliance with laws and regulations. Access to certain kinds of information is illegal in many countries, and trade in certain kinds of products is illegal in different areas.

- Taxes

  Governments get paid through taxes and so have a strong interest in ensuring col-lection of taxes and in closing loopholes.

Governments must be cognizant of the ubiquity of the Internet. An attempt by govern-ment to over-regulate the conduct of business may simply drive business elsewhere. Businesses may make a worldwide *choice of law* and conduct transactions in a legal venue most favorable to their needs.[2] Businesses incorporate in Delaware and register ships in Liberia for exactly these reasons.

The Role of Standards

In information technology, a *standard* is a set of specifications that help enable sys-tems built by different parties to interoperate. In Internet commerce, standards serve two primary functions.

1. Standards are a way of transferring power from vendors to customers.

   It is generally to the benefit of the vendor to have a proprietary technology base. Proprietary systems can lock in customers by raising extreme switching costs and can reduce vendor costs by removing the necessity of testing against the products of other vendors to ensure standards compliance.

2. Standards are a way of assembling a complete system from multiple vendors.

   In an early-stage market, it may be that no single company can build the "whole product." To the extent that the complete system relies on components from oth-ers, standards help everyone. Individual vendors build components that comply with appropriate standards, and this permits system integrators to use components from multiple vendors to assemble a complete system.

---

2. As described by Daniel E. Geer Jr. in testimony before the House Science and Technology Committee, February 11, 1997. The statement is available at http://www.house.gov/science/dan_geer.html.

The success of the Internet itself is a tribute to standards. In a way, the definition of the Internet is based on a standard. Systems that comply with the Internet standards such as TCP/IP *are* the Internet.

The main problem with standards is that it is difficult to make them simple enough to be widely adopted and yet complex enough to be useful.

Late Versus Early Standardization

Standards efforts tend to follow one of two paths: late or early standardization.

Late Standardization

In late standardization, various parties work together cooperatively to build the market, or competing technologies arise and the market decides on a leader. Only after some market stability is reached do the parties get together and declare the result a standard. Most of the Internet-related communications standards have evolved in this way, with experimentation and interoperability testing followed by mutual agreement on standards. The primary benefit of late standardization is that the resulting standards tend to be simpler and at least are known to match real requirements.

A second form of late standardization occurs when a proprietary system acquires such a dominant market share that it becomes a standard, even though this may not happen in a cooperative manner. Standards arrived at in this way tend to work effectively but are more complex because of their origins.

Early Standardization

In early standardization, the parties involved get together and jointly agree on specifications. This can work out for the benefit of everyone, especially when the growth of the market would be greatly delayed by a period of fragmentation. On the other hand, early standardization tends to result in overly complex standards that attempt to answer customer needs that are not well understood. The parties involved sometimes add complexity merely so that all vendors will be equally inconvenienced. The standards efforts for music and data compact discs are an example of early standardization intended to grow the market, whereas the International Standards Organization (ISO) suite of internetwork protocols is an excellent example of a runaway standards process that ultimately failed in the market.

Standards for Internet Commerce

Are standards important for Internet commerce? As frequently happens, sometimes they are and sometimes they aren't. We don't sort the following list by good versus bad; these are merely ideas to think about.

- Standards aid interoperability.

  Unless one is able to obtain a complete system from one vendor, it is essential that the components interoperate. This problem is exacerbated when the system operator does not even control which components are used. For example, in a business-to-consumer Internet commerce system, the seller may rely on the customer to obtain an adequately functional Web browser, which must then interoperate successfully with the seller's Web server and content layout.

- The best is the enemy of the good.

  In the early stages of a market, system designers experiment with many different technologies and mechanisms. However, when each commerce site is completely different in style, design, function, and customer experience, the user base may be limited to those who thrive on newness and complexity. There is a strong benefit from consistency and standardization that leads to ease of use.

- The good is the enemy of the best.

  Standardization, and particularly premature standardization, restricts innovation. In addition, the more widely adopted a standard, the more resistant it is to change and evolution. In an early market, no one has any idea (or everyone has lots of ideas) about what technologies and design principles will ultimately succeed. At best, standardization will slow down the rate at which the market discovers and converges on successful principles.

Standards of Good Practice

A different sort of standard is one of performance or functionality. Security and privacy standards frequently fall in this area. For example, basic system requirements should be universal, such as using encrypted communications for private and financial information and exercising due care that customer credit card numbers are not exposed in databases. Lack of these facilities would not cause interoperability problems, but buyers of systems and their users should demand adherence.

Privacy Versus Merchandising

Consumers would like to retain their privacy, releasing as little information as possible to sites on the Net, whereas commercial interests, beyond collecting information necessary to provide a service, frequently combine that information with other sources of data to build up very detailed pictures of their customers and sometimes resell that information to others. In addition, the very technologies that can be abused in profiling and exploiting consumers are necessary to build Web applications and make them easy to use.

The first problem is not the transfer of information alone, but how that information is used. A consumer will understand the necessity of entering a shipping address to order online, but that same consumer may be very unhappy if that address is sold to another organization for marketing purposes.

The second problem is that privacy does not seem amenable to purely technical solutions. As discussed later, the Web cookie facility has acquired a bad reputation, and many users now turn off cookies in their browsers. This prevents many Web sites (that use cookie technology for quite legitimate reasons) from providing any service at all.

Platform for Privacy Preferences

The Web community's reaction to the privacy issue combines technology and trust. The World Wide Web Consortium developed a system called the Platform for Privacy Preferences (P3P). The group's Web page (http://www.w3.org/P3P/) introduces the system as follows.

> The Platform for Privacy Preferences Project (P3P), developed by the World Wide Web Consortium, is emerging as an industry standard providing a simple, automated way for users to gain more control over the use of personal information on Web sites they visit. At its most basic level, P3P is a standardized set of multiple-choice questions, covering all the major aspects of a Web site's privacy policies. Taken together, they present a clear snapshot of how a site handles personal information about its users. P3P-enabled Web sites make this information available in a standard, machine-readable format. P3P enabled browsers can "read" this snapshot automatically and compare it to the consumer's own set of privacy preferences. P3P enhances user control by putting privacy policies where users can find them, in a form users can understand, and, most importantly, enables users to act on what they see.

From a technical point of view, the idea is that whenever a site requests personal or profile information from a user, it can be provided automatically. This is true so long as the site's stated intentions for using the information conform to the user's preferences. P3P began to see some significant deployment in 2001, particularly with the addition of P3P support to Microsoft's Internet Explorer Web browser.

Cookies

One technology caught up in the debate about privacy is the *cookie*. Cookies are an interesting technical innovation added to World Wide Web browsers in 1995. In 1996, as knowledge and use of cookies spread, a controversy erupted about their privacy implications.

Cookies are a technology for turning stateless Web hits into *sessions*, for automatically recognizing a particular browser when it returns to a site after an extended interval, and for storing user profile information in the browser. These capabilities are enormously useful to both service operators and users, but they also introduce concerns about the privacy of information about users.

What Are Cookies?

Cookies are a Web protocol and browser mechanism that permits a server to tell a browser to store a block of information on the user's hard disk, and to give it back on subsequent visits to the same server. No information in a cookie is sent to a server that wasn't first put there by the same server. When a browser connects to the server, the server says, "Take this envelope, and bring it back with you the next time you come in."

This capability can be used to accomplish three things.

1. Tracking of a particular browser through a site—a session of related Web hits
2. Automatically recognizing that a browser has returned to a site at a later time
3. Providing the ability to store user profile information at the browser

To the extent that the ability of cookies to store user profile information has caused a lot of concern, it should be noted that a profile can easily be stored at the server and indexed by anything unique about the browser, such as a browser serial number or a cookie containing a unique ID. Some sites attempt to use the browser's IP address as a unique number, but this leads to problems because many users are shielded by proxy servers or use dynamically assigned addresses.

What Are the Benefits?

Cookies can provide the technical underpinnings for sessions, automatic user recognition, and user profile storage. Each of these capabilities provides valuable services for the user as well as the service.

- Sessions

  Without sessions, it is essentially impossible to provide a Web-based service that has more than one form. If a succession of forms is needed, there needs to be a place to store the state of the process between hits, and as a consequence a way to retrieve (index) that state on the next hit. In addition, if, during the succession of screens comprising a service, the user wants to branch off into other Web content (help screens, for example), then there needs to be a way to pick up the service where the user left off. So one benefit to both service and user is that sessions permit an application to use a series of Web screens with embedded help. Another benefit is that the service can conduct log analyses to see what parts of the service are used, and how, so as to improve service.

  Obviously, sessions can provide extremely valuable information for advertisers and auditing bureaus, especially when coupled with demographic information, but whether this is a benefit to the user is arguable.

- Automatic user recognition

  Automatic identification of a particular user is the cornerstone of any secure service (that needs authentication) and also of any service that offers personalized views to individuals. Without hit-by-hit authentication, a service cannot offer secure content, because you don't know who is getting it. Without authentication, a service cannot offer any degree of personalized service.

  There is also a place for recognizing a returning user—even anonymously. For example, if an online mall wants to provide a shopping basket that is preserved across sessions, an anonymously issued user ID can accomplish it.

- Client-side user profiles

  The final application of cookies is for storing items such as user profiles or application state. One benefit of using a cookie for this purpose is that the service does not suffer the performance impact of referencing a server-side database on each hit. Another privacy benefit is that there need be no central storage area where all sorts of information on all sorts of people is collected.

What Is the Downside?

- Unknown tracking

  Cookies can be used by Web sites to store information on personal preferences and behavior without the permission of the person. Because the cookie uniquely tracks a particular browser, a Web site can obtain accurate information on repeat visits. But the information stored can also be inaccurate, particularly if a computer is shared by more than one person. This can lead to personal information of one user being revealed to another.

- Cross-site tracking

  Cookies can be generated by services (such as advertising services) that are shared by multiple Web sites. These cookies can be aggregated to track a single browser across multiple sites.

- Employer search

  When company-owned computers are used by employees to surf the Web, cookie files may be stored on the company computer. The company may be able to search those files in order to obtain evidence of improper use of the machine. Indeed, one enterprising newspaper has sued a local government in Tennessee to obtain staff cookie files under the theory that they are official government records.

Summary

Whenever different participants in a system have different goals and requirements, there is a potential for conflict. This is particularly true in a new industry such as Internet commerce, where there are few established standards. Our advice is to build a list of the participants in your system and to be very clear about their goals, interests, and agendas.

Understanding the participants, their goals, and their interests is very important in framing both the business problem and the technical challenges to be overcome. Framing those problems and developing a core approach to solving them is the process of developing an *architecture* for the system, which we consider in the next chapter.

CHAPTER 6

Functional Architecture

Architecture . . . the adaptation of form to resist force.
—John Ruskin[1]

What Is Architecture?

The architecture of a system defines its basic components and important concepts and describes the relationships among them. There are many different ways to approach systems for Internet commerce, ranging from the simple to the complex. In part, the architecture depends on the nature of the business, and the system architecture developed for a consumer retail system might be very different from that for a publishing system. We believe that many design ideas span a wide range of commercial requirements, and that the similarities among systems for Internet commerce are much greater than the differences. This chapter describes a core architecture for Internet commerce systems, which can be adapted for many applications.

Why should we have a general architecture? Why not simply build the systems focused on a single application? For us, a practical answer is that, in our experience building systems for Internet commerce for several years, reusing the architecture and design work where possible is best for the customers. More important, however, is that as businesses refine and evolve their goals for Internet commerce, their systems need to evolve as well. That evolution may go well beyond the original requirements for the system, so the flexibility of the architecture is critically important in making that growth possible. For example, a software store may begin by taking orders over

---

1. John Ruskin, *Val d'Arno* (1874).

the Internet and sending out boxes with manuals and CD-ROMs. Later, it may want to deliver software over the network as well. If the original system does not handle online delivery, the store may find itself facing significant development or upgrade costs to add this capability. Note that the original system might not have implemented the online delivery subsystem, but it should be straightforward to add it if the original architecture and design were done with that idea in mind.

In this chapter, we describe the kinds of thinking that go into creating an architecture, explore some of those areas in more depth, and present some examples of practical architectures for Internet commerce.

Core Architectural Ideas

Architectures for commerce systems may look very different, but they all have to address the same issues. These issues must be understood no matter what approach is taken. In some cases, these common questions are considered explicitly during the design phase; in other cases, the questions and their answers are reflected in assumptions about various components in the architecture. In this section, we examine some of the primary elements that go into a commerce architecture, and we hope to make most of the issues explicit rather than leaving them as assumptions.

One word of caution: it may sometimes seem that what we describe in the architecture is so obvious that it need not be written down, or that we are drawing unnecessary distinctions. In our experience, leaving the obvious as implicit can often lead to later confusion and misunderstanding, precisely because everyone thought it was obvious but had different ideas of what was obvious. If we are to be successful at designing and building computer systems, we must be very precise, not only in describing the computational steps but also in our understanding and description of what we are trying to do. The processes of doing business may seem natural because they are so familiar to us, and because people can handle many unusual situations easily and effectively. When we design computer systems to manage some of those processes, we must be especially careful because computers cannot figure out how to keep a customer happy when something unexpected goes wrong.

Understanding of Roles

Two of the most basic questions for any computer system are "Who uses it?" and "What do they do with it?" For some programs, there are a few kinds of users who share similar goals. For example, novices and experts both use word processors with the same goal—producing documents. Internet commerce systems are more complicated: their users include the buyers of goods and services, the sellers of goods and services, and the people who operate all of the machinery.

Understanding the various roles and kinds of users for a system helps us to focus our attention on making sure that all users can use the system effectively to accomplish their goals, whether that is making a purchase or creating accounting reports.

Decomposition of Functions

A second important part of the system architecture is the way it decomposes the system into functional units. The specification of these functional units and the interfaces between them defines the architecture of the system. One of the differences between architectures is often the way that they group functions into units. Are all of the components integrated in a single system? Are the components distributed across multiple systems? What are the interfaces between functional units?

Linking Content to Transactions

The first two considerations for the system architecture, roles and decomposition, apply to the design of almost any computer system. A third part of the system architecture of an Internet commerce system is the way that content, such as a catalog, is linked to the transaction processing. In a paper-based system, the buyer transcribes item numbers and quantities onto an order form or requisition. Obviously, we would like to do this electronically.

There are several key issues in this linkage.

- How the user makes the transition

  In many cases, the user sees a **Click here to buy** button or can add items to a shopping cart for later purchase. The transition to the transaction takes place either at the **Buy now** point or at **Checkout** for the shopping cart.

- How the information is verified

  Depending on the underlying technology, it may be necessary for the transaction system to verify that the purchase information, such as price, item identification, and so on, was not modified when it was sent over the network. Because (as we shall discuss in more detail later) the Web uses a stateless protocol, a commerce system built on top of the Web must manage its own state. If that state is carried by the client in some way, the server must be able to ensure that it was not modified in transit.

- How the information matches up

  Some Internet commerce systems include a real-time inventory check to assure customers that items are in stock. If the system indicates that an item is in stock, however, how long is that indication valid? If the customer puts the item in a shopping cart for purchase at some later time, does the system promise that the item will be available when the purchase occurs? If the system does make such a promise, how long is it valid? What if the customer never returns to the site to buy the items in the shopping cart?

The answers to these questions help make design decisions for the system. Because different answers can lead to very different designs, it is important to think through the issues early in the design process.

Trust Models

In any distributed system, different components trust each other to a greater or lesser extent. Some components may trust others completely for all kinds of access (for example, both reading and writing data elements), whereas other components may disallow any remote access to their data. The specification of these relationships is called the *trust model* for the system. Any system has at least an implicit trust model, but specifying a trust model explicitly helps us to understand the details of the relationships between components when we need to analyze the security of the system.

Roles

Many different people interact with an Internet commerce system, and they need to do different things. Buyers require one set of operations; catalog designers, customer service representatives, and system operators each have their own sets as well. Even though these latter groups may all work for the merchant, they have different tasks to perform. For some businesses, especially smaller ones, the same person may perform all these tasks. Larger businesses have different people fulfilling different roles. Considering roles separately enables us to satisfy the requirements of businesses of all sizes, as well as making it possible to design a system that allows a smaller business to grow smoothly without having to reconsider what people do at each stage.

Speaking in terms of roles also helps to avoid confusion. For example, simply referring to the customer does not distinguish the cases when one person is selecting a product to be purchased and another arranges payment. By defining the operations required by a particular role, we can ensure that everything needed by the role is present in the system, rather than relying on the ability of one person to act in multiple roles.

It is important to keep in mind that there might be individuals playing many different roles in some organizations, and that there might be many individuals playing the same role in a larger organization. For example, larger organizations commonly have many people in the customer service role.

Next we describe some of the primary roles for both the buyer and the seller.

Customer Roles

In any commercial transaction, there is a buyer and there is a seller. We use many different words for the buyer: *customer, consumer, purchasing agent,* and so on. On the Internet, we sometimes refer to the buyer as a *client* or *browser* as well, referring more to the software than to the person. But there are some subtle differences among these words, and the distinctions reflect different roles on the buyer side. In some cases, such as a consumer purchase, the same person plays all of the roles without even thinking about the differences. Businesses, however, often make purchases in different ways, so it is useful to consider the various roles.

- Specifier—this person selects what is to be purchased.
- Approver—this person approves a purchase recommended by the specifier.
- Buyer—this person negotiates the terms and conditions of a purchase and arranges for payment.
- Recipient—this person receives the delivered goods or services.

In addition, we can distinguish different kinds of buyers based on their relationships with the seller. An *anonymous buyer* (sometimes referred to as a *walk-in customer*) has no prior relationship with the seller and may not ever create one beyond making a simple purchase. A *member customer* is one who repeatedly buys from a seller and has established some kind of relationship, which we will call *membership* here. A member may sign up because an account is convenient, because it offers some special benefits, or because there is a business relationship that is reflected in the membership.

Membership accounts give rise to another role, the *member administrator.* A person acting in this role may modify or update any stored profile information about the member. If the membership encompasses several individual accounts, such as for different members of a family or multiple purchasing agents for a business, the member administrator may also be able to set limits on the use of the individual accounts. These limits might be on the kinds of items that can be purchased, the amounts that can be spent, the time of day for purchases, and so on.

In practice, of course, a single individual may fulfill more than one role. For example, a consumer buying a sweater selects one in a store, pays for it, and takes it home. In this case, the consumer plays all three roles, and we generally make no distinctions among them. In contrast, consider the electronic components example described in Chapter 2. The specifying engineer determines which part will be purchased, a purchasing agent negotiates the payment terms, and the manufacturing group receives the components for inclusion in the final product.

What this breakdown tells us is that a general-purpose Internet commerce system needs a way for different people to handle different parts of a transaction, but it should also be very simple for a single person to handle all of them. Consumers do not expect to change roles explicitly at every stage, but they do expect to have a quick and easy process for buying. Companies, on the other hand, that make distinctions in the various roles want to be able to hand off the transaction from one role to another smoothly and efficiently. Even consumer systems get value from a good implementation of roles. A wish list is something a specifier would use, and most systems permit orders to be shipped to different addresses.

Business Roles

On the other side of a transaction is the seller. There are many roles in an Internet commerce system for sellers. Smaller businesses, and even larger ones beginning with small-scale efforts in Internet commerce, may have just a few people playing all the roles—so much so that the different roles enumerated here may seem overly complicated. Thinking about the roles early, however, makes it possible for an Internet business to grow more smoothly as more people join the team and the roles become more distinct in reality. For the seller, there are two main groups of roles: the business and content creation team and the operations team. The most important business roles are as follows.

- Business manager

  The business manager is responsible for the business approach on the Internet, creating and operating the Internet presence for the business, deciding which products and services are to be sold online, determining pricing, and establishing the key business relationships needed to make the venture successful. (We will discuss implementation strategies for these kinds of operations in Chapter 7.) This is primarily a business role, with particular attention paid to the success of the online business and the bottom line.

- Internet commerce architect

  The Internet commerce architect is generally a systems analyst who turns the business requirements into a system design that incorporates the creation and management of content (such as catalogs) and the transaction processing, fulfillment, and technical aspects of customer service. In short, the architect fills in the next level of detail for the commerce value chain.

- Content designer

  The content designer is responsible for the look and feel of an Internet commerce system, including graphic design, page layout, user experience, and so on.

- Content author

  The content author creates or adapts product information in a form that can be used for Internet commerce, working within the design laid out by the content designer.

- Implementor

  The implementor is responsible for creating any programs or software extensions needed to make the Internet commerce system work. For example, an implementor might write the software that takes product information from a database and dynamically renders it into a Web page.

- Database administrator

  If a database of product information is used, the database administrator (DBA) manages the creation and operation of the database to ensure its correctness, integrity, and performance.

- Sales and marketing team

  The sales and marketing team is responsible for focused efforts in promoting Internet-based commerce for the business.

- Customer service representative

  Customer service representatives for the business answer questions about products, assist buyers with registration or the purchasing process, respond to inquiries about order status and problems after the sale, and handle product returns and payment disputes. A business may have different people specialized in different areas of this role.

Of course, a particular organization may have more than one person in one or more of these roles, or one person may act in many of them. Some of the decisions may be determined by software purchased from a particular vendor, in which case many people on the commerce team described previously must select which product to buy and how it fits in with their plans for Internet commerce. Some members of this team may be outside consultants, depending on the skills and availability of the organization's staff.

The operations team installs and operates the Internet commerce system, making sure that it is running and available for customers. Some specific approaches to system operation are discussed in Chapter 7. The roles include the following.

- Operations manager

  The operations manager is responsible for managing all service activities for the Internet commerce system.

- System supervisor

  The system supervisor manages the system staff.

- System administrator

  The system administrator is responsible for the technical operations of the computer systems and networks.

- Security officer

  The security officer ensures that appropriate security measures have been taken in the design and implementation of the Internet commerce system.

- Fulfillment agent

  The fulfillment agent is responsible for shipping and handling of physical goods or delivery of services. In the case of digital goods, the fulfillment agent is responsible for overseeing the operation (and staff, if any) of the fulfillment system.

- Accountant

  The accountant is responsible for ensuring that the proper accounting procedures have been followed for Internet-based transactions, managing the relevant business records, creating reports on the transactions handled by the system, and other accounting functions.

Roles and Reality

The roles we have described are probably not exactly the roles found at any particular business, and it is unlikely that there is any one-to-one correspondence between these roles and people doing real work. Thinking about roles instead of people, however, enables us to ensure that all of the work gets done and that we are not missing an important function as we design a system and put together a team to operate it. Making these distinctions also helps if some of the work will be outsourced. As we shall see in Chapter 7, there are many approaches to implementing a system, and sometimes it makes sense to outsource all or part of the operation of an Internet commerce system. Some of the roles here—the operational ones, for example—can be outsourced relatively easily. Others, such as deciding which products are to go into the online catalog, are business decisions that cannot be handed off to others.

Components

Another important aspect of the system architecture is the set of components that comprise the system. For Internet commerce, we frequently try to take advantage of general-purpose Internet applications, for three reasons.

1. If general-purpose applications can be used, we need not build them again.
2. General-purpose applications are widely distributed, so we need not create the distribution channels to put a specialized tool in the hands of customers.
3. Customers are already familiar with the application, so they do not need to learn how to use a specialized tool.

In the next two subsections, we introduce the basic components used for Internet commerce systems. We will present a more detailed technical discussion of these components in Parts Two and Three of this book. Although our focus is on using general-purpose tools, such as the browsers and servers of the World Wide Web, there are, of course, times when it is appropriate to create and distribute a specialized tool for commerce. Even so, we think the components described here are a good starting point for designing such tools.

Customer Components and Clients

For customers, the primary tool for using the World Wide Web is a *browser,* sometimes called a Web *client.* We discuss browsers and other Web clients in Chapter 8. The system architecture is clearly influenced by the basic structure of the Web, and in particular by the capabilities of browsers. As we shall see, one of the important questions in deciding exactly how to structure a system is "What browsers do the customers have, and what are their capabilities?"

Some companies have also designed specialized client applications for commerce, particularly for payment. These applications, often called *client wallets,* are designed to implement one or more payment methods that require additional processing, such as cryptographic operations, on the client computer. Client wallets may also be used to keep track of what transactions have been made, to check on order status, or to manage other information related to transactions. The main problem with client wallets is that hardly any customers have them. Over the past several years, companies have not succeeded in distributing them on a large scale, so they are essentially irrelevant for most Internet commerce systems. An important lesson from these attempts is that new client software is a barrier for customers, and they will likely look for alternatives rather than proceed with installing new software. We look at different payment systems, including their requirements for client software, in Chapter 15.

Sometimes customer components can reside on third-party systems. For example, server-side wallets are Web sites at which consumers can register payment credentials and release them to sellers without having any special client software. Another example is a buyer home community system that provides authentication and customer service facilities in a federated commerce system, as we shall see later in this chapter. Such systems are not yet common, but many companies continue to build them.

Seller Components and Servers

On the other side of a transaction is the seller, whom we might also call the *merchant* or *vendor.* The seller provides all of the components of the commerce value chain, from content to customer service. In practice, a seller may provide some of the stages in the value chain directly and contract with others to provide the rest. Different sellers may make different decisions about which stages to provide directly, and these decisions may even change over time. Again, therefore, we separate the stages of the value chain in the general architecture so that different components can be handled differently.

Some components of the value chain are more easily outsourced than others. Content, for example, is a presentation of the actual products or services offered for sale by a business. Although a company may look outside for creative presentation ideas or development of the actual content, what the products are and how they are sold are the foundation of the business. Payment services, on the other hand, are very important to the business, but the details of the processing can be hidden as long as the results are correct. Here are some of the components.

- Content management system

  This can refer to the seller's catalog or to the entire corporate Web presence. Content management systems permit the creation and management of dynamic and continually updated content.

- Transaction processing system

  The seller's transaction processing system keeps track of all information related to transactions: what was ordered, who ordered it, how much it cost, the status of payment, the status of fulfillment, and so on.

- Payment processors

  Payment processors manage the movement of money or other payment instruments in the system. For example, when a consumer pays with a credit card, the seller connects to a credit card payment processor to authorize the transaction (by checking for sufficient available credit) and, later, to settle the transaction.

- Fulfillment systems

  Companies operating mail-order businesses often contract with a fulfillment company to handle packing and shipping orders. A business taking orders over the Internet for tangible goods might do the same. Indeed, a business selling digital goods over the Internet might even work with a fulfillment company to operate the servers used to deliver the online products. Or, in both cases, a business might choose to manage the fulfillment process in-house.

One logical grouping of these functions results in what we will call the *front office* and the *back office*. The front office is concerned with marketing and selling goods and services. Content and presentation are very important, and the focus is on attracting the customer to buy the product or service. The back office is concerned with managing the details of the transaction, from placing the order to payment to fulfillment. Proper handling of the transaction is important, such as ensuring that the relevant information is delivered to the right places and that the payment is collected correctly.

Examples of System Architecture

As we have suggested previously, different answers to different issues can result in very different system architectures. In this section, we look at four different architectures and discuss how they are constructed. The four architectures are a Web server with an order form, an approach to distributed transactions originally created at Open Market, a large-scale federated commerce system, and an approach to business-to-business commerce originally developed by the Open Buying on the Internet (OBI) Consortium. There are, of course, many other approaches to Internet commerce; we chose these to illustrate many of the points discussed in this chapter.

For analysis of architecture, we have found it convenient to consider four primary components of Internet commerce systems.

1. Client

   The client is a computer system, typically a personal computer, connected to the Internet either directly, through an Internet service provider (ISP), or indirectly, through a corporate network. The buyer uses the client computer for browsing and purchasing.

2. Merchant

   The merchant is the computer system or systems that contain the seller's electronic catalog and, in the case of online goods, products for over-the-Net fulfillment.

3. Transaction system

   The transaction system is the computer system or systems that process a particular order and that are responsible for payment, record keeping, and other business aspects of the transaction.

4. Payment gateway

   The payment gateway is the computer system that routes payment instructions into existing financial networks such as for credit card authorization and settlement.

Various architectures use these four components in different ways. In some systems, some of these components are combined into a single computer system, whereas in others these four system components are implemented by separate computer systems.

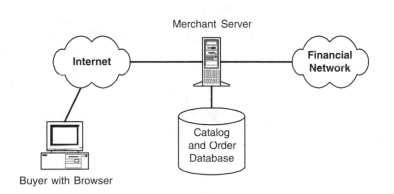

FIGURE 6-1. **Merchant Server: Physical View**

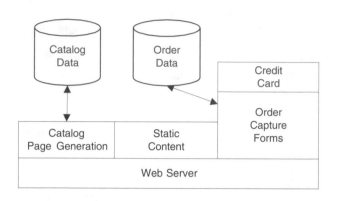

FIGURE 6-2. **Merchant Server: Logical View**

Once the designers of a commerce system have selected a gross division of function, there are still many decisions to be made at lower levels of functionality. For example, the order aggregation function, which permits the assembly of individual items into a complete order, can be implemented as part of the merchant, the transaction system, or the client.

Web Server with Order Form

Building a Web server with catalog pages and an order form is one of the simplest ways to construct an Internet commerce system. This approach is typically called a *merchant server.* A diagram of a representative system is shown in Figure 6-1, and a logical diagram of the structure of the merchant server is shown in Figure 6-2. Many of the technical details will become clearer as we discuss the technology in later chapters, but we will sketch the basic ideas here.

In this example, a single Web server provides both the catalog content and the order form. In other words, the merchant server and transaction server are combined into one system, and there is no explicit payment gateway. The catalog might consist of a set of Web pages describing items for sale, with embedded pictures, drawings, specifications, video or audio clips, and so on. The Web pages might be created as static pages using an HTML editor, or they might be created dynamically from a database of items and descriptive information. Next to each item is a button that the customer can click to buy the item or add it to a shopping cart for later checkout. When ready to buy the item (or items, if more than one is present in a shopping cart), the customer clicks a **Checkout** button that starts the payment part of the transaction.

Payment by credit card is by far the most common method used on the Internet today for consumer transactions (as we discuss in detail in Chapter 15). A simple order form might consist of a listing of the items being purchased and a set of fields for the cus-

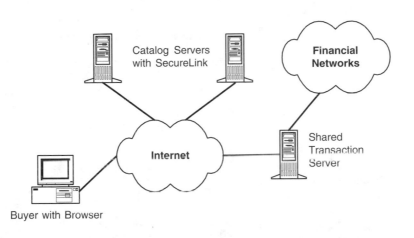

FIGURE 6-3. Open Market Distributed Commerce Architecture: Physical View

tomer to enter credit card payment information, including the card number, the expiration date, and the address for delivering the items, if they are physical goods. The form might also ask for the billing address, because some credit card systems use the billing address as part of the verification of the holder of the credit card.

It is possible, of course, that the Web server might use a different payment mechanism. In the simplest version of this model, the Web client has no special capabilities for commerce, so the commerce application does not require additional software for payment mechanisms. Credit cards, purchase orders, and other kinds of account-based payments may be used with such systems, thus taking advantage of the basic security capabilities common on the Web today.

This basic architecture may be appropriate and sufficient for some kinds of Internet commerce applications. Its primary virtue is its simplicity. On the other hand, it may be more difficult to expand it as the online business grows, or to incorporate new technologies and components as they become available.

Open Market Distributed Commerce Architecture

The core architectural idea of this architecture is to separate the management of content from the management of transactions through a technology called *SecureLink*. This idea permits multiple catalog servers to share the capacity of a single transaction engine and allows the content-oriented parts of the system to scale independently from the transaction-oriented parts of the system. Separation of these functions allows separate management of several system facilities—most notably, security. This approach also permits service organizations to provide transaction management services on an outsourced basis for other companies. Figure 6-3 shows the physical architec-

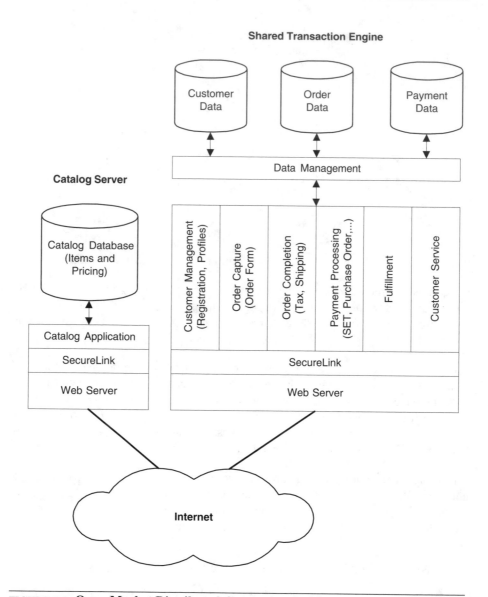

Shared Transaction Engine

Catalog Server

Catalog Database (Items and Pricing)

Catalog Application

SecureLink

Web Server

Customer Data

Order Data

Payment Data

Data Management

Customer Management (Registration, Profiles)

Order Capture (Order Form)

Order Completion (Tax, Shipping)

Payment Processing (SET, Purchase Order,....)

Fulfillment

Customer Service

SecureLink

Web Server

Internet

FIGURE 6-4. **Open Market Distributed Commerce Architecture: Logical View**

ture of this approach, and Figure 6-4 shows how functionality is distributed across different elements of the system. In this architecture, the transaction server is separated from the merchant server, and there may or may not be a separate payment gateway depending on which payment methods are supported.

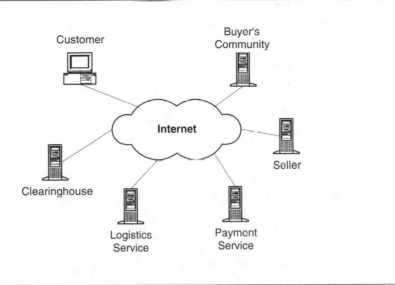

FIGURE 6-5. Federated Commerce System

Federated Commerce System

A federated commerce system (FCS) is a system made up of servers operated by different organizations and tied into an overall, perhaps global, commerce system by Web services and a collection of service agreements. In this system, consumers are members of communities of interest, which provide authentication services and customer service points of presence. When a consumer buys something, the necessary payment and shipping information is routed from her home community to the seller. The seller may also use some of the federated services for payment and other functions. At the conclusion of the transaction, a record is posted to the consumer's online statement held by her home community. From the consumer's point of view, only the home system is responsible for keeping online information. The essential architecture of this system is shown in Figure 6-5.

The federated commerce system includes

- Clearinghouse

   The FCS clearinghouse is responsible for tying the network together. It permits the seller to locate a buyer's home community and helps establish peer-to-peer connections among the various participants.

- Customers

   Customers browse for information, make purchases, and request customer service.

- Home communities

  Consumers join home communities on the basis of interests, services offered, or the degree of privacy protections offered.

- Sellers

  Sellers include merchants, service providers, and publishers.

- Payment provider

  The payment provider provides support for various payment mechanisms as a Web service. It uses a common interface, which helps make sellers more independent of the payment systems.

- Logistics provider

  The logistics provider handles shipping, returns, and other services.

We will return to this example in an extended form in Chapter 21.

Business-to-Business Purchasing

A closely related problem is managing purchases between businesses using the Internet. One architecture for such systems was proposed by the Open Buying on the Internet (OBI) Consortium, which was formed in 1996 to develop standards in this area. The consortium is a group of buy-side organizations, sell-side organizations, payment organizations, and technology companies that is addressing the problem of business-to-business commerce on the Internet. The core idea of OBI is to split the functionality of the commerce system between buy-side activities and sell-side activities so that each organization manages those functions logically connected to it.

The OBI design is based on a model of business commerce shown in Figure 6-6. In this model, the logical breakdown of activities is to place the customer database, requisitioner profiles, and approval processes on the buy side, and to place the catalog, order management, fulfillment, and payment activities on the sell side. This structure results in the architecture shown in Figure 6-7. The key idea in OBI relevant to our functional components is the splitting of the transaction server into its sell-side and buy-side parts.

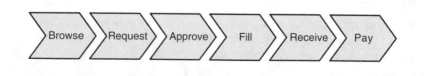

FIGURE 6-6. OBI Business-to-Business Purchasing Process

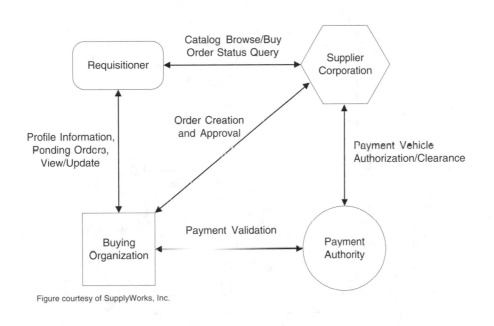

Figure courtesy of SupplyWorks, Inc.

FIGURE 6-7. OBI Architecture

In order to make this architecture work, two elements of interoperability are needed between the buy-side and sell-side components: requisitioner authentication and order handling.

1. Requisitioner authentication

   Because the buy-side organization assumes the responsibility in the OBI model for managing the pool of requisitioners, the sell side must have a standardized means of authenticating prospective requisitioners as authorized by the buying organization. OBI uses public-key certificates for this purpose. When the requisitioner browses the supplier catalog, he presents a certificate signed by the buying organization to validate himself. This approach implies that at the time the trading relationship between the companies is set up, the supplier catalog must be configured to accept the certificates.

2. Order handling

   In OBI, the requisitioner builds up an order by interacting with the supplier catalog. That order is then sent in a standardized format called the *OBI order request* from the sell-side OBI server to the buy side. Once it is there, any necessary approval processes proceed. After the order is finalized, it is returned to the sell side as an OBI order for fulfillment.

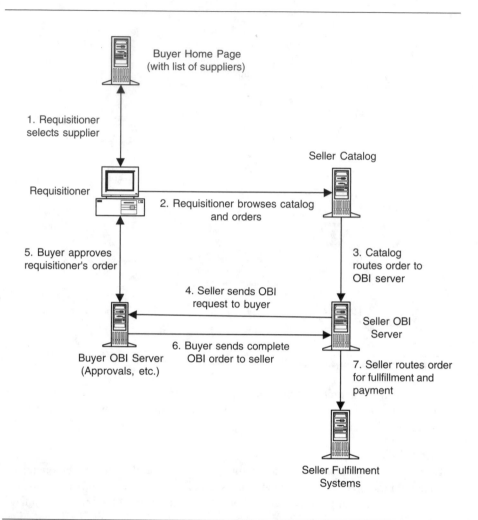

FIGURE 6-8. OBI Transaction Flow

The real benefits of the OBI choice of placing functionality can be seen only when there are multiple buy-side companies trading with multiple sell-side companies. When this happens, the buy side is able to manage its requisitioner database and approval system centrally, and it can use those systems seamlessly with multiple trading partners. Similarly, the selling organization can leverage a master catalog and order management system against multiple purchasers. In this ideal situation, information is not duplicated on either side.

Transaction Flow in the OBI Model

In this section, we walk through an OBI transaction. The descriptions in the following list correspond to the numbered arrows in Figure 6-8.

1. The requisitioner uses a Web browser to connect to the buying organization's purchasing server and selects a hyperlink to the selling organization's catalog server.

2. The selling organization's catalog server authenticates the requisitioner based on a digital certificate and then allows the requisitioner to browse, select items, and check out.

3. The content of the order is transferred from the catalog server to the selling organization's OBI server.

4. The sell-side OBI server maps the order into an OBI order request, encapsulated in an OBI object (with optional digital signature), and transmits the order request to the buying organization's OBI server over the Internet.

5. The requisitioner specifies any necessary annotations to the order, and internal approval processes take place.

6. The completed and approved order is mapped to an OBI order format, encapsulated as an OBI object, and transmitted back to the selling organization via the Internet.

7. The selling organization obtains payment authorization, if necessary, and begins order fulfillment.

For additional information on OBI, see www.openbuy.org.

Summary

Ultimately, the architecture of an Internet commerce system (like the architecture of any complex computer system) has a tremendous effect on the long-term success of a project. It is almost always easier to slap something together quickly to solve a particular problem, but the resulting system won't be able to handle the challenges of tomorrow and will quickly become obsolete, even for its original purpose. By carefully creating an architecture, taking into account the business challenges to be addressed and possibilities for change over time, the system can evolve and adapt to growth, new challenges, and technology changes. Over the long term, the up-front investment can have enormous return. Trading those advantages against "let's get it running now" is an important decision that should be made very carefully. Indeed, one lesson from the dot-com craze of the late 1990s is that moving too quickly is not always an advantage, particularly for established businesses with loyal customers.

Assuming now that there is an architecture—at least a simple one—in place, we can consider some strategies for implementing the commerce system, the subject of the next chapter.

CHAPTER 7 _____ *Implementation Strategies*

Rome wasn't built in a day. If it were, we would've hired
their contractor.
>   —Billboard for the Boston Central Artery project

Organizing for Internet Commerce

Who owns Internet commerce in the organization? Is it sales and marketing? Is it MIS? Is it corporate or divisional? We addressed this issue briefly in Chapter 1. Regardless of the reporting structure, the requirements for organization seem clear. The team will need to

- Draw on resources enterprise wide with sufficient priority to make progress.
- Have access to suitable technical and business skills.
- Be comfortable with rapidly changing technologies.

Planning the Implementation

As anyone who has ever operated business computer systems knows, the hard part is not the design or even writing the code—it is operating the system reliably and effectively over the long haul. Conceptually, taking credit card numbers over the Internet is straightforward, but what happens when the connection to the financial processor isn't working in your West Coast office at 6 A.M. and your East Coast customers are trying to buy something? This chapter considers some approaches to implementing and operating an Internet commerce system. During different phases of design, develop-

	In-House	**Outsource**
Project design	Marketing and IT staff	Business consulting
Software development	Custom development	Off-the-shelf software / Web services
Content development	Marketing staff	Web developer
Hosting and operations	IT staff	Internet service provider / ASP
Transaction Services	IT staff	Commerce service provider

TABLE 7-1. **Implementation Options**

ment, and operation of a commerce project, choices must be made regarding the use of internal resources or outsourcing. Table 7-1 summarizes some of the options considered in this chapter.

In planning an Internet commerce system, there are five phases to consider.

1. Project design
2. Software development and integration
3. Content development
4. Deployment
5. Long-term operation

Within each phase, it may be appropriate to do the work in-house or to outsource it. In our discussion, outsourcing may include, for example, using off-the-shelf software from a vendor, either as a packaged application or as Web services, as compared with doing in-house development.

Outsourcing

With any ongoing service, it is useful to ask whether it is best performed in-house or outsourced to a specialized organization. Internet commerce is no different, and the rapid evolution of Internet technologies can often make it difficult to keep up without some assistance. Forrester Research developed one model of an outsourcing strategy, shown in Figure 7-1. It consists of four phases.

1. **Early outsourcing.** In the beginning stages, an IT organization can create a system more quickly and begin to develop the requisite skills by calling on the expertise of outside specialists. Such specialists typically develop expertise in new technologies more quickly than do large corporate users.

2. **Internalization.** If the first phase is successful, IT groups who have already begun to develop the necessary skills can take over from the early outsourcing. The new skills, combined with detailed knowledge of the business, make it possible to expand deployment as well as customize the application to meet the specialized requirements of the business.

3. **Centralization.** As a technology spreads, it becomes possible to support the systems across the enterprise. This requirement, combined with the need to limit expenses, moves responsibility for the system to a central IT group.

4. **Late outsourcing.** As an application moves to legacy status, it may be important to continue operating it, but it may no longer be a core part of the business. In addition, it may also distract an IT team from learning new technologies and developing new business opportunities. At this stage, outsourcing it to a specialized company may be especially attractive because the outsourcers can create economies of scale for operating similar applications for many customers.

This model is useful for many applications, but it is particularly appropriate for Internet commerce applications. Outsourcing the implementation and operation of an Internet commerce system allows an organization to establish its presence and direction more quickly. The early experience is invaluable in developing follow-on applications, which can be brought in-house as the internal teams learn the new technology skills and begin to integrate the commerce applications more closely with other parts of the business.

An alternative method of analyzing outsourcing versus internal development is to consider how closely the project is aligned with the business.

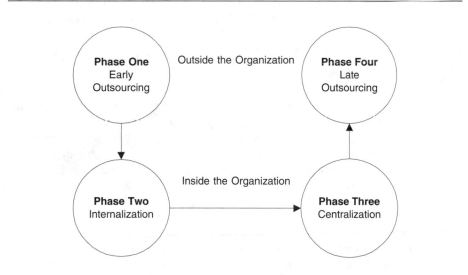

Figure courtesy of Forrester Research, Inc., Cambridge, MA, USA

FIGURE 7-1. Life Cycle of Technology Outsourcing

- Is the project a core competency?

  Are the development and operational skills required already available in-house? If not, would this project alone justify the hiring and training necessary for success? If the answer to these questions is no, then outsourcing may be appropriate.

- Is the technology a commodity?

  This is a difficult issue. If the technology involved is not a commodity, then the necessary development skills may be available only from a few specialized sources. Commodity technology may be less expensive to manage internally, especially if excess capacity is available. Operational considerations may be the reverse—if the operations of the project are a commodity, then outsourcing operations may have an economy of scale that makes them superior to in-house operations.

- What are the technology and project rates of change?

  Are the technology and the project expected to change rapidly? If so, then internal development, closely coupled to the business, may be indicated. Slowly changing applications may be safely outsourced and (nearly) forgotten.

- To what extent does the project need to be integrated?

  If a project has few and well-defined interfaces with one's core business systems, then it may be a good candidate for outsourcing. On the other hand, if complex and custom integration work is required to interface the application with existing in-house systems, internal development and operation may be more pragmatic.

Custom Development

One approach to developing an Internet commerce application is to create a custom application, with the development inside or outside the organization. The advantage, of course, is that the application, if developed successfully, will presumably meet the requirements of a specific business. In addition, a custom application may be better integrated with other systems at a particular business. These advantages are especially strong when the market for packaged application products for Internet commerce applications is still young and the products are evolving quickly.

On the other hand, there are several potential problems with custom solutions, and they should be considered carefully in a "make or buy" decision. First, rapid development is not always quality development. One of the attractions of custom development for Internet commerce applications is to "get something up fast." Indeed, it is not very hard to put together a simple catalog on a Web server, perhaps with a basic order form to collect credit card numbers. Sometimes it is important to get a system running quickly—to establish a presence on the Internet—but that short-term system may not be what is needed in the long term. How does it integrate with other systems? How is customer service handled? How does the system evolve with new technology? How are the security issues addressed? If Internet commerce is a strategic direction for the business, and not just a tactical demonstration, it should be approached with an idea of the long-term directions.

Second, custom development may now take longer than using off-the-shelf products. The ranges of features, cost, and quality in products for Internet commerce applications are expanding rapidly, so there may be a product that meets, or almost meets, the requirements of a particular business.

Third, how will a custom application be maintained? Will an in-house staff continue to work on it, or will they have new projects to undertake? Or will the outside consultants or integrators maintain it? Are they committed to long-term maintenance?

Fourth, custom development often has hidden costs. There may be ideas or features that were missed in the original definition of the project and that will require expensive changes later. Getting effective maintenance for a custom system—by definition, the only one like it in the world—may cost more than expected.

Fifth, the business requirements will undoubtedly change over time, and those changes will require changes in the software. Such changes will go well beyond maintenance, requiring modifications of the software, extensions to new applications, solutions to new problems, and so on. Although it is often difficult to predict how the requirements may change and what the implications for the software will be, we can predict with great confidence that such changes will happen.

Finally, the technology will change, and probably will change quite rapidly. Will the custom application be flexible enough to evolve? Will the team working on it learn about the new technology quickly enough? Does a shift in technology require a rethinking of the way the entire application is structured?

These questions are important ones to understand in developing any important application for a business. In some cases, the requirements of the business are so specific that the custom development is justified. In others, the long-term costs suggest that building on off-the-shelf products, with some integration and modest customization, is a more effective approach, even if not all of the initial goals can be accomplished.

Packaged Applications

In the early days of Internet commerce, almost every system was unique, developed to particular specifications as a custom implementation. Over time, of course, many software products for creating commerce applications have appeared on the market. The applications available today vary considerably in price, capabilities, and the amount of work the application developer must do. Products for Internet commerce fall into several broad categories.

- Content creation and management

- Order processing
- Fulfillment
- Integrated systems

Even within these categories, there are wide ranges of products. Content tools, for example, range from simple HTML editors to sophisticated systems for creating, managing, and mapping entire Web sites.

The details of these kinds of products are discussed elsewhere in this book, but there are a few general issues to consider in choosing any given product.

- Does the product meet the requirements as a component of the application? (For example, does a content creation tool handle the desired kinds of content?)
- How does the product integrate with other products (if it needs to do so)? In particular, does it integrate with the best of the other categories?
- Can the product be integrated with necessary legacy systems (such as inventory management)?
- Does the product have a plan for its long-term evolution in Internet commerce applications?
- Can the product be customized to meet specific requirements?
- Is the product extensible?
- What kind of support is behind the product?

Whenever possible, it is important to look at the choices of products for Internet commerce applications in terms of how they fit in with the overall direction of the commerce project, rather than in isolation. The best tools are the ones that will be used to get the job done, which may be very different from the most sophisticated tool in each category. Finally, hybrid approaches may be appropriate, with packaged applications providing the core functions and with custom software integrating the applications to existing business systems.

Working with System Integrators

System integrators (SIs) can be of great value to any Internet commerce effort. However, there are minuses as well as pluses. Integrators can bring skills to the project that may be missing or overcommitted in-house. They've probably done this before. On the other hand, SIs often build what they know how to build, not necessarily what you need. Integrators like to reuse solutions they already have. The technology used may be proprietary or idiosyncratic, locking you in to the same SI indefinitely.

The Roles of Internet Service Providers

First and foremost, Internet service providers, called *ISPs*, connect individuals and organizations to the Internet so their customers can communicate with other Internet users. Second, they often provide *hosting services* for Web sites or other Internet applications, where the ISP installs and operates the server computers and software that make up the Web site. In such cases, the server systems are usually located on the ISP's premises, not on the customer's. Third, ISPs may provide transaction services, such as payment systems, for the commerce operations of their customers. We refer to ISPs that supply such services as *commerce service providers*, which we discuss in more detail later.

Communications Services

The core of the ISP's service is providing communications.Typically, this includes the fundamentals of Internet systems, including the routing of Internet Protocol (IP) packets, the Domain Name System (DNS), and electronic mail. The communications services may be available by dialup, broadband, or a dedicated data circuit such as T1, and they are available in many different bandwidths. The bandwidth effectively measures how much data can flow over the connection per unit time. How much bandwidth you need depends on your application, but experience suggests that a T1 connection (providing 1.54 megabits per second), or at least a reasonable fraction of a T1 connection, is required for adequate performance in Internet commerce systems.

The Domain Name System is used to translate hostnames such as *www.serissa.com* to an IP address such as *10.250.92.7*. Most ISPs will also take care of registering a domain name so that others can find it.

When you are selecting an ISP, there are several important issues to address.

- Cost of the desired bandwidth

  The ISP can usually help size your application, enabling you to select the most cost-effective bandwidth.

- Outbound connections

  The Internet is a collection of networks that interconnect with each other. This means that some ISPs are closer to the Internet backbone—the high-performance core of the Internet—than others. The effective bandwidth between your site and your customers depends not only on your ISP but also on your customers' ISPs and all the other ISPs in between.

- Reliability

  How reliable is the ISP's service? How quickly does the ISP respond to problems? As with any other service, it is frequently a good idea to talk with other customers of the ISP to learn about their experiences. Of course, higher reliability and better customer service may also cost more, so be prepared to take that into account.

Some ISPs can provide redundant connections (at higher cost, of course) that may improve overall reliability. If so, be sure to check how much redundancy there really is. For example, there may be two circuits between the same routers at your site and the ISP's site. Although this may guard against certain kinds of circuit failures, it certainly will not handle router failures. And because it is hard to tell where the circuits are physically routed, it may even be the case that they end up using the same fiber-optic cable in the telephone system, which means there is hardly any redundancy at all.

- Extra services

  What additional services does the ISP provide? Do you need those services for your application? If not, will you be paying for services that you do not use?

The performance and reliability of your ISP are fundamental to the performance and reliability of your Internet commerce application, so it is very important to find an ISP that can provide the level of service you require at a price that fits your budget.

Hosting Services

Hosting services provide locations and communications for Web sites or other Internet applications. The hosting company installs and operates the server computers and software that make up the Web site. In such cases, the server systems are usually located on the hosting company's premises, not on the customer's.

- The hosting company has a trained staff available for the operations.
- The hosting company (usually) can provide round-the-clock operations and support, which may be difficult for smaller businesses to justify. (In other words, the hosting company may have an economy of scale in hosting.)
- Because the Web site can be connected directly to the Internet backbone, greater bandwidth may be available to the users compared with hosting at a corporate site.
- The cost of the operation may be amortized over a longer period of time or over many hosting customers, resulting in a lower cost of ownership for the business.
- The hosting site can be physically secure, have redundant power and environmental controls, and have Internet security systems carefully kept up-to-date.
- The hosting site can be located close to customers not at a corporate site.
- The hosting company may be prepared to scale the service rapidly for anticipated demand.

There are also some disadvantages, of course. The biggest one is lack of control: one is relying on another company to provide the critical operational services. The hosting company may also constrain when and how one can update the content on the Web server. Even taking these limitations into account, however, it is very common to use hosting services.

There are several issues to evaluate when selecting a company for hosting services.

- What kind of hardware will be used for the Web server? Can it run the kind of software you will need?

- What kind of software will be used for the Web server? Will it support your requirements? Can you provide your own programs for your application? Who controls the configuration of the software?

- What commitments for reliability will the ISP make? What has been the experience of other customers?

- What performance can be expected from the hardware, software, and network? Is it sufficient? What will happen if the performance turns out to be inadequate in practice? Will your application have its own system, or will it share a computer with other applications? Can the ISP handle peak loads for you as well as average loads?

- How do you update the content of your Web server? Can you use the tools you want to? If not, are the tools required by the hosting company sufficient for your application?

- How is the security of the system managed? Are the operating systems reasonably well secured? Are they carefully managed? Is there a firewall in place? How does the ISP staff handle potential security incidents? Are the software components kept up-to-date with security-related patches from the software vendors?

- Is the hosting staff capable of providing the service you require? Are they too busy with other customers to give you the necessary attention?

- How much will it cost to get the level of service you require? Are there extra costs beyond the basic ones?

As with the basic communications services, it is important to select a hosting company that can provide the services you require at a reasonable cost. Although it is possible to change hosting companies, managing the transition can be difficult. It is therefore worthwhile to invest some time and effort in understanding what the ISP can do for you before you set up the site.

Application Service Providers

An application service provider (ASP) supports and operates enterprise applications on behalf of other companies. For example, most ERP companies offer their applications as a service as well as a product. An ASP that specializes in commerce is a commerce service provider, which we discuss in the next section.

Commerce Service Providers

Beyond simple hosting services for Internet commerce applications are transaction services, which provide the infrastructure for order capture, payment, and fulfillment. We call an entity that provides such a service a *commerce service provider* (CSP). Internet service providers are often CSPs, but other kinds of organizations may also be

CSPs. A bank, for example, may provide transaction services for Internet commerce as an extension of the services it provides to its merchant customers. Some *Internet malls* provide similar services as well.

It is common for CSPs to provide hosting services as well, although this is not always required. Some system architectures (as discussed in Chapter 6) require that content servers and transaction systems be located together, but others do not.

Here are some important questions for commerce service providers.

- What kinds of payment systems are supported now? What kinds may be added in the future?

- Does the CSP handle the kind of business model you require (for example, information commerce, consumer retail, and so on)?

- What is the cost structure? Is the pricing based on a flat rate, transaction volume, transaction value, or something else?

- What kinds of reports are available to sellers?

- How and when are funds transferred to sellers?

- What customization of the ordering and payment processes can be performed for each seller? Does this meet your application requirements?

- Can the look and feel of the ordering and payment processes be customized for appropriate branding of the site?

- Which tasks are managed by the seller, and which by the CSP?

Web Services

A new category of outsourcing is Web services, which we discuss in more detail in Chapter 11. A Web service is essentially some chunk of business logic that is made available remotely over the Internet. Some commerce-related examples are payment services and logistics services. Web services offer the possibility of making outsourcing decisions along functional lines, perhaps keeping content management and order management in-house but outsourcing payment processing and sales tax calculation.

Project Management

It may seem trite to say, but one of the keys to a successful Internet commerce application is getting the work done. A typical commerce project will involve software from several vendors, some custom development (or at least customization) by an in-house team or outside consultants, the operational services of several organizations, the integration of the new application into existing business models and practices, and many other activities. Without effective project management, it is unlikely that all the pieces will come together for a successful system.

This is not the glamorous part of Internet commerce, but it may well be the most important. Although projects will differ greatly in the details, there are some common issues for Internet commerce projects.

- Estimating costs

  What are the real costs of the project likely to be? These costs include those of software products, the time and effort required to customize or extend the products, information about the actual products and services for sale up on the Internet, Internet access, personnel requirements for developing and operating the application, and so on. A common mistake is to look primarily at the up-front cost of the software as being the dominant cost, when in fact the costs of customizing or adding on to the base software may be much higher. The operating costs may also be much higher, depending on the details of the application. It is important, therefore, to look at the cost of ownership for the project, not just the initial software costs.

- Measuring benefits

  What are the expected benefits from developing the commerce application? Is this project a strategic investment or one for immediate return? Are the primary benefits expected to be lower costs (from having to print and mail fewer catalogs, for example) or increased revenues? Is this a pilot project to be replaced by a larger-scale (and possibly different) system, or is this the primary system? Having a good idea of the expected benefits and making sure that the expectations are shared across the organization make it possible to measure them over time and to ensure that the organization can evaluate whether or not the project is successful.

- Sizing and performance

  It is especially hard to predict the required levels of performance and sizes of the server systems for any Internet service, not just for commerce systems. The usual problem is that an interesting site can attract a large number of people over a short period of time: word of mouth can spread very quickly on the Internet. When the site is overloaded, it can get a reputation for poor performance just as quickly. This phenomenon of intense periods of heavy use is sometimes called a *flash crowd*.[1] What this suggests is that we should plan systems for high peak loads with desired service requirements and a different set of expectations for average loads and service requirements. These plans should be separate from what would be considered a successful load or number of users on the system, because the goal of the planning is to handle the potential load. The potential load may be well in excess of what would be considered successful.

- Personnel

  Does the project have the necessary staff with the right skills to implement the application? Does it need consultants or contractors with specialized knowledge? Does the team need additional training on the software or technologies to be used?

---

1. The term *flash crowd* was coined by science-fiction author Larry Niven in a short story by that name (in *The Flight of the Horse,* Ballantine, 1971).

- Maintenance, support, and upgrades

  What is the expected evolution of the commerce application? Are the software components on track with the expectations for the evolution? Who performs the maintenance and support on custom components or extensions? Will upgrades of software components have stable programming interfaces to enable reintegration with other systems? All too often, commerce applications are developed without long-term plans, and shifts in products and technology can leave them isolated over time. Although such shifts may happen even to the best-planned projects, careful planning in advance can avoid many such problems. Indeed, this is why we advocate paying attention to the architecture and long-term questions for Internet commerce in this book, rather than focusing on the details of what can be done to-day.

Staying Up-to-Date

One of the truisms of technology is that it changes. Especially in the Internet world, the technology is evolving quickly. We want to stay up with the latest and greatest technologies, whether they be the Web, real-time audio, Java, or exciting ideas yet to be invented. There is tension between the desire for stability and the drive for rapid evolution, and between the cost of change and the fear of being left behind. Therefore, it is worth thinking through the benefits, costs, and implications of incorporating new technologies into an Internet commerce application.

Issues for the Business

- How will the proposed change affect the existing system? In many cases, the change may have little or no direct effect on the application already running. Other possible changes may risk the stability of the running application; such changes must be evaluated and tested carefully.

- Will your team have the necessary skills? Changing technology requires continual development of new skills for the team implementing the application. Although the continuing education of the team is important, this must be balanced against a treadmill of technology change. One useful question here is whether or not the technology—or the skills—are strategic to the organization.

- What are the costs? What does it actually take to implement the new technology in the application? These costs might come from software, new or custom development, staff training, new hardware to run the new software, or added routine operations. No matter what the components of the cost, it is important to look at the overall cost of the new technology, which may be far greater than the cost of simply acquiring a new software package.

- How much change can the customers and the organization handle every year? Even when all the other factors line up—the customers like (or at least don't mind) the change, the technology looks like a long-term winner, the costs aren't out of line, the team has (or can acquire) the needed skills—there may be a limit to how much change the customers (or an organization) can handle in a given period of time. Sometimes absorbing the change may be too much in the context of all the other activity going on.

Issues for the Customers

- What software will your customers have? Some new technology features require that customers have additional software on their systems. For example, real-time audio applications may require special software for playing back audio files. To get the benefit of the new software, not only must the application be modified, but the customers must also install the extra components on their systems. In some cases, distributing the client software must be done as part of the application, which can result in added development and customer service costs. Do not forget that the required client software must also be available for the platforms (operating systems and other core software) that the customers are using. It is also important to keep in mind that the customers who use your system may not be the owners and managers of their computer systems. If the application requires particular client software, it may be necessary to negotiate with the IT department of each of your business customers to make sure the appropriate software is loaded and operable.

- What do your customers require? Some customers may want very much to have a site with the latest technologies—multimedia audio and video, Java applications, and so on—whereas others may have no interest in such technologies at all. Understanding your customers is therefore extremely important in making decisions about these technologies. A Web site aimed at teenagers, for example, will probably make much more extensive use of multimedia applications to attract customers than a Web site that will be used by electronics engineers to select parts.

- How will your customers react to change? Some groups of customers are uncomfortable with rapid technology evolution. Familiarity and stability are important to them, so changes in the application are likely to put them off.

- What are the expectations? Do your customers expect rapid deployment of new technology as a matter of course, or do they expect a steady and deliberate evolution? Matching the technology development with the expectations can help customers have a sense of how your business operates, making it possible for them to plan more effectively.

- Is the latest technology a fad or a trend? Some technologies have short lives, whereas others become core parts of business computer systems. In the early stages, it is often difficult to tell them apart. Jumping into a fad can be a costly exercise in unusable technology, whereas missing a fundamental trend may cause you to lose valuable time to competitors. Although it is not always possible to tell which is which, thinking through this question may help you make a decision about the investment. This is particularly important when you are evaluating an exciting new technology that may or may not have significant long-term effects on the business.

These questions are intended to help guide the process of adopting new technologies into commerce applications. In many ways, they represent a pragmatic view that is often opposed to the excitement and vision of new technology. On the other hand, it is easy to get caught up in such excitement, and asking these questions helps one arrive at a realistic understanding of the benefits as well as the costs.

The Role of Standards

Part of the core philosophy of the Internet is the use of standards to ensure interoperability among components from different vendors. TCP/IP, the core protocols of the Internet, are defined independently of any one vendor, and that definition is what makes it possible for two computers owned by different people, manufactured by different companies, running different software, to communicate with each other.

Just what is a standard, anyway? In the computer business, we often talk about two kinds of standards, *de jure* and *de facto*. The first kind, *de jure* standards, are the standards specified by designated organizations that are recognized to have some authority. These include organizations such as the International Telecommunications Union (ITU) and the American National Standards Institute (ANSI). These groups develop standards as a collaborative process among representatives from companies and other organizations that are involved in developing a particular technology area.

By contrast, *de facto* standards are those that have become "standard" through widespread use. Sometimes such standards evolve from a particular company's technology becoming widely used by many vendors; the Network File System (NFS) developed by Sun Microsystems is one example. In other cases, such standards arise out of collaborative development, often including work from researchers and university labs. The TCP/IP family of protocols is an example of such development.

The Internet Engineering Task Force (IETF) is somewhere between de jure and de facto. The IETF operates on the standard of rough consensus and running code, rather than elaborate paper designs. This process tends to lean toward designs that are cleaner and simpler than the results of traditional standards bodies, yet the de facto submissions of groups with running code are frequently improved by the scrutiny of the IETF process.

For our present discussion, standards serve two main purposes: they provide the basis for building interoperable applications, and they provide a certain stability for longer-term development. In addition, some kinds of standards allow applications to be ported easily from one platform to another, which can simplify the evolution and deployment of an application. Building applications using a foundation of standard protocols can take advantage of years of work by others to develop a common approach to a problem, or to create other applications that work together. For example, using the standards of the Web as the base of a commerce application means that the user interface can be provided by commonly available Web browsers and the communications managed by a Web server.

Standards cannot always be a hard-and-fast requirement, however. When a technology area is developing rapidly, it often takes standards some time to catch up. In the early stages of such development, it may be difficult to predict which of several competing products will emerge as a standard (or at least as the basis for one). In such cases, it may be necessary to choose a technology solution in advance of standardization, based on the best available information and understanding of both the risks and the potential benefits.

In other words, standards are another tool for getting the job done. They can be very effective at times, but we must not be trapped into using only standards when new opportunities present themselves.

24/7 Operation

As we have said, the Internet is open for business around the world, 24 hours a day, 7 days a week. Customers (and potential customers) from Australia are likely to be browsing sites in the United States at times when a normal storefront would be closed. Even within the same time zone, customers may be using the Internet for business late at night, whether for convenience or simply because they can't sleep. Many businesses, especially smaller ones, are not accustomed to operating under such conditions, so it is especially important for them to consider these aspects of the operation.

It might be observed that telephone order businesses have many of these same characteristics: their catalogs are available to customers at any time, and the telephone may be used throughout the day or night. There are, however, some important differences, especially in terms of what customers are coming to expect from Internet businesses. In most cases, telephone order companies that are open during business hours have some geographic limitations for their bases of customers. For example, almost all of their customers may be in the United States. Geography therefore limits the most common times of interest—during the day. On the other hand, many telephone order companies are providing 24-hour service, because they recognize that customers will call around the clock.

Second, if the catalog is the Web site and the Web site isn't available, then the catalog isn't available. Part of the service—perhaps the main part—is providing the information to customers whenever they would like to get it.

Staffing is the most difficult part of providing service 24 hours a day, 7 days a week. If operations are not fully automated, then appropriate personnel need to be available at all times. It takes about five full-time-equivalent staff to keep one person on duty on a round-the-clock basis. Computer systems and network connections will operate around the clock unless something goes wrong, so there are two main questions for providing round-the-clock service.

1. Are there any routine operations that require a person to do them outside normal business hours? This question applies to any part of the Internet business that is not automated. For example, if a purchasing system requires a person to approve a purchase order, and this function must be available at any time, then someone must be present at all times to perform the task.

2. What should happen if the automated systems fail outside normal business hours? When something goes wrong with the computer systems or networks, it usually takes a knowledgeable person to diagnose the problem and repair it. How is the problem detected? How are the right people notified? Are there specific requirements for how long the failure can last? For example, a project plan might specify that certain kinds of failures must be repaired within an hour, other kinds within four hours, and so on.

Of course, different businesses will have different requirements for their availability and responsiveness, depending on the nature and expectations of the customers, the way that the Internet is being used for business, the availability of trained staff, and the amount the business is willing to invest in providing such a level of service. The important thing is to think through these requirements and make some decisions at the outset about what is desired for service, rather than to be caught by surprise when a computer or network connection fails.

Finally, as we discussed earlier, outsourcing the operation of the Internet commerce system is one way to provide a high-availability system. Most organizations that handle such outsourcing have plans and staff to make the systems available around the clock. It is important, of course, to ensure that they do and that both parties agree on the expected level of service and responsiveness to problems.

Security Design

Surveys often show that security is one of the primary areas of concern for those creating systems for Internet commerce. Indeed, the security of the system is of critical importance in a successful system over the long term. There are important security issues in the design, implementation, and operational phases of any Internet commerce project.

We discuss security issues, technologies, and solutions in detail in Chapter 14. In implementing and operating an Internet commerce system, however, we must emphasize the importance of continual monitoring and evaluation of the system from a security point of view. It does no good to set up a system correctly at the outset and then undermine the security with careless operation, in much the same way that it does no good to install a lock on a door if no one ever locks it.

Multiorganization Operation

Over time, developing a robust Internet commerce system will almost certainly involve coordinating the efforts of many organizations. In this chapter we have already looked at several possible participants.

- Internet service providers
- Commerce service providers
- Web services operators
- Web and content developers
- Payment processors
- Software vendors
- System integrators
- Different organizations within a company

These participants are often involved not only with the creation of the Internet commerce system but also with its day-to-day operation. So when problems arise, as they inevitably do, it is exceedingly important for the different groups to work together smoothly on solving them. Problems with networked computer systems are often difficult to diagnose, so the complete team must be able to cooperate to find them instead of blaming each other. Once the problem has been found, of course, it may be clear who is responsible for solving it, or it may require a team working together to do so.

Performance problems in particular are often extremely hard to find. Part of the problem is that it may be difficult to find the bottleneck in a complex system, with many components and a structure that may not be fully understood by anyone on the project team. Another part of the problem is that network systems are commonly designed to tolerate many kinds of faults, typically by sending data again if an expected result does not occur within a given period of time and by having redundant services. When these features are combined, the failure of one service may go undetected, because the sender finds a different service after some time interval. Thus, a fault in the system (the failure of the service) appears to the users as a performance problem (the extra time taken to retransmit the data).

To maximize the chances for successful operation, then, there are several steps that can be taken in advance of problems.

1. Ensure that all participants understand both their own roles and the roles of the other participants in the operation of the system.

2. Bring all (or most) of the participants together to work on the routine operation as a team, so that when problems arise, the people and the organizations are used to working with each other.

3. Plan in advance how to handle particular problems, so that there will be known solution paths for at least the predictable problems.

4. Establish a set of problem-solving procedures—from detection to diagnosis to solution—that are familiar to all participants. These procedures will then help the team work together in solving the problem, rather than trying to figure out who should do what in an ad hoc fashion.

5. Prepare for problems by acquiring—by development or purchase— tools for monitoring the system and diagnosing faults. It is much easier to use well-understood tools to find a problem than to apply primitive tools and debugging techniques haphazardly. And the monitoring tools, if used correctly, can provide early warnings of many faults before they become serious.

For the most part, these suggestions have little to do with technology; they are about working with people, teams, and organizations. In making an Internet commerce system a real success for the business, however, these are some of the most important issues to be solved. The most wonderful technology in the world won't succeed if the team operating it doesn't work together.

Summary

It is easy to be seduced by the lure of computing technology, whether for Internet commerce or any other application. The technology, however, is only one factor—albeit the flashiest—in the effective use of computer systems. In particular, an Internet commerce system must enable a business to deliver value to its customers. With the technology components in place, they must be operated in a way consistent with delivering that value and with the reliability, security, and performance expected by the customers. The operational task may not be glamorous, but it is absolutely fundamental to the success of the business, which is, of course, what the effort is all about.

The first part of this book has focused on the nontechnology parts of an Internet commerce system: understanding the business issues, focusing on the customer, developing an architecture, and executing a plan. With that view, we now turn to the technology components of Internet commerce systems.

Part Two

The Technology of
Internet Commerce

CHAPTER 8   *The Internet and the World Wide Web*

Technology . . . the knack of so arranging the world that
we don't have to experience it.

    —Max Frisch[1]

The Technology of the Internet

Part One of this book was primarily about the business issues for Internet commerce. Understanding the business is really the first step in planning a successful system for Internet commerce. In Part Two, we delve into the technology used to make those business plans real. We will be discussing both the core principles underlying the technology (such as how to think about security for Internet commerce) and some current technology components (such as some of the communications protocols used on the Internet today). The core principles provide some guidance for making decisions in the face of rapid technological change, whereas the discussion of current technologies provides some understanding of how to put them to work, as well as demonstrating how the core principles can be applied.

In this chapter, we begin with a look at the fundamental technologies of the Internet, starting with the core protocols (TCP/IP) and moving to some of the main applications, such as the World Wide Web. We also examine some of the fundamental design principles of the Internet. Understanding these principles not only helps us understand the technology but also helps us build on the accumulated experience of the Internet for designing new systems.

---

1. Max Frisch, *Homo Faber* (1957).

In the remainder of Part Two we examine some technologies that are particularly important for Internet commerce. We look at the key building blocks for commerce systems, the problem of system design, some particulars of XML and Web services, the creation and management of content for commerce systems, the uses of cryptography to provide security, issues of system security, payment systems, order management, and transaction processing. In addition, we will examine the place of Internet commerce systems in the context of other enterprise information systems, as well as emerging mobile and wireless technologies that may affect how commerce is done on the network. We then work through some examples of how these components can be put together in an effective system design.

Development of the Internet

The Internet grew out of a research network originally funded by the U.S. Department of Defense. Development of this network, known as the ARPANet after the *Advanced Research Projects Agency* (*ARPA*), began in 1969. Over time it grew slowly, as universities, defense agencies, and a few companies joined the network, mostly as participants in various research projects funded by ARPA. As the network grew, it was used for applications beyond research, such as electronic mail. With these other applications came increasing use by research groups working on other kinds of projects.

In the early 1980s, the current versions of the core Internet protocols, TCP and IP (which we discuss later), were introduced across the network. Shortly thereafter, as ARPA reduced its role in supporting the network, the term *Internet* came to be used as the name for the now global entity. The term *Internet* itself comes from the word *internetwork*—an interconnected set of networks. As we shall see, the Internet can grow with very little central control as networks are connected to each other.

The term *internet* (with a lowercase *i*) is sometimes used to describe an internetwork distinct from the Internet (with a capital *I*). For a time this term was commonly used to describe networks belonging to individual organizations, such as large companies, that used Internet technology. More recently, the term *intranet* has become the common term for such internal networks. We shall have more to say about intranets later in this chapter.

Design Principles of the Internet

The Internet has been successful because of some fundamental decisions about its design that were made early in its history. These decisions are often invisible to the end user, and even to application developers, but understanding them provides insight into why the network is the way it is. In addition, we often find that such insight helps in

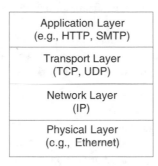

FIGURE 8-1. **Layering of Internet Protocols**

making choices about building new applications. Even when such applications seem far removed from the core design principles of the Internet, those that match the spirit of the Internet design are more likely to succeed than those that do not.

The main design principles of the Internet are as follows.

- Interoperability

    Independent implementations of Internet protocols actually work together. This may seem obvious today, but it took significant work in the early days of the Internet to make that happen. In fact, the Interop conference began as an event for vendors to test the interoperability of their products. Today, interoperability means that systems can be assembled using computers and software from different vendors. In the context of Internet commerce, interoperability means that buyers and sellers do not have to buy and upgrade software simultaneously from the same vendor to conduct commerce. Of course, this is true only if the software from different vendors is based on open standards and does, in fact, interoperate.

- Layering

    Internet protocols are designed to work in layers, with each layer building on the facilities provided by lower layers. For example, TCP builds on IP to create reliable byte streams, and application protocols such as those for the Web or electronic mail build on the capabilities of TCP. This layered architecture is shown in Figure 8-1.[2]

- Simplicity

    One way to look at the layering of the Internet is that it grows both up and down from IP. IP itself is very simple, providing only the addressing, routing, and formatting of packets. Below the level of IP, there is the complexity of many different

---

2. Some readers may note that this model differs from the common Open Systems Interconnection (OSI) reference model for network layers. Internet applications typically do not fit the OSI model exactly, so we have used the simplified model here.

kinds of network hardware and topologies, such as Ethernet, dialup connections, and so on. IP hides that complexity from applications. Above IP, higher-level protocols such as TCP offer abstractions that are easy for application programmers to understand and use. As a consequence, both application developers and users are insulated from the complexities of different network devices as well as from the complexities of implementing low-level network protocols.

- Uniform naming and addressing

The IP layer offers a uniform addressing structure that assigns a 32-bit address to each computer connected to the network. These addresses are commonly written in *dotted quad* form, such as 16.11.0.1. Numeric addresses are hard for people to remember, so the Domain Name System (DNS) offers a uniform way to translate human-readable names for computers, such as *www.serissa.com*, to the numeric address for that computer. These two systems, together with interoperability of implementations, let the Internet function. The IP layer is also evolving; a newer version called *IPv6* is now being deployed. Among other changes, IPv6 uses 128-bit addresses for computers on the network, enabling many more systems and networks to be interconnected.

- End-to-end protocols

The Internet is designed around end-to-end protocols. That is, the interpretation of the data happens on the sending and receiving systems, but nothing in the network needs to look at anything but the destination address and a few other control bits for delivering the packet. This is somewhat like mailing a letter: you put the recipient's address on the envelope and drop it in a mailbox. The postal service does not care what is inside (as long as it is not hazardous), and you do not care if it travels by truck, jeep, or airplane, as long as it arrives in a reasonable amount of time. By contrast, when you travel to a faraway city, you might take a taxi to the airport, an airplane to the other city, and a bus to the hotel. Each of these steps is booked and paid for separately. The analogous design in networking is a hop-by-hop system, in which intermediate computers are processing the data at the application layer. End-to-end protocols have several advantages. They hide the internal structure of the network, including the wide range of physical hardware used on the Internet, from users and applications. In addition, they can provide simple abstractions to programmers, shielding them from such things as the messy details of recovering from low-level errors. The most important fact about end-to-end design, however, is that the end systems are ultimately responsible for error recovery and success. This makes the network much simpler, and it winds up making the overall system much more reliable.

From these simple principles comes a powerful, robust, and reliable network that has scaled to a global level. The standards and specifications for the Internet protocols are developed by the Internet Engineering Task Force (IETF), which is open to participation by anyone who would like to contribute. Over time, the IETF has brought together vendors, users, researchers, governments, and others to develop and improve the technology of the Internet.

Core Network Protocols

The Web depends on a number of lower-level protocols, particularly IP, TCP, and DNS. Several comprehensive works on the networking and protocol technology of the Internet are listed in Resources and Further Reading, which follows Chapter 22.

Physical Layer

The Internet, as the name suggests, is a network of networks. At the physical layer, no single technology is used. Various parts of the Net run over local area networks using Ethernet, token ring, Fiber Distributed Data Interconnect (FDDI), Asynchronous Transfer Mode (ATM), and other technologies. Wide area networks have been built with point-to-point data circuits, dialup, frame relay, ATM, and other services. All of these network technologies are used to transport and route Internet traffic. Within one of these lower-level networks, routing is handled by whatever means are built into that network. In most cases, even the addressing is distinct from Internet addressing. For example, Ethernet uses 48-bit universal identifiers for addressing and routing. When an IP network is built using an Ethernet, the end systems use a special protocol, the Address Resolution Protocol (ARP), to translate IP addresses into Ethernet addresses.

Internet routers are used to connect these constituent networks. These routers forward packets from network to network until they reach the network connected to the destination system, whereupon the router can deliver the packet directly. Each router has a local map of the network that tells it where to forward a packet next, based on the destination address in the IP header. The information about where to forward a packet next, which can be quite complex in a large network, is distributed using specialized routing protocols.

Security at the physical layer depends on the network technology being used. Some network systems, for example, include encryption of all data on the physical network. This encryption does not, however, extend to data when it travels off that particular physical network. The security of router configurations depends for the most part on simple passwords, on the obscurity of these devices, and on the detection of the side effects of tampering (which are usually obvious).

Routers are often used as the first line of defense against network attack. In particular, routers may be configured as part of a network firewall in order to provide careful segregation of "suspect" traffic that originates outside an organization, from presumably authorized traffic that originates on the inside. We shall have more to say about firewalls in Chapter 14.

Internet Protocol (IP)

The term *TCP/IP* is commonly used as the name of the fundamental networking protocol of the Internet. In fact, TCP and IP are two separate protocols, although most applications on the Internet use both. *IP* is the *Internet Protocol*, and it is the one that most defines the Internet. IP deals only with small packets of data, which are labeled with the network addresses of the source and destination computers. The network is responsible for trying to deliver packets to their destinations, but it does not guarantee that it will do so. Within the network, packets may be lost or duplicated, and they may arrive out of order. This "best efforts" approach may not seem useful at first, but in fact it is a very powerful substrate for building networked applications. Other protocols can build on the foundation of IP to meet the needs of different kinds of applications. Such protocols are identified in an IP packet by a protocol identifier, which enables a destination system to select the correct protocol for processing at the next higher layer.

IP itself does not offer any security services. In theory, attackers with physical access to the network can listen to packets going by, introduce forged packets, or intercept and alter legitimate packets. Addresses can be forged easily, so many applications must be careful about believing the addresses on a packet. Ultimately, it is the responsibility of higher-level protocols to manage these problems, but network layer techniques such as firewalls are often used to create protected network environments in which applications simply do not worry about these sorts of attacks.

IP has been used in its current form for many years. More recently, the IETF has defined the next generation of IP, IP version 6 (or IPv6). IPv6 includes many improvements on IP, including a larger address space, better scaling for the routing system, and security services. It has been carefully designed to allow a gradual transition, because the Internet is already so large. There will probably be a lengthy period of conversion to IPv6 as vendors upgrade their software and as network users install it at their sites. During the transition, some of the improvements, particularly the security services known as IP Security (IPSEC), are being deployed with the current version of IP.

Unreliable Datagram Protocol (UDP)

The two most common transport protocols on top of IP are the Unreliable Datagram Protocol (UDP) and the Transmission Control Protocol (TCP). UDP provides a very simple datagram (or packet) service to applications. It gives them access to the facilities of IP, along with a few additional features. These features include a checksum for basic data integrity and a *port number,* which is used to identify which application is the real destination of the packet (recall that the IP address identifies only the system, not the application running on the system). UDP does not provide any services for reliable delivery or ordered delivery, so packets may arrive out of order, or they may never arrive at all. Applications that use UDP must provide the level of reliability they need, but they also have great flexibility in how to do so. Two notable Internet applications that use UDP are the Domain Name System (DNS), which we discuss in more detail below, and Sun Microsystem's Network File System (NFS).

Transmission Control Protocol (TCP)

The Transmission Control Protocol (TCP) is the most common transport protocol on the Internet. Building on the packet-oriented foundation of IP, it provides the abstraction of a reliable byte stream. That is, an application sends data, and the receiver gets it in the order it was sent (unless, of course, an error occurs that is too serious for TCP to recover from). It also provides a flow control mechanism to ensure that a receiver is not overwhelmed by a sender transmitting data too fast. TCP works by having the receiver send back an acknowledgment for the packets it receives. If the sender does not get the acknowledgment within a certain period of time, it transmits the packet again. Each packet also contains a sequence number, so the receiver can put them into the right order. TCP thus creates an illusion of a continuous ordered stream of data for application programmers, who need not worry about the details of how the data gets through the network. Most familiar applications on the Internet use TCP, including the Web and electronic mail.

TCP itself does not contain any native security mechanisms, although its operation does have implications for security. An eavesdropper can pick up individual packets and easily reconstruct the conversation, but it is much harder for an attacker to change the data in a TCP stream. More unfortunately, it is easy to attack an end system by sending many requests for new connections without following through on the rest of the protocol. This so-called denial-of-service attack ties up critical resources of the operating system and can block legitimate connections. Because several such attacks have occurred, vendors are currently deploying countermeasures to these and related attacks. To a certain extent, network firewalls can also help limit the problem.

Domain Name System (DNS)

The Internet uses 32-bit numeric addresses to route packets to a particular network adapter on a particular machine somewhere on the Net. Humans, however, like to use names rather than numbers for networked machines and services. Aside from relieving users of the necessity of remembering and transcribing numeric addresses, names serve some valuable purposes.

1. A service can move from machine to machine (and, hence, from address to address) while keeping the same name, and thus people (and other systems) need only remember the name of the service.
2. A service can be supported by multiple machine that have independent addresses but share the same name.

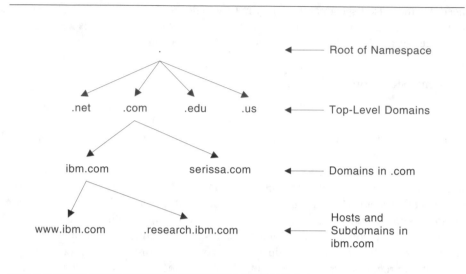

FIGURE 8-2. Structure of the DNS Naming Hierarchy

The problem of translating human-sensible names into numeric addresses is handled by the Domain Name System (DNS). The DNS is a very fast, very scalable method of translating names into addresses. A DNS name such as *www.serissa.com* consists of a machine name, in this case *www*, and a hierarchy of domains, *serissa* and *com,* separated by periods. Generally speaking, a *domain* is the name of an organization that assigns names to computers and services, whether it be a company, a university, or some other kind of entity. As shown in Figure 8-2, DNS names are structured in a hierarchy. The name is processed from right to left, with the root of the hierarchy represented as a dot at the end. When a program needs the network address for a machine, it queries local DNS servers, which may, in turn, query remote servers as well. Root DNS servers are responsible for top-level domains such as *com, edu, gov,* and *mil,* as well as geographic domains such as *us, ca,* and *jp* (which designate the United States, Canada, and Japan, respectively). These root servers know only which other lower-level servers know about the *com* domain. DNS servers for the *com* domain then know which lower-level servers are responsible for the *serissa* domain, but they do not know anything about names within the *serissa* domain. Finally, the *serissa* DNS servers are responsible for knowing the IP address of the machine *www*.

In addition to these authoritative servers, DNS information may be temporarily cached by other systems, and most clients are configured to accept such nonauthoritative information (nonauthoritative because it is not necessarily up-to-date).

The DNS is also used to translate IP addresses into names. If we want to find the name associated with the address *204.152.184.147*, for example, we reverse the order of the numbers and use the *in-addr.arpa* domain for the lookup, resulting in *147.184.152.204.in-addr.arpa*. This looks almost like a regular domain name, and we get back the answer *www.serissa.com*. This process, often called a *reverse lookup,* works because the hierarchy of network addresses (which read from left to right) is very similar to the hierarchy of DNS names.

This ability to translate addresses into names is often used for both access control and logging. An incoming connection has no name associated with it, only the IP address of the sender. Because logs and access control rules are often read and written by people, it is much easier for them to read and write names, so applications commonly translate addresses into names.

Using DNS information for access control can be risky, however. DNS is very widely used on the Internet, but the security of Web systems that use it depends on both the source information fed into DNS and the security of intermediate DNS servers between the client and the server. As an example, consider a Web server configured to provide access only to hosts in *serissa.com.* A connection arrives from IP address *204.152.184.147,* and the server uses a DNS reverse name lookup to find out if indeed this address is assigned to Serissa. One problem is that this works well if in fact the address is one of Serissa's, but if it isn't, then the DNS inverse lookup will retrieve the answer to this question from the attacker's DNS server. One way to guard against this is to look up the name again in the DNS to see if the address entries match. For most applications, the usual course is to use DNS to translate names into addresses but not to depend on the DNS results for authenticating the source of the messages.

The World Wide Web

In 1992, Tim Berners-Lee at CERN released the first implementation of the World Wide Web. Because of its power and accessibility, the Web has grown in popularity to the point that many people do not distinguish between the Web and the Internet itself.

Web Fundamentals

The World Wide Web is a global hypertext network of millions of Web servers and even more millions of Web browsers connected by the HyperText Transfer Protocol (HTTP) and its variants. Like the Internet, the Web is growing rapidly, so it is hard to say exactly how big it is at any given time. Web servers supply, and browsers display, pages of multimedia information. These pages are usually defined by the Hypertext Markup Language (HTML) and can contain text, graphics, audio, video, and even pieces of software called *applets* that are automatically downloaded from the server and run on the desktop. The most important elements of Web pages are hypertext links to other pages on the same or different servers. These links appear as highlighted text invoked with the mouse, but portions of images may contain hypertext links as well. By simply clicking the links, a user can easily move from page to page without having to worry about the location of the information or about the underlying details of communications.

World Wide Web—Summary

The WWW project merges the techniques of networked information and hypertext to make an easy but powerful global information system.

The project represents any information accessible over the network as part of a seamless hypertext information space.

W3 was originally developed to allow information sharing within internationally dispersed teams, and the dissemination of information by support groups. Originally aimed at the High Energy Physics community, it has spread to other areas and attracted much interest in user support, resource discovery, and collaborative work areas. It is currently the most advanced information system deployed on the Internet, and embraces within its data model most information in previous networked information systems.

In fact, the Web is an architecture which will also embrace any future advances in technology, including new networks, protocols, object types, and data formats.

—Tim Berners-Lee describing the World Wide Web, circa 1992
From *http://www.w3.org/Summary.html*

Each hypertext link contains a visible part, called the *anchor*, which the user sees on the screen. The anchor usually describes the link or gives a title for the referenced page. Hyperlinks can also be represented by images, so Web pages can be created with icons representing links. The target of the link is described by a *Uniform Resource Locator* (URL) such as

    http://servername.domain/path/name/of/object.html

which can refer to a page on the same server or to one anywhere on the Web.

The World Wide Web is a nearly pure client-server system. Content is held by Web servers and requested by clients. With a few exceptions, servers do not initiate activities, and clients merely display the content they have retrieved from a server. Exceptions include *server push*, in which a client holds open a network connection and the server continually updates the client, and *applets*, in which code is automatically downloaded for the client to execute, usually to provide more complex interactive behavior.

Uniform Resource Locators

The structure and flexibility of the URL is central to the use of the Web for many applications, including electronic commerce. As shown in Figure 8-3, a URL such as *http://www.w3.org/example/path/index.html* is composed of several parts.

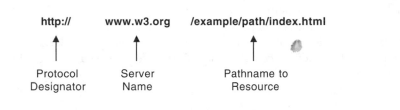

FIGURE 8-3. Components of a URL

- Protocol designator (*http:*)

  This tells the browser what protocol to use in connecting to the server, in this case HTTP. Most Web browsers can use other protocols as well, such as FTP (*ftp:*) and SMTP (*mailto:*) for file transfer and electronic mail, respectively.

- Server name (*www.w3.org*)

  This is a Domain Name System (DNS) name. The browser will use the DNS to translate the name into an IP network address.

- Pathname (*/example/path/index.html*)

  This is frequently the full name of a file on the Web server, but it may be interpreted by the server to mean that a program or database query should be executed to generate the results for the client. By convention, the extension (in this case, *.html*) means that this is an HTML document, but this convention is not required.

This particular URL refers to a static HTML page of information somewhere in the filesystem of a server. Much of the power of the Web comes from two additional capabilities: pages can be constructed dynamically by application software, and information can flow in both directions. When a page is constructed dynamically, the Web server passes the path portion of the URL to an application program, which can return an HTML page or other content constructed on the fly by the application itself. In addition, HTML pages can contain forms to be filled out by the user, and the input data for the forms sent back to the server. The Web can also be used by programs to pass information to other programs and return results. These are called *Web services*, and usually the information is encoded in XML rather than HTML; we discuss XML and Web services in more detail in Chapter 11.

Web Protocols

The Web actually employs several network protocols. Some of them, such as the File Transfer Protocol (FTP), originated elsewhere but have been assimilated into the Web. Others, such as the ones described here, have been created for the Web itself.

HyperText Transfer Protocol (HTTP)

The HyperText Transfer Protocol (HTTP) is the original Web communications proto-col. With HTTP, the client opens a TCP connection to the Web server and transmits an HTTP header. The header contains an HTTP command, such as **GET**, **PUT**, or **POST**, and the path portion of the URL. The HTTP header may also include information for authenticating the user, as well as information about acceptable document formats. This information allows the client and server to negotiate about what formats will be returned by the server, so that (for example) a client that can handle images only in the GIF format will not receive images that use the JPEG format.

Clients use the **GET** command in HTTP to retrieve documents, and **PUT** to upload files to the server. The **POST** command is used by the client to send the results of a form filled out by the user. With the **PUT** and **POST** commands, the client simply transmits the information immediately after the HTTP header and a blank line.

When the server has finished processing the request, it transmits a reply header back to the client followed by the page to be displayed. One of the header fields sent by the server specifies the format of the data being returned, which permits the client to lo-cate the proper module or application for it. This capability enables Web browsers to display many different kinds of data (for example, text, HTML, images, and so on). Moreover, a browser may be *extensible*, which allows it to invoke plug-in modules or other applications to handle data formats it does not itself understand.

Secure Sockets Layer (SSL) and Transport Layer Security (TLS)

The Secure Sockets Layer (SSL), originally developed by Netscape Communications Corporation, is the most widely used security protocol on the Internet. In our simpli-fied model for protocol layers, SSL fits in between TCP and the application, where it can provide security services for any stream of data. In addition to encrypting the communications, SSL provides for the use of digital certificates for authentication. The Internet Engineering Task Force (IETF) has also defined an open standard ver-sion of SSL called Transport Layer Security (TLS), which is the evolutionary succes-sor of SSL. URLs that begin with *https:* are using SSL or TLS for a secure connection. For convenience, we will refer to this family of protocols as *SSL/TLS*, and we discuss them in more detail in Chapter 14.

Over time, the Web has grown to embrace more and more protocols, making it possi-ble for a Web browser to become the primary interface to the Internet for many users.

Other Web Tools

The foundations of the Web—HTTP, HTML, URLs, and so on—have become the ba-sis for many applications. Search engines, for example, are one of the most popular applications. A search engine is a tool for finding information on a web, whether that web is the World Wide Web or a web used internally by a company or other organization. The index created by a search engine may be created in different ways. Some are created and maintained by people, giving the engine the organized feel of a library. Others use *Web robots* to download information from all over the Web, indexing the pages in some fashion. Web robots typically work by keeping a list of Web pages to index and downloading them one by one. Each one is indexed from the text, and any hyperlinks on the page are added to the list of pages to index, if they have not already been indexed recently. On a well-connected web, then, a robot can index nearly all of the static pages that it can read.

Other Web tools make it possible to use the Web when you are not connected to it. For example, mobile computers (such as laptops and notebooks) are typically connected to the network only part of the time. For many users, then, an *offline browser* enables a user to download Web content in advance and in bulk, rather than downloading each page as it is clicked. Later, while the system is disconnected, the user can browse the pages just as if the network were present. (Of course, this does not work well for interactive applications or dynamic pages with changing content.)

The Web has become so powerful and ubiquitous that many applications have embraced it in one way or another. For example, some programs offer help by linking back to the vendor's Web site for information, rather than providing it with the program. Or they may augment the help files with updates and frequently asked questions on a Web site. Word processors, spreadsheets, and other applications may allow the user to embed other documents into their own by providing a URL, so the data is fetched over the Web as appropriate.

From the point of view of Internet commerce, these are all components that we think about when designing a system. For example, does the commerce system need to work with offline browsers? What about with the Web embedded in other applications? Does the commerce-enabled Web site work well with search engine robots that may try to index it? The answers to these and other related questions should be part of the requirements definition for commerce services.

Agents

The term *agent* has been used to mean many different things, ranging from spell checkers that work as you type to artificial intelligence programs that find the information you need before you ask for it. To be practical today, agents are typically more limited in capability, although many research projects are exploring what agents might be able to do.

In the realm of Internet commerce, the most common conception of an agent is something like a personal shopper, which finds various items you might be looking for and presents them with comparison information. Taken a step further, such an agent may even be authorized to make purchases under certain conditions.

Personal shoppers may sound interesting to buyers, but they are worrisome to sellers. Agents that discriminate primarily on price, for example, tend to drive a market toward only low-price sellers. Because the agents are automated, it is difficult (if not impossible) to build a relationship with the actual customer. Already, the Net has seen sellers react against prototype agents of this type. In most cases, the sellers developed countermeasures to keep agents from using their systems. Agents are still too new to the Internet, and especially to Internet commerce, for predictions to be made about how they will ultimately be used in commerce applications. It is very likely that they will be put to such use, and the developers of any evolving commerce system should keep an eye on where this technology is going.

There are, however, a number of comparison shopping sites on the Internet, which survey commerce sites for pricing on computer components and other items.

Intranets

The term *intranet* has come to be used for applications of Internet technologies on internal networks of companies and other organizations. Intranets most commonly include Web technology in one way or another. For Internet commerce, intranets have two interesting properties. The first is that the intranet can be used to create a unified experience for customers by drawing on the resources of many different parts of the company, pulling together functions such as product information, technical details, customer service, ordering of products and services, as well as any other specialized organizations within the company. Second, Internet commerce applications can be deployed for internal use as well, making it possible to use the same applications for internal ordering, transaction processing, and service for internal "customers."

Extranets

Similar to the word *intranet,* the term *extranet* has come to be used to describe a network connecting an organization with its partners, suppliers, and close customers. Sometimes the term simply means communication among such organizations using the Internet, but frequently it refers to networks that connect them together more closely than a typical Internet connection does. The network may use the Internet, or it may use Internet technology on a private physical network. Typical applications include sharing of information for joint projects, direct connections into a supplier's ordering system, and direct access to customer service and support.

Such activities include many that we have discussed for business-to-business Internet commerce. Indeed, an Internet commerce system may be the basis for an extranet, resulting in closer relationships for both buyers and sellers. In a sense, the extranet provides an exterior security boundary that protects the organizations from the open network while providing lower security boundaries for greater sharing of information between the partners.

Related to extranets are Virtual Private Networks (VPNs). VPNs use encryption technology to tunnel private data securely through a public network. The most common use of VPNs is to permit workers on the road or at home to connect to the public Internet as a way of reaching the intranet of their own company.

Consumer Devices and Network Computers

As the Web has grown, so has the range of devices that can connect to it. Many of these devices do not have all the capabilities we associate with desktop computers; they may be limited in computing power, storage, network bandwidth, display capabilities, and so on. Some of these devices, such as WebTV and Web-capable mobile phones, are aimed at a broad consumer market. Others, such as various kinds of network computers, intend to take full advantage of the Web and related technologies. They are based on the premise that the useful resources for users are all on the network somewhere, and the primary goal of the desktop device is to connect the user to those resources. These so-called thin clients are really built around the Web as the basic interface to computing.

Thin clients of various kinds have some important implications for Internet commerce applications. In particular, application designers must understand the range of devices they expect to be used with the application. For example, an application built using Java for execution in a browser rules out the use of any browsers that cannot run Java. Such a limitation may be an acceptable trade-off for some applications, but others may want to reach the broadest possible group of customers. As the various types of devices develop further and gain broader use in the marketplace, application designers should consider how to evolve their applications to keep up with what their customers are using. In particular, we examine some implications of mobile and wireless devices in Chapter 20.

The Future of the Internet: Protocol Evolution

Like other technologies, the Internet is evolving quickly, and changes are inevitable. Although many of the core principles remain the same, the details will be different. All of the technologies mentioned in this chapter are changing to some degree.

TCP/IP is evolving with the development of IPv6, the next generation of the Internet Protocol. IPv6 builds on the long experience with IP (which is officially version 4) and provides improvements in scalability, security, and support for real-time media. Because it changes the fundamental protocols of the Internet, it will be quite some time before the entire Internet is running IPv6, although many IPv6 products are on the market today. In fact, some of the security technology developed for IPv6 is also being deployed for use with the current version of IP.

From a system design point of view, IPv6 has little direct effect on Internet commerce. Because of the layered architecture of the Internet, applications for commerce are largely insulated from the changes in the lower layers. Thus, as IPv6 is deployed, commerce applications will continue to work while the overall network benefits from the new capabilities. Over time, as the IPv6 security infrastructure comes into widespread use, commerce applications will be able to use the IPv6 security features to enhance their security as well.

The Web is changing, too—both HTTP and HTML are active areas of work. New versions of HTTP promise better performance and more flexible interactions between clients and servers. The changes in HTTP may affect applications more than IPv6 does, simply because HTTP provides capabilities closer to the application's logic. Because the changes are designed to be compatible with earlier versions, applications need not change right away, and they can be modified when it is appropriate to take advantage of what is new in the protocol.

As for HTML, the follow-on development gaining rapid acceptance is the Extensible Markup Language (XML), which is discussed in Chapter 11. In effect, XML allows applications to define their own markup extensions, which (among other things) enables them to define documents that include application-specific tags for data items as well as rules for displaying them on a screen. For example, a commerce application might use XML to define an order form, where the prices, descriptions, quantities, and so on are tagged appropriately. This enables a display application, such as a browser, to show a nicely formatted form on the screen, while the application can parse the order form to extract the information needed to process the order.

Although changes in the technology of the Internet are inevitable, it is not necessary to adopt each one immediately as it becomes available. Each evolutionary step (and the occasional revolutionary one) must be evaluated in terms of how it affects the value delivered to customers by the commerce application and in terms of the costs of implementing the change. There is also some risk that such changes will not become common in the marketplace, leaving an application at a dead end. For Internet commerce applications, we recommend aggressive caution and prudent revolution.

Summary

Although the Internet has become widely used only in the last few years, its roots go back more than three decades to work in academia and research. Some key architectural principles of the Internet, such as interoperability, layering, and common addressing and naming, have created a network that could grow to a worldwide scale, supporting a tremendous variety of applications. The core protocols of the Internet make it possible for computers around the world to communicate with each other.

Building on this foundation, the World Wide Web brought a new generation of information management and usability to the Internet. The Web is itself another layer in the foundation for many kinds of applications, such as the Internet commerce systems we describe in this book.

In the next chapter, we look at some of the primary building blocks for Internet commerce systems.

CHAPTER 9

Building Blocks for Internet Commerce

I found Rome a city of bricks and left it a city of marble.

—Augustus Caesar[1]

Components in an Internet Commerce System

The building blocks of Internet commerce are the technologies of the World Wide Web: its protocols, browsers, and servers, along with application development structures such as Java, ActiveX, and CGI. This chapter begins with a look at the basic content machinery of the Web and then surveys the protocols and mechanisms for getting content to the user. We then turn to current technologies for building content pages at the server and the evolving technologies for adding programmability to the browser. We conclude with a look at the changes in basic Web technology that are important for adding commerce facilities to the Web.

Content Transport

There are two ways for content to get from a server on the Internet to the screen of the end user: either the user's client program (browser) goes to the server and retrieves the content, or the server initiates the connection and delivers content to the desktop. These two delivery mechanisms are called *pull content* and *push content*, respectively. Some systems for pulling content actually pull from peer systems on the network,

---

1. From Suetonius (c. 70 – c. 140), *Augustus.*

rather than the original server; these systems are called *peer-to-peer networks*. A common variant of push content is *broadcast*, in which the same content is delivered to many clients simultaneously. This last approach is sometimes called *multicast,* because the content is actually received by multiple clients but not all possible ones.

Pull Content

Pull content has been the traditional mode for the World Wide Web: the client opens a connection to a server whenever the user clicks a hypertext link. Most Web browsers can use several different network protocols to retrieve content, but the HyperText Transfer Protocol (HTTP) is the most common. The fundamentals of HTTP were described in Chapter 8. We will now discuss some of its more subtle points.

Protocol Variations

In the original design of the Web, a browser used a separate HTTP connection for each component on a page. For example, each included image (the most common kind of component after the Web page itself) required a separate connection, with its own overhead.[2] Of course, when the page components come from different server systems, separate connections are necessary; but when the components all come from the same server, a single connection can suffice. The HTTP 1.1 protocol permits multiple requests on a single connection while also reducing the overhead of the protocol in many other ways.

Caching

Fetching a document, especially a large one, from a remote server can take some time, especially with a slow Internet connection. To improve the performance as seen by the user, many browsers save temporary copies of Web pages and their components. The repository of copies is called a *cache.* There are several obvious situations in which browser caching is effective.

- An image such as a logo or toolbar is used on multiple pages in the same site.
- The user clicks the **Back** button on the browser, causing a recently seen page to be redisplayed.
- A site is visited repeatedly over time.

In addition to the browser cache, Web contents are often cached in proxy servers. A proxy server typically sits between a group of users on an organizational network and the Internet at large. They are also sometimes used as part of an Internet service provider's network. Used as part of a firewall, proxy servers provide some security advantages. By providing caching, proxy servers can also reduce the network traffic

---

2. This is the reason why some sites have a single image with an *image map* for a toolbar—it is more efficient than using separate small images for the different buttons.

between internal users and the Internet, as well as providing better performance for the users.

There are two big problems with caching.

1. The cache is missing something you wanted it to have.

   When the browser makes a request, and the requested page or image is located in the cache (called a *cache hit*), the user gets fast and predictable performance. When the requested item is not in the cache (called a *cache miss*), the user has to wait for the main content server to respond. The net result is unpredictable performance. Statistically speaking, caches tend to improve the average performance of the Web but increase the variance. This effect can irritate users.

2. The cache has something you did not want it to have.

   When the browser makes a request, and the item is in the cache, the user gets a response right away, but the real page back on the content server may have changed. The HTTP protocol has some ways to deal with this problem, but they are not always successful.[3] As the Web continues to grow, caching is likely to become more common in the quest for good performance. On the other hand, the software must also evolve to do a better job of caching correctly. Web browsers typically have a **Reload** button that forces a page to be fetched from the primary server, but users have to guess when they need to select it. HTTP 1.1 has more elaborate cache control mechanisms than HTTP 1.0.

Effects of Caching on Commerce Applications

Caching can have bad effects on commerce applications. An outdated page can confuse users, disrupting their use of the commerce application. Here are some examples.

- A catalog page is cached and does not display current prices.

- A catalog application displays different prices to different corporate customers, but because of proxy caching, a user from one company sees prices relevant to another.

- An order form page does not display the correct total, because the user receives a cached copy reflecting an earlier stage of the order.

- The application uses *hidden fields*[4] to store part of the application state. The user resubmits a cached copy of a form containing information inconsistent with the rest of the application.

---

3. The **HEAD** command in HTTP can be used to ask a server if a page has changed since a specific time, and various header fields such as **PRAGMA NOCACHE** can inform proxy servers and other caches when and for how long it is safe to cache.

4. HTML forms provide hidden fields as a way to carry information in the form that is posted back to the server, but this information is not displayed to the user. For example, a form might be asking for a customer's payment information, with the order number carried in a hidden field so the application can match up the payment data with the right order when the user submits the form.

The solutions to these problems are different. For example, one way to solve the last problem is to avoid using hidden fields that store part, but not all, of the state of the application. In other cases, it is important to make sure that the Web server is sending the appropriate HTTP cache directives so that Web pages are cached properly.

Offline Browsers

Like many Web users, we are often frustrated by slow or unpredictable performance of the Web. We often know ahead of time what we want, and it would be easy to say simply, "Computer, turn on overnight and make a copy of Web site such-and-such on my local hard disk." In the morning, we can browse through it quickly, and we can even read the Web pages without being connected to the network. This magic is what *offline browsers* do. An offline browser is a desktop application that can preload content onto the local hard drive in a way that is transparent to normal operations of the Web. Offline browsers are especially useful for laptop users and for those who visit the same sites over and over again. However, they do not work well for dynamic or interactive sites. Increasingly, offline capabilities are being integrated with browsers as a basic function.

Some offline browsers require end users to specify what content they want to retrieve automatically, whereas others allow creators of content to create *packages* to which the user subscribes. Such packages turn a *pull model* offline browser into something more like a *push model,* because the content creator defines exactly what is distributed to the users. The user decides when to download the package, however.

A similar set of tools can be used for a different application: replicating a Web site. In order to provide higher effective performance or to enhance reliability, a Web site may actually consist of multiple Web servers with identical content. Replication can be difficult when the site is dynamic, because the underlying applications and databases, and not just a collection of HTML Web pages, must be replicated. It is also difficult for users to find the "best" replica, because there is no good way to find the least-loaded server or the one that is "nearest" on the network. However, users benefit even from simple replication schemes, because they generally perceive improved performance and reliability.

Push Content

The Web began with users requesting documents from servers. As an alternative, a server might deliver content to the end user proactively, without a direct request. From a technology perspective, a user signs up for a *channel* of content and the relevant information is automatically delivered to the desktop. Like a television or radio channel, a push content channel can contain material meant for real-time viewing, but unlike television or radio, a channel can contain arbitrary information bundles. By way of analogy, imagine that the television station could control your VCR, automatically recording for you the programs you signed up to see. More dramatically, push systems, if implemented for the physical world, could automatically update all the books, magazines, videotapes, and music recordings in your entire house. Push technology can be applied to any kind of content, including multimedia intended for end users and software intended for computers.

If a push system is used to deliver applications and databases to the desktop, or in conjunction with real-time server connections, it can be effective for dynamic and interactive content as well as static information.

Peer-to-Peer Networking

In the early days of the Internet, there were few client computers. Most machines on the Internet were time-sharing systems with terminals. These systems communicated over the Net with FTP, Telnet, and e-mail as equals. The rise of the personal computer reordered the landscape into clients (PCs) and servers (usually minicomputers and mainframes). Clients operated at the behest of the user, and servers responded to them. In the late 1990s, however, personal computers became powerful enough that programmers remembered they were also general-purpose computers that could act as servers themselves, and peer-to-peer networking was (re)born.

The general idea of peer-to-peer networking is that every participant is both a client and a server. Several variations of peer-to-peer networking have emerged, most often for sharing files—particularly music files. In the Napster system, for example, there is a central directory of files, but the files themselves reside on various participating machines. A client wanting a file consults the directory for a list of nodes containing the file. The client then selects a server based on performance or other properties and requests the file directly. The actual file transfer takes place between end systems. Gnutella is another variation, which has a distributed directory of content in addition to a distributed repository.

It is not yet clear what effect peer-to-peer technology will have on Internet commerce. While it is true that today's personal computers would outperform powerful server machines from a few years ago, it is prudent to consider the security issues of peer-to-peer technology. In a sense, servers are machines that you control, whereas clients are machines that you do not control.

Extension Mechanisms

Web browsers typically include built-in support for HTML and many other data types such as images, text, and audio. Most browsers also include various extension mechanisms so that additional capabilities can be added in the field, either with user intervention or automatically. Some of these mechanisms are as follows.

MIME Type	Description
text/html	HTML document
image/gif	GIF image
image/jpeg	JPEG image
text/plain	Plain text
application/pdf	Adobe Portable Document Format (PDF)
audio/x-pn-realaudio	RealAudio
video/mpeg	MPEG video
video/quicktime	Apple QuickTime video

TABLE 9-1. **Examples of MIME Types**

MIME Types

MIME is an acronym for *Multipurpose Internet Mail Extensions*, an Internet standard for multimedia electronic mail. With MIME, each document is tagged with a type to identify what kind of data it is, such as HTML, text, images, and so on. Some common MIME types for the Web are shown in Table 9-1. HTTP has borrowed much of the MIME mechanism from its original application, although the details are occasionally different. The browser interprets the MIME type to decide how to display the downloaded data. If the MIME type is not handled directly by the browser, most browsers can be configured to launch an independent viewing application. For example, a user may install a video application that can display video clips downloaded from the Web. The installation process configures the browser to start the application when the clip is downloaded. When it is launched, the helper application operates independently of the browser

HTTP also allows the browser to inform the server of its capabilities by listing the MIME types it can handle. This makes it possible for a server to deliver data in different formats, depending on what the browser can handle.

Unfortunately, the extra installation and configuration, as well as the separate operation, mean that this mechanism can be awkward for users. For many applications, it may be better to use one of the other extension mechanisms. However, the MIME mechanism allows extension applications to be independent of the underlying browser, which can be advantageous as well.

Plug-ins

Some browsers, such as those from Netscape Communications Corporation, have a *plug-in* mechanism, which permits software developers to add new capabilities to the browser using a defined programming interface. One such capability is the display of a new type of data using the browser window itself rather than starting a separate application. The software containing such add-on capabilities is itself called a *plug-in* and must be installed by the user, manually or automatically, before the new data type can be used. Another similar approach is the use of Microsoft's Object Linking and Embedding (OLE) technology, which is used in Microsoft's browser.

Browser plug-ins can modify the behavior of the browser in very complex ways, such as adding new toolbar commands and menu items. They must be implemented to work with a specific version of a specific browser (although a browser vendor may provide good upward compatibility). Consequently, plug-ins are powerful but inconvenient for many commerce applications, unless they gain widespread use among buyers who can use them for many different sellers.

Scripting

Browsers such as Navigator, Internet Explorer, and others permit executable scripts to be embedded in Web pages. Scripts are written in languages such as JavaScript and VBScript and are executed by an interpreter in the browser when the page is displayed. For security reasons, these scripts have limited power, but they can modify the display and increase the interactivity of the Web. A common application, for example, uses a script to check the validity of form entries supplied by a user. This allows errors to be corrected more quickly, without a visit to the server to verify the input.

Applets

Netscape's Navigator, Microsoft's Internet Explorer, and other browsers are able to execute applets written in Java. A Java applet is downloaded on demand from a server when a Web page requires it. The applet then executes in the Java virtual machine supplied by the browser, which limits the ways in which the applet can affect the system. We discuss Java and Java applets in more detail later.

Controls

Microsoft's Internet Explorer introduced the notion of ActiveX controls. ActiveX controls are software modules that are automatically downloaded and installed when a Web page containing them is encountered. Unlike Java applets, however, ActiveX controls have free run of the user's computer. ActiveX controls are discussed in more detail later.

These extension mechanisms can all be used to make the Web a more dynamic and interactive environment. Using them, however, may require a fair investment in development and maintenance as browsers evolve over time. In addition, it is still difficult to write extensions that are at once easy for users to obtain and install while still being portable across different browsers. Understanding your customers, their software, and their willingness to be flexible is important in making decisions about how to take advantage of browser extensions.

Client Software Requirements

This discussion of browser software leads us to one of the most difficult problems in Internet commerce: should the commerce experience be designed to use only the capabilities common to nearly all browsers, or should it take advantage of more advanced features? If advanced features are required, then one can restrict the set of users to those who have the corresponding software, or one can make it possible for users to obtain the necessary software easily. In either case, there is an additional problem when the user population is split among different platforms, such as Windows, Macintosh, and UNIX. There are a several possible approaches.

- The commerce site adapts to the capabilities of a particular user. For example, it may dynamically select between presentation that makes heavy use of images and one that is limited to text. This selection may be automatic if the site can identify the capabilities of the browser, or it may ask the user to choose the style of interaction by clicking an appropriate link.

- The commerce site requires the user to have particular software installed, such as an animation plug-in, a commerce module, or a particular version of a browser. This solution may be appropriate in a closed user community, where a single organization has substantial influence over the users.

- The commerce site "looks best" when viewed with particular software, such as a particular browser version. It may or may not look good, or even work, with other software. If one or two types of client software have a dominant market share among the targeted user base, this may be an acceptable system.

Note that it is possible to shift among these approaches, both as you gain experience with customers and as the software evolves. Some years ago, for example, few users had browsers capable of rendering tables in HTML, but now almost all browsers can do so. Therefore, a choice that was appropriate at one time may not be appropriate as the available software changes.

Media and Application Integration

As the Web grew, it has come to be integrated with other media, including e-mail, television, and print publications.

E-Mail and the Web

Because Web browsers now include e-mail and newsgroup functionality, it is now common for electronic mail to be sent in HTML format. Obviously this results in a richer display than plain text, but it also means that electronic mail can be fully integrated with the Web: e-mail can include images and hypertext links to Web content. This capability has many applications to Internet commerce.

- Advertising

  Advertising sent via e-mail can include direct links to the seller's online store or can even originate a transaction.

- Reference material

  E-mail newsletters can include links to references and additional information.

- Interaction

  E-mail can include links that permit the recipient to do something. For example, an online sale confirmation e-mail can include a link to the seller's customer service page or even to the online order status page for the particular transaction.

One great downside, however, of HTML and Web-enabled e-mail has been the great number of related security and privacy problems. For example, mail programs capable of handling HTML have often been tricked into executing arbitrary code for attackers. On the privacy side, a mail program displaying an inlined image from an HTML message will have to request it from a Web server. That server can then track who has opened the e-mail message that was sent out, especially if it generates messages using unique IDs for the image URLs.

Television and the Web

Almost every television advertisement, it seems, displays a URL or Web site name on the screen. This permits the viewer, if so inclined, to go to the Web for additional information on the product advertised. In addition, some consumer equipment permits special coding in a television broadcast that automatically launches the user's browser to display relatedWeb content.

Print and the Web

Many print publications are available on the Web. Indeed, many are freely available online, even when they have paid subscriptions for their print editions. There are some paid subscription sites, such as the *Wall Street Journal* (www.wsj.com), and the number is now growing. In addition, most print advertising now includes a URL or Web site name as a link to more information available online.

Server Components

The original concept of the World Wide Web was very simple. Web servers stored pages coded in HTML in their filesystems. These pages could be retrieved by browsers using HTTP. The URL of a page was simply the hostname of the server plus the filename of the document.[5] Later, it was realized that HTML Web pages could be pro-

---

5. Actually, Tim Berners-Lee's original concept of the Web included the ability to create, update, and annotate content from the desktop—capabilities that have only recently become common.

duced by programs as well as stored as files. In this mode, the URL specifies the hostname of the server, the name of the program to be run, and possibly some arguments for that program. In the most general case, a Web server is free to attach any interpretation at all to a URL and to use any mechanism to create and return the page contents to the browser.

The Common Gateway Interface (CGI)

The Common Gateway Interface (CGI) defines a standard interface between a Web server and an independent application program that is responsible for some portion of the URL namespace. These applications are sometimes called *gateways* because one of the first uses of CGI was to create gateways between the Web and a variety of existing applications. CGI has also served as the interface for entirely new applications designed for the Web but not integrated directly into a Web server.

CGI was originally designed and implemented for UNIX platforms, but it has been carried across to most other Web server platforms as well. In CGI, the path portion of the URL identifies the application, which is launched by the Web server as a separate program. The standard input and output streams of the application are wired to the network connection from the browser. The input from the browser (such as a posted form) thus goes to the application, and the output of the application is sent to the browser. The server mediates this connection and ensures that the HTTP protocol is followed. In addition, the server provides some details about the request to the application using environment variables. Examples of some common CGI environment variables are shown in Table 9-2.

Beyond CGI

CGI is very general, because the application is completely decoupled from the Web server. Unfortunately, this generality comes at the cost of performance, because the application must be launched independently for each request. In addition, because the application exits after a request, there is no convenient place to store state between Web requests. These limitations of CGI have led to the development of several other interfaces between Web servers and applications.

All server APIs, CGI included, must solve the following problems.

- Starting and stopping application
- Passing data from the client to the application
- Passing data from the application to the client
- Status and error reporting
- Passing configuration information to the application
- Passing client and environment information to the application

CGI Variable Name	Meaning	Sample Value
GATEWAY_INTERFACE	Version of CGI in use	CGI/1.1
SCRIPT_NAME	Name of the CGI program being executed	/payment.cgi
PATH	Search path for finding other programs	/sbin:/bin:/usr/sbin:/usr/bin
HTTP_USER_AGENT	Version identifier of browser	Mozilla/4.0
REMOTE_HOST	Name of client machine	mypc.serissa.com
REQUEST_METHOD	HTTP command	GET
REMOTE_ADDR	IP address of client machine	10.0.25.10
HTTPS	Indicates SSL/TLS in use	OFF

TABLE 9-2. Examples of CGI Variables and Values

Server APIs

Netscape, with NSAPI, and Microsoft, with ISAPI, have each defined application programming interfaces that permit application software to be integrated directly with a Web server. Although they differ in detail, both permit application code to be loaded and executed in the same process context as the server itself. This structure yields high performance, but it removes the security of isolating the application process from the server as well as isolating multiple applications from each other. Server APIs also generally limit the application programmer's choice of programming language and may limit other aspects of the application design.

FastCGI

FastCGI, originally developed by Open Market and now supported by several servers (including Apache and Zeus), is an attempt to deliver the performance of an integrated server API while preserving the isolation and safety properties of CGI. In addition, FastCGI permits applications to run on separate systems, remote from the Web server. FastCGI works by communicating between the application and the Web server using a lightweight protocol carried over TCP or other stream protocol, such as local interprocess communication. The use of a communications link between the FastCGI application and the Web server permits the application process to be persistent and yet provides a high degree of isolation for reliability and security. A persistent application provides both a convenient way to keep track of the state of a multirequest process and the performance advantage of starting the application only once.

Server-Side Scripting

There is a middle ground between pages of static content kept in the filesystem and pages of dynamic content created by a complete application: server-side scripting. In these schemes, base pages (also called *templates*) are kept in the filesystem, but these pages contain a mix of HTML and instructions in a scripting language that are executed by an interpreter embedded in the Web server itself.

- Server-side includes

  Server-side includes represent a very simple form of scripting in which certain tags in a page are replaced by the results of running a program or by certain information, such as a timestamp, already known to the server. Such scripting languages are limited to specifying these program names and their arguments.

- Server-side scripting

  It is possible to embed a language interpreter in the Web server. Web pages stored in the filesystem can contain scripts or programs that are interpreted on the fly. The plain HTML portions of the Web pages are combined with the output of the script sections to produce the final page sent to the browser. Common embedded languages include Java, JavaScript, PHP, and VBScript. Embedded languages must run in some environment to be useful. Microsoft's Active Server Pages (ASP) is an execution environment for server scripts and control. ASP permits the page designer to combine JavaScript and VBScript scripting with ActiveX controls written in any programming language. Java scripting is done in Java servlets and Java Server Pages (JSPs), which are discussed later. The Apache Web server supports modules for various languages, including Perl, Python, and PHP.

Database-Driven Templates

Mechanisms for connecting the Web to database systems are structurally similar to server scripting. The usual approach is to define a template language for the pages, which are stored in the Web server filesystem. Special tags in the templates permit embedded statements using the Structured Query Language (SQL) to create database queries. Results from the queries are then substituted in the pages delivered to the browser. There are many systems on the market for linking databases to the Web, and they can be an effective part of an Internet commerce system.

Programming Clients

Before the Web, systems intended for geographically distributed users were usually built in one of two ways: as mainframes with networks of terminals or as client-server systems. In the case of mainframes, the application programs ran on the mainframe, and the terminals had few, if any, capabilities beyond local editing and printing. In contrast, client-server systems took advantage of the processing capabilities of the client computers, which are typically PCs. The application data remained on the server, and the processing of that data moved to the client.

Early Web browsers were much like very fancy terminals with some multimedia capabilities. They had excellent displays, local editing, and complex forms, but no programmability. Web browsers were termed the *universal client,* but at the cost of moving application logic back to the server. Web applications tend to have three tiers, with Web browser clients fronting a tier of application servers, which in turn front database servers.

The current generation of Web browsers goes very much further, offering essentially full programmability to the application designer. As we have seen, clients can be programmed in different ways, including scripting, Java applets, and ActiveX controls.[6] Adding application logic to the browser is problematic from a security perspective. Client code to improve interactivity or provide better data display seems fine, but designers must remain aware that code running on computers "outside the firewall" cannot be trusted. All data coming from clients must be independently validated or even recomputed before acceptance.

Scripting

Scripting refers to the practice of embedding small programs in the source form of an interpreted language directly in a Web page. Scripts run when encountered on a page or when specified events happen, such as the user clicking a button or editing a field of a form. They can be very useful for performing interactive functions such as checking form contents for consistency and validity.

Netscape and Microsoft browsers support scripting in the JavaScript language, which is an object-oriented scripting language developed by Netscape. It resembles Java in some ways but does not have Java's strong type system.

Scripting languages are very powerful for rapid development of simple applications, but their lack of compile-time checking makes it difficult to do adequate testing of even a moderately sized script. Beyond a modest complexity, it is better to use Java applets or ActiveX controls.

Java

Java is an object-oriented programming language developed by Sun Microsystems. It is now being widely adopted for general programming tasks as well as for creating browser applets for the Web. Java includes not only a specification of the language but

---

6. We limit our discussion here to programming mechanisms that automatically deliver and integrate new functionality to the browser. Browser plug-ins certainly add functionality, but the user must explicitly install them or approve their automatic installation.

also a specification of the *virtual machine* that forms the execution environment for Java programs. Rather than being compiled to the native instruction set for a particular processor (such as a Pentium or SPARC), Java applications are compiled to an instruction set that executes on a well-defined abstract machine. The language and virtual machine together permit a Java program to be completely portable. A Java program compiled to Java byte codes will run the same way on any platform that implements the standard Java virtual machine.

Browsers from Netscape, Microsoft, and others include a Java virtual machine and extensions to HTML that permit Web pages to contain references to Java applets and their parameters.[7] When an applet is encountered, it is automatically downloaded into the browser virtual machine and executed. The virtual machine includes Java class libraries that let the applet draw on the screen, interact with the user, and communicate with the server from which it came. The virtual machine implements a so-called *sandbox*, which prevents the applet from reading the user's hard drive or from taking over control of the user's computer.

The portability of Java applets and the standardization of the virtual machine mean that applet creators do not need to worry about supporting many different versions of the applet for different client computers in use by the users. A single applet will run exactly the same way on all platforms. Java and the Java virtual machine are still evolving rapidly, so the applet author does need to worry about different versions of the Java environment.

Security for Java applets is based on a sandbox model, in which the applet is prevented from doing anything that might be dangerous. Unfortunately, this also prevents the applet from doing many things that are useful. Extensions to Java, such as signed applets in Java 1.1, make Java applets useful for some commerce applications.

ActiveX

In 1996, Microsoft introduced ActiveX. ActiveX is an evolution of Object Linking and Embedding (OLE), which Microsoft developed earlier to enable diverse applications to work closely together. ActiveX controls are software objects referenced by a Web page, which can be automatically downloaded and installed on a user's PC at the time of first reference. On future references, the control is automatically activated without being downloaded again. Unlike Java applets, ActiveX controls have full access to the resources of the client system.

The security model for ActiveX is based on code signing rather than on a sandbox. ActiveX controls have full access to the user's computer. In order for users to be willing to install such potentially dangerous pieces of software, each control is digitally

---

7. Because of disagreements about control over the Java language, Microsoft plans to stop including Java with Internet Explorer, although it will still be possible to add a Java plug-in.

signed by its authoring organization (digital signatures are described in Chapter 13). Before running the control, the user decides whether or not to trust the organization that created it.

ActiveX controls are very powerful, but they contain binary computer code, making them dependent on particular platforms. At this time, ActiveX is restricted to various versions of Microsoft Windows. In addition, the flow of a user's experience at a Web site may be disrupted when an ActiveX control is installed if the user must interrupt the process to answer a question about trusting the creator of the ActiveX control. ActiveX currently has no provision for removing controls once they are installed, so frivolous or seldom-used controls will accumulate and consume the user's system resources.

Sessions and Cookies

The HTTP protocol is designed to be stateless. Each request is intended to be independent of every other request. As the Web has come to be used as the foundation for complex applications (for commerce and other areas), cookies and other technologies have been developed to maintain persistent application state on top of the stateless protocol.

Why Sessions Are Important

As originally conceived, the Web was a very large collection of documents. Browsers would request a document, the user would work with it for a while, and then the user would request another document. In this environment, a stateless protocol makes sense. With many browsers and few servers, it is appropriate to make the server stateless so that it uses few resources per request. Today, however, almost any interesting Web-based application, particularly an Internet commerce application, requires a whole series of actions by the user and the server, working through a number of different Web pages. Therefore, it is important to treat such a series of actions as a single session of work.

State and Sessions

What is really going on in an application that has a series of interactions with the user? At the most basic level, the application has to remember state, and to make changes to the stored state as a result of interactions with the user. The situation is also complicated by the fact that there may be many users whose interactions with the Web application are interleaved with one another. Sessions are a way to remember which state information is associated with which user.

The way to approach this problem is to consider the possible places to keep application state. The general context is shown in Figure 9-1. A Web browser communicates

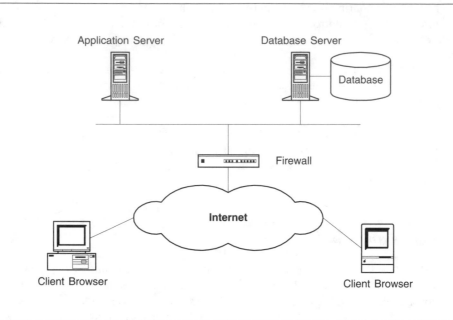

FIGURE 9-1. A Generic Web Application

with an application running on a Web server, which may also use a database. The state of the application can be kept in the database, in the application, or in the client.

State Kept in Database

In this model, the application itself is stateless, perhaps implemented as a CGI program that is executed anew on every client request. If the application requires a series of interactions with the user, intermediate application state is stored in the database. On each client request, it is necessary to locate and read the state from the database. This can be done by using Web basic authentication, which supplies a username and password on each request, or it can be done with a cookie or other session mechanism (discussed later).

State Kept in Application

If the application intermediate state is substantial, and the intermediate state does not require transaction safety, it may be kept in allocated storage inside the application. In this case, the application must be persistent (not restarted between client requests), as is possible with FastCGI, ISAPI, and NSAPI. Again, a session mechanism must be used to associate the particular user with a particular block of stored state information.

State Kept in Client

For simple applications, it may be appropriate to keep application state in the client between requests. In this model, when the application server responds to a client request with some intermediate results, it also sends to the client any intermediate application state that will be necessary to resume the application on the user's next request. This requires a mechanism for handing state information back and forth between client and server.

Session and Client State Mechanisms

There are several techniques for identifying a set of user requests as belonging to the same session and for passing state information back and forth between client and server. In addition, it is important to note that the difference between a session mechanism and a state mechanism is subtle. State is the application information itself, whereas a session identifier is a reference to state stored somewhere else.

Authentication Mechanisms

Any authentication mechanism, such as basic authentication or client certificates, can serve as a session mechanism. Because these authentication systems identify the user to the server on each request, state information can be stored at the application or application database and looked up on each request by using the user identification.

Dynamic URLs

If a user ID or other information is embedded in every URL used for a sequence of pages, the URLs in use by a particular user will be different from the URLs used by any other user. This creates a session mechanism. The difficulty is that these dynamic URLs can be easily lost if the user clicks out to some other Web site for a while and then reenters the application later. In addition, dynamic URLs can present a security challenge unless they are cryptographically protected from forgery or tampering.

Cookies

Most of the current generation of browsers support cookies, an idea originally introduced by Netscape. A cookie is a block of information transmitted from server to browser and stored there. On subsequent requests to the server, the browser sends back the cookie along with the Web request. Cookies can be used to store session identifiers or to store application state. In addition, cookies can be set to be persistent across browser sessions. The privacy implications of cookies are discussed further in Privacy Versus Merchandising, which begins on page 77. Because cookies are accessible to the savvy browser user, they must be protected from tampering.

Forms

If the Web application consists of a series of HTML forms, application state or session identification can travel along with the form as a hidden field. A hidden field is a special type of HTML form field that is not displayed to the user but merely returned as is to the server when the form is submitted. Like dynamic URLs and cookies, hidden fields are subject to tampering if not protected.

Applets

As Web applications evolve from simple HTML with forms and become more like client-server systems, it will become more common to use applets, controls, and client scripting to store session identifiers or application state.

Object Technology

Object technology has become the subject of intense marketing, as competing companies apply the label to whatever they were doing anyway. Consequently, it is necessary to dig fairly deep to understand exactly what is going on. The essential idea of a software object is a package containing both some *data* and the *methods* that operate on that data. This packaging has several good results.

- Encapsulation—objects hide the details of their implementation.

  Objects are a step beyond subroutine libraries, or Application Programming Interfaces (APIs). The programmer who develops software using APIs must understand how data is represented and stored. With object technology, the object is responsible for the data, not the programmer making use of the object to accomplish some higher goal. Encapsulation not only makes it unnecessary for the programmer to learn about the internal details of the object, it makes it impossible. This sounds heavy-handed, but it greatly reduces both immediate problems and latent bugs.

- Polymorphism—there can be multiple implementations of an object.

  Once a particular concept, such as a bank account, has been represented as an object, variations of the concept, such as a checking account or a savings account, can be represented as different implementations of an object, each with the same interface. When this is done, applications that operate on the account, such as the application that computes interest due each month, do not even need to know that there are different kinds of accounts.

- Language binding—objects can be implemented in different languages.

  The internal communications between one part of a program and another part are usually orchestrated by the language and its compiler. However, because the object technology carefully defines the ways in which one object can call another, there is no need for all the objects in a system to be coded in the same language. Instead, each language system provides a translation to the standard communications machinery defined by the object system.

At one level, object technology is about better and more efficient ways to construct large software applications; disciplined use of abstraction and encapsulation make software more reliable, whether or not development is done using an object-oriented programming language, such as C++ or Java. At quite another level, object technology provides the possibility that complex systems can be built using software piece parts designed and implemented by different groups or different companies. This idea is called *component software*.

An object model alone is not sufficient to achieve component software. The object model supplies a base set of assumptions and conditions needed to achieve interoperability—similar to a standard gauge for railroad tracks. Having the rails the same distance apart is obviously necessary, but not sufficient, for cars to run on different railroads. Component software systems also impose additional sets of standard interfaces that compliant objects must obey in order to ensure interoperability. Returning to our railroad example, standard interfaces for car coupling and brakes are also necessary for interoperability.

Beyond component software is the notion of distributed object computing, where the application is composed of software objects located on multiple computers connected by a network. Distributed object computing requires not only an object model and language bindings but also wire protocols, naming, and a security model.

- Wire protocols

  When objects communicate over a network, they must agree on the format and order of transmission of information. Network communication is related to the problem of object persistence, in which an object can record its data on disk. In achieving object persistence, the object serializes itself on disk, essentially writing out a copy of its data in a linear format. In object network communications, the source object creates a serialized message in a standardized format so that the recipient object, potentially running on a computer of a completely different architecture, can successfully receive and interpret the message.

- Naming

  In any distributed system, the software components of an application must establish communications with each other. Since on the network any pair of computers can potentially communicate, objects use a naming and addressing system to look up each other's network addresses and establish the proper communications channels. This problem also arises in the nondistributed world of component software; but in traditional applications, the binding together of all the objects is done by the programming environment at build time, rather than dynamically at runtime.

- Security

  In a distributed system that must operate over open networks, such as the Internet, security is a major issue. Software components must ensure that they are communicating with the correct objects (authentication) and that their communications are private (via encryption) and trustworthy (via integrity checking). In Internet commerce, an additional aspect of security—trust—becomes essential. In many situations, not all the software objects making up an application are running on computers controlled and operated by a single organization. The system designer must determine precisely what degree of trust to place in computations done by computers run by customers or by different organizations.

CORBA

The Object Management Group's Common Object Request Broker Architecture (CORBA) is the result of a 15-year effort by a consortium of companies to define a reference model for objects as well as to encourage companies to produce interoperable implementations for multiple languages and platforms.

CORBA is based on the idea of an Object Request Broker (ORB), which is the basic mechanism through which objects make requests to and receive responses from other objects. The ORB provides naming and communications services. CORBA objects are described by an Interface Definition Language (IDL) that formally defines their interfaces. IDL is a language for defining objects. It solves the language binding problem through language-specific translators that take an IDL description of an object and translate it into a specific set of language bindings.

CORBA also supplies object services, common facilities, and a number of domain interfaces that define common objects for particular application domains such as finance and health care. CORBA works over the Internet using the Internet Inter-ORB Protocol (IIOP), which defines the way CORBA objects communicate over a TCP/IP network.

COM

Microsoft's Component Object Model (COM), which is an essential part of its operating systems and applications, is the most widely used object system. Beyond the basic object model, which defines communications standards, Microsoft provides several other levels of functionality under the blanket name *Object Linking and Embedding* (OLE).

- OLE automation

  OLE automation defines a set of standard interfaces that, if implemented by an object, make that COM object scriptable so that it can be used from a scripting language such as Visual Basic. The ability to link potentially complex objects by using veneers of script can enable rapid application development. Scripting languages may have high overhead, but because the bulk of the execution time is spent in compiled objects, an application built in this way may not suffer from poor performance.

- ActiveX

  Once known as OLE controls, ActiveX objects are COM objects that implement additional sets of standard interfaces that make it possible to use them as component software. One of the most interesting aspects of ActiveX is a definition of both design time and runtime behavior. ActiveX controls can be configured at design time through one set of interfaces in an integrated programming environment such as Visual C++ and then operate at runtime through another set of interfaces. This distinction between design time and runtime helps to make well-designed ActiveX controls useful as component software.

- Distributed COM (DCOM)

  DCOM uses a version of DCE RPC (Distributed Computing Environment Remote Procedure Call) for its wire protocol, permitting COM objects located on different computers to communicate.

- Microsoft .NET

  Microsoft .NET is Microsoft's implementation of Web services, which we will discuss further in Chapter 11. In this context, the important point is that .NET provides remote access to objects using the remote procedure call system called the *Simple Object Access Protocol* (SOAP).

JavaBeans/RMI

Java is an object-oriented programming language, and Remote Method Invocation (RMI) is the standard way for a Java object to communicate with another across a network. As an object-oriented language, Java has a built-in object model. The other key feature of Java is *Write Once, Run Anywhere*. Java applications are built to run under the control of the Java virtual machine, a kind of abstract computer. Platforms that support Java (almost all platforms, these days) implement the virtual machine, and then any Java program can run.

JavaBeans is the Java version of component software. JavaBeans implements a set of standard interfaces and behaviors that, similar to ActiveX, permit programmers to customize the behavior of Beans at design time. JavaBeans can also use a set of bridges that permit Beans to interoperate with RMI-based objects, ActiveX controls, and CORBA objects.

Web Services

We shall have more to say about Web services in Chapter 11. Web services are a way to make distributed applications work across the Internet, using XML and SOAP. SOAP is constructed using XML and standard Web protocols.

Implications of Object Technology for Internet Commerce

Object technology has several implications for the design of systems for Internet commerce.

- Rapid application development

  Object technology generally permits more rapid application development than earlier methods of programming. Obviously, this advantage is not at all unique to Internet commerce.

- Distributed applications

  Object technology permits applications to be distributed across multiple computers without the development staff necessarily having to be experts in all aspects of network communications and security.

- Flexibility of deployment

  Object technology, particularly its availability in the Web context of downloadable applets and controls, provides great flexibility for the designers of Internet commerce applications. In particular, designers of multitier applications can use object technology to place functionality at different servers or to migrate functionality all the way to the client desktop. Automatically moving part of the application to the desktop can provide great advantages of interactivity and interoperability but also introduces some complex security and trust problems, because the desktop computer may not be a trustworthy computing platform.

In practice, object technology will probably have a role in almost all Internet commerce projects.

Application Servers

As Internet applications grow more complex, they require infrastructure that is more complete and more reliable and that provides greater services. Whereas a typical Web application of a few years ago required operating system services, a Web server, and connectivity to a database, the list is much longer today.

- Operating system

  Provides filesystem, logging, initialization, and communications
- Web server

  Provides protocol support for HTTP and SSL/TLS, security, access control, and logging
- Database connectivity

  Provides SQL-compliant database and language bindings
- Transaction service

  Provides transaction monitor for linking multiple SQL databases and middleware

- Page generation

  Provides Web page scripting and dynamic Web pages

- Software components

  Provide a rich set of existing software functions that can be combined as needed for a particular application

- Middleware

  Provides connectivity to enterprise applications

- Application scaling and deployment

  Provide a scalable platform without requiring application redesign

As technology advances, the application platform incorporates more and more services that once were the province of the application. This leaves the designers of applications more freedom to concentrate on business logic. The functionality of the application floats on the rising tide of application server functionality.

The leading contenders for the architecture of the application server are Microsoft, with its full suite of products, and Sun Microsystem's Java 2 Enterprise Edition (J2EE), with implementations provided by many vendors. Table 9-3 provides a brief comparison of these two architectures.

Commerce Client Technology

The ability to program browsers has been applied in many ways to Internet commerce. As discussed in the section on Object Technology, commerce functionality can be distributed to the desktop, with advantages in privacy, convenience, and interactivity, but also with potential disadvantages in security, universality, and reliability.

For some aspects of client technology, there are alternatives such as server-side wallets, which can be implemented in a system such as the federated commerce architecture example in Chapter 21.

Advantages of Clients for Commerce

- Privacy

  Information such as the user's profile, preferences, and purchase history can potentially be stored on the desktop rather than becoming part of a central database. If the proper care is taken to protect these sorts of information, client storage can enhance personal privacy.

	J2EE	Microsoft
Vendor	BEA, IBM, others	Microsoft
Operating system	Java VM	Windows NT, 2000, XP
Web server	Apache, Sun, others	IIS
Database	JDBC + Oracle, others	ODBC + SQL Server
Transactions	JTS	MTS
Page generation	Java Server Pages	Active Server Pages
Object model	Java	COM
Components	JavaBeans, EJBs	Active X
Middleware	JMS, connectors	Microsoft Message Queue
Scaling and deployment	Servlets and containers	Windows NT Services

TABLE 9-3. **Application Server Architecture: JavaVersus Microsoft**

- Convenience

  Commonly used information such as billing and shipping addresses can be stored by desktop software and automatically supplied to merchant servers. This can relieve the user from the burden of repetitively entering the same information at site after site and can also help ensure that the information is accurate when used. Of course, for these benefits to be realized, the information storage and supply mechanisms must be standardized. Although some browsers have limited capabilities to remember how forms have been filled in, there are no standards that make it possible for them to provide information when presented with a new form.

- Interactivity

  Perhaps the key benefit of moving functionality to the desktop is interactivity. Because the software is running directly on the user's computer, a high-bandwidth, low-latency channel is available between the user and the application. This permits the use of highly interactive techniques, such as drag-and-drop operations, that would be impossible to use with a purely server-based implementation.

Disadvantages of Clients for Commerce

- Security

  The security technology for Java and ActiveX applets is designed primarily to protect the desktop computer and its user from hostile software. Neither Java nor ActiveX does much to protect a distributed application from a hostile user or untrustworthy client computer. Any use of client software for Internet commerce must be carefully evaluated to make sure that errors, accidental or malicious, in the operation of the client software cannot damage the integrity of the application.

- Universality

  Until client technologies such as Java are universally available, requiring client capabilities can merely reduce the audience for a commerce application. If a user does not have the equipment or environment for the client software, that user cannot use the application. More subtly, if the user must take special action such as installing a plug-in or control, the barrier is set higher for use of the server application.

- Reliability

  Many of the potential benefits for client software require that persistent state must be maintained on the client computer. This can cause problems in usability and reliability. If the user habitually uses several computers—an office desktop and a laptop, for example—the stored state on the two computers may be incomplete and incompatible. If the user's computer crashes, which is not unusual, stored state may be lost. It may not be adequate to depend on the user for backup of application-critical information.

Client Functionality

In designing a commerce system, it is appropriate to consider each element of functionality for potential deployment to the desktop. We discuss some possibilities here.

- Receipt and coupon storage

  The desktop is a natural place to store Internet commerce purchase receipts and coupons. If these items are not stored and indexed on the desktop or a server-side wallet, then the user has the problem of remembering all the various commerce locations she has visited.

- Payment credentials and applications

  Some Internet payment protocols, such as Secure Electronic Transactions (SET), require client software to function. Others, such as entering a credit card number into a secure HTML form, can benefit from desktop software that could, for example, enter one's information into the form automatically.

- Shopping carts

  The functions of a shopping cart may be placed at the transaction engine to simplify cross-store purchasing, at the catalog server to support complex pricing, or at the user's desktop to provide maximum interactivity. With client software, drag-and-drop item selection can be implemented, as well as highly interactive pricing calculations and order modification.

- User profile

  User profile information, from shipping addresses to preferences in colors and styles, is a natural candidate for client storage. If such information is kept at the client, it can be used for multiple Internet sites and potentially kept more private.

Commerce Client Examples

There have been several examples of client software for Internet commerce.

- Wallets

  CyberCash, IBM, JavaSoft, Verifone, and others have built *electronic wallets*. These applications store user payment credentials for SET and similar protocols and may also play a role in receipt storage. Most of these efforts have faded, however.

- Shopping application

  Peapod, among others, has created a specialized commerce application for the desktop. Peapod software is specialized for the needs of grocery shopping. As such, it is highly interactive and has excellent support for repeat and recurring orders.

- Applets

  A number of sites use Java or ActiveX applets to display the contents of the user's shopping basket. These display applications typically also make use of browser frames to provide a separate windowpane for the shopping cart, distinct from the frame used for catalog information.

Delivering Digital Goods

As discussed in Chapter 4, fulfillment for digital goods is accomplished online. In information commerce, the content itself is the product.

Securing Delivery

When the content is the product, the commerce system must provide the link between the sale and fulfillment. Once payment is made, fulfillment must be automatic. Several mechanisms are available.

- License key

  In the case of software purchased and fulfilled over the network, the software package may be freely downloadable but not operable without a specific license key. Rather than purchase the download, the customer in effect purchases a license key. The key is usually tied both to the software and to a particular computer, so that the same key will not work for more than one copy of the software. This technique is also applied to purchasing specific rights for information databases located on a CD-ROM or on a network server as well as for secure containers (discussed later).

- Access control database

  Once payment is taken for a particular content package, the commerce system can make an entry in the access control database for the content server. Thereafter, the end user logs in to the content server using traditional Web access control mechanisms, such as name and password, via basic authentication. This scheme has a number of problems, notably that the user's credentials are kept in lots of different places, making it difficult for him to remember which password is used where or to update all the servers when a new password is chosen. It may also be awkward for the system operators to maintain all the access control databases when multiple content servers are involved.

- Digital receipt

  Once the payment transaction for digital goods is complete, the commerce system can create and sign a *digital receipt*, stating that payment has been received and that delivery is authorized. This approach was taken by Open Market's products. An Open Market digital receipt is a URL that points to the electronic fulfillment area and that contains a *ticket*. The ticket is analogous to a movie theater ticket: if you have one, you get in; otherwise, you don't. The digital ticket contains information on the access rights given, the term of those rights, and a reference to the transaction that created it, for auditing purposes. In this system, a central transaction engine can provide commerce services for distributed digital goods fulfillment servers. Because the receipt is a URL, it is automatically managed by Web browsers and can be bookmarked and saved by the user.

- Public-key attribute certificate

  Many Web browsers offer the ability to use X.509 version 3 public-key certificates for security purposes. These certificates primarily offer authentication but can also be used for access control. Version 3 of the X.509 specification allows for an extensible set of attributes to be attached to the certificate, which can be used to specify access rights for digital goods fulfillment. In this model, when digital goods are purchased, the commerce system can prompt the user to create a new public key and then turn that key into a certificate by signing it (acting as a certificate authority) and attaching attributes describing the necessary access rights for digital fulfillment. This approach can work, but it is awkward because of the complexity of creating, installing, and using a certificate. This topic is discussed more fully in Chapter 13.

Failure Recovery

Customers tend to object when they pay for things and then don't get delivery. From the buyer's perspective, this is a usability issue: delivery should be reliable or at least easy to retry. If it isn't, the customer will go elsewhere. From the seller's perspective, the reliability of fulfillment is a cost issue and a customer satisfaction issue. If delivery is unreliable, customers may be lost. If the mechanism for retry or failure recovery is too expensive, then it becomes a cost and a customer service problem.

The approaches to failure recovery are as follows.

- Too cheap to complain

  If payment for digital goods is on a per-page basis using microtransactions, then it may be acceptable simply to charge for all pages, whether successfully viewed or not.

- Time-based charging

  If payment for digital goods is based on the time spent connected to the service, and if unsuccessful downloads are infrequent or resolved quickly, then it may be acceptable to charge for all time used, whether productive or not.

- Separate bulk transfer from the transaction

  Permitting free downloading of bulk data in encrypted or inactive form and then charging for an unlocking key or license key can improve the reliability of fulfillment. Because the downloading of the bulk data is not protected, the consumer can retry as needed. The downloading of the particular license key needs to be reliable, but at least it is small and fast.

- Permit retry based on transaction records

  If the transaction records are persistent, the commerce software can automatically redeliver after a failed download attempt. The buyer will have to authenticate himself to the satisfaction of the commerce system as in fact being the original purchaser. Open Market's software, for example, provides persistent proof of purchase in the form of online statements and digital receipts.

- Grant access, not a download attempt

  Upon payment, the commerce system can make an access control entry stating that "This customer has access to the download area for the next hour," on the basis that an hour is enough time for several download attempts, even if the first is unsuccessful. Subscriptions work this way, as do digital receipts.

Auditability

Related to the concept of failure recovery is the concept of auditability. Generally, a commerce system is auditable if the system stores enough records so that a reasonable person would agree that a particular transaction happened as claimed. These sorts of records are valuable for several purposes.

- Dispute resolution

  Customer disputes frequently involve nondelivery of a product or service or the charging of an incorrect price. If the commerce system provides adequate records, there will be a complete audit trail of all essential features of the transaction: date and time, means of authenticating the customer, price, description, and evidence that indeed the product was delivered or service rendered. This information can refresh the customer's memory or assist a customer service representative in resolving the dispute.

- Failure recovery

  One interesting case arises when the audit trail provides an indication that service was not rendered to the buyer. In this case, for digital goods, the goods or services can be redelivered. The system may err in this direction since the marginal cost of delivery is near zero.

- Audit

  Audit has a precise technical meaning, but in this context we refer to a more general sense of checks and balances that help ensure that all customers have paid, that all payments are matched by buyers, and that goods and services have been successfully delivered.

Rights Management

One important aspect of digital goods is the management of intellectual property rights. Information is fundamentally different from physical artifacts in that exact copies can be made. If Erica gives a copy of an electronic document to Samantha, they both have it. This fact has always been true of information, but the advent of the photocopy machine and the subsequent advent of electronic documents have greatly lowered the cost of copying. Improper use and redistribution of copyrighted materials is such a sufficient problem that content owners are reluctant to make their information available on networks unless there are controls to prevent or discourage misuse.

Rights management refers to the problems associated with intellectual property rights and in particular to the problem of ensuring that, in a commerce setting, payment is made for a particular use of content and that the use made does not exceed the use authorized. For example, the content owner may want to charge one price for searching a database and viewing the results on a screen and a higher price for printing the search results.

In discussing rights management, it is very useful to draw a distinction between facilitating compliance and enforcing rights. In a business-to-business context, the buyer might have no particular incentive to steal content, particularly if the charges would be passed on to the buyer's client. Instead, what is needed is an easy way to pay. Facilitating compliance involves many design issues, but the problem is much easier than operating in a potentially hostile business-to-consumer environment in which software designed to let users steal commercial content may be widely available.

Generically, rights management requires some means of specifying which rights are desired and which rights are granted, plus a means of paying for those rights (in the case of facilitating compliance) and a means of securing the content against unauthorized use (in the case of rights enforcement).

Secure Container Technology

The generic name for rights enforcement technology is *secure container technology.* The general idea is that the content is carried around the network in encrypted form and is unlocked only at the point of use. In addition to the concept of unlocking information only at the point of use, secure container technologies can also control some aspects of the computing environment. For example, the container application might disable the **Print** button if the document does not convey the right to print. It is always possible for the end user to transcribe manually information received off the screen and to rekey it, but secure containers can make it difficult or uneconomical to misuse protected content. These technologies can also offer *superdistribution,* which can implement an entire distribution chain from author to publisher to distributor to end user with economic and security models maintained at every point.

In practice, such technologies have not become common, and it is often possible to circumvent them.

Fingerprinting and Watermarks

As discussed previously, it is useful to distinguish between facilitating compliance and enforcing rights. At some level, these are opposing concepts: facilitating compliance is about making it easy to pay, whereas enforcing rights is about making it difficult to copy. There is also a middle ground: making it possible to trace improper use. For example, suppose a protected document were improperly copied and republished on the Internet. If it were possible to identify the original purchaser of that copy, it would serve to discourage improper use. It turns out that this kind of tracing is possible through digital techniques called *fingerprinting* and *watermarking*. In these schemes, each copy of a document is made subtly different in a way that is not obvious and that encodes a serial number or other tracing information.

Here are some simple examples of fingerprinting methods.

- For images, a trivial amount of *noise* can be added to the encoding of the image. This noise can have no effect on the appearance of the image, but a decoding computer that knows what to look for can recover the added noise and decode it to a serial number.
- For text, slight variations in the spacing of the words or the line breaks can encode a serial number.

The technical name for hiding a message in another message in such a way that the existence of the hidden message is also hidden is *steganography*. Watermarks do not have to be hidden, but if they are not, a technically astute attacker might be able to remove them. Indeed, many schemes for watermarking have been proposed and subsequently broken by attackers. It is usually a good idea also to place an explicit copyright notice in a protected document. The notice, together with the real prospect of improper use being discovered and traced, helps to set the social context of copyrighted information in electronic form.

Summary

Unlike many systems based on information technology, systems for Internet commerce depend on client software and server software that may be supplied by different vendors and operated by different organizations but still must interoperate across an open network. This chapter has focused on basic client and server technologies, digital goods fulfillment, and a brief survey of object technologies. These components provide the basic wiring and Internet infrastructure for commerce systems. The chapters that follow discuss the architecture of Internet commerce systems and the various supporting technologies such as cryptography, security, and transaction processing.

CHAPTER 10

System Design

The contact with manners then is education. . . . history is philosophy
learned from examples.

—Dionysius of Halicarnassus[1]

The Problem of Design

The chapters to come will examine many of the key technology areas for developing
systems for Internet commerce. A logical question, of course, is "How do they go together?" In this chapter, we consider the problem of design: given a set of components, how do we put them together to create the most effective solution? Although we
are saving details of the components for later, the discussion in this chapter is intended to frame an understanding of the role each component plays in the overall
system.

From a software engineering point of view, there are many possible design methodol-
ogies to use. Such techniques as object-oriented design, rapid prototyping, formal
methods, extreme programming, and so on can all be used in the design of Internet
commerce systems. We do not advocate any particular method or set of methods. The
methods appropriate for your team depend on your own views and experience, the
views and experience of the team, the tools available to you, and many other factors.

In this chapter, we look at some of the main design issues that have arisen in our own
experience with Internet commerce systems. For the most part, these issues are not

---

1. Dionysius of Halicarnassus (c. 54 – c. 7 B.C.), *Ars Rhetorica*, XI.

unique to Internet commerce systems, but they do tend to be very important in such systems. We begin first with some principles of design—those ideas that are mostly independent of particular choices of technology and that apply to a wide range of systems.

A Philosophy of Design

The design of a computer system, like any engineering design, is really part art and part science. The science is very important for computer systems. It tells us what kinds of problems can be handled successfully by computers and how to evaluate, measure, and select algorithms for specific problems. The discipline of software engineering provides some guidance in the proper development of computer programs. Designing a complex system, however, requires insight, experience, and good taste as well as science.

Understanding the Customer's Requirements

There is no substitute for a good understanding of the target customers and what they want. In many cases, they cannot say explicitly what they want, so it is necessary to ferret it out in other ways. Is convenience important? What about access to good information? What inconveniences might customers tolerate in exchange for certain services? How much are they willing to pay? The result of such understanding may be a product or service that never occurred to the customers, but it is obviously just what they want once they see it. A particular challenge in Internet commerce is that there are many new and unforeseen opportunities. It's impossible to predict with certainty what buyers will prefer, so flexibility becomes very important as well. Indeed, it is often necessary to adapt techniques and customer experiences from other Internet commerce sites into your own.

Planning for Evolution

If a computer system of any kind is going to be around for a long time, we should plan for it to incorporate technology changes and to evolve over time. The performance of computer hardware, such as processor speed or memory density, tends to double approximately every two years, for approximately the same cost. Network performance, measured in bandwidth, is also increasing. By planning for this evolution, we can take advantage of these changes so as to provide superior service and performance over a long period of time. In addition, software is changing rapidly. Only a few years ago, for example, almost no one had heard of the World Wide Web. Although we may not foresee every technology change that arrives, we can imagine that some kinds of changes are possible and plan appropriately so that the system can evolve in many different directions.

Starting Small

It is often tempting to build a large, comprehensive system that will solve all known problems. Such systems frequently take a long time to design and build, and they often end up being canceled before they can deliver anything at all. Getting started with a small system provides an opportunity to learn from those first explorations and to adapt the evolution of the system appropriately. This approach is particularly important in the rapidly changing world of the Internet, because a large and complex system is likely to be obsolete by the time it is deployed. Incremental development, by contrast, allows a system to take advantage of technology changes as well as improved understanding of the customers and the business.

Keeping Options Open

The design process is largely about making choices. We often find, however, that some choices limit our future options more than others. For example, we might design our system around a particular payment method, such as credit cards. Although credit cards might be quite sufficient today, they might not be sufficient in the future. We might not be able to predict what else we might need, but we could design the system to handle payment methods in a generic fashion, with a particular module that implements credit card payment. In that way, we have the option of adding other payment systems later. If this is done early enough in the life of the system, the added flexibility frequently has little additional cost. In making design choices, then, when all other things are (nearly) equal, it may be wise to choose the path that allows the most flexibility in the future.

Developing an Architecture

As we saw in Chapter 6, the architecture of a system contributes a great deal to its long-term development and evolution. Early attention to creating the architecture, with particular focus on design issues such as the ones we discuss here, paves the way for a system that can grow and develop over a long period of time. A system architecture is a framework for solving individual design problems. There is obvious benefit from such a framework at the time of initial design, but an architecture is even more powerful later, as a framework for solving problems that were not envisioned at the time the original system was built.

An Architectural Approach

In the following sections, we discuss some of the most important issues in system design. These issues cut across many phases of Internet commerce system development (and, of course, they are relevant to many other kinds of computer systems as well). By this we mean that each issue must be considered as part of the overall architecture, the detailed system design, the implementation, and the operation of the system. For example, an architectural decision to build on a distributed system has implications for how the system will scale in comparison with a centralized system, but a perfect architecture for scaling may not mean much in practice if the detailed system design does not provide for the necessary facilities or if the implementation omits them.

The fundamental design issues we consider here are as follows.

- Performance and scaling
- Reliability
- Transactions
- Managing state
- Security

Each of these issues is fundamental in the sense that it is important in an Internet commerce system and also cuts across the different phases of development, as we have discussed.

Performance and Scaling

Simply put, scaling is the question of how big a system can grow in various dimensions to provide more service.[2] There are many different ways we can measure the scale of a system, such as the total number of users, the number of simultaneous users, the transaction volume, and so on. These dimensions are not independent, and scaling up the size of the system in one dimension typically affects other dimensions as well. The side effects may help other areas or hurt them, depending on the changes made. For example, increasing the CPU performance of a system often helps in several areas. In contrast, increasing the size of a database to handle more users may sometimes decrease the performance.

Therefore, it is important to evaluate possible changes in the system to improve the scaling or performance in the context of the entire system, not just for one component. Having a clear set of priorities for the system (such as "the most important thing is to serve millions of users") makes it easier to make trade-offs when needed, as well as to justify investments in new hardware or software changes to make the desired improvements.

Often the system architecture itself enables or limits certain kinds of changes for scaling. As an example, if a system is designed to operate all of its components (catalog

---

2. Anecdotal evidence, as well as our own experience, suggests that something unexpected becomes a serious problem every time a system increases its size (in some dimension) by a factor of 10. This tells us that system designers, in general, have some difficulty looking beyond order-of-magnitude changes. We can compensate for this either by trying harder (since we know about this problem) or by planning to deal with something unexpected at the points where the system has grown that much. This also means that a particular design problem can be addressed only when the order of magnitude of the problem is known and planned for.

server, payment system, user account management, and so on) on a single computer, the primary means of scaling up the system is to buy a larger computer. Such a system is therefore ultimately limited by the size of the available computers. In some cases, the natural evolution of computer technology (faster CPUs, bigger memory systems, bigger disks) will allow the system to scale to the required level of service, but often it will not, especially because the basic software (operating system, database, and application) often consumes a considerable part of the additional resources. Distributed applications, in contrast, may often be less efficient for small-scale systems, but they may scale up much better as demand grows.

One additional (and often overlooked) point about scaling up Internet services is how fast the scaling can be done. Internet services often become popular very quickly (the *flash crowd* effect mentioned in Chapter 7), so it may be important to add capacity to the system rapidly in order to keep up with the demand. If, for example, a system can be scaled up by adding additional servers as needed, the increased capacity may often be added without disrupting operation of the existing service.

For many systems, poor performance is often an inconvenience and perhaps a source of complaints, but the users keep using the system. In Internet commerce systems, performance problems are much more than an inconvenience—they can be a disaster for a business, putting off customers and giving competitors an advantage.

The performance of a system can be measured in many ways, so it is important to decide what measurements are important and relevant. Two common kinds of metrics examine *latency* and *throughput*. Latency is a measure of how long it takes to complete a given operation. For example, how long does it take to download a Web page? Throughput is a measure of how many operations can be completed in a given time: how many Web pages can the server deliver in an hour? These two measures may seem almost the same, but they actually tell you very different things. Latency tells you about the experience of a particular user (on average), whereas throughput tells you how many users the system can handle. Also, the two measures may interact with each other: as throughput increases, for example, the latency as seen by any given user may increase. This is like driving on a highway in heavy traffic: the number of cars moving down the highway is greater than normal (that is, greater throughput), but the average speed is lower (yielding higher latency).

To get a good characterization of a system's performance, you should decide what you want to measure in advance, and then measure it and work to improve it. Although your ideas of what is important to measure may change over time, this is the only way to make real improvements in the system. All too often, the performance metrics for a system are chosen to make it look good, without regard to getting an accurate idea of how the system performs for its users.

Reliability

Many business computer systems require a high degree of reliability, and this is particularly true of Internet commerce systems. The special challenge of Internet commerce is the risk of being embarrassed in public. When the system is not working, neither is the business. In other situations, people can work around the computer's failures. The frontline operators for a mail-order business, for example, can write orders on paper if needed, but at least the phones are being answered. On the Internet, if the server is down, one may not even be able to tell easily if the company is still in business.

Reliable systems are often built by using redundant components, so that when one fails, another is available to take over. In many network protocols, such as TCP, the sender of a message on the network expects an acknowledgment and will retransmit the message until it receives one (or until it gives up after trying too many times). Such attempts to recover from difficulties may also mask failures. But if those failures are not reported to the operators, the system may not be repaired—until the last redundant component fails. At that point, all the redundant design is for naught. Keep an eye on the system to make sure that broken components are fixed soon after they break.

Transactions

The term *atomicity* comes from the world of transaction processing. In many applications, it is important that a transaction be atomic. That is, it must not happen that one part of a transaction was completed and another part was not. For example, when money is transferred from one bank account to another, we can think of this transaction as consisting of two parts: debiting the amount from one account and crediting it to the other. It seems clear that we want either both parts to happen (in which case the transaction succeeds) or both parts not to happen (in which case the transaction fails). If only part of the transaction is completed, such as the debit operation, the result is both incorrect and confusing. Such failures can also result directly in unhappy customers (and errors that may be hard to correct), so it is well worth the effort to avoid them. Here we introduce a few key concepts about transactions before diving into more details about transaction processing in Chapter 17.

Transactions for Internet commerce often have this requirement: they must be atomic. In addition, they must satisfy three other requirements: consistency, isolation, and durability. *Consistency* means that all parties have the same view of the outcome of the transaction. *Isolation* means that independent activities don't interfere with one another. *Durability* means that the outcome of a transaction cannot be undone by a hardware failure.

In a distributed system, such as a client-server system for Internet commerce, the client and server may exchange several messages in order to complete an operation. If so, the system should be resilient against network failures that may lose, duplicate, reorder, or maliciously modify the messages. We can think of a transaction as beginning with the first message and ending with the last one, so that the complete transaction should be atomic. If the network fails in the middle of the transaction, the state of the system should remain consistent. Ideally, it should also be clear to both sides whether or not the transaction has succeeded, but when it is not, it is usually straightforward for the two sides to sort it out.

It is easy to see how this property of atomicity should apply to a payment transaction— the transfer of money should clearly be atomic, as in the previous banking example. Atomicity is also important in other parts of a complete purchase transaction. For example, payment is just one part of the purchase transaction; it must also include the recording of the purchase as being complete. If the money has moved but the merchant loses track of what has been purchased, the goods may never be delivered.

The general problem of recovering from various kinds of failures is related to atomicity. Indeed, we can consider the implementation of certain transactions as atomic transactions to be a way of avoiding or recovering from certain kinds of failure. The most common types of failures for an Internet commerce system are network failures and system crashes. Let's look at the problems caused by each type.

In a network failure, there is some problem in communication between two systems, although both of them are functioning correctly otherwise. If some care is not taken in designing the application, the consequences of a network failure may be rather confusing. For example, a client might not get service that it requested, or a server might have delivered a response that never reached the client. More specifically, suppose that a customer has purchased a software package for downloading. If the download is interrupted by a network failure, how can the client complete the download?

Different systems may have different ways of handling this problem, but it is an important one to address. One way, for example, for a system to recover is for the server to have an account for each customer that contains a listing of all completed transactions. After customers experience a network failure, they can identify themselves to the server, examine the listing of transactions, and resume a failed delivery. Another approach might be to issue the equivalent of a store receipt, which could be used to resume downloading the software after a failure.

System crashes, on the other hand, must be handled somewhat differently. The crucial issue in preparing for a crash is ensuring that important information is *durable* and is recorded on stable storage at the proper times.[3] By *stable storage,* we mean a storage medium, such as a disk, that will hold the information across crashes and power failures. For example, the system should record that a purchase has been completed

---

3. Of course, another approach is to ensure that systems never crash. This approach usually requires special hardware and software as well as careful attention to seemingly mundane issues such as redundant sources of power. This approach is discussed in more detail in Chapter 19.

before informing the client of this fact. This ensures that if the server crashes before completing delivery, at least the server is certain about what happened, and the client does not think that the operation completed when, in fact, it did not.

How a system recovers from failures is not just an abstruse technical issue. It can have real consequences on the way that customers perceive the system and on the kinds of problems that must be solved with customer service. When evaluating a product for use in a commerce system, understanding how a system deals with these problems can often provide useful insight into how carefully the system designers worked through the difficult issues in creating an application.

Managing State

In any distributed system, a key question is where different pieces of information, called the *state* of the system, are stored. One way to think about this is that the underlying information is stored in a database, whether it be a "real" database system or a collection of files that represent the information stored by an application. When we talk about managing the state of the system, we are really talking about the variables in the process of being modified. For example, there may be several steps in making a particular transaction, and the system must keep track of the progress of each step and its results. Eventually, those changes are committed to the database as updated information, or they are discarded.

With a client-server system such as the Web, the choice is essentially about which of these two stores specific information. In a three-tier Web application, there are three possible places: the client, the application logic, and the third-tier database. Some of the choices are clear: information that is private to the client or that may be relevant for several different services may be stored at the client. The server is a good place to keep information that is not specific to a particular client or user. In between, there is a range of information about the state of completed transactions, user account information, and transactions in progress that must be stored somewhere. Such information is often kept at the application server in a three-tier system, but it may be split between client and server if only the two systems are involved.

Because early Web browsers provided few, if any, methods for keeping track of user-specific state, commerce systems have typically managed all of the state information themselves. Some applications, notably payment systems, have attempted to manage more of the state on the client side. Each of these approaches has its advantages. Here are some of the advantages for the server.

- No special client software is required.
- Customers can use the system from wherever they happen to be, whether it be home, office, a kiosk, or someone else's computer. They are not tied to the computer with the right software and configuration.

- The server can control the security of the information, based on business and application security requirements.

- The set of information recorded can be extended without requiring updated software to be distributed to clients.

- Customers do not need many different pieces of software to do business with different Web sites.

- The server may have an aggregation of information that can be used for applications such as special marketing programs.

Storing information on the client side has some strong advantages for customers. The primary advantage is that important information about payment credentials, transactions in progress, and perhaps a transaction history are kept private on the customer's system. A client application may also store such items as receipts for online purchases. Of course, some of that information will be tracked by merchants for accounting and marketing purposes no matter where the official copy used by the customer may be.

For many applications, the costs of developing a client component have been prohibitive. The real value of a client-side application becomes clear when that application provides some unique functions not possible with a pure server implementation or when the client application (with some real utility) can be used across many different servers. How best to use client components is still a matter for the system designer to weigh carefully.

In the world of federated commerce (see Chapter 21), other servers, operated by third parties, may hold some of the application state. Server-side wallets, network single sign-on, and users' home portals may all be involved in a transaction. In this sort of situation, it may be easier to get the technology to work than to understand what all the moving parts are doing.[4]

Security

Security is often cited as the biggest concern regarding the technology of Internet commerce. A common question is "Is the Internet safe for commerce?" In a sense, this is the wrong question; a better one might be "Can the Internet be safe enough for my business?" Just as we use different locks for houses than for bank vaults, there are many different technical components used for security in Internet commerce, and they depend on such issues as risks, costs, and the value of the information involved.

---

4. Leslie Lamport said this about distributed systems: "A distributed system is one in which the failure of a computer you didn't even know existed can render your own computer unusable" (private communication, 1987).

We can break down the issues of security into four main areas.

1. System security

   How secure is the operating system of a computer? Can unauthorized users log in to it? Can information be protected from different users on the system, or can any user on the system read (and modify) any information on the system? Is the system physically secure? Who can get into the room? These are basic questions about the system underneath an application, and they are extremely important because it is impossible to build a secure application on an insecure foundation.

2. Communications security

   It is often important to protect the contents of a message from eavesdroppers or others who might otherwise see the message. A common example for commerce applications is protecting a customer's payment credentials, such as a credit card number, when the customer sends it to a merchant's server. In such cases, we typically use some kind of encryption mechanism to keep the messages private.

3. Data security

   After data has been communicated securely, we must worry about how it is protected on the end systems. In some cases, it is processed immediately and discarded, so no additional protection is needed. In other cases, we rely on the protection mechanisms of the operating system to safeguard the data. For particularly sensitive data, such as a customer's credit card number, we may choose to encrypt that data when it is stored on a disk.

4. Authentication and authorization

   Authentication is the means of answering the question "Who are you?" in a reliable manner. Passwords are a common method for authenticating users to computer systems, although there are others. Authorization is the means of answering the question "What are you allowed to do?" For example, a system may contain a list of people allowed to perform a particular task. In a commerce system, authorization often consists of having proof that you paid for something.

These aspects of security are important for any Internet commerce system, and they should be included as part of any system design or product evaluation.

Building on these core ideas, there are three main principles of security to keep in mind when designing or evaluating a system.

1. ***The security requirements are determined by an understanding of the business requirements and the associated risks.*** We create different security systems for applications that handle million-dollar transactions and those that handle $10 transactions. We never assert that a system is absolutely secure. Rather, we look at whether or not it has an appropriate set of security technologies in place for the perceived risks and threats.

2. *Securing a system means securing the entire system, not just individual components.* It is easy to put together a number of components that have their own security properties, but the resulting system is not necessarily secure. Different components may interact badly with each other, or between different components there may be gaps that can be exploited by an attacker. Designing a secure system requires attention to the complete system.

3. *The operation of a secure system is the most important element in keeping it secure.* If you don't lock the front door of your house, it doesn't matter whether the door has a lock or not. Similarly, the continuing operation of a secure system must include detailed attention to whether or not the users and operators of the system are using it as intended. In particular, users may sometimes subvert the security of the system (intentionally or not) in order to make it more convenient or easier for them to use. It is therefore especially important for the system operators to be vigilant about how the system is used, so they can detect misuse as well as attempts to break the system.

Understanding these principles goes a long way in helping ensure that a secure commerce system can be designed, implemented, and operated. In Chapter 13, we discuss in some depth the subject of cryptography, which is used to create many components of a secure system. Building on the use of cryptography, we examine detailed issues of security technology for Internet commerce in Chapter 14.

Design Principles Versus Technology Fads

One of the hardest parts of buying a PC today is knowing that it is obsolete the moment it is unpacked. The rate of change in computer hardware is breathtaking, and that of computer software is dramatic as well. In only a few years, the Web has become the basis for most Internet commerce systems as well as many other applications. The technology of the day changes very quickly, so it is impossible to say in this book what technologies, or what products, are best suited for a particular commerce application.

Therefore, instead of focusing on specific technologies, we have examined the fundamental issues in designing a system for commerce. These principles can be applied to many different technologies and can be used to evaluate many different products in order to develop a specific application that satisfies specific business requirements. More important, when one steps back to look at these principles, it becomes possible to see what is really important about the system and how it will evolve over time. Rather than choosing components and building an application around them today, only to be faced with potential obsolescence in a very short time, we think it is important to develop an approach to strategy and design that enables a business to design the system it needs and then bring in the products or custom development required to realize that vision.

As we discussed earlier, this is why system architecture is so important. The architecture provides a framework for evolution and for making decisions about what technologies to adopt, and when. It helps keep evaluations focused on the business problems that must be solved rather than on the hype that often surrounds new technologies.

Summary

This chapter has discussed the important aspects of designing a system for Internet commerce. Although these issues are common to the design of many kinds of computer applications, they are especially important for Internet commerce applications. Of course, different applications will ultimately have different designs that are appropriate for the requirements and architectural approaches chosen for those projects. Even though the answers may be different in each case, any successful design must confront these problems at one point or another.

With these basic principles in mind, we now turn to more detailed descriptions of some of the main technology areas for Internet commerce. Throughout the succeeding chapters, the principles and design issues discussed in this chapter form the backdrop for how the technologies fit into an overall system for Internet commerce.

CHAPTER 11

XML and Web Services

text parser absorbs
spaces brackets and tokens:
meaning springs to life

—Philippe Lourier[1]

What Is XML?

The Extensible Markup Language (XML) is a standardized way of representing structured data as text files. Many readers will be familiar with HTML, which uses markup tags such as `<H1>` and `</H1>` to denote a block of text that is a heading of level 1. XML is similar in that it uses tags to mark up the file, but it is very different in that it lets one define new tags and new document types for new purposes. Consider the following XML fragment.

```
<?xml version-"1.0"?>
<Address>
  <Name>Larry Stewart</Name>
  <Street>11 Serissa Circle</Street>
  <City>Wayland</City>
  <State>MA</State>
  <ZIP>01778</ZIP>
</Address>
```

---

1. From an entry in the 2001 XML Haiku Competition, sponsored by alphaXML Ltd.

This XML version of an address in the United States uses tags such as `<Name>` to identify the parts of the address. This arrangement makes XML very easy for disparate software tools to create and use.

XML is now being used for content intended for people, for content intended for computer systems, and as an underlying interchange format for communications. For people, the address format denoted by that XML fragment would be processed by a stylesheet into an appropriate display format for the user's device, be it a Web browser or a Web-connected cell phone. For computers, the fact that the individual fields of the address are delimited and identified makes it easy for applications to transform the address into the appropriate internal format. For communications, the standardized format makes it easy for disparate systems to exchange information.

The World Wide Web Consortium (W3C) has published "XML in 10 Points," which is a good introduction.[2] Some of the most important are excerpted here.

1. XML is a method for putting structured data in a text file.
2. XML resembles HTML, but it is not HTML.
3. XML is text, but it is not intended to be read by people.
4. XML is actually a collection of technologies.
5. XML is supposed to be verbose.
6. XML seems new, but its roots go back over 20 years.
7. XML requires no license or particular platform.

XML Content for People

Before the Web, most standard documents were stored on paper or microfilm, and most computer documents were stored either in the proprietary format of a word processor or as printable files—plain text or PostScript. In all of these cases, the documents were not well suited either to interactive display (on the Web) or to searching and indexing. The one great exception was the commercial online databases such as LexisNexis, which did contain millions of articles for search and display. The encoding standard of choice for these large systems was the Standard Generalized Markup Language (SGML).

When developing the original World Wide Web, Tim Berners-Lee realized that display and search were essential, and he also realized that SGML was too hard to understand and to use. He created a simplified version of SGML: the Hypertext Markup Language (HTML). HTML was well suited to display (up to a point) and somewhat well suited to searching. Once the Internet became popular, however, it became evident that while HTML was workable for simple documents in small communities, it mixed up the ideas of the structure of a document and the display of that document.

---

2. See http://www.w3.org/XML/1999/XML-in-10-points.html.

One of the great contributions of XML is the strong separation of structure and presentation. The structure of a document is encoded in XML, and the display is managed by stylesheets. XML is essentially a language for defining other languages, and it has been used to define such varied items as the Mathematical Markup Language (MathML), the Synchronized Multimedia Integration Language (SMIL), and Scalable Vector Graphics (SVG), among many others.

XML as an Interchange Format

In every area of business, documents need to be exchanged between disparate computer systems. Sometimes the systems are different parts of the same enterprise, and sometimes they are parts of different enterprises. It also happens that a single system needs to save a document and read it back later—this is communications through time rather than through space.

In all of these cases, agreements are needed about the syntax and semantics of the information. Owing to its ease and acceptance, XML has all but eliminated arguments about syntax, leaving the debate mostly about what the various fields mean rather than how they are represented. Even when there are multiple XML vocabularies for the same kind of document, technologies such as Extensible Stylesheet Language Transformations (XSLT) make it straightforward to transform one into another.

The value of XML as a basic interchange format on which everyone can agree has led to an enormous number of XML vocabularies being defined by various groups. Some good places to start are the Web sites of the W3C (www.w3.org) and XML.org (www.xml.org).

Why XML Is Successful

Informally, XML is nothing more than a standardized way to represent structured data as text files. By itself this is nothing new—standardized serial encodings for complex data have been around for more than 25 years—but XML has been more successful than any of the preceding attempts. Here's why.

- XML is a text format. Because XML documents are just text files, they can be created, handled, and processed by text-oriented tools. XML can be created or examined with a text editor and does not require any special tools.
- XML is extensible. Information specific to an industry or domain can be captured in XML either by creating new document types or by extending old types.
- XML is competitively neutral. Because XML did not start as a proprietary specification and then be endorsed by a standards group, it has been endorsed and adopted by everyone.
- XML tools are widespread. Both proprietary and open source tools for XML are widely available, speeding adoption.
- XML is simple.

- XML is sufficient. The potential benefits of alternatives are so small, and the cost of developing an alternative so high, that architects and developers find it easy just to adopt XML.

Origins of XML

XML is a restricted form of the Standard Generalized Markup Language (SGML), which is described in ISO standard ISO 8879. XML was developed starting in 1996 by a working group of the W3C. The purpose of the effort was to address two related problems. The main problem was SGML itself. Although SGML had been successful in parts of the publishing industry, it was so complicated that it was accessible only to experts. The XML group aimed to simplify the basic model of SGML. The second problem was HTML. HTML itself was a subset of SGML intended for markup on the Web. HTML had become wildly successful as a result of its simplicity and accessibility, but it was being extended in haphazard and incompatible ways by Netscape and Microsoft.

What the XML group came up with was inspired, given the intensely competitive times. XML was new, so no one would have a competitive advantage; simple enough that it was easy to adopt; and extensible, so it could be used as the basis for formats specific to any industry or topic.

Other Options

If not XML, then what?

- EDI. Electronic Data Interchange formats such as XNSI X.12 and EDIFACT have been around for a very long time. These formats are positional: a record consists of fixed elements of fixed size in a fixed order. This leads to a compact representation, which is good but also results in extreme difficulties between trading partners because they must agree on a large number of small details in order to establish communications.

- ASN.1. Abstract Syntax Notation is a standardized representation of data structures that is heavily used in the telecommunications industry and in protocols like the Z39.50 information search and retrieval protocol. ASN.1's encodings are small but binary, and consequently they are difficult to produce and parse.

- S-expressions. Symbolic expressions originate with the LISP programming language. S-expressions can easily represent arbitrary data structures and are text-based, so they are very easy to process. Arguably, S-expressions would be better for XML than the current SGML-derived syntax.

- RPC. Remote procedure call systems, which connect a subroutine call on one system to a subroutine on another system, necessarily have a way to serialize the function parameters. Some examples of RPC systems are Java's RMI, CORBA, and Microsoft's DCOM.

With the exception of S-expressions, XML differs from these alternatives in key respects: an XML document can be parsed and processed without its document type being known, and an XML document can be extended or *subclassed* easily.

Basic XML Standards and Technologies

Much of the ongoing development and standardization of XML technologies is proceeding under the auspices of the W3C. The W3C is concentrating on basic XML technologies and on XML for presentation and is mostly leaving XML for data exchange and communications up to other groups. The W3C effort in XML is managed by the W3C Architecture Domain and is divided into several working groups.

- The XML Core Working Group is responsible for the core syntax of XML and such auxiliary areas as the XInclude recommendation.
- The XML Schema Working Group is broadly responsible for data types and structural constraints in XML, including the XSchema recommendation.
- The XML Linking Working Group is responsible for XML variants of hypertext links, particularly for the XLink and XPointer recommendations.
- The XML Query Working Group is broadly responsible for information retrieval from XML data sources and specifically for the XQuery recommendation.
- The XSL Working Group is under the aegis of the W3C Document Formats Domain rather than the Architecture Domain. It is responsible for the XSLT transformation language, the XPath expression language, and XSL Formatting Objects, a particular XML vocabulary for formatting documents for display.

XML

The starting point for XML standards is the XML 1.0 specification, released by the W3C in February 1998. It defines the syntax of XML documents. This standard defines an XML documents as *well formed* if it is syntactically correct and as *valid* if it specifies a particular document type definition (DTD) and complies with the constraints expressed in it. If an XML document is well formed and valid, an XML parser will be able to process it, even if the parser does not have the DTD available. This idea is vital to the broad use of XML, because it means that general-purpose code can be written to handle well-formed documents, without regard to their specific document types.

Namespaces and Schemas

As we have said, every XML document type is described by a DTD, or *document type definition*. The original design for DTDs did not provide for the reuse of sections of XML vocabulary in multiple document types or for the ability to embed one XML document inside another. The solution to these problems is the concept of namespaces for XML vocabulary. Rather than having the DTD define a single flat namespace of tag names, XML namespaces introduce a hierarchical design in which tags can have fully qualified names to identify them uniquely. By using this hierarchy, a section of a document can be assigned a namespace so that internal tags and attributes can use short names within that section.

The XML schema effort is after bigger fish. DTDs provide only a modest level of syntactic specification of XML document types, and DTDs themselves are not encoded using XML. The schema effort aims to provide a new DTD structure that is more detailed and is itself encoded in XML.

DOM and SAX

The W3C Document Object Model (DOM) and the Simple API for XML (SAX) are really APIs for XML parsers and for access to parsed representations of XML documents. These APIs give applications some independence from the wide variety of available XML parsers and provide some standards for program access to XML documents. These two APIs are substantially different in design. SAX is an event-driven API. The client of the API supplies functions to be called whenever specific XML constructs are encountered during parsing. The in-memory structure is left to the programmer. DOM is focused on the data structure itself, providing functions that the client uses to traverse the structure of an XML document and functions for creating and altering the in-memory structure of a new document.

XPath

XPath, the XML Path Language, is a recommendation of the W3C that provides a common syntax for addressing parts of an XML document. XPath is used particularly by XPointer, the XML mechanism for a link to an internal section of a document, and by XSLT, the XML technology for document transformations.

XPath actually has two parts: a path language much like a URL, which can be used to traverse the tree structure of an XML document to reach a specific section, and an expression syntax that can be matched against sections of an XML document.

XLink and XPointer

XLink is a W3C recommendation for the encoding of hypertext links within XML documents. As with hypertext links in HTML, XLink links can specify one-way links that point to other documents, but XLink can also perform the following functions.

- Specify relationships among more than two resources.
- Associate metadata with a link.
- Specify links that are bidirectional.
- Specify indirect links, which are fully specified elsewhere.

```
<?xml version="1.0" ?>
<quotes>
<stock>
  <symbol>AMZN</symbol>
  <price>7.50</price>
</stock>
<stock><symbol>EBAY</symbol><price>58.33</price></stock>
</quotes>
```

FIGURE 11-1. Stock Quotes in XML format

In HTML, a URL can point to an internal section of a document only by using the odd "#" syntax. XPointer permits the use of XPath expressions as part of URLs that point "inside" an XML document.

XSL and XSLT

The Extensible Stylesheet Language (XSL) is a flexible way of defining stylesheets for formatting XML documents. XSL Transformations (XSLT) is the language used to specify how source XML documents are to be translated into other XML formats or into other formats altogether. XSLT was originally conceived as part of the process of transforming XML documents into HTML for human use, but it is now assuming a central role in transforming XML documents between the various formats used by different systems that are tied together on a network.

Let's consider an example in which stock quotes are obtained in a special stock quote XML vocabulary as shown in Figure 11-1. Our objective is to transform documents of this type into HTML for rendering in a Web browser. To do this, we can use an XSLT engine and the stylesheet shown in Figure 11-2. This document is itself an XML file using the XSLT vocabulary. The XSLT production `xsl:template` is used to match the root note of the stock quote document and generates the basic output page. The production `xsl:for-each` matches each of the stock quote nodes as an enumeration. Finally, `xsl:value-of` is used to match and extract the stock symbol and value for each quote. Figure 11-3 shows the output HTML file produced and rendered by Internet Explorer.[3]

XML for Presentation

Most content on the Web is coded in HTML, which started out as a very simple language that expressed the basic structure of the document. Rendering the content was left to Web browsers. In the early days of the Web, there were many browsers, and most Web content could be viewed by any of them. As the Web grew, however, content producers wanted to have greater control over how their content would be displayed. This led to a rapid and haphazard evolution of HTML, particularly as Netscape and Microsoft competed to add new features that would make their software

---

3. This example was processed using Michael Kay's Instant Saxon XSLT processor.

```
<?xml version="1.0" ?>
<xsl:stylesheet xmlns:xsl="http://www.w3.org/1999/XSL/Transform"
version="1.0">
  <xsl:template match="/">
  <html> <body>
  <H1>Stock Quotes</H1>
  <table border="2" bgcolor="white">
    <tr><th>Symbol</th><th>Price</th></tr>
    <xsl:for-each select="quotes/stock">
      <tr>
        <td><xsl:value-of select="symbol" /></td>
        <td><xsl:value-of select="price" /></td>
      </tr>
    </xsl:for-each>
  </table>
  </body></html>
</xsl:template>
</xsl:stylesheet>
```

FIGURE 11-2. XSLT Stylesheet Example

```
<html>
    <body>
        <H1>Stock Quotes</H1>
        <table border="2"
bgcolor="white">
        <tr>
            <th>Symbol</th>
            <th>Price</th>
        </tr>
        <tr>
            <td>AMZN</td>
            <td>7.50</td>
        </tr>
        <tr>
            <td>EBAY</td>
            <td>58.33</td>
        </tr>
        </table>
    </body>
</html>
```

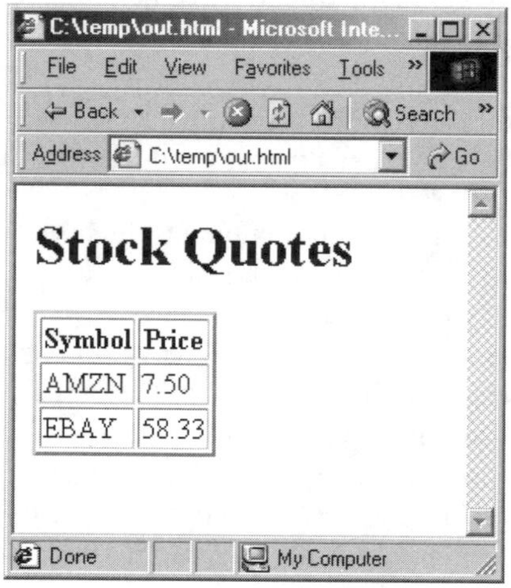

FIGURE 11-3. Generated HTML and Internet Explorer Rendering

stand out. In some cases, the two companies added unique HTML tags; in other cases, they implemented differing interpretations of the same tags. In combination, these forces have encouraged content creators to design Web pages that require a specific browser for proper display. In part, the continuing evolution of the HTML standard has mitigated this trend, but many Web sites today will work properly only with specific browsers.

The use of XML can solve these problems by stronger separation of form and content. Content is best expressed in domain-specific XML, whereas form will be handled by transformations and stylesheets for different purposes. At this writing, we're still in the transition from a fragmented HTML universe to a unified XML universe. On the content side, the W3C has reformulated HTML 4.01 into strict XML as XHTML 1.0. This doesn't add new capabilities, but the regularity of XML and the availability of processing tools will greatly simplify content processing. For formatting and rendering, the use of XHTML immediately provides a baseline parity with HTML, and the use of cascading style sheets provides better control over rendering. XSLT provides transformations from domain-specific vocabularies to XHTML, and the forthcoming XSL Formatting Objects recommendation will provide precise control over rendering to multiple devices.

XML for Data Exchange

In the same way that ASCII unified the representation of computer data, XML is unifying the representation of structured computer information. There are many reasons for this.

- XML is soothing.

  Competitive groups find it possible to agree on standardized document formats for domain-specific information, either because XML isn't viewed as anyone's proprietary baliwick or because it is flexible enough to be inclusive.

- XML lets general-purpose software handle variant data.

  XML is designed to carry many different document formats in a uniform way. Software that processes XML can therefore handle multiple document types without modification while still being able to modify and process the parts of documents that they understand. The alternative approaches require opaque objects or high degrees of complexity.

- XML simplifies application architecture.

  Many business applications require communication, processing, and storage of many different document types. The use of XML for all of these functions provides a uniform framework for information that both simplifies the application architecture and increases the degree of reuse of code.

In this section we examine three efforts that use XML for business purposes: the Open Applications Group, Inc. (OAGI), ebXML, and RosettaNet.

OAGI

The Open Applications Group, Inc. (OAGI) has taken on the problem of developing XML business document type definitions for common business activities. To date, more than 200 Business Object Documents (BODs) are available. Each BOD is an XML document containing a control area that is standard and a data area that varies according to the type of the document.

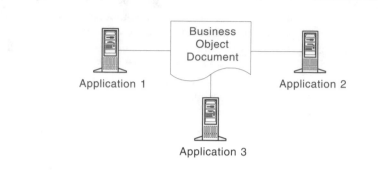

FIGURE 11-4. OAGI Vision of Common Business Documents

The vision and objective of the OAGI, shown in Figure 11-4, is simple: if applications all use a common set of business documents, application integration can be turned from an $O(n^2)$ problem[4] to an $O(n)$ problem, greatly reducing the effort.

ebXML

The Electronic Business XML (ebXML) effort is sponsored by OASIS (Organization for the Advancement of Structured Information Standards) and UN/CEFACT (United Nations Centre for Trade Facilitation and Electronic Business). Its mission is to provide an open infrastructure to lower the barriers to entry for electronic business. With this goal in mind, ebXML has created an architecture with three levels.

1. CPP—Collaboration Protocol Profile

    CPPs for ebXML companies are stored in a distributed registry. The CPP contains information about the business processes supported by a company, their business service interface requirements, and their message service requirements. The CPP registry supports discovery, in that a business seeking trading partners can use the registry to locate likely candidates and evaluate their services.

2. CPA—Collaboration Protocol Agreement

    The CPA represents the intersection of two CPPs. It is a mutually agreed upon description of the messaging services and business processes to be used by trading partners.

3. Business processes

    Business processes, such as *purchase a product*, describe the required business data and the business document choreography of the process.

---

4. The notation $O(n^2)$ means that the cost of solving a problem grows with the square of the size of the problem, as measured by n (bad). Similarly, the notation $O(n)$ means that the cost of solving a problem grows linearly with the size of the problem (good).

The use of XML goes a long way toward reducing the costs of establishing electronic document interchange, mostly because XML is self-describing and extensible. However, XML business documents by themselves do little to help trading partners get connected to each other. The ebXML standard takes several more steps by formalizing the representation of business processes—what documents go where, and what happens to them?—and by formalizing the representation of business capabilities (in the CPP) so that prospective partners can perhaps automatically make agreements and begin to transact business.

RosettaNet

RosettaNet was founded by several information technology companies in 1998 to assist in the rapid development of e-business by developing common standards for Internet commerce. This effort has resulted in standards in three areas.

1. The RosettaNet business and technical dictionaries are an attempt to reduce confusion resulting from differing terminology among trading partners. The business dictionary specifies properties for defining transactions, whereas the technical dictionary specifies properties for defining products and services.

2. The RosettaNet Implementation Framework (RNIF) provides XML exchange protocols between trading partners that cover the areas of packaging, transport, routing, security, and trading partner agreement.

3. The RosettaNet Partner Interface Process (PIP) is an XML-based dialog between trading partners that implements a business process. A PIP includes a business document, its XML vocabulary, and the choreography of messages that implement the business process. PIPs are available for product information, order management, inventory, marketing, service, and other key processes.

For its initial efforts, RosettaNet concentrated on the needs of the computer and component industries, reasoning that they were close to the Internet, and yet e-business was difficult because of the complexities of products and their descriptions.

XML for Communications—Web Services

Web services are simply application logic made accessible over the Web. As a rather trivial example, consider a shipping rate calculator provided by a logistics company. Such calculators have been available as interactive Web pages for several years. As shown in Figure 11-5, turning such a calculator into a Web service requires the following steps.

1. Encapsulate the logic of the calculator, but not the user interface, into a subroutine.

2. Define the API for the calculator using the Web Services Definition Language (WSDL).

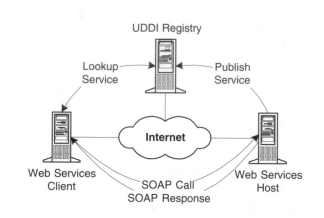

FIGURE 11-5. Web Services Environment

3. Host the subroutine on a Web server supporting the Simple Object Access Protocol (SOAP).

4. Publish the calculator definition to an appropriate UDDI (Universal Description, Discovery, and Integration) directory.

At this point, a programmer who wants to use the rate calculator from an e-commerce system can do the following.

1. Look up the service in the UDDI directory.

2. Use SOAP to make a remote call from the client application to the rate calculator.

3. Use the results of the call in the application.

Web services make it easy for service providers to make business logic available for remote use and for application developers to locate and use such remote logic.

The Vision of Web Services

Web services provide a straightforward and interoperable means for programs to communicate with each other over the Web, as well as directories so that providers can advertise and users can search for services. At a minimum, this means that a market can be developed for heavyweight remote services, such as payment systems, logistics, and business messaging. Somewhat more speculative are applications that knit together disparate applications by the use of service discovery and negotiation: imagine making theater and dinner reservations from your Web phone, automatically matching schedules with your prospective guests.

Remote Procedure Calls

There is a certain buzz about Web services being a "new thing." They are and they aren't. The technological underpinnings of Web services are now 20 years old. Web services are built on the concept of remote procedure calls (RPCs), a concept that has been around since 1981. However, there are two new factors. First, Web services are generally understood to be remote and therefore less reliable than local procedure calls. Historically, RPC implementations have focused heavily on modeling the exact behavior of local calls, although this frequently causes confusion for programmers. Second, Web services are being built on open standards, leading to wide interoperability among different implementations.

In an RPC, the calling program, rather than invoking a local subroutine, instead invokes a *client stub*, which has the same API as the desired routine. The client stub communicates with a remote server, where a *server stub* makes the actual call to the actual subroutine. In addition, the program must bind its interface to the appropriate server, typically by using a network directory service. In contrast, the binding for a local procedure call is made by the programming environment linker or by dynamic linking to a shared library.

The earliest RPC systems were built using single-language environments, and the definitions of the remote APIs were maintained by the language system. Later, systems such as CORBA evolved, in which an explicit Interface Definition Language (IDL) was used, so that the caller and callee could be implemented in different languages on different platforms. All of these systems used binary transmission formats to provide the best performance.

Web services still follow the basic RPC model. The role of the service directory is implemented by one using the UDDI standard, and the APIs are defined using WSDL, which is an XML schema. Actual parameters and return values are not marshaled into tight binary formats, but rather are encoded in text form in XML. Finally, rather than using a specialized binary wire protocol, Web services are built on standard Web servers and HTTP. Taken together, these decisions have the effect of permitting nearly frictionless use of the existing Internet infrastructure for communications between programs.

SOAP

The Simple Object Access Protocol (SOAP) is essentially the specification of how RPCs are implemented over the Web. There are three aspects to SOAP: calling conventions for remote procedure calls, encoding rules for parameters and return values, and the envelope. The SOAP RPC conventions explain how to represent calls to remote procedures and their responses. The SOAP encoding rules explain how to represent application data—namely, the arguments and return values from the remote procedure calls. Finally, the SOAP envelope defines the contents of a SOAP message

```
POST /StockQuote HTTP/1.1
Host: www.stockserver.com
Content-Type: text/xml; charset="utf-8"
Content-Length: NNN
SOAPAction: "Some-URI"

<SOAP-ENV:Envelope
xmlns:SOAP-ENV="http://schemas.xmlsoap.org/soap/envelope/"
SOAP-ENV:encodingStyle="http://schemas.xmlsoap.org/soap/encoding/">
<SOAP-ENV:Body>
<m:GetQuote xmlns:m="Some-URI">
<symbol>AMZN</symbol>
</m:GetQuote>
</SOAP-ENV:Body>
</SOAP-ENV:Envelope>
```

FIGURE 11-6. SOAP Implementation of Stock Quote Request Carried by HTTP

and the rules for processing it. SOAP is almost always used with HTTP as the transport protocol, but it can also be used with other communications systems.

Returning to the XML example from Figure 11-1, Figure 11-6 shows the stock quote request inside a SOAP envelope, which in turn is carried by an HTTP POST request. Figure 11-7 shows the SOAP response to the request, carried in an HTTP response.

The SOAP encoding rules specify how to encode programming language data types—including numeric types, strings, structures, and arrays—in XML. SOAP's RPC conventions model the remote procedure call as a structure that contains the procedure's formal parameters and whose name is the name of the method. Similarly, the RPC response is also modeled as a structure that contains the response values and whose name is derived from the name of the method.

WSDL

The Web Services Description Language (WSDL) is the interface definition language for Web services, playing much the same role that IDL does for CORBA. Most commonly, WSDL is used to describe services that are accessible via SOAP and HTTP, but WSDL can also be used to describe a broad range of more general services that use either message-oriented or procedure-oriented approaches. WSDL files define Web services in terms of the following six concepts.

1. Types—the data type definitions that are used to describe messages
2. Message—an abstract definition of the data being transmitted
3. PortType—a set of abstract operations, each of which has input and output messages
4. Binding—the concrete protocol and data format specifications, operations, and messages
5. Port—an address for a single communication endpoint
6. Service—the aggregation of a set of related ports

```
HTTP/1.1 200 OK
Content-Type: text/xml; charset="utf-8"
Content-Length: NNN

<SOAP-ENV:Envelope
xmlns:SOAP-ENV="http://schemas.xmlsoap.org/soap/envelope/"
SOAP-ENV:encodingStyle="http://schemas.xmlsoap.org/soap/encoding/"/>
<SOAP-ENV:Body>
<m:GetQuoteResponse xmlns:m="Some-URI">
<Price>7.5</Price>
</m:GetQuoteResponse>
</SOAP-ENV:Body>
</SOAP-ENV:Envelope>
```

FIGURE 11-7. SOAP Message for Stock Quote Reply Carried as HTTP Response

In practice, this is probably too many levels of abstraction with excessive flexibility. Abstraction is good, but it isn't necessary for every level of every system to include its own support for extensibility. However, the complexity of WSDL and UDDI has not unduly slowed the deployment of Web services.

UDDI

Universal Description, Discovery, and Integration (UDDI) is not a protocol so much as a process. The idea is to operate directories or registries of business entities, business services, and service specifications so that people and programs can find suppliers of needed Web services and their characteristics. For further information, see www.uddi.org.

XML for Applications

The discussion so far gives the impression that XML is closely related to the Web, but XML is equally valuable for internal use in applications.

XML Data Storage

XML is a candidate for storage of business documents. Many current systems usually store information from business documents (such as order forms) in a relational database, in which the parts of the document are broken into various columns and tables, or in an object-oriented database, in which the document itself stored as an object. With the relational approach, it is easy to search for information in any part of the document, but it is expensive to store or retrieve the whole object. In contrast, object-oriented databases make it easy to store and retrieve the entire document, but searching is generally more expensive. When business documents are represented in XML, the entire process can be simplified by storing the complete document in the database and also storing index fields in relational tables.

Some vendors are adding XML features to their databases, including the ability to search stored XML documents, and other vendors are producing specialized products for storing XML.

XML Processing

Enterprise applications frequently involve the execution of various processing steps on a business document. These applications often represent the documents as complex data structures or, in more modern systems, as objects with operations defined on them. Both approaches can impede the ability of the application to evolve. For example, when new fields are added to the document, it may be necessary to modify many different parts of the system.

An alternative approach is to represent business documents in an application as preparsed XML documents conforming, for example, to the W3C Document Object Model. With this structure, several tasks become straightforward.

- Validation—Schema validation allows a generic verification that a document contains all required structure and fields.
- Extensibility—Data elements can easily be added to a document and ignored by existing code that doesn't need the new functionality.
- Breadth—Many document types can coexist in the system, conforming to different schemas.
- Storage—XML business documents can be stored as described under XML Data Storage above.
- Transformation—Many types of required processing can be accomplished by document transformation using XSLT.
- Communication—XML business documents will be in the right format for exchange with other systems.

For example, in Java 2 Enterprise Edition (J2EE), the standard way to implement business logic is as Enterprise JavaBeans (EJB). One variation of this approach is to have the EJB system use a uniform mechanism for passing data—namely XML. Front-end systems access the business logic layer by composing XML queries, which are sent to the appropriate EJB component. Data responses are also in XML and can frequently be presented back to the user by an XSL transformation to XHTML.

XML Transformation

Once business documents are represented as XML data structures, XML tools such as XSLT may be used for conversions and transformations. This makes it possible to handle several different XML formats for a single concept such as an order or invoice, because the different forms probably can be converted to one another using XSLT.

XML Data Access

It is certainly true that maintaining business documents as XML text objects would execute more slowly than traditional methods, but active business documents can be preparsed into DOM data structures and passed from module to module as in-memory data structures. Accessing particular fields of a document can be as easy as writing an XPath specification for it. In this way, the additional overhead is minimal, and it more than pays for itself in the resulting ability to maintain and extend the application.

Summary

XML is successful because it is simple and powerful and doesn't offend any proprietary interests. The key technical issues are that new XML document types can be readily defined for application-specific purposes and that XML documents are extensible and therefore more flexible than fixed formats. XML is being used for presentation, for data exchange, for communications, and even as a main internal structure for applications and databases.

CHAPTER 12

Creating and Managing Content

To him who in the love of Nature holds
Communion with her visible forms, she speaks
A various language.

—William Cullen Bryant[1]

What the Customers See

The first point of contact for customers doing business on the Net is *content:* the information, catalog, brochures, and so on available on a Web site. For most Web sites, compelling content that draws in customers and encourages repeat visits is essential, and commerce sites are no exception. The precise look and feel of Web content is a creative and marketing design issue, but the design of Internet commerce systems requires a general understanding of the mechanisms of Web content and the tools available to create and manage it. This chapter provides an overview of Web content technology and how it works with Internet commerce.

The technology of content creation and management has evolved rapidly over the past few years. Specialized tools for creating Web content have become widely available, and many other programs have been adapted to generate output for the Web as well. In addition, as more and more people throughout companies have become involved in producing Web sites, it has become harder simply to manage all of the content being created. This problem has led to the development and deployment of sophisticated

---

1. William Cullen Bryant, *Thanatopsis* (1817).

content management systems that help take documents and other materials from conception to delivery on the Web.

In this chapter, we first review the basic elements of the Hypertext Markup Language (HTML) and other media types for the Web. Some systems use *static* HTML pages, which rarely change, and other systems use *dynamic* Web pages, which are generated on demand, usually by a combination of application software and a database. In general, dynamic pages are most useful when parts of the content change frequently or when the content is tailored to particular users or classes of users.

Basic Content

Content in the World Wide Web is made up of multimedia hypertext pages typically described in HTML. Web pages are *multimedia* because they can include text, images, audio, video, and other kinds of data. In fact, the Web protocols are extensible to deal with any kind of media. Web pages are *hypertext* because instead of following a linear sequence like the pages of a book, any Web page can link to any number of other Web pages, in arbitrarily complex ways.

HTML is a description language for structured documents similar to SGML (Standard Generalized Markup Language), which has been the standard for professional publishing for many years. A fragment of an HTML document is shown in Figure 12-1, and a browser's rendition of it in Figure 12-2. Tags in the document source[2] describe the semantics of the document, and the details of the visual representation are left to the client software. This is a distinctly different model of description than a system such as PostScript, which describes the appearance of a document but not its structure.

In the most common mode of operation, a Web browser retrieves pages coded in HTML from one or more Web servers. Web pages are identified by Uniform Resource Locators (URLs). Part of the URL tells the browser how to locate the proper server and what protocol to use to retrieve the page. The rest of the URL is sent to the server to locate the particular page on that server.

If a page is merely linked to the next page, there will still be a linear ordering of pages. In HTML, however, any location on a page can contain a link to another page on the same server or on another server anywhere in the world. The location of a link is called an *anchor*. Anchors can occur in a list of pages, such as a table of contents or index, in running text, or as portions of clickable images. This ability of each page to link to many other pages turns the collection of pages on servers around the world into a web.

---

2. With HTML, a tag is marked by `<tagname>` in the document. If a tag is used to mark a region of text, the region will start with `<tag>` and end with `</tag>`.

Basic Formatting

Using HTML, Web browsers have built-in abilities to handle several standard types of content.

Text

Text encompasses a variety of facilities for structuring documents such as headings, typefaces in different sizes and styles, and layout directives such as centering.

Lists

HTML provides support for lists of items with arbitrary nesting levels. Standard HTML provides for three kinds of lists: unnumbered (bulleted) lists, numbered lists, and definition lists, which are used for text such as glossaries.

Images

Web browsers handle images in several ways. A document may just be an image, in which case the MIME type of the document specifies the format of the image. As an alternative, an HTML page may embed images inside it using special tags, and the browser retrieves separate files that actually contain the images. In addition to displaying pictures or diagrams, Web pages often use images and small graphics for icons, toolbars, and visual appeal. Such techniques give the Web page designer a great deal of flexibility in creating the appearance of Web pages.

Forms

Much of the Web's power comes from its ability to create interactive applications. The simplest form of interactivity is the *form*. An HTML form can contain such elements as check boxes, menu selections, and text entry fields. The user can fill out such a form and submit it to the Web server, which can then return information based on the contents of the form. Forms are discussed in more detail later.

Advanced Formatting

In addition to these basic capabilities, most browsers today can handle more advanced features of HTML.

Tables

A table is a mechanism for achieving more control over the representation of arrays of content. In early versions of HTML, for example, the only way to line up a column of figures was to switch to a fixed-pitch font for that region of the document. The table formatting capabilities of HTML use a very general description of rows and columns of content, giving the designer many choices for layout.

```
<!DOCTYPE HTML PUBLIC "-//IETF//DTD HTML//EN">
<html>
<head>
<meta http-equiv="Content-Type"
content="text/html; charset=iso-8859-1">
<meta name="GENERATOR" content="Microsoft FrontPage 2.0">
<title>HTML Example</title>
</head>
<body bgcolor="#FFFFFF">
<h1>HTML Example</h1>
<p>This page contains HTML examples for <u>Designing Systems for
Internet Commerce</u>.</p>
<p>An HTML page can contain headings, text, lists, graphics, and
so forth. This page was prepared using Microsoft FrontPage.</p>
<p>Here is an HTML Unnumbered List:</p>
<menu>
    <li>This is the first item</li>
    <li>This is the second item</li>
</menu>
<p>Here is an HTML table with two rows and three columns:</p>
<table border="0" cellpadding="3" cellspacing="4">
    <tr>
        <td>Row 1</td>
        <td>Column 2</td>
        <td>Column 3</td>
    </tr>
    <tr>
        <td>Row 2</td>
        <td>Cell 2,2</td>
        <td>Cell 2,3</td>
    </tr>
    <tr>
        <td>Row 3</td>
        <td>Cell 3,2</td>
        <td>Cell 3,3</td>
    </tr>
</table>
<p>Right below this line is a graphic image of a line of rocks.</p>
<p><img src="Rocks80E3.gif" width="528" height="30"></p>
<p>Here is a simple &quot;request for assistance&quot; form:</p>
<form action="sendmessage.cgi" method="POST"
name="sendmessage.cgi">
    <p>Priority: <input type="radio" checked name="R1"
value="V1">Normal
    <input type="radio" name="R1" value="V2">High <input
type="radio" name="R1" value="V3">Emergency</p>
    <p>Message: <input type="text" size="44" name="T1"></p>
    <p><input type="submit" name="B1" value="Submit"></p>
</form>
<hr>
<p>The end.</p>
</body>
</html>
```

FIGURE 12-1. An Example of HTML Source

Frames

A frame is a structuring mechanism that permits several independent Web pages to share display space in the same browser. One application of this capability is to maintain different views on a set of pages. For example, a site might keep a navigation view in one pane while displaying detailed content in other panes.

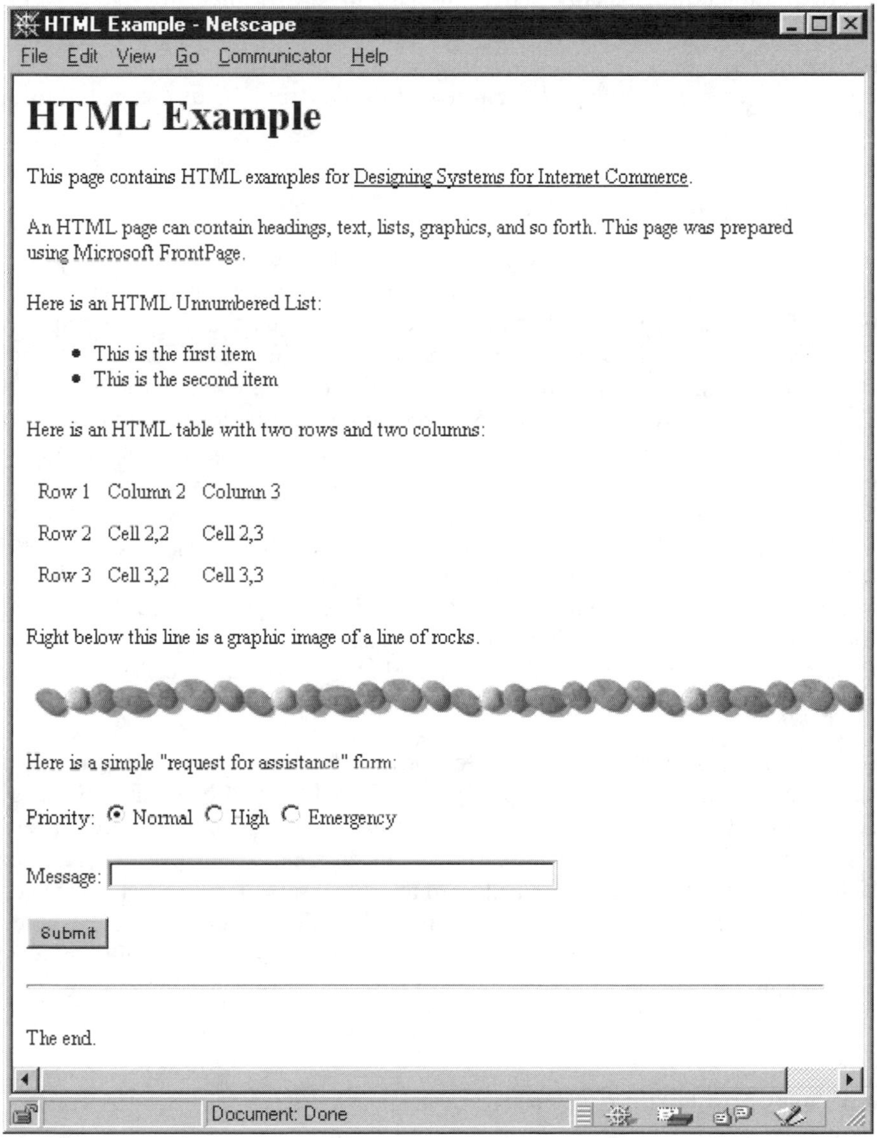

FIGURE 12-2. **Screen Shot of the Rendered HTML from Figure 12-1**

Image Maps

Web browsers usually display hyperlinks as highlighted text, indicating that clicking the text will call up the linked Web page. Often it is possible to click an image as well, making small images useful as icons to represent hyperlinks. An image map is an alternative means of representing and activating links. When an image map is used, parts of a graphic image can be active, so that a hypertext link can be activated by clicking a portion of an image. Image maps can be handled at the server, in which case the browser sends the click coordinates to the server, or at the client, in which case the server sends along a description of the *hot* regions of the image to the browser.

Controlling Appearance

Unlike many document description languages, HTML describes the structure of a document rather than its appearance, and browsers control how the various tagged elements of an HTML page should be displayed. This means that HTML documents can be displayed on a wide variety of devices, because the browser can render them differently depending on the capabilities of the device. It is even possible to render HTML for the visually impaired while still providing information about the structure of the document. This means, however, that the designer of a page does not control its ultimate appearance.

Historically, obtaining close control over the appearance of a Web page on the user's display has been a big problem for Web authors. Frequently, page creation teams must test their HTML pages using the most popular browsers, adjusting the HTML coding as needed. Sometimes they even use peculiar techniques to control appearance, such as inserting transparent or invisible images on the page to obtain precise control over spacing.

For some applications, this lack of control can be a frustrating limitation. In order to give authors greater control over the display of HTML, the Web community has developed *cascading style sheets*. This system permits a Web page to reference a set of style sheets, which describe how the various elements should be displayed. Even more advantageous, an HTML page can be linked to several sets of style sheets, which can define the preferred representations of the page on different devices. For example, a high-resolution PC display could use one set of style sheets, a low-resolution television set could use another set, and an Internet browser for the visually impaired could use a third set.

Web Pages and Forms

The use of fill-out forms is a powerful method of interactivity on the Web. Forms consist of HTML tags that create on the browser screen an editable set of fields intermixed with standard HTML markup. Each field has a name, which is not displayed for the user but is used by the server to keep track of the various fields. The form is created by the Web server, either as a static page or as the dynamic output of a program. Dynamic forms might be used to vary the set of fields to be completed, as appropriate for the application. The initial values of the fields may be filled in by the server, or they may be left blank. After completing the form, the user clicks a **Submit** button (which may have a different display). At this point, the field names and contents are sent to the Web server as a series of name-value pairs. An application running on the Web server receives and interprets the form contents.

HTML forms can contain the following kinds of fields.

- Check box—used to select options
- Option button—a set of command buttons, only one of which can be activated (like the station selector on a car radio)
- Text line—an editable line of text
- Scrollable text line—an editable line of text that can be larger than the box shown to the user
- Text area—an editable text box with multiple lines
- Command button—a button used to submit the form or reset its contents to their original values
- Image—a command button that is rendered as an image instead of as a button with a textual label
- Drop-down menu—a menu that contains a list of alternatives

These elements can be combined in different ways to create many interactive Web applications.

Images

HTML documents can contain embedded images in formats such as GIF, JPEG, and PNG. Embedded images are not stored by encoding the image itself within the HTML file, but are stored as separate image files on a Web server. The author of the HTML file merely inserts an *image source* tag within the HTML source:

```
<img src="Rocks80E3.gif" width="528" height="30">
```

When the Web browser encounters a tag such as this, it retrieves the image using HTTP and then renders it in place. The **width** and **height** attributes are hints to the browser about the size of the image, so that the browser can leave the right amount of space for the image and proceed with rendering the rest of the page. The image can be filled in later, since it may take some time to download. This technique lets the text portions of pages display faster on slow Internet connections without the need to reformat the display when the actual image is finally available.

Image Maps

In HTML content, the anchor for a hypertext link can occur in text, as an image, or as part of an image. A common Web paradigm is to use an image containing multiple links to other pages. The geometric definitions of the regions (or *hot zones*) of the image can be kept at the server or sent to the client. Image maps were originally interpreted only by the server, but most browsers today can use the client-side version as well. Client-side image maps have several advantages: they take load off the server, different parts of the image can be linked to different servers, they can be more interactive for the user, and they can be used more effectively by text-only browsers.

Multimedia

Web content is not limited to text, graphics, and images. Audio, video, and animation are also available. Animated images can be built using features of the GIF image encoding format, client scripting, dynamic HTML, or even with extension languages such as Java. Audio, video, and other media types may be handled by external applications or by adding a plug-in to the browser to render the data in place.

Other Types of Content

HTML, along with its programmable extensions such as Java, JavaScript, and ActiveX, is the most widely used data type on the Web. Some others are becoming increasingly popular.

VRML

The Virtual Reality Markup Language (VRML) is used to define a three-dimensional virtual world. Once a VRML model is downloaded to a suitably equipped browser, the user can navigate the world interactively on the desktop.

PDF

The Portable Document Format (PDF), developed by Adobe Systems, is a further development of the popular PostScript language, which describes documents for printing. The objective of PDF is to make PostScript a useful environment for browsing documents online. PDF adds searching, interactive use, hyperlinks, and annotation to PostScript. The key difference between HTML and PDF is that HTML describes the structure of a document without controlling its rendering, whereas PDF tries very hard to give the author full control over the appearance of the document on the screen. The objective is that a document should look exactly the same online as on paper. PDF has become popular as a means of distributing paper forms, journal articles, and other carefully formatted items online. Today, many businesses use PDF for documents whose precise appearance is important, and governments use PDF for distribution of official documents and materials such as tax forms.

Flash and Shockwave

Macromedia Flash is a Web format for dynamic presentations and graphics. The Flash player is a free download, whereas the authoring tools are not free. Macromedia Shockwave provides both dynamic graphics and interactivity. It is widely used for online games, interactive training, and similar activities. By April 2002, Web users had made more than 400 million downloads of Flash and more than 250 million downloads of Shockwave.

Tools for Creating Content

There is a wide range of tools available for creating content. Each of the following is described in more detail later.

- Many desktop publishing tools have been extended to create Web content. They are intended for use by end users, and they are generally most useful for static content that does not change frequently.

- Database connectors can be used to publish content dynamically from a database by using templates for page layout that are combined with the results of database queries. They are mainly intended for use by Web developers.

- Authoring environments have been developed specifically for creating and managing more complex Web sites. They are mainly intended for use by Web developers, but they may be appropriate for some end users as well.

- Complete applications have been created for specific purposes such as banking or Internet commerce catalogs. These applications tend to be used by specialists in the specific area, but they can be very useful in simplifying some of the work.

In addition, the basic technology of the Web, described in Chapter 8, permits Web pages to be created dynamically by an arbitrary application. Such systems often use relational databases for storing primary data, and the Web is used as an engine for querying the database and rendering the results.

Desktop Publishing Tools

Although HTML can be created by manually entering the tags with a text editor, there are many desktop publishing tools that provide *what you see is what you get* (WYSIWYG) editing. These tools allow the creation of HTML pages while displaying them as they will be rendered by a Web browser. There are many such tools on the market today. Some are specialized for editing HTML and creating Web sites, whereas others are publishing tools that have been adapted to generate HTML as well as other output formats.

Database Connectors

When a Web site must publish hundreds or thousands of very similar pages, such as stock quotes or catalog items, it makes sense to store the basic page layout as a template with the actual information stored in a database. Database connectors are used to manage this process by defining a language for writing page templates, which are stored in the Web server's filesystem. Special tags are used to embed database queries in the templates. Results from the queries are then substituted in the pages delivered to the browser. This technique has the following advantages.

- By changing the template in one place, the look and feel of thousands of Web pages can be changed at once.
- The generated pages automatically track changes in the information stored in the database.
- Complete pages are never stored, thus saving storage space on the server.
- The same data can be provided in different forms to different users, or shared by many applications.

As with HTML publishing tools, many database connector products are available.

Managing Content

Creating content has an essential creative aspect, but it also has a procedural aspect in which the path from the creative keyboard to a production Web site is carefully defined and scrupulously followed. This procedural work is sometimes called the *editorial process flow* or the *publishing phase* of Web content. This section follows content through its life cycle: creation, editing, staging, testing, production, and archiving.

Creation

Content must come from somewhere. It may be written from scratch, collated from other sources, or delivered by a live feed from other sources. Beyond the creative part of creating content, the procedural part consists of a series of conversion and formatting steps that different items go through before they are ready to become part of the live Web site.

Format conversions move documents from various desktop publishing or source formats into HTML or whatever standard format the site may use. These steps may be manual, using desktop conversion tools, For they may be automated. In either case, there is some danger that the output document may not look at all correct. Desktop publishing documents are formatted to achieve a certain appearance when printed, and there are usually several ways to achieve this appearance. For example, a section heading may be coded as a section heading paragraph with a standard type style, or it may be coded as a body paragraph with a nonstandard type style. HTML, in contrast, expects section heads to be coded only as section heads. Automated conversion tools can sometimes give unexpected results, especially if the input format lacks the semantic information used for HTML. Issues such as this must be solved with a combination of experience, standards, training, and testing.

Formatting applies standard templates to documents that will become part of a site. These templates may be applied in the creation of individual documents if desktop publishing tools are used to prepare content, or they may be used in the generation of content by automatic tools driven from a database. In both cases, the value of the templates comes from consistent presentation to the user as well as from making it easier to use repeated elements such as logos, toolbars, and navigation aids.

Editing

After an item has been created and converted to the correct format, it will go through the following editing steps.

1. Does the item conform to corporate standards of look and feel?
2. Are the spelling, grammar, and other aspects of the presentation correct?
3. Are all the facts correct?
4. Are the correct links for hypertext in place?

Except for the hypertext links, these steps are similar for both print and the Internet. The challenges of these processes in the Internet case are to achieve a fully electronic process and to meet the real-time demands—the deadline for new content may not be weekly, but every 10 minutes.

Staging and Testing

Of course, not all sites need to be updated continuously. If changes are made less frequently, it may be useful to make all changes on a "staging" system before any modifications of the production system are made. The content on the staging system can be extensively tested before it is made available on the production site.

Content Testing

If the site's content is HTML, it is a good idea to check the HTML for syntactic correctness. For example, every tag must have a matching closing tag, with appropriate nesting, and only sanctioned tags should be used (because some organizations may have policies on HTML style). Such checks are especially important for HTML written by hand. In some cases, it may be possible (and appropriate) to use automatic tools for preparing versions of the content for display by different browsers as well as a text-only view for those users with lower-speed network access.

Link Testing

Few things irritate Web users more than stale or disconnected hypertext links. Links that are internal to a site are straightforward to manage, although it is useful to test them for consistency. Links to other sites should be tested periodically to ensure that you catch problems before your customers do. Some Web publishing environments, such as Microsoft's Active Server Pages, provide mechanisms for making links correct by construction, by creating and inserting the link only when the page is viewed.

Commerce Testing

If the site is commerce-enabled, then staging is the right moment to check that all items are enabled correctly, with accurate prices, sales tax classifications, and so forth. In addition, test transactions can be run to verify that fulfillment of both physical goods and digital goods works properly and that all reports are correctly generated.

Indexing

If the site uses a full-text search engine to help user navigation, withdrawn pages must be dropped from the index, and new or changed pages must be added. Ideally, the production index always exactly matches the production pages.[3]

Editorial Review

Because the staging system represents a fully functional but private version of a Web site, it is an appropriate place to run any final human editorial checks on content.

Production

The Internet is not like a magazine or newspaper. In print, each new issue is assembled completely while still hidden from public view. Only the full issue is delivered, all at once, to the subscriber. In contrast, Web content can be visible to subscribers at all times. If a site attempts to exploit the ability of the Internet always to deliver content that is up-to-date, the site can literally be changing under the eyes of the reader. Careful design is required to be able to update the content of a production site while at the same time ensuring that the content is internally consistent, that all the links actually work, and that all required testing has been done. Not only must the system be designed to accommodate such updates, but the processes that go along with doing the work must also be designed and followed carefully. Here are two particular dangers.

First, there is the danger that more than one person will attempt to change the same document at the same time. Depending on the details of how this is done, one of them may "win" while the changes of the others are lost. In the worst case, the resulting document may become scrambled. The usual solutions to this problem include the application of *source control* tools that lock documents before update or the use of a document repository that can maintain multiple versions and identify conflicts.

---

3. A related issue is that content on one's own site may be searched and indexed by a central search engine such as Google or AltaVista. These massive search engines poll individual sites only occasionally and may be out-of-date.

Second, a change in a Web site often means that many individual pages must be updated. Unless this is done carefully, an active user may see the pages in an inconsistent state, viewing old versions of some pages and new versions of others. This problem is sometimes exacerbated by caching in browsers and proxy servers, which may show old versions for some time after the new ones are available. A common approach to solving this problem is to change all affected pages in one atomic action, such as by renaming a directory or committing the changes in a database. In addition, it is important to make sure that the appropriate hints for caches are provided.

Archiving

It is an excellent idea to save at least one old version of a site, with a procedure for rapidly putting the archived version into production. The archived version serves several purposes.

- The archives form an audit trail of changes.

- The ability to access archived copies of individual documents (or even the entire site) may be of value to some users.

- An archived version is useful if the production content version is damaged or vandalized. The archived version can be put back in production, providing a means of rapid recovery from such problems.

Multimedia Presentation

By far the largest amount of Web content is HTML, but other data types are also in widespread use. A hypertext link in HTML can be linked to an arbitrary data type. When the Web server returns a page, an HTTP header carries data type information to the browser. Browsers have built-in support for many data types, can accept plug-in extensions to handle other data types, and can launch a completely different application for still others.

- Built-in

  Popular browsers implement native support for HTML and image formats such as GIF, JPEG, and PNG.

- Plug-in

  Adobe Systems provides a freely distributed reader for Acrobat format files. When installed, the reader plugs into the browser to add support for the Acrobat data type. When the user clicks an Acrobat document, the reader plug-in takes over the browser window and displays the document in place.

- Separate application

  A Web document catalog might contain a Microsoft PowerPoint presentation. When the user clicks on the associated link, the user's copy of PowerPoint is launched to handle the file.

There are some widely used data types.

- Animated images

  Some image formats, such as GIF, can be used to sequence through a series of images. These formats are widely used for creating small animations.

- Applets and scripting

  Applets and client scripting can create animation effects and other interactive behavior in the browser. Dynamic HTML has similar capabilities.

- Video data

  Video clips can be integrated with other Web content, using standard encoding types such as MPEG, QuickTime, and AVI. To date, most video is distributed as downloaded clips that are played locally, but as network bandwidth improves, streaming video[4] will become increasingly common.

- Audio data

  Audio clips can be put on the Web using WAV files, SND files, and the aforementioned AVI files. In addition, protocols such as RealAudio permit streaming audio to be used.

- Shockwave

  Shockwave files are complete multimedia animations, produced by the popular Macromedia Director animation creation tool.

Personalization

One of the most interesting things about the Internet is that an information creator can interact directly with an information consumer, instead of having intermediaries such as publishers, distributors, and so on. To some, this aspect of the Internet spells doom for middlemen, but it also represents an opportunity to strengthen customer relationships. In business-to-consumer commerce, for example, businesses compete for customers on the basis of price, convenience, and service. Because the network gives more or less equal access by the consumer to all businesses, price and convenience may quickly reach parity across providers. At that point, the primary basis for competition will be service and relationships, and the network provides excellent tools for improving both.

Unlike a broadcast channel such as print, television, or radio, where most consumers receive the same content, each Internet user has an individual channel to the online

---

4. Streaming audio or video can be tricky. Historically, browsers downloaded an entire audio or video file to the client machine, and then launched an application to play it. Streaming media works by starting to download the media file, and then starting to play it before the download is complete. As long as the download stays ahead of the playback, this works well, with lower playback latency.

presence of a business. Instead of providing the same content to everyone, a site can provide individually personalized content to each user.

Personalizing a site may be done for business functions or for unabashed merchandising purposes. Users of a business-to-business catalog, for example, may see the different prices negotiated for their respective companies. A retail site may send personalized electronic coupons to frequent shoppers.

There are three key elements to personalizing a site: authenticating the user, creating a user profile, and generating custom content.

Authentication and Identity

The first step in personalizing a site is authenticating the user. In this context, it may not be necessary to know an individual's true identity. Instead, it is sufficient to ensure that a series of visits by a user represents the *same* person, even if the precise identity is unknown. In other cases, it is important to have formal authentication, as in the preceding business example. In this kind of application, techniques for authentication include the following.

Browser Cookie

Once a user has registered, the site may record a persistent cookie in the user's browser. This technique provides automatic sign-on at future visits, but it breaks down if the user disables the use of cookies or tries to use the service from a different computer. Cookies have the advantage that they can track users through a site, and even identify users on subsequent visits, although there may be no explicit registration or identification at all. (There are other techniques for maintaining session state that do not use cookies, but they have similar properties.)

Name and Password for a Single Site

One common technique is to register each user of a site with a name and password on the first visit. On future visits, the user is prompted for the name and password before being permitted to enter the site. Unfortunately, this can be a burden for the user, who ends up with individual accounts at many different sites. This result poses several problems. If the user chooses the same name and password for many sites, it may be easy to remember, but a compromised password exposes all of those sites. In addition, all of those sites know the password, so an unscrupulous operator can abuse that knowledge. On the other hand, users who choose different names and passwords for each site are more likely to lose track of them. Users with lost passwords can be a significant source of customer service problems.

Central Authentication Database with Delegation

Many sites may share a central authentication database. The customer has one set of credentials, so they are easier to remember and protect. The affiliated sites get greater security, can share the costs of the authentication database, and may gain access to a larger group of users. For Internet commerce, organizations that offer commerce services to multiple businesses may also offer a registration database, such as that in Open Market's Transact engine. Another place where a single authentication database occurs is in a large online service such as America Online, where affiliated businesses can rely on the central registration service. However, because there is no standardized Internet authentication and registration system, a business cannot count on obtaining user authentication from an arbitrary Internet service provider.

Several efforts are underway to provide central user accounts. Microsoft's Passport service, Sun's Liberty Alliance, and AOL's Magic Carpet are examples.

Personal Digital Certificates

Public-key digital certificates are digital objects in which a trusted third party attests to the binding between a username and a security key. Whenever the security key is used to set up a secure connection, the server at the other end can find out the associated name and which organization stands behind it. Certificates were just beginning to get acceptance in 1997, and they are still awkward to use. The use of certificates for authentication is discussed further in Chapter 14.

User Profiles

After the system has identified a user, it can retrieve a stored profile about that user. Sometimes, if the profile is small, a site may use a browser cookie to store the profile on the client, rather than storing it in a database. User profiles can contain a wide variety of information. We now discuss some common categories.

Registration Information

Many Web sites have registration forms. Users may fill out these forms in order to gain access to the site or as part of making a purchase. There is a wide range of information that is collected, ranging from name and address to payment credentials (such as credit card numbers) and demographic information.

Optional User-Supplied Information

Profiles help to personalize sites. Sites frequently request information about the preferences of users in order to provide better service. For example, Amazon.com sends notices of new books to buyers who have registered for news about favorite authors. Such profiles are optional and generally linked to a specific benefit for the user.

Linked Information

Once authentication is available, profile information can be automatically generated. For example, if an authenticated user completes a commerce transaction, the user and transaction become linked. Appropriate reporting software can record actual or contemplated purchases in the associated user profile for merchandising purposes. Profile and transaction information obtained online can also be linked to personal information obtained from sources off the network.

Browsing Information

At the finest level of detail, individual browsing patterns in a site can be collected into the user profile along with such information as search keywords entered. The Web is the first medium in which such finely detailed tracking of individual activities is possible, and it is not yet clear how best to use the information for personalization. At a minimum, areas that are frequently visited by a user might be given links on a personalized home page for the user.

Storing Profiles

There are several ways to keep and maintain profiles.

- Browser cookie

  As mentioned previously, cookies can be used to store user identification information, often for tracking sessions. Cookies can also be used to store profile information directly. The advantages are that the site need not allocate storage for profiles and that the profile data is directly available to Web applications at the site without querying a database. The disadvantage is that if a user switches computers (or simply deletes the cookie), the profile information is lost. The site also will not have all users' profile information available at once for reporting or marketing analysis.

- Site local storage

  User authentication information can be used to retrieve profile information from a local database. This works well until the Web site grows to more than one location.

- Shared storage

  A shared system can store user profile information. For example, a transaction engine or authentication system that serves multiple sites can also provide a common user database with shared profile information. The advantage is that the information need be kept up-to-date in only one place. This approach, sometimes called a *server-side wallet*, has not become common on the Web. This situation may change as Web services are deployed and provide standard interfaces for exchanging information.

- Client wallet

  One additional storage site for profile information is a browser-based wallet. This method is not widely used, but it may become more common. Originally invented as a way to store payment credentials for commerce, browser wallets can also store profile information such as name, address, and personal preferences. These can be released to requesting Web sites automatically, on approval of the end user, or under the control of privacy software such as the Open Profiling Standard.

Custom Content

Given user authentication and profile information, the final problem to be solved is how to generate personalized content. The details will necessarily vary with different applications, but here are a few examples.

Personal Newspaper

The objective of our example personal newspaper site is to attract users by offering a custom-tailored newspaper. The concept is to save users time by putting the information they want on a personalized front page. The site could be funded either by paid subscriptions or by advertising.

Users are asked to register an interest profile, which includes the following elements on a registration form.

- Name and password, for signing on to the site on future occasions
- E-mail address, to be used as a location for sending an e-mail version of the personal newspaper, if desired
- Postal code, to be used for creating a custom weather report for the user's home city
- Favorite sports teams, for selecting news items about the teams, including up-to-date scores
- Stock market ticker symbols for companies of interest, for generating a custom portfolio report and news items about the companies

The user profile and authentication information are stored in a database at the Web site. When a user clicks into the site, a sign-on screen asks the user to sign on or register as a new user.

After the user signs on, the Web application uses the user's name to retrieve the user's profile from the database. The standard front page is a template with placeholders for weather, sports, and business, but no content in those areas. The Web application uses fields from the user's profile to select an appropriate weather report, team scores, and company news, and populates the template, which is then returned to the user. A periodic batch job searches the database for users who have selected the e-mail option and queues personalized e-mail messages for transmission.

If the site is supported by advertising, advertisers can learn a great deal from the profile, such as the postal code. The profile can be used to place advertisements that are more likely to be of interest to the user.

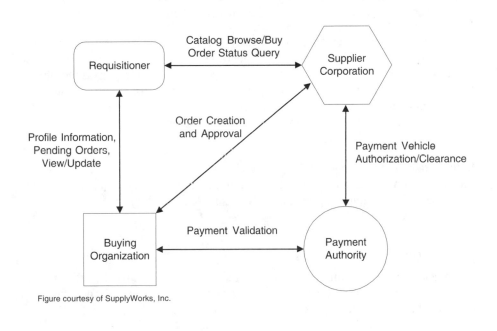

Figure courtesy of SupplyWorks, Inc.

FIGURE 12-3. OBI Architecture

Custom Catalog

The objective of our example catalog site is to sell office supplies to medium-sized corporate customers. The purpose of the Web ordering system is to reduce ordering costs by having the end-user requisitioners order supplies directly. This service is provided to several customers, and the supply catalog must be customized for each buying organization. The customizations include an order form reflecting the look and feel desired by the respective buying organizations, a set of offered supplies that is limited by contract, and a set of prices and discounts that reflect the volume of orders. Personalization for individuals also reflects individual purchasing limits.

In this example, which follows the design of the Open Buying on the Internet (OBI) standard, the selling organization operates the catalog and provides organization-level customization. The buying organization is responsible for authenticating requisitioners and for authorizing purchases according to individual purchasing limits. For convenience, Figure 12-3 reproduces the OBI architecture diagram from Chapter 6.

To create a purchasing relationship, the buying and selling organizations agree on services, items covered, and contract pricing. This information is placed in a buying organization profile stored at the seller's catalog system.

The buying organization creates digital certificates for requisitioners, which record their usernames, as assigned by the purchasing department.

When a requisitioner enters the seller's catalog, the site uses the information in the digital certificate to select the proper discounts, price tables, available items, and the proper order form for the buyer. When the order is complete, the catalog routes the order to the buyer's approval system, along with the username from the certificate. The buyer's approval system uses the username from the certificate to select the proper purchasing limit. If the order is approved, it routes the order back to the seller along with the proper shipping address.

In this example, the storage of the profile is split between buyer and seller systems. This division makes sense for this application, because the same requisitioners may purchase from multiple suppliers, and there is no need to store the same profile in multiple places.

Merchandising

The objective of our example merchandising site is to attract traffic by offering coupons and special offers to create repeat customers. In order to be as unobtrusive as possible, there will be no registration or sign-on requirements.

For this system, authentication will be done by using a browser cookie to store a unique ID number. If a browser comes to the site for the first time, no cookie will be present, so a new ID number will be allocated and stored as a cookie. The purpose of the ID number is to recognize repeat visitors and to adapt site behavior over time.

At first, the user profile will be empty, and the site home page will display generic special offers. Should the visitor make a purchase, however, the ID number will become linked to the user's profile (particularly the postal code) and transaction records.

The postal code will be used to select special offers appropriate for the user's apparent demographics, which is already common practice. After the first transaction, when the user visits the site, the home page will display offers more likely to be of interest to the user.

The order form for the site will also permit the user to enter an optional e-mail address, in case the user wants to be informed of a delay in shipping or of any special offers. A notice indicates that the site will not resell address or e-mail information, in order to assure the user of privacy.

A weekly batch job uses the available profile and transaction information to send occasional electronic coupons to the users who have registered e-mail addresses. The electronic coupons are URLs that bring the user back to the site.

Summary

Personalized content depends on the identification or authentication of the customer, storage of appropriate profile information, and a site architecture that permits the dynamic construction of content according to that profile. Custom content is an important mechanism for sites attempting to build stronger relationships with customers, which can help the competitive position of the site in an environment that tends to flatten other competitive factors such as price and convenience.

Integration with Other Media

As the Internet becomes more and more integrated into everyday life, there are increasing opportunities to link other media into the Web for commercial purposes. Four essential characteristics of the Internet make this exciting.

1. Capacity. Except for modest storage expense, the marginal cost of Web content is essentially zero. Product information can be voluminous and detailed.

2. Currency. Content on the Internet can be kept up-to-date. Catalogs, pricing, inventory, and financial and regulatory information all change frequently.

3. Transactions. In other media, an advertisement exhorts one to telephone for a transaction. On the Internet, the transaction is right there.

4. Bandwidth. Internet bandwidth is large and increasing, but not unlimited. Individual access to the network is frequently over dialup telephone lines using modems running at 28.8 Kbps or less. In addition, many laptop users work in a disconnected mode while traveling, with no immediate access to the Net. Many users, however, are able to access the Net using high-speed corporate LANs, 56-Kbps modems, cable modems, DSL, or satellite links.

With these factors in mind, several types of cross-media integration seem particularly important.

URLs in Advertising

In traditional print and broadcast media, space is at a premium: every square inch of print advertising and every minute of broadcast advertising come with a substantial price tag. With ubiquitous Internet access, print and broadcast advertising can concentrate on brand recognition and link to online sources for detailed product information. Today, most magazine and television advertisements include URLs, linking these media to the Web.

CD-ROMs and DVDs

CD-ROMs are already in wide use for distributing applications, catalogs, and reference information. CD-ROMs have the advantages of large capacity and bandwidth, and they work even when disconnected from the network. CD-ROMs lack currency and transaction capability, but by integrating network access (when available) with local CD-ROMs, an application can have the capacity and bandwidth of the CD-ROM and the currency and transaction capability of the Internet. Updates to CD-ROM content can be pulled from the network or pushed by servers to client systems, and applications delivered on CD-ROMs can be easily linked out to transaction and information systems on the Internet. Digital Versatile Discs (DVDs) are similar to CD-ROMs except that they have much greater capacity.

E-Mail and the Web

E-mail is a familiar medium to Internet users, but it has only recently been integrated with the World Wide Web. The current generation of e-mail clients can display most messages formatted in HTML, and they can activate a Web browser from a URL in an e-mail message. These capabilities make it easy to use e-mail to communicate with customers and to distribute special offers and coupons. The recipient can easily store and forward these messages, as well as jump immediately to interactive or transactional Web sites.

Wireless and Mobile Devices

As the Web has been extended to wireless and mobile devices, ranging from laptops to cell phones, it has become common to reuse Web content for them. We discuss mobile and wireless systems in more detail in Chapter 20.

Summary

Creation and management of content that is compelling and easy to use are as important on the Internet as in other communications media. With any new medium, however, we find new capabilities, new tools, and new constraints. The Web offers powerful mechanisms for integrating many kinds of media and for providing a user experience that is rich in detail. Moreover, the presentation can be tailored to the personal interests and characteristics of an individual customer, an ability unmatched by any other medium.

Discussions about the Internet and the Web often focus on technology, but ultimately it is compelling content that brings customers back to a site. Take advantage of the technology, but focus on the content.

CHAPTER 13

Cryptography

The King hath note of all they intend,
By interception, which they dream not of.
—Shakespeare, *Henry V*

Keeping Secrets

Cryptography, from the Greek word for "secret writing," is the science of communication over untrusted communications channels. Historically, cryptography has been associated with spies, governments, and the military. It has been used in warfare for thousands of years, with some of the most famous cases, including the German Enigma machine, coming from World War II. Over the last 50 years, however, cryptography has acquired a sound mathematical and practical foundation and has moved from being a tool of military and diplomatic application to one that embraces commercial applications as well.

When used properly, cryptography can keep a message secret, positively identify its sender, and assure the recipient that it was not modified in transit. In some cases, cryptographic techniques can help prove that a message was sent in the first place, and by whom.

As a short example, let us apply these attributes of cryptography to a problem of electronic commerce over a network. Alice, a purchasing agent, wants to order some widgets from her supplier, Bob. What are the requirements for this transaction?

- Alice wants to be sure that she is really dealing with Bob and not an impostor (authentication).

Privacy	The message is secret: only the sender and intended recipient know the contents of the message.
Authentication	The recipient knows that the message is not a forgery but was in fact sent by a particular sender. The sender knows that the message is going to the proper recipient.
Integrity	The recipient knows that the message was not modified (intentionally or accidentally) while in transit.
Nonrepudiation	The author of the message cannot later deny having sent the message.

TABLE 13-1. **Functions Provided by Cryptography**

- Bob wants to be sure that Alice is really Alice and not an impostor (authentication), because Alice gets special prices as part of a contract already negotiated.

- Alice wants to keep the order secret from her competition, and Bob does not want other customers to see Alice's special prices (privacy).

- Alice and Bob both want to ensure that crackers cannot change the price or quantity (integrity).

- Bob wants to ensure that Alice cannot later claim that she did not place the order (nonrepudiation).

These are some of the properties that Alice and Bob may want to have for their communication, and cryptographic techniques can be used to provide them. We will return to Alice and Bob's communication as we delve into the details of these properties, which are summarized in Table 13-1.

In this chapter, we discuss some basic principles of public- and private-key cryptography and then discuss how these technologies are used to create secure communications channels, digital signatures, and other solutions. We close with a discussion of key management, the little-appreciated linchpin of cryptography.

Types of Cryptography

In cryptography, an ordinary message (the *plaintext*) is processed by an encryption algorithm to produce a scrambled message (the *ciphertext*). The receiver uses a matching decryption algorithm to recover the plaintext from the ciphertext. If these algorithms were known to everyone, there would be no security, because anyone could decrypt the ciphertext. Therefore, in addition to the algorithm, there is an additional piece of input data called a *key*. The key is secret, even though many people may know the algorithm. The principle is the same as that of a combination lock. Many people may use locks with the same design, but each one chooses a different combination. The combination of the lock is equivalent to the key of the encryption algorithm.

There are two basic types of cryptographic algorithms: secret-key systems (sometimes called *symmetric*) and public-key systems (sometimes called *asymmetric*). In secret-key cryptography, both encryption and decryption operations use the same key (that is, the key is used symmetrically). Systems for public-key cryptography use related but different keys for the operations of encryption and decryption operations (in other words, the keys are asymmetric). As we shall see, having two keys means that one can be published—that is, made *public*—which gives public-key cryptography its name. The other key is kept secret and is sometimes called a *private key*. Secret-key systems have been around for many hundreds of years; public-key systems are a recent invention, dating from the mid-1970s. Both types of systems allow for secret communications, but public-key systems can more easily grow to worldwide scale and more easily permit unaffiliated persons to communicate securely. Public-key systems can also be used to provide *digital signatures,* which are analogous to handwritten signatures on letters, contracts, and other documents. We shall have more to say about digital signatures later in this chapter.

In practice, cryptographic systems often use secret-key and public-key cryptography together. Secret-key algorithms are usually much faster than public-key algorithms, so it is more efficient to use a secret-key algorithm to encrypt the actual data. The system generates a random key for the symmetric algorithm and then encrypts that key using the public-key algorithm. The receiver first decrypts the secret key using the public-key algorithm and then decrypts the data using that newly decrypted key.

Algorithms, Modes, Protocols, and Key Management

There are four main components in the use of cryptography for practical systems: cryptosystems, modes, protocols, and key management. The term *cryptosystems* refers to the cryptographic algorithms and their characteristics. *Modes* refers to how the cryptographic algorithms are initialized and used to manage messages that are longer than a single block. *Protocols* refers to the ways in which cryptographic algorithms are composed and applied to real problems, such as the securing of a communications channel or information in a database. Finally, *key management* refers to the essential problems of creating, distributing, and storing keys.

The process of designing and analyzing cryptosystems is extremely specialized, so we limit ourselves to a brief survey of those systems that are commercially relevant today. Protocols are very important for electronic commerce, because they are used for protecting content and information as well as for payment systems. Finally, key management, perhaps the least-appreciated component, is actually the most important for the attainment of real security in a hostile environment.

We begin with a discussion of how to think about the security of systems using cryptography and then continue with a discussion of algorithms, protocols, and key management.

How to Evaluate Cryptography

The operational security of a system that uses cryptography depends on the security of the cryptographic algorithms in use, the correct design of the cryptographic protocols, and, above all, proper key management.

- Algorithms

  The design of cryptographic algorithms is very specialized. Don't try this at home. Instead, choose an established and well-understood algorithm that offers the features you need and that is sufficiently strong for your purposes. Because cryptography is still a rapidly developing field, it is prudent to be prepared for unpleasant surprises. When possible, design systems so that the cryptographic algorithms can be replaced with new ones. If you choose an algorithm that can use keys of different lengths, be prepared to use longer keys in the future. Someone may try to sell you a new cryptographic algorithm with claims of better security, better performance, or some other advantage. Using such an algorithm can be dangerous, because you can't really tell how good it is. It may seem boring to use algorithms that are well known and well understood, but it is certainly safer.

- Modes

  Many cryptographic algorithms are block-oriented, meaning that they process the plaintext in blocks that usually range in size from 64 bits to 256 bits. When the message is longer than a single block, the algorithm runs as many times as needed to encrypt the entire message. The mode of an algorithm determines how the processing of one block affects the processing of other blocks. There are several ways to do this, and they are very subtle. Use of the wrong mode can render the entire system subject to easy attack.

- Protocols

  The design of cryptographic protocols is perhaps more accessible than the design of algorithms, but even the simplest-appearing protocols are fraught with an amazing number of subtle bugs. Don't try this at home either. Whenever possible, use established protocols (and when it is not possible, try harder to find one that works). As with algorithms, the use of modular components allows you to introduce new protocols from time to time. This is especially useful if weaknesses are discovered in an older protocol, which sometimes occurs.

- Key management

  Key management is the most difficult part of cryptography, and it is also the least discussed. Don't even consider trying to design it yourself, except that you may have to if the systems and components you want to buy don't do it. Key management includes the generation, distribution, storage, and updating of keys. Because modern cryptographic algorithms and protocols are very strong, key-management systems are a tempting target for attackers. When evaluating a system for secure communications, it is important to ask hard questions about the workings of the built-in mechanisms for key generation, storage, and distribution. Sometimes, however, these functions are left to the user of the system, and there is no choice but to design and implement them yourself.

Cryptographic Strength

The right way to think about the security of a cryptosystem is that the key encapsulates the entire security of the system as long as it employs a sufficiently strong algorithm. In particular, we would be suspicious of any system that depends on the secrecy of an algorithm. A published algorithm that has withstood years of study by cryptanalysts is a much better bet.

How, then, does one measure the strength of a system? One way to attack a cryptosystem is to try all possible keys to decrypt a message. This kind of attack is known as an *exhaustive search* or a *brute force attack*. It is impossible to prevent a brute force attack, but an attacker may find that mounting one is prohibitively expensive if the number of possible keys is extremely large.

Another attack is known as a *chosen plaintext attack*. First, suppose that the algorithm itself is available to all. Second, suppose that the attacker has access to the system and is therefore able to submit plaintext and receive the corresponding ciphertext, encrypted using the current key, which remains secret, of course. Such a system would seem to give the attacker every advantage, other than knowing the key ahead of time. If the attacker still cannot decrypt your messages by any means other than trying each possible key, you are in good shape.

If a system can be attacked only by trying each possible key, then there must be enough possible keys to make this task computationally infeasible. Key length is measured in bits. For example, the Data Encryption Standard (DES), which was specified by the U.S. government in 1977, has a 56-bit key. For a key with n bits, there are 2^n possible keys. Every bit added to the key length doubles the work required of the attacker. For example, DES with a 56-bit key has 2^{56} possible keys, or about 72,100,000,000,000,000 different keys. This may seem to be a sufficiently large number, but this turns out not to be the case. Several years ago, a research group at Digital Equipment Corporation built a chip capable of 16,000,000 DES operations per second. If one were to build a machine with 1,000 such chips, a DES-encrypted message could be broken in less than 8 weeks. On June 17, 1997, a team led by Rocke Verser broke a DES-encrypted message by marshaling the efforts of some 78,000 computers on the Internet over a period of several months. On July 15, 1998, the *DES Cracker* machine of the Electronic Freedom Foundation (EFF) took less than 3 days to solve the problem posed in the RSA Laboratories DES Challenge II. Such an effort may be beyond the reach of a casual cracker, but it is easy for a criminal syndicate and has almost certainly been done by the code-breaking agencies of national governments.

A related piece of bad news is that the performance of computers at constant cost is doubling about every 18 months. This technology trend, known as *Moore's Law*, has held for nearly 30 years and shows no sign of letting up. In round numbers, by 2010, machines and their components will be at least 1,000 times faster per dollar than they were in 1996. More speculatively, nanotechnology or biotechnology may make massively parallel code-breaking efforts possible at some future time. Fortunately, the computational cost of attacking a cipher increases exponentially faster than the cost of improving its strength.

In January 1997, RSA Laboratories announced the RSA Secret-Key Challenge, a series of symmetric key cryptographic contests. The first challenge to fall was a 40-bit key version of the RC5 algorithm—in less than 4 hours. A stronger 48-bit version of RC5 took 313 hours and DES took 140 days, as mentioned previously. Note that RC5 has a variable key length, and some stronger challenges remain unsolved.

Operational Choices

Leaving aside for a moment the issues of protocols and algorithms, the first choices to be made are the cryptographic strength of the system, embodied by choices of algorithm and key length, and some of the key-management questions. It is most important to choose truly random keys that are sufficiently long, keep those keys secret, and change keys "often enough." Again, this all supposes that you have selected a good cryptosystem; all the security of the system lies in the keys, and none in the algorithm itself.

We will consider key randomness and key secrecy shortly. For now, let us consider the selection of key length and the frequency of key updates.

Key Length

Given a reasonably strong algorithm, how well the data is protected depends largely on the length of the encryption key. Fundamentally, an encrypted message must remain secret for the useful life of the information. To a large extent, the value of the information in the encrypted message will govern the resources used to attack it. For example, an attacker would be foolish to spend $1 million to obtain information worth $1,000, but he might spend $1 million to obtain a secret worth $2 million. Here are some examples.

- Financial credentials must remain secret beyond their validity period.
- Contract bids must remain secret beyond the contract award.
- Editorial material must remain secret until published.
- Confidential personal information must remain secret beyond the lifetime of the individual.

Today, it is common to use 128-bit keys for symmetric algorithms, both for communications security and for the security of data to be protected for 20 years. The necessary key lengths for public-key algorithms vary considerably. The current recommendation for the RSA public-key algorithm, for example, is to use a minimum length of 1024 bits, with 2048 bits used for especially sensitive applications or long-term keys.

Key Updates

Cryptographic keys do not last forever; they need to be updated from time to time. The proper lifetime of a key is a function of the value of the items encrypted, the number of items encrypted, and the lifetime of the items encrypted. We have already discussed lifetime. If a key can be broken by a properly equipped adversary in 2 years, and the lifetime of information encrypted using the key is 6 months, then the key should be changed at least every 18 months so that an attack mounted on the first item encrypted will not succeed until after the last item encrypted loses its value.

The number of items encrypted is an issue for two reasons. First, if individual encrypted items have a market value, then the sum of the values of all encrypted items is the proper measure against which to balance the resources an attacker may bring to bear. Second, some cryptosystems can be attacked more easily when a large body of ciphertext is available. This effect is more difficult to quantify, but again, it is a good idea not to use a key for too long.

Another factor that leads to frequent key updates is paranoia. The longer a key has been in use, the greater the chance that someone has compromised the key storage system and obtained the key by subterfuge rather than by brute force attack.

It is important to note that changing a key does not increase the time that an attacker will need to find it using brute force or any other method of cryptographic attack. Changing keys does, however, limit the amount of information revealed if any particular key is found. For example, if the encryption keys are changed every month, then only one month's worth of information is disclosed if a key is discovered.

One-Time Pads

Is there a perfect cryptosystem? Surprisingly, the answer is yes. It is called the *one-time pad*. The idea of the one-time pad is to have a completely random key that is the same length as the message. The key is never reused, and only the sender and the receiver have copies. To send, for example, a 100-bit message, the message is exclusive-ORed[1] with 100 bits of the key. That portion of the key is crossed off, never to be used

---

1. The exclusive-OR operation produces a "1" if exactly one of the two input bits is a "1."

again. The receiver reverses the process, exclusive-ORing the ciphertext with her copy of the key to reveal the message. If the one-time pad key contains truly random bits, this scheme is absolutely secure. The attacker does not know what is on the pad and must guess—but there is no way to know when he is right. By changing the guess, the attacker can decode the ciphertext into *any* message, be it "attack at dawn" or "negotiate surrender."

The one-time pad offers perfect security and is indeed used when perfect security is needed, but the system has many disadvantages.

- The pad must be truly random. Any structure at all can be used to break the system. Creating truly random characters is difficult, and creating a vast quantity of them is more difficult.

- The pad must never be reused. If a sheet is used twice, then the two sections of ciphertext encrypted using the same page can be compared, possibly revealing both.[2] Since the pad is consumed as messages are sent, the pad has to be very long or frequently replaced.

- The pads must be distributed, stored, and used with absolute secrecy. Because the ciphertext cannot be successfully attacked, the obvious point of attack is to copy or substitute a pad.

- Every pair of correspondents must have a unique pad, leading to immense practical difficulties of distribution.

These practical difficulties effectively restrict the use of one-time pad systems to situations in which cost is no object. For most other situations, cryptosystems are used in which the length of the key is fixed, and the key can be attacked by exhaustive search.

Secret-Key (Symmetric) Cryptography

In a symmetric cryptosystem, shown in Figure 13-1, the message, sometimes called the *plaintext*, is encrypted using a key. The resulting ciphertext is sent to the recipient, who decrypts the message using the same key. Note that the same key must be known to both parties. Perhaps the best-known secret-key system is the Data Encryption Standard (DES), now supplanted by Triple DES and by the Advanced Encryption Standard (AES). Table 13-2 shows how symmetric cryptography achieves privacy, authentication, integrity, and nonrepudiation.

Suppose that Bob and Alice want to communicate using secret-key cryptography. To get started, they must agree on a key, which only they will know and which they will

---

2. This has actually happened. In an effort to save money during World War II, the Soviet Union issued duplicate pads to multiple offices. By intercepting both ciphertexts, the United States was eventually able to decode many of these *Venona* messages. See http://www.nsa.gov/docs/venona.

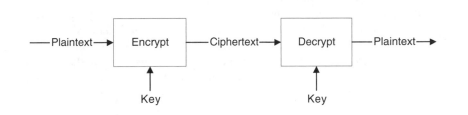

FIGURE 13-1. Symmetric Cryptosystem

Privacy	Only those who know the key can encrypt or decrypt messages.
Authentication	If separate keys are used for each pair of communicating parties, then the receiver of a message can be assured that the sender was authentic. The sender knows that only the intended recipient can decrypt the message.
Integrity	Symmetric encryption does not provide message integrity without some effort. However, a message integrity code (MIC) can be added to the message. A MIC is a message digest of the message combined with the secret key.
Nonrepudiation	Symmetric cryptography does not provide nonrepudiation, because either the sender or the intended recipient could have created the message.

TABLE 13-2. Functions Provided by Secret-Key Cryptography

keep secret from all others. Once Bob and Alice have a key in common, each one can encrypt messages to the other. Authentication is ensured, because each person knows that only the other person has the key. When a message arrives, there is only one person who could have sent it. The integrity of the message can also be ensured, provided that a message digest or message integrity code is included with the message.

Block Ciphers and Stream Ciphers

A block cipher algorithm is designed to take a fixed-length block of plaintext, perhaps 64 bits or 128 bits, and encrypt it with the key to produce a fixed-length ciphertext. A stream cipher algorithm uses the key to produce a pseudorandom key stream, which is then typically exclusive-ORed with the plaintext to produce the ciphertext. Both methods have some practical disadvantages. Because each block of a block cipher is independent, an eavesdropper may notice that certain ciphertext blocks are repeated and will therefore know that corresponding plaintext blocks also repeat. With the simple application of a stream cipher, the key stream repeats with each new message, making analysis easy. To combat these problems, an initialization vector (IV) is used. For block ciphers, the IV is prepended to the message and encrypted. Then the first block of ciphertext is exclusive-ORed with the second block of plaintext, and so on. This technique is called *cipher block chaining* (CBC). The IV is different for each message. With a stream cipher, the IV and the key are used to initialize the key stream generator so that it produces a different sequence for each message. The IV itself is sent in the clear before the first part of the ciphertext is sent.

Secret-Key Cryptosystems

This is by no means an exhaustive list of current symmetric cryptosystems, but is rather a quick list of interesting and commercially important systems.

- DES

  The Data Encryption Standard (DES) is a block cipher that uses a 56-bit key to encrypt a 64-bit plaintext block into a 64-bit ciphertext block. DES is defined by Federal Information Processing Standard (FIPS) 46, published in November 1976. The most common mode of operation of DES is CBC. In this mode of operation, each output block of ciphertext is exclusive-ORed with the next plaintext block to form the next input to the DES algorithm. The process begins with a 64-bit IV. Without CBC, individual blocks of ciphertext can be replaced by an attacker to disrupt communications. Also, because 8-character blocks of 8-bit data such as ASCII fall naturally on 64-bit boundaries, a cryptanalyst can identify when blocks are repeated and can gain substantial insight into the plaintext. Although DES has been in widespread use for more than 20 years, withstanding intense scrutiny from cryptanalysts, its 56-bit key length is too small to resist brute force attacks by modern computers. Consequently, DES should not be used in new systems, and it should be retired from older systems.

- Triple DES

  A recent variation of DES, called *Triple DES* or *3DES*, uses three 56-bit DES keys to encrypt each block. In a Triple DES encryption operation, the data block is encrypted with the first key, decrypted with the second key,[3] and encrypted again using the third key. The middle operation is a decryption, so that if the three keys are chosen to be the same, then Triple DES reduces to ordinary DES. In its three-key mode, Triple DES requires a 168-bit key. A second variant, in which the first and third keys are the same, requires a 112-bit key.

- IDEA

  The International Data Encryption Algorithm (IDEA) is a block cipher developed by Lai and Massey in 1991. IDEA uses 128-bit keys to encrypt 64-bit blocks. IDEA was used as the bulk cipher in older versions of Pretty Good Privacy (PGP).

---

3. By "decrypted with the second key," we mean that the DES algorithm is run in decryption mode with that key. Clearly, the decryption operation does not yield the plaintext, because a different key was used.

- RC4

  RC4 is a variable key length stream cipher designed by Ron Rivest for RSA Security. RC4 is widely used on the Internet as the bulk encryption cipher in SSL/TLS, with key lengths in the range of 40 bits to 128 bits. RC4 is a proprietary cipher of RSA Security, but the source code of a program that appears to duplicate the function of RC4 was published anonymously on the Internet in 1995. As a consequence, the RC4 algorithm is receiving much more cryptographic scrutiny.

- Blowfish

  Blowfish is a variable key length block cipher designed by Bruce Schneier of Counterpane Systems. Blowfish is freely available and is very fast, running nearly three times faster than a DES implementation on an Intel Pentium processor. Blowfish is widely used in file encryption applications for personal computers, secure tunneling applications, and others. The key length is variable from 32 bits to 448 bits, which makes it interesting for variable security applications. For more information about this algorithm, see http://www.counterpane.com/blowfish.html.

- CAST

  CAST is a variable key length block cipher designed by Carlisle Adams and Stafford Tavares for Entrust Technologies. The key length is variable from 40 bits to 128 bits. CAST is the standard bulk encryption cipher in some recent of versions of PGP. In January 1997, Entrust released a version of CAST for free use in both commercial and noncommercial applications.

- AES

  The Advanced Encryption Standard (AES) is an effort of the National Institute of Standards and Technology (NIST) to develop and standardize a replacement for DES. The effort was launched on January 2, 1997. On October 2, 2000, NIST announced that it had selected the Rijndael algorithm. Rijndael is an iterated block cipher whose block length and key length can be independently set to 128 bits, 192 bits, or 256 bits. NIST published FIPS 197 for AES in 2001.

Unless there are compelling reasons to choose a specific algorithm, AES is now an especially good choice for new applications. Because it is now a standard, it is receiving careful scrutiny by cryptographers, and it continues to resist attack.

Public-Key (Asymmetric) Cryptography

In an asymmetric cryptosystem, shown in Figure 13-2, the encryption key is different from the decryption key. Typically, each participant in a public-key system randomly creates her own pair of keys. Then one member of the pair, called the *private key*, is kept secret and never revealed to anyone, whereas the other member of the key pair, called the *public key*, is distributed freely. Either key may be used for encryption or for decryption, but the most important point is that the private key should never be revealed. The best-known public-key cryptosystem is RSA, named after its inventors

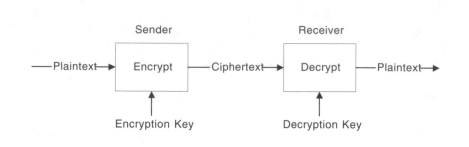

FIGURE 13-2. Asymmetric Cryptosystem

(Rivest, Shamir, and Adleman). A public-key system is somewhat like a safe with a slot in the top. Anyone can put items into the safe, but only the person who knows the combination can get them out. Table 13-3 shows how public-key cryptography achieves privacy, authentication, integrity, and nonrepudiation.

A Public-Key Cryptography Example

Suppose that Bob and Alice want to communicate using public-key cryptography. To get started, Bob and Alice each create a key pair, and each pair consists of a public key and a private key. Next, Bob and Alice publish their respective public keys in the town directory. If Bob wants to send Alice a message, he encrypts the message using Alice's public key. The ciphertext can be read only by Alice, because only she knows her own private key. Alice decrypts the message using her private key, revealing the original message.

Privacy	A message is encrypted by the recipient's public key. Only the recipient has the proper private key to decrypt the message.
Authentication	The recipient can authenticate the sender of a message by verifying a digital signature—a message digest of the message encrypted using the sender's private key.
Integrity	A digital signature of the message provides message integrity. A message digest of the message is encrypted using the sender's private key.
Nonrepudiation	Nonrepudiation can be provided using digital signatures. However, long after the fact, a dispute can arise about whether the signature was created at the same time as the message. For this problem, a digital timestamping service may be useful.

TABLE 13-3. Functions Provided by Public-Key Cryptography

The first problem with this scheme is that anyone could have sent the message. Because Alice's public key is published in an open directory, anyone can send a message to her. If the message reads, "Meet me at the trellis at midnight—Bob," how can Alice tell if the message is really from Bob or if it is perhaps from her father who is testing her? An answer to this problem, and an application of authentication, is for Bob to apply a digital signature to the message. Suppose that Bob takes the message and encrypts it using his private key, creating a signed message. Anyone can decrypt this signed message by using Bob's public key, so it isn't secret; but only Bob could have sent it, because only Bob knows his private key.

The solution to Bob and Alice's problem—sending a secret, authenticated message—lies in the combination of these techniques. Bob first signs his message using his own private key, and then he encrypts the signed message using Alice's public key. Only Alice can decrypt this message, and once she has, she can verify that Bob sent it.

The next problem with public-key cryptography is the authenticity of public keys. When Bob sends a message to Alice, he looks up Alice's public key in the directory. Suppose Alice's father has substituted his own public key in the directory. Now, when Bob sends a message, he unwittingly encrypts it using not Alice's public key, but her father's key. If Alice's father is clever, he will decrypt the message, and then reencrypt it using Alice's public key. The substitution may not be discovered unless Alice thinks to check the directory to see if the key listed under her name is the right one.

One solution to the problem of the security of key directories is the use of public-key certificates. A public-key certificate is a document containing a name and the corresponding public key, signed by a trusted certificate authority. Suppose the town clerk is operating as a certificate authority. Alice, when she first creates her public key, appears in person before the clerk with a document attesting that the public key is really hers. The clerk signs the document using her private key. The resulting signed document is a public-key certificate. Anyone can verify its authenticity by checking the signature using the clerk's public key. Of course, the clerk's public key must be beyond reproach. Once Alice has a certificate, she can place it in the directory, and Bob can be assured that the key he uses to send messages is really Alice's key.

Certificate authorities are often organized in a hierarchy (similar to that of the DNS), which enables administrators to distribute the process of issuing the certificates. To create the hierarchy, higher-level certificate authorities sign certificates for lower-level authorities. The certificate authority at the top of the hierarchy is called the *root,* and its public key is called a *root key.* A hierarchy of certificate authorities and widespread use of public-key certificates are what is meant by a *public-key infrastructure* (PKI).

Public-Key Cryptosystems

The two main public-key cryptosystems are RSA and some variants of elliptic curve algorithms. Readers who are not interested in the mathematical details of these algorithms may skip to the next section.

RSA

The preeminent public-key cryptosystem is RSA. The security of RSA is based on the fact that it is very hard to factor large numbers. An RSA public key consists of two parts: a modulus n and a random encryption key e. The corresponding decryption key d is kept secret. The keys e and d are chosen randomly, but they are related such that $ed = 1 \bmod (p - 1)(q - 1)$, where p and q are prime numbers and $n = pq$. Encrypting a message using RSA is the mathematical operation

$$c = m^e \bmod n$$

where m is the message, c is the ciphertext, e is the encryption key, and n is the RSA modulus. Decryption is

$$c = c^d \bmod n$$

There are several important things to know about the RSA algorithm.

- The numbers p and q must be primes, and certain "weak" forms must be avoided.
- A particular choice of p and q must never be used with multiple keys e and d; if this is done, the cipher is easily cracked.
- RSA is a block cipher in which the size of the block is the size of the modulus n. The information to be encrypted must be shorter than a block, or the message must be broken up into multiple blocks.
- The message cannot be too short. If m^e is smaller than n, or wraps only a few times, then the message is easily decoded.
- There are several formatting rules for one-block messages, which make life difficult for cryptanalysts.

The best source for recommended use of RSA cryptography is the Public-Key Cryptography Standards (PKCS) series published by RSA Security, Inc.

As mentioned previously, other than the "be careful about this" items above, the security of RSA is equivalent to the problem of factoring. If the (public) modulus n can be decomposed into its factors p and q, then the private key d can be recovered. In recent years, mathematical researchers have made substantial progress in factoring, with the best current algorithms being the General Number Field Sieve (GNFS) and the Special Number Field Sieve (SNFS), which is applicable only to numbers of a special form. Table 13-4 shows some estimates of the amount of computing power necessary

Number Size (in Bits)	Arbitrary Integers (Using GNFS)	Special Integers (Using SNFS)
512	3×10^{4}	–
768	2×10^{8}	1×10^{5}
1024	3×10^{11}	3×10^{7}
1280	1×10^{14}	3×10^{9}
1536	3×10^{16}	2×10^{11}
2048	3×10^{20}	4×10^{14}

TABLE 13-4. **Computer Power Required to Factor (in MIPS-Years)**[a]

a. From Andrew Odlyzko, "The Future of Integer Factorization," *Cryptobytes*, Summer 1995. The unit *MIPS-Year* means a 1-million-instruction-per-second computer running for 1 year. A personal computer running at 1 GHz is approximately 1,000 MIPS.

to factor numbers of certain sizes popular in the use of RSA. Generally speaking, the RSA modulus must be longer by a factor of 10 than a symmetric cryptosystem key of equivalent security. The constant 10 is only illustrative and changes upwards as improvements are made in algorithms for factoring.

Elliptic Curves

Cryptosystems based on elliptic curve algorithms are now being introduced. Elliptic curve cryptosystems are based on the difficulty of a mathematical problem known as *discrete logarithms*, rather than on the difficulty of factoring. Barring unusual progress in solving this problem, elliptic curve systems can achieve a particular level of security with shorter keys compared with systems based on the difficulty of factoring. Several standardization efforts are under way for elliptic curve systems in groups such as ANSI X9, ISO/IEC, and IEEE.

The major problem with elliptic curve systems is that they are new. They have not survived years of intense scrutiny as RSA has. However, what passes for popular opinion in the cryptographic community is that elliptic curve systems are coming up fast.

Modes

When the message to be encrypted is longer than the block length of the cipher, it is necessary to execute the algorithm several times and to combine the results in some way. The method of combination is called the *mode of operation*.

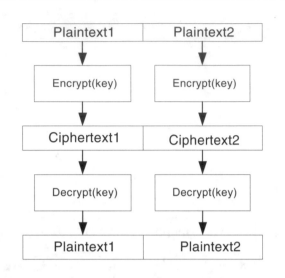

FIGURE 13-3. Electronic Codebook Mode

Electronic Codebook Mode

In electronic codebook (ECB) mode, shown in Figure 13-3, the encryption algorithm is applied independently to each block of the message. This approach is obvious, straightforward, and almost always a bad idea. The main problems with this mode are that the same input block is always encrypted as the same ciphertext and that an attacker can substitute blocks to alter part of a message. Suppose, for example, that messages are being used to make payments. If the payment amount appears in a fixed place in the message, an attacker can change the payment amount by substituting ciphertext blocks from previous messages that use the same key. ECB mode can be appropriate for some uses, however, such as the encoding of random data (such as cryptographic keys) and the encryption of plaintext that is no larger than a single block.

Cipher Block Chaining Mode

In cipher block chaining (CBC) mode, shown in Figure 13-4, each plaintext block is exclusive-ORed with the preceding block of ciphertext before the plaintext is encrypted. The process is bootstrapped using an initialization vector (IV). CBC mode solves the major problems of ECB mode. In CBC mode, each block of plaintext is scrambled by XOR with a block of ciphertext. Because these blocks are different, if the same plaintext occurs in multiple places, it will be encrypted to different ciphertext. The IV provides this function for the first block of plaintext. The IV must be random and different for each message, but it doesn't need to be secret. Often the IV will be transmitted in the clear as the first part of the message. CBC mode also makes the

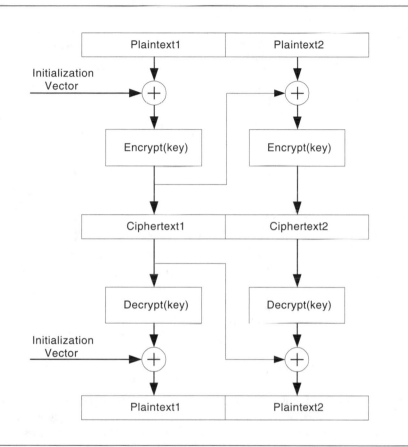

FIGURE 13-4. Cipher Block Chaining Mode

overall message more resistant to tampering. If an attacker switches blocks around, duplicates blocks, or attempts to substitute old blocks in new messages, the chaining that occurs during decryption will result in the output plaintext being gibberish.

Cipher block chaining can also be used to create a message authentication code (see Message Authentication Codes, which begins on page 246). Because every block of ciphertext depends on all previous blocks, the final block of the ciphertext depends on both the entire message and the secret key, so it is a MAC. This is known as the *cipher block chaining-message authentication code* (CBC-MAC) mode.

Cipher Feedback Mode

Cipher feedback (CFB) mode is a way to turn a block cipher into a stream cipher, which allows such a cipher to be used for encrypting a continuous stream of data. It

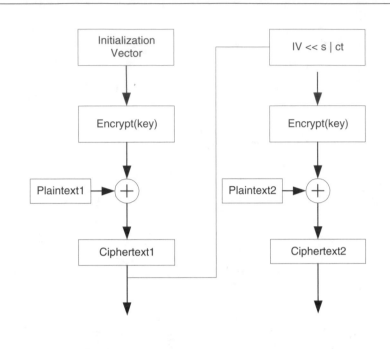

FIGURE 13-5. Cipher Feedback Mode

operates as shown in Figure 13-5. The initialization vector is encrypted to produce the first block of the cipher stream. Successive inputs to the encryption algorithm are produced by shifting in the previous block of ciphertext. CFB mode can be used for any size of plaintext that is no larger than the block size of the encryption algorithm. Only the encryption operation is used by cipher feedback. The decryption procedure is not needed. (Figure 13-5 shows how a message is enciphered using CFB; the method of deciphering is left as an exercise for the reader.)

Output Feedback Mode

Output feedback (OFB) mode, shown in Figure 13-6, is another method of turning a block cipher into a stream cipher. In OFB mode, the IV is encrypted to produce the first block of the cipher stream, which is then used as the key for the second encryption operation to produce the next block of the cipher stream, and so forth. It is critically important in OFB systems that a different IV be used for every message. If the IV is reused, then the cipher streams for the two messages will be identical and the two messages can be jointly solved by an attacker, just as when a one-time pad is reused. Like CFB, OFB requires only an encryption operation and does not use decryption. Again, the process of deciphering is left as an exercise for the reader.

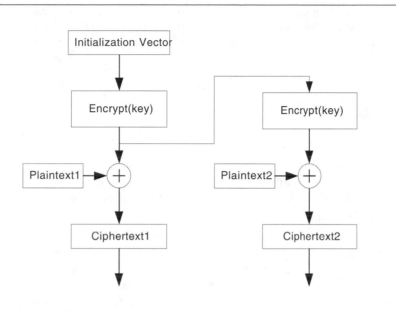

FIGURE 13-6. Output Feedback Mode

Protocols

A protocol is a series of steps taken to accomplish a task. In fact, this is also the definition of an algorithm, but we use *algorithm* to refer to the attainment of internal, mathematical results such as encrypting a block, and *protocol* to refer to the attainment of user-visible results such as secret communication and digital signatures.

Communications

Obviously, most of the previous discussion of secret-key and public-key cryptosystems has been about their use in communications, but complete application of cryptography to communications also addresses some issues beyond the simple encryption and decryption of blocks.

- Session keys

  A session key is a cryptographic key adopted for use for a particular message or during a particular session of communications. Session keys are used for two reasons: to achieve greater performance and to limit the amount of data encrypted with a master key. Frequently a communications system will use a relatively low-performance public-key cryptosystem only to communicate a session key, which is then used for high-performance symmetric-key encryption of the bulk message data. The second reason for using session keys is to limit the amount of information available for cryptanalysis of the master key. Because only the random session keys are ever encrypted by the master key, the attacker cannot exploit any statistical properties of the actual messages to assist in the attack on the master key.

- Message integrity

  It may be possible for an attacker to alter or substitute different ciphertext somewhere along the communications channel between sender and intended recipient. It is therefore necessary to ensure that the message received is the same as the message sent. Sometimes an alteration would be obvious because the received message would decrypt to gibberish, but computers are much worse than people at detecting gibberish. To solve this problem, one may add a message digest to the plaintext before encrypting the message or include a MIC or digital signature as part of the ciphertext.

- Protection against replay

  It may be possible for an attacker to record an entire message and then replay it later. If duplicate messages are not detected and discarded, the attacker can cause considerable mischief. For example, if an encrypted order for widgets with instructions to charge a credit card can be replayed, then the attacker could run down the seller's widget supply or cause the buyer an overdraft. Duplicate messages can also arise accidentally. For example, if the communications channel goes offline during a transmission, the sender may retransmit the most recent message. But was the message lost or just the acknowledgment that the message had been received?

- Data compression

  Data compression and encryption do not mix—or rather, they mix only when combined in the right way. *Data compression* refers to the problem of encoding a message in the minimum amount of space. In order to do this, data compression algorithms such as the familiar ZIP and COMPRESS algorithms exploit statistical properties of the source file to encode the same information with fewer bits. Good encryption destroys these statistical properties that compression algorithms exploit, so in general it is not possible to compress an encrypted message. It is, however, possible to encrypt a compressed message. This odd property has two readily apparent effects. First, a modem that depends on data compression for achieving a high bit rate will get a much lower bit rate on encrypted materials. Second, compressing file systems such as the popular Stacker and Doublespace systems for PCs will not achieve any space savings when used on encrypted files. Arguably, compressing a file before encrypting it may slightly improve security, because compression reduces the redundancy that may be exploited during cryptanalysis. The main point here is that encrypted files are essentially incompressible.

Chapter 14 describes some secure communications protocols in use on the Internet.

Message Digests and Hash Functions

Hash functions, also known as *one-way functions*, take a variable-length message and collapse it to a fixed length, such as 128 bits or 160 bits. The result is often called a *message digest* or a *hash* of the message. Hash functions are an essential element of digital signatures and of message authentication codes. Rather than create a digital signature by, say, encrypting the entire message with one's private key, one encrypts the hash of the message instead. This creates a signature with a small fixed length that is independent of the length of the message. Good hash functions have the property that, given a particular hash, it is infeasible to guess a message that would have the same hash. In addition, it should be infeasible to find any two messages that have the same hash. Here are some widely used hash functions.

- MD5

  MD5 (the *MD* stands for *Message Digest*) is a public-domain algorithm designed by Ron Rivest. It accepts as input a message of arbitrary length and reduces it to a 128-bit output. Some recent cryptographic research has found some weaknesses in a variant of MD5, which makes it prudent to choose alternative functions when possible. To date, these weaknesses do not apply to the use of MD5 for message authentication codes, so MAC algorithms based on MD5 continue to be acceptable. Other recent research is beginning to question nearly any 128-bit hash algorithm, so it is appropriate to choose algorithms with outputs of at least 160 bits for new system designs.

- SHA-1

  SHA-1 (the *Secure Hash Algorithm*) was developed by the U.S. National Institute of Standards and Technology (NIST), with assistance from the National Security Agency. The output of SHA-1 is 160 bits in length.

- RIPEMD-160

  RIPEMD (for *RACE Integrity Primitives Evaluation Message Digest*) is a 160-bit hash algorithm developed by the European Community's Research and Development in Advanced Computation Technologies in Europe effort.

- MDC-2 and MDC-4

  MDC-2 and MDC-4 are hash algorithms that use DES block encryption. MDC-2 was designed by IBM and is specified in ANSI X9.31 for use in financial-security applications. MDC-4 uses four DES encryptions per 64-bit block of input data to produce a 128-bit output.

SHA-1 and RIPEMD-160 have been accepted as part of the international standard ISO/IEC 10118-3:1998.

Message Authentication Codes

In communications, messages are often protected against accidental damage by attaching a checksum, cyclic redundancy check, or error-correcting code. The sender uses the message to compute the checksum and then sends both to the recipient. The recipient uses the message as received to recompute the checksum. If the received checksum is different from that locally computed, then a transmission error has occurred. Checksum algorithms are designed to guarantee that all errors involving fewer than so many bits are detected, and to detect all other errors with very high probability.

A message authentication code (MAC) does a very similar job but protects the integrity of the message against both deliberate and accidental tampering. A MAC algorithm uses the message and a secret key (which is not transmitted with the message) as input and produces a fixed-length output. MACs are constructed using hash functions. An attacker may know the message but cannot reproduce the computation without the secret key. Message authentication codes are sometimes referred to as *message integrity codes* (MICs), because the secret key can be used to ensure both the authenticity and the integrity of the message.

Early MAC algorithms simply concatenated the key with the data and hashed the combination. Such simple approaches turn out to have cryptographic weaknesses, so recent work has been focused on developing stronger algorithms. An example of a MAC algorithm is HMAC, which can work with nearly any hashing algorithm. It is commonly used with MD5 or SHA-1. HMAC is defined as follows.

$$HMAC = H((k \oplus opad) \, \| \, H((k \oplus ipad) \, \| \, message))$$

In this formula, H is the base hash function, k is the key, and *ipad* and *opad* are special padding strings defined in the specification of the HMAC algorithm (IETF Request for Comments 2104).[4]

A hash function may also be constructed using a symmetric cryptosystem operated in CBC-MAC mode, as previously discussed in Cipher Block Chaining Mode, which begins on page 240.

Digital Signatures

A digital signature is an information block attached to a message that could have been created only by a particular individual. One can use public-key technology to produce such a digital signature by creating a message digest of the message and encrypting the message digest with one's private key. Anyone can validate a signature using the

---

4. In the formula, the notation $x \oplus y$ means the exclusive-OR of x and y, and the notation $x \, \| \, y$ means the concatenation of x and y.

corresponding public key. A trusted digital timestamp can be used to ensure that the signature was created at a particular time. Such a trusted digital timestamp is important, because attackers could create and backdate arbitrary signatures if they ever obtained a private key.

Timestamps

If nonrepudiation is important to the parties in a transaction, it is necessary to use an unforgeable method for digitally timestamping a document. For example, suppose that Alice digitally signs a contract but later wishes she hadn't. She might declare that her private key has been lost or stolen and that some unknown miscreant has used her (now public) private key to sign and backdate the contract. A timestamp can prove that the document was signed and delivered before Alice claims her key was stolen. There are various ways of constructing digital timestamps; one way is for the timestamping service to create a digital signature of the document being stamped combined with a clock value. Obviously, one could argue that the private key of the timestamping service itself is suspect, but a solution is to place all the timestamped documents into a sequence and to create a running message digest of them. Periodically (weekly perhaps), the current digest value is widely published, so even the timestamping service itself cannot cheat. Surety, Inc. operates such a *digital notary* service (www.surety.com).

Certificates

A public-key certificate is a digital document containing a public key, the name of the key's owner (called a *distinguished name*), dates of validity, and other information, all digitally signed using the private key of a certification authority. This subject is so sufficiently important to have an entire section devoted to it; see Certificates and Certificate Authorities, which begins on page 252.

Key Exchange

Because public-key algorithms are slow compared to symmetric-key algorithms, the two systems are often used in combination. A public-key system is used for authentication and to convey an encrypted *session key*, and a symmetric algorithm is used for bulk data encryption with that key. However, if another method of authentication is available, then a key-exchange algorithm can be used to establish a session key. The best-known key-exchange algorithm is Diffie-Hellman, named after its inventors. Such an approach may offer advantages in certain circumstances.

Secret Sharing

From a security point of view, the safest way to keep a document secret is to have only one copy of it (that is, put all your eggs in one basket, and then watch that basket). However, such an approach runs the risk that a natural disaster or other catastrophic event will destroy the only copy. It is also risky to keep multiple copies, because doing so increases the chances that one will be lost. Now suppose the secret is broken up into three parts, such that any two can be used to reconstruct the secret. Such a scheme is called *secret sharing*. In general, a secret can be divided into n parts, and any m parts can be used to recover the secret (with $m \leq n$). If fewer than m parts are available, no information about the secret is revealed. This technique provides safety for the secret, since any $n - m$ parts can be lost before the secret itself is lost, and it provides substantial security, because m independent attacks must be made to gather enough parts. Of course, even one attack may give warning that evildoers are afoot.

A related idea is known as *secret splitting*, which is equivalent to secret sharing with $n = m$. Secret splitting is sometimes used for key distribution, with the parts of the key being sent through different communications channels. One way to split a secret into n parts is to choose n numbers, such that the exclusive-OR of all of the numbers yields the original secret.

Key Management

Key management is the hardest part of cryptography. Key management has to do with the creation, distribution, storage, and destruction of cryptographic keys. A key is at least as valuable as all of the information legitimately encrypted with it. We say "at least" because if an attacker has a key, he can also create unauthorized messages and introduce them into the system.

Key Generation

The main requirement for cryptographic keys is that they be chosen at random. Unfortunately, true randomness is very difficult to achieve. Because of this, many systems attempt to mix changing data from several sources, but this approach is often unsuccessful. For example, an early version of a popular secure Web browser created cryptographic keys that were based in part on the time of day, as given by the machine's clock. The attackers in this case knew the approximate time that the keys were generated, so they were able to test a small set of possible keys using only a few minutes of computer time.

There are true random number generators, which are based on such natural physical phenomena as radioactivity and shot noise. These devices are not broadly deployed and are often expensive. For keys generated by computer software, two solutions are popular.

- User input

  For long-term keys, key generators rely on input from outside the computer. Typically, the user is asked to type randomly for a while. The letters typed are ignored, and instead slight random variations in the interarrival time of keystrokes are used.

- Pseudorandom

  For moment-to-moment creation of short-term keys, key generation is pseudorandom, combining unpredictable pieces of information such as the process identifier, the computer's real-time clock, the number of hardware interrupts received, and so forth. None of these items alone is random enough, but they can be combined into a *randomness pool*. This pool can then be used to generate keys that are sufficiently random for most purposes.

Even when the keys are randomly generated, there may be some additional challenges in creating them. Sometimes a cryptosystem will have some keys, or some patterns of keys, that are known to be weaker in some way than an average key chosen at random. The key-generation procedures must avoid these weak keys.

Passwords intended for human use are also keys. Unfortunately, when people choose their own passwords, they tend to choose poor ones. Just as unfortunately, if users are assigned passwords by a computer, they write them down. (Actually, in an era of network threats to security, writing down a really good password and sticking it in your purse may be the best choice. To protect against individuals with physical access, write down only part of the password and remember the rest.) The usual advice is to use a long, memorable password, such as a multiword *pass phrase* or a password composed of multiple words separated by weird punctuation.

Key Storage

After good cryptographic keys are generated, they must be stored somewhere. Proper storage for both short and long periods of time is essential to good security. During the lifetime of a key, it may be used and stored in many different places, such as the following.

- In memory

  When a key is used by a computer, it must necessarily be in memory. This is a problem on most computers, because the contents of memory may be available to other software running on the same system. On a PC, there is no real defense against this threat, because PC operating systems provide no protection. Traditional multiuser operating systems prevent users from reading or writing the memory allocated to other users. Often, however, a privileged user or a debugger necessarily has access to the memory of other processes. For these reasons, keys used on a system are only as secure as access to the machine and the password of the system administrator. To mitigate the risks of online storage, good practice includes zeroing out all storage used for keys as soon as they are no longer needed.

- On disk

  Cryptographic keys are frequently stored in disk files, because they are too long and too random to be entered by hand. Key files on disk are frequently stored in encrypted form. The good news is that stealing the encrypted file may not benefit the attacker. The bad news is that the security of all the keys in the file is only as good as that of the master key, which is frequently a human-sensible password, not a true random key. In addition, one should understand where the file password itself is kept. If the system needs to be able to restart automatically after a power failure, the password for the key file must be online somewhere. If automatic restart is not required, the system might prompt an operator to enter the key file password. In this case the operator might wonder if the prompt is from the real key unlocking software or from a clever imitation seeking only to steal the key file password. Because of these limitations, security for encrypted key files generally also reduces to the physical security of the computer combined with the security of the administrator password. And do not forget that the key file will be present on backup tapes. How are backups handled and stored?

- In protected hardware

  Commercial systems often use protected hardware devices such as cryptographic accelerators and smart cards both to store keys and to perform cryptographic operations. Because the key never leaves the device, which is designed to be tamper-proof, the key is physically protected. This approach is not entirely without risks, however. Although it may be impossible to steal a key stored in this way (at least not without being detected), it still may be possible for rogue software to command the use of the keys to decrypt or encrypt messages on behalf of unauthorized parties.

- In offline storage

  Some systems take a different approach for truly valuable keys. In these systems, the key is not kept online at all but is used only on isolated computer systems and stored in a vault when not in use. If having even a single copy is too risky, secret sharing may be used to split the key into a number of separate parts, some subset of which are needed to re-create the key. When keys, or the keys to unlock encrypted key files, are kept offline, there must be documented procedures for access to the keys as well as for how they are handled, stored, and destroyed.

Key Destruction

In many cases, cryptographic keys remain valuable long after they leave service. An attacker might record all the ciphertext encrypted under a key and hold it for a long period. If the key becomes available later, all the saved ciphertext can be decrypted easily. Here are some suggestions for destroying keys when they are no longer needed.

- Keys stored in memory—Zero immediately after use.
- Keys stored on disk—Overwrite multiple times with 0s, 1s, alternating patterns, and random patterns. It turns out that it is possible to analyze "erased" magnetic media several layers deep, so this process must be especially thorough.
- Keys stored on paper—Burn or shred with a confetti shredder, not a strip shredder.

- Keys stored on backup tapes—If you must keep backup tapes of keys, keep them on segregated tapes that contain no other vital information. Then they can be easily destroyed when they are no longer needed.

Key Distribution

Sometimes keys do not need to be distributed. For example, when cryptography is used to encrypt files on the disk of a personal computer, there is no need to distribute the key to anyone. For communications security, however, two or more persons, located at some distance from one another, must exchange keys. When two people are involved, the situation is fraught with peril. When a whole network of keys must be distributed, the situation gets complicated.

There are several methods of sharing a key between two people.

- Meet in person.

  This procedure is the simplest to understand, but it doesn't scale well to thousands of people, and it is expensive. An entire set of keys can be exchanged in advance in this way, but then they must all be stored securely.

- Send the key by courier.

  The essential problem is whether or not to trust the courier. One can split the key and send the parts by different routes, but this adds to the expense. This method also does not scale well.

- Use a master key, also known as a *key-exchange key*, to encrypt session keys.

  This is a time-tested method, especially if the key-exchange keys are stored in protected hardware.

- Use public-key cryptography or a key-exchange protocol.

  These schemes permit the secure exchange of keys with someone—but with whom? The problem is translated from privacy to authentication. For public-key systems, the usual solution is to use certificates. For key-exchange protocols, common solutions include both digital signatures and out-of-band confirmations, such as telephone calls. It is particularly important to guard against man-in-the-middle attacks, in which an attacker impersonates each party with respect to the other.

When more than two parties must communicate, pairwise key exchange quickly becomes unmanageable. In such cases, it is common to use either a key-distribution center (KDC) or public-key certificates.

A KDC is a central, trusted authority that shares a separate master key with each member of the network. When two parties want to communicate, they use a session key provided by the KDC. The KDC may distribute the pairwise session keys in batch, or it can operate in real time to create keys as the need arises. The Kerberos system, originally developed at MIT, uses this basic scheme. A KDC-based system can be constructed entirely with symmetric cryptography.

When public-key systems are used, the usual technique is to create an infrastructure of public-key certificates. As mentioned previously, a certificate binds a public key to a name by having a trusted third party (the certificate authority) sign the certificate. These certificates can be freely published and exchanged over open communications channels. Parties wanting to communicate use the public key from the certificate of their chosen correspondent to encrypt a session key.

Both of these schemes require a central authority of some sort. Either an online KDC creates keys as needed, or an offline KDC distributes keys, or an offline authority certifies public keys. The trade-offs are in the details. Is a reliable online service required? How are keys revoked if they are lost or stolen? Does the KDC have the ability to read all messages? Is it trusted not to do so? The public-key systems seem to be the most powerful when two parties with no prior relationship want to communicate, provided that each is willing to trust a third party to authenticate the other.

Certificates and Certificate Authorities

A public-key certificate is a message containing a public key, a name, and some dates of validity, all signed by the private key of a trusted certificate authority (CA).

The primary purpose of a certificate is to attest to the connection between the public key and the name of its owner. One should read a certificate as, "I, the certification authority, attest that the attached public key belongs to the entity named herein." Certificates are very useful because they offer a solution to the problem of authentication without requiring an online KDC. Alice and Bob can go to the CA independently for their public keys to be signed. When Alice wants to communicate with Bob, she sends Bob her public-key certificate along with her signed message. Bob is able to validate the certificate because the public key of the CA is (and must be) known to everyone. The other situation in which a public-key certificate is very useful is when Alice wants to send an encrypted message to Bob. If Alice does not already have Bob's public key, she first obtains it either from Bob directly or from a directory service. In both cases, Alice wants to be sure that the key really belongs to Bob, because it is possible that someone has tampered with the directory service. Fortunately, a certificate stands by itself—built into it is the statement from the CA that the public key is Bob's. Alice might then wonder if the person using Bob's certificate is really Bob. She can be sure of this because only Bob has the private key that matches the public key in Bob's certificate.

The standard format for certificates is the ITU standard X.509. Two versions are in common use. X.509 version 1 certificates contain a public key, the distinguished name (an X.500 name) of the owner, dates of validity, the distinguished name of the certificate authority, and the signature of the CA. X.509 version 3 certificates also contain a flexible set of attribute/value pairs.

The best-known commercial CA is VeriSign (www.verisign.com). Several companies sell public-key systems, including certificate-issuing systems, which can be used to set up a complete public-key infrastructure.

Summary

Cryptography provides the essential tools for establishing privacy, authentication, message integrity, and sometimes nonrepudiation on an open network. Cryptography provides the machinery that makes possible such technologies as SSL/TLS for secure communications on the Web. In effect, cryptography makes it possible to accomplish at a distance, over an open and untrustworthy network, what would otherwise require face-to-face meetings.

CHAPTER 14   *Security*

You can wear a flak jacket, but still be hit by a bus.
—Shikhar Ghosh[1]

Concerns About Security

Lack of security is often cited as one of the greatest barriers to Internet commerce, but in fact the possibility of security is one of the great enablers of Internet commerce. Security of systems for electronic commerce is a business problem involving risk management and ease of use, not merely a technology problem. Technologies such as public-key encryption provide critical components of an overall solution, but they are not enough. In this chapter we suggest some ways to think about the security of the entire system; we review the technologies of security; and we discuss several related areas, such as export control. Although many of the topics here are relevant for Internet security in general, not just for commerce, our focus is on what is necessary to build Internet commerce applications.

Although there are good reasons for caution regarding security issues, it is possible to do business on the Internet today with a secure system, using the principles described in this chapter. These principles apply both to systems designed from scratch as well as to systems built around off-the-shelf products for Internet commerce.

Readers less interested in the technical details should read the first few sections to gain an understanding of the basics and then skim the remainder of the chapter. Those interested in more depth than we provide here should refer to the references at the end of the book.

---

1. Overheard in the office at Open Market, Inc.

Why We Worry About Security for Internet Commerce

Many people have heard vague stories and statements about the security of Internet commerce, and their first reaction is caution (sometimes paralyzing caution). Others wonder what all the fuss is about, because we do not spend much time worrying about the security of transactions in the physical world. Why is the Internet different? Why does it inspire such worries? There are actually many reasons why the Internet is different, and why we should be cautious.

The Physical World Does Worry About Security

Many of the issues we call "security problems" for Internet commerce are the online analogs of real-world business issues. We want certain kinds of business communications to be private, we expect to be paid with real money, we require personal signatures on contracts, and so on. These expectations, and the means by which we accomplish them, have been developed over thousands of years—through the entire history of commerce. On the Internet, we are faced with these issues in a different context, so we are forced to make them explicit and to develop new solutions, all over a comparatively short period of time.

Our Computers Are Connected

Throughout most of the history of computers, one had to be in the same room as the computer to use it, or at least on a directly connected terminal. As long as only trusted users had access to the rooms and the terminals, the security of the system itself was not so important. On the Internet, we are allowing anyone in the world to use our computers, if only (we hope) in a small way, such as to fetch a Web page. But now we have created a hole in the dike, and we must be careful how we design, implement, and operate our systems to ensure that the entire dike is not swept away.

The Network Is Public

An *internetwork* is an interconnected collection of networks, and the *Internet* (with a capital *I*) is the biggest interconnected data network in the world. The individual networks are owned by thousands of different individuals and organizations, and there is no central control of the network at all. What holds the Internet together is an agreement on common protocols and the fact that networks carry traffic for each other. For example, in the early days of the Internet, it was common for network packets to traverse university networks where any sufficiently motivated and clever undergraduate could read them. By contrast, in most countries, the telephone system evolved under the control of a single entity. But even in the early days of the telephone, privacy was a problem. Party lines were common, with multiple people sharing the same line. Telephone operators, especially in small towns, could—and did—listen to conversations. As the system evolved over many years, the technology and the organizations changed so that we now expect our telephone calls to be private. Indeed, so strong is this expectation that many people are surprised when cellular phone conversations are recorded, despite the fact that cellular phones are radios.

The Network Is Digital

Given access to the telephone system, it is still difficult —or at least time-consuming—to get useful information by listening to telephone calls. If one can target a particular person directly, of course, it is much easier. But if one simply listens to random telephone calls, it may be quite a while before one gets so much as a credit card number. A computer network, on the other hand, makes it possible to listen to many "conversations" simultaneously. Moreover, a computer can sift through the conversations looking for particular patterns, such as the numeric pattern of a credit card number, without the attacker having to do any work personally.

Computers Collect Data

Suppose that we keep a (paper) file on each customer in our file cabinet, and that one item in each file is a credit card number. An attacker with access to the file cabinet can go through each file and collect a list of credit card numbers—a feasible though tedious attack. If, on the other hand, we have a single sheet of paper listing all the customers and their credit card numbers, then the attacker's job is much easier. Computer systems are frequently like that: the desired (and sensitive) data is easily accessible, or programs can be used to perform searches. The use of the computer by itself may make certain kinds of attacks possible, so we must address problems that are not "realistic attacks" in a world without computers.

Computers Can Be Programmed

As we have just seen, one of the problems is that an attacker can use a computer to sift through data looking for important information. Computers can also be programmed for other nefarious activities, such as submitting hundreds (or thousands) of fraudulent orders or probing for ways to gain access to a computer system. In particular, sophisticated attackers can write and distribute programs that are used by unskilled attackers (sometimes called *script kiddies*). Such tools make unskilled attackers much more dangerous. It is as if one could easily get a simple-to-use machine for picking locks, rather than having to learn and practice in order to be an effective lock picker.

Without Good Security, Computer Fraud Is Untraceable

On an insecure computer system, an attacker may leave no traces. Crimes in the physical world always leave some physical evidence—a witness, footprints, fingerprints, pictures on a security camera, and so on. Security and cryptographic subsystems both protect the system and provide some traces of what actions have been performed, and by whom. Because we create the entire environment on the computer, we must also create these subsystems—there are no properties of nature to help us. Such subsystems may be built into the computer system, or they may be built to observe its behavior from outside.

Computers Are Not Perfect Replacements for Humans

In many respects, computerized order taking is cheaper and more efficient than having a person answer telephone calls and write down orders. On the other hand, a person can be more flexible in working with a customer or can observe something unusual about an order or a pattern of orders. Machines do not have such flexibility. It may even be the case that some people are more willing to lie to a computerized system than they are to a person on the telephone, making the set of possible attackers much larger.

The Internet Seems Anonymous and Distant

In many ways, communication over the Internet seems more abstract, more impersonal, or less real than communication in person, or even over the telephone. This "virtualness" means that some people may try to defraud, confuse, or play a prank on a distant, faceless Web site when they would never think of doing such a thing to a neighborhood store. Conversely, this distance means that it is all the more important that consumers be assured that they are dealing with the business they intend to deal with. It is hard in the physical world to fool people into thinking they are at a well-known department store, but such deception can be much easier online. Even in the physical world, problems like this can arise: there have been instances in which fake ATMs were set up to collect account numbers and PINs.

Information Commerce Is Different

Many of our security concerns are especially true for information commerce. Online information is easy to copy, distribute, and modify. If we are selling information, we want it delivered only to the buyer, not to anyone who happens to be eavesdropping. In the physical world, a mail carrier can copy a magazine, but doing so requires a fair bit of effort, whereas copying the electronic version requires just a few keystrokes. As buyers of information, we want to be sure that the information sent is what we receive. Again, it requires substantial effort to intercept and modify a piece of physical mail, but it is much easier electronically. Sellers of information usually want to deliver the digital goods immediately, so they have no opportunity for later checks as they do in mail-order retail. They do not even have a delivery address in the physical world, so it is exceedingly difficult to track down a fraudulent transaction.

The Legal System Must Catch Up

Many of the problems that we have described here are handled by the legal system, which generally relies on many pieces of physical evidence—contracts on paper, signatures, delivery addresses, and so on—in establishing a case. We take it for granted that a person's signature is so difficult to forge that it is very hard to prove that one did not sign something if the signature appears to be legitimate. What substitutes for the signature in Internet commerce? In most cases (if at all), we use digital signatures, which is a new technology with its own complex and subtle properties. Similarly, other areas of the law—many of them so familiar that we hardly think about them— are challenged by the changes in technology.

There Are Proven Paths of Attack

Computer systems have proven vulnerable in the past to attackers, so we must be careful and vigilant with new systems for Internet commerce. There is a perception that there is a problem. Internet security has become front-page news for the *New York Times* and the *Wall Street Journal,* so many people—both buyers and sellers—are concerned about the security issues. Even where the risks may seem lower than some in the physical world, today the perception is that the risks are much higher, so it is important that they be addressed in the design and implementation of systems for Internet commerce.

Because We Can

One of the remarkable things about cryptography is the kind of protection it gives us for many applications. Internet commerce applications are among the easiest to secure with cryptography, but cryptography will increasingly be used in the physical world as we understand better how to combat many kinds of crime by judicious use of the strong security systems originally developed for the online world.

Risk of the Unknown

Finally, we always worry about diving into uncharted waters. Our current business and legal systems are so familiar that we tend not to think about how we got to where we are today. It is often useful to recall the evolution of money, bank vaults, the law of contracts, and the telephone system as we recapitulate much of that evolution over a very short period of time.

Thinking About Security

Most experienced practitioners find it appropriate to think of security as a problem of managing risk. This is true for three reasons. First, the security you need depends on what you are trying to protect. Banks use different security systems than retail stores, for example. Second, additional security almost always comes with additional cost, inconvenience, or delay. At some point, the costs of adding security outweigh the advantages. Third, there is no point in making the security of a system much stronger in one area than in another, because a chain is only as strong as its weakest link.

In reality, security is a property of the entire system. The security of a bank, for example, depends on its vault, guards, video cameras, motion sensors, the vigilance of employees, and the procedures for operating all of the equipment and handling problems. Similarly, the security of an Internet commerce system requires appropriate technology, a clear understanding of what is being protected, and careful operation and monitoring by the people running it.

Technology

In effect, technology components are the tools in the security toolbox that are to be used in constructing a secure system. These components include cryptographic mechanisms, secure communications protocols, means of storing sensitive information, and so on. Most discussions about security, especially for Internet commerce, focus on these components, and we describe them in more detail later in this chapter.

Policies and Procedures

A security policy defines what is being protected, and why. It outlines the threats against the system that we want to defend against. By doing so, it allows us to design a security subsystem to protect the application as well as to evaluate the resulting implementation to see if the security goals are being satisfied. Over time, the policy can also be used to guide an evaluation of whether or not the system is operating correctly. Of course, the policy itself may evolve over time, with corresponding changes in the implementation of the security subsystems. It is especially important for the policy to evolve along with changes in the business, because such changes may alter the nature of the risks involved. For example, a large business may simply attract more of the wrong kind of attention than a small one.

Procedures record how the system should be operated to comply with the policy. Writing them down allows the right things to be done again and again, instead of being done when (or if) someone remembers to do them.

People

It is often said that people are the weakest link in any computer security system, because they can be tricked, persuaded, or coerced into assisting attackers.[2] Much of the time, they might not even be aware of what they are doing. This is why proper training about security issues is essential, and not just for the operators. Everyone involved with the system should be aware of the security policy, the mechanisms used to implement the policy, and his or her own responsibilities for safeguarding information. We outline some specific ideas later in this chapter.

---

2. This is often called *social engineering*.

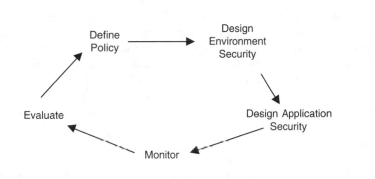

FIGURE 14-1. Security Design Cycle

Security Design

With these issues in mind, we turn to the high-level design of secure systems. The security design should be part of a project from its very beginning, because it is much more expensive to add security after the fact than to design security into the system from the start. We recommend following a five-step process for the security design of a system for electronic commerce.

1. Create the security policy.
2. Add appropriate security mechanisms to the application.
3. Design the security of the physical, network, and computer system environment.
4. Develop feedback, monitoring, and auditing mechanisms to observe the system in operation.
5. Use the results of monitoring and auditing to refine the design, implementation, and operation of the system.

This cycle is depicted graphically in Figure 14-1.

Creating the Security Policy

The first step in a security design is the creation of the security policy. A policy should cover the entire system, including information systems (computers and networks), data (development, production, and backup information), and people (operators, maintenance personnel, and customers). The policy should include a discussion of what is being protected, what kinds of protection are needed, who is responsible for different parts of the system, any necessary training, and what kinds of monitoring and auditing are required.

Designing the Environment

The second step is to design the environment for the application. The environment design includes all of the components outside the application itself, such as the computers, operating systems, networks, and physical location. Often the environment may provide some capabilities or protection for the application, so the application need not duplicate them. (Note, however, that such capabilities should be documented so that the application can be re-created elsewhere should the need arise.) In other cases, the environment may constrain the application in certain ways or require that special security measures be taken by the application because they are not part of the environment.

For example, suppose an application operates on systems protected by strong physical security. Furthermore, the operators perform all of their work on local consoles. In this case, the application may place less emphasis on authentication and access control for management operations, because it can assume that the operators must have been authenticated to gain access in the first place. An application designed to be managed remotely, however, will have a very different set of concerns. Note, however, that we did not say that the application would have *no* emphasis on authentication and access control. It is still good practice for the application to have its own means of authentication and access control, because it is possible for the physical security mechanisms to fail.

In practice, the design of the environment and the design of the application security mechanisms may interact a good deal. Some security problems may be easier to solve in the application than in the environment, and vice versa. In some cases, especially in product design, the application may impose some requirements on the environment in which it will be used. The important thing is to consider the design of the entire system—application and environment—in developing the security design.

Designing the Application Security Mechanisms

The third step in security design is providing security mechanisms for the application itself. The general design of the application, along with the security policy, should already provide the requirements for what is being protected and give some guidance on the kind of protection needed. The security design, then, can apply technology components, such as cryptography, authentication, and authorization systems. In addition to these generic mechanisms for controlling access to information, there may be some specific requirements of the application itself. For example, if the application involves the sale of software over the network, the security system might include product keys that permit the software to run only on the particular customer's computer. As in this example, the security required for an application often goes well beyond simply encrypting communications on an open network or protecting against attackers breaking into a computer system.

Monitoring and Auditing

Beyond even the special requirements of a particular application, security requires feedback mechanisms to ensure that the security mechanisms are working correctly, containment mechanisms to limit the extent of damage, and recovery mechanisms in the event of a problem. In the physical world, there is still a role for the human security guard, who makes sure that the locks on the doors are actually locked. In the electronic realm, these checks and balances take the form of audit trails, velocity checks, and customer service. The information provided by such mechanisms can be used in many ways: re-creating what happened if a problem occurs, checking to ensure that attacks are unsuccessful, verifying that the operation complies with the security policy, and evaluating whether or not the security policy, design, and mechanisms are effective for the application.

Computer security experts often point out that security is a property of the entire system. The designers and operators of a service must think carefully about the application, the risks, and the value at stake before deciding on the level of security to be provided, and within each level they must think about the relative strength of the security mechanisms deployed.

Analyzing Risk

Part of designing an appropriate security policy is determining what level of protection is warranted against what kinds of threats. A bank, for example, faces different risks than a home owner, and the bank is therefore willing to pay more to protect itself against those risks. Many choices in computer security are determined by how much the security measures cost (in terms of money, performance, or inconvenience). Without a good understanding of the benefits of particular security measures, it is impossible to evaluate the choices from a business point of view. In this section, we look at how to analyze computer security risks and evaluate means of reducing those risks.

Adversaries

The first step is to "know thy enemy." People often begin by focusing on types of attacks and the ensuing damage, but the means of attack are merely tools. A determined attacker, for example, may be willing to work very hard to penetrate a system, whereas a casual attacker may give up easily. Both may try the same kinds of attacks, but the persistence of the attacker can make a big difference. Hence, it is important to ask the following questions.

1. Who are your adversaries?
2. What are their intentions?
3. What are their resources?

Here are some potential groups of attackers to consider.

- Crackers

  Crackers are the *cyberpunks* who like to break into computer systems for fun, to commit vandalism, or to show off. Crackers may use off-the-shelf attack software from the Net or from magazines, perhaps without really understanding it. Crackers typically do not have powerful computing resources, and their intentions are frequently not malicious. They often cause substantial damage, whether by vandalizing systems, disrupting operations, or just taking up the time of systems staff trying to identify the damage and repair it.

- Researchers

  Researchers may work very hard to expose weaknesses in secure protocols and publish those weaknesses on the Net. Their revelations cause publicity and embarrassment but lead indirectly to more secure systems. Researchers typically have access to substantial computing resources, ranging from networks of idle networked computers to special-purpose hardware or supercomputers.

- Criminals

  Even without the Internet, there is an immense amount of white-collar crime, much of it exploiting weaknesses in computer systems. Because the Internet is both ubiquitous and anonymous, it has become an attractive venue for crime. Internet crimes range from simple fraud with stolen credit card numbers to sophisticated attacks for access to money or information. Criminals may not have the resources to break encryption schemes, but they can easily afford to bribe employees or other individuals with access to electronic commerce systems. The usual motivation of criminals is financial gain.

- Competitors

  Competitors probably will not break into your computer systems to steal money or destroy records, but they might want to gain access to your customer lists or business plans. In addition, a competitor who learns of weaknesses in the security of your systems might use that information against you in competitive sales situations or to generate bad publicity for you. Although corporations may have large resources, they are not likely to spend large amounts of money in illegal or unethical ways.

- Governments

  In an intensely competitive world economy, more and more government intelligence agencies are working to the economic advantage of domestic industry at the expense of foreign industry. Such organizations typically are not after direct financial rewards; instead they focus on proprietary design information, pricing information, and accurate intelligence about competitive sales situations. Government intelligence agencies have immense resources at their disposal.

- Insiders

  Disaffected, disgruntled, or greedy employees may pose the most serious threats to the security of electronic commerce systems. Insiders, by definition, have access to sensitive systems and information. There are technical ways to safeguard systems, such as protected hardware devices, but audit trails, cross checks, and good employee relations are essential. One of the most important decisions in designing an application is how much security is oriented toward external threats and how much toward internal threats.

- Anyone with physical access

  Anyone with physical access to facilities is a potential security threat. Cleaning crews, delivery personnel, contractors, visitors, and temporary workers all have access but may not be subject to the same training, scrutiny, and supervision as full-time staff.

Different organizations will assess the risks posed by each of these groups differently, but it is important to consider all of them as well as any others you might think of.

Threats

With some idea about who the potential attackers are, we can consider the types of possible attacks. For example, communications over open networks are exposed to many threats, such as eavesdropping, masquerading, and others. Furthermore, the client and server computers may be attacked, and an application itself may be subject to attack entirely outside the client-server realm. Here are several types of attacks that could be mounted against these systems.

- Service interruption or degradation

  This type of problem can be caused by failures of equipment such as disks, computers, or networks. More ominously, a denial-of-service attack from the outside may disrupt operations. For example, an attacker could exploit a bug in the operating system of a server—perhaps one unrelated to the commerce application—to crash the system. In such an attack, no private information is disclosed, but the attack interferes with the effective operation of the business. Distributed denial-of-service attacks are especially interesting because they do not necessarily exploit flaws in the system—thousands of remote machines merely overwhelm the application with requests that are individually reasonable. The attacker tries to make it difficult to distinguish real requests from those of the attack.

- Theft and fraud

  An unauthorized user may be able to obtain goods or services fraudulently. This could happen if the authentication system fails, enabling an unauthorized user to impersonate an authorized user. For example, an attacker, by guessing passwords, may be able to gain access to another user's account. In a more complex situation, a user may be able to manufacture unauthorized discount coupons.

- Misappropriation

  Payments from legitimate users may be directed to an unauthorized party. Although this may be difficult when credit cards are used, other payment systems may be more susceptible. For example, one seller, appearing to be legitimate, might sell access to another seller's content. The payment would go to the wrong party, with both the buyer and the legitimate seller being unaware of the diversion.

- Data contamination

  Records kept by the system may be destroyed or rendered untrustworthy. This may be caused by a software bug or an equipment failure, or it may be an active attack. Such an attack can take several forms: the attacker might alter legitimate records or inject false information into the system. A problem with contaminated data may go well beyond any actual modifications. For example, if business records are lost, anyone who is aware of the problem can challenge transactions, knowing that the records cannot be used to defend against the dispute.

- Theft of records

  An attacker may gain access to your business records, confidential information about your system, or private information about your customers. For example, an intruder may steal customer files, perhaps including credit card numbers.

- Content alteration

  Attackers may break into a system and modify its content. For instance, crackers may break into a Web site and paint graffiti over its image files.

- Masquerading

  Attackers create a look-alike Web site, which draws unsuspecting users. For example, attackers might spoof the Domain Name System (DNS) to lure customers to a false site.

The methods used to implement these sorts of attacks are complex and varied. Here are some of the attack mechanisms, which can be combined in interesting ways.

- Eavesdropping

  An intruder listens to the messages going by on the network. The messages may or may not be encrypted, but even if they are, they can still be recorded for later analysis.

- Traffic analysis

  An intruder learns that certain clients are talking to certain servers. Historically, traffic analysis has been very valuable in military and diplomatic situations. For example, a sudden increase in message traffic between the command center and units in the field may indicate that an attack is imminent, even if the messages cannot be decoded. In commercial situations, it may be useful to know that two supposed competitors are talking. Most electronic commerce systems, and Internet systems in general, make no attempt to avoid traffic analysis.

- Cryptanalysis

  An intruder tries to decode encrypted messages. There are many different techniques in this category, including brute force attempts to guess decryption keys, attacks on algorithm and protocol weaknesses, and attacks on the systems for generating and distributing keys.

- Authentication attack

  An intruder masquerades as the server you think you are talking to, or as a legitimate customer. This is also a broad category, including guessing of passwords, stealing a legitimate user's credentials, and so on.

- Substitution attack

  An intruder substitutes all or part of a message with something different.

- Skimming

  An intruder may attack the system a little at a time, spread out to such a degree that the overall impact remains undetected. For example, if an attacker has a large supply of stolen credit card numbers, each may be used only once.

Basic Computer Security

Computer security is a subject worthy of several books, and some good ones are listed at the end of this book. In addition, computer security is always changing. New hardware and new software arrive constantly, and the rapid evolution of Internet technologies only compounds the problem. New systems, and even changes in existing systems, require new security analyses. Beyond the technology evolution, changing business requirements demand system changes as well.

Key Security Issues

Computer security has many enemies, including complexity, flexibility, and people. Complex software has bugs, which can be exploited by an adversary. Very flexible software is difficult to configure correctly, which leads to errors. An excessive number of users leads to diffusion of the responsibility for security.

- Complexity

  Software has bugs, and more complex software has more bugs. Sometimes bugs are fairly harmless. When they are not, they may open paths of attack. This kind of bug often occurs when software is given unexpected inputs. Although the software may work when the input is within bounds, it may fail in dangerous ways when an adversary drives it outside its intended regime. For example, a network application may fail to check the length of character strings submitted over the network. An adversary sends a very long string, which overwrites the application's stack, causing it to execute code sent by the attacker. The adversary now has all the privileges of that application, which may include access to the entire system.

- Flexibility

  Complex systems are often difficult to configure correctly. Configuration entries may appear innocuous but have great consequences for security. Systems that are changed frequently are particularly vulnerable to such problems, and frequent change is common for Internet systems responding to changing business requirements. For example, suppose that a user asks that a file be made readable to everyone temporarily. When the immediate need is over, no one remembers to change it back, leaving a part of the system unprotected.

- People

  Generally speaking, the more people who have access to a computer, the less secure it will be. Although most multiuser computers go to some trouble to isolate users from one another, that isolation is effective only if carefully administered.

Security Principles

When constructing applications for networked computers, the following principles are useful to help ensure the security of the system.

- Keep the security system very simple.

  Complex applications may be unavoidable, along with their attendant bugs. One way to help protect such a system is to isolate it from some kinds of network access with a *firewall.* A firewall limits the kinds of network traffic allowed through to the end system. In practice, a firewall system should be simple enough so that the correctness of the firewall implementation and configuration can be easily evaluated. *If you have some complex software, protect it from the bad guys with some simple software.*

- Limit changes in system configuration.

  Every change in the configuration of the system is a potential source of security problems. Obviously, a mistake in configuration may open a hole, but sometimes even a seemingly correct change may cause a problem in combination with other configuration options. In any event, careful records of changes are essential. *If you do not understand the configuration of the system, you do not understand its security.*

- Consider new versions carefully.

  New versions of software may offer attractive new features, but they may also have unknown security problems. You may need some time to learn how to operate them securely. Of course, it is important to track and install patches for security problems as quickly as possible, but other changes should receive cautious deliberation. *New software is seductive, but it may be dangerous.*

Basic Internet Security

The Internet is a worldwide collection of interconnected computer networks. Generally speaking, a computer is connected to the Internet if it has an Internet Protocol (IP) address and can exchange packets with other similarly connected computers. This is possibly too strict a definition, because many machines located on corporate, government, or university networks are partly isolated from the general network by firewalls. These partly isolated machines may not have the ability to exchange network packets directly with the main Internet, but we will consider them to be connected if they have the ability to send and receive electronic mail and the ability to connect to World Wide Web sites.

For convenience, we divide the computer population into clients and servers. Generally speaking, a client is a desktop computer whose function is to accomplish a wide variety of computing tasks for an individual. Server computers, on the other hand, are set up to deliver a more constrained set of services to a wide variety of users. This difference leads to Internet clients and servers generally operating in widely different environments, running different application and communications software, holding different kinds of data, and being subject to different sorts of security problems.

Client Security Issues

The typical Internet client computer is an Intel PC, Macintosh, or desktop workstation, with a TCP/IP protocol stack and a variety of Internet client applications. (If the PC is running server applications, we will consider it to be a server.) There are two key client-security issues to consider: how does the attacker get at the client, and what does he or she do once there?

Methods of Attack on Client Computers

The following are potential methods of attack on client computers.

Physical Access to the Computer

Take a few minutes to wander around your company's offices. Count the unattended computers. If machines are left logged in but unattended at night, they are accessible to the cleaning staff and whoever else has physical access at night. Even if unattended machines are a problem only during business hours, what are the site policies on escorting visitors? Are those policies followed? If visitors are not a problem, insiders who might not want to use their own computer accounts for mischief might feel free to use those of others. Physical access also makes it easy for the attacker to install such things as hardware or software keyboard sniffers.

Opportunistic Introduction of Software (Viruses)

Because personal computers were not designed to be multiuser machines, they are quite vulnerable to computer viruses. The problem is that any program running on a PC has essentially complete access to all hardware and software on the system. A virus can flash messages on your screen, alter other programs to propagate itself, or erase your hard disk. Antivirus software attempts to combat these problems by matching new software against a library of known viruses and by intercepting suspicious system calls.

Classically, viruses get into PCs by riding along with new software as it is loaded. Whenever a floppy disk is written by an infected machine, the virus adds itself to the disk. When the disk is run on another system, the virus has a new home.

Software in the original packaging is not immune. It is possible for viruses to be introduced into software during manufacturing if the master disk becomes infected before duplication. When this happens, it is a source of huge embarrassment to the vendor, but that doesn't help the victims.

Network Security Problems

Personal computers are capable of using network file servers and are usually capable of exporting or publishing the content of the local hard disk to the network. If the security settings of such network file systems are set improperly or not set at all, the computer or the information on it may be compromised. Moreover, because client computers sometimes run network servers, such as personal Web servers, many of the security aspects of operating server computers apply also to clients.

To the extent that clients use insecure communications over their local networks, they are accessible to any machine connected to that LAN. This is particularly important with the widespread use of 802.11b wireless LAN technology. 802.11b incorporates security technology known as *Wired Equivalent Privacy*, but recent exploits have found the built-in security of 802.11b to be essentially worthless.

Directed Attack over the Network

After more than a decade of computer viruses, PC users are beginning to appreciate the dangers of loading new software on their machines. A computer connected to a network, however, is subject to additional forms of attack, based on content and automatically installed software rather than user-installed software.

PC mail software has the ability to transmit attachments in addition to straight text. Attachments are arbitrary documents intended for manipulation and display by particular applications. If the application has security holes, such as unguarded scripting languages, a virus can be sent along with the document. When the unwary user clicks the document in order to see what is in it, the associated application is launched and the virus is in. Some e-mail applications may be subject to e-mail viruses even if the user does not click the attachment. These viruses (or worms) spread by remailing copies of themselves to yet other e-mail addresses found in the local address book.

World Wide Web applets have similar problems. An applet is an executable program attached to a page of Web content. Applets are typically written in the Java programming language or as ActiveX controls. The designers of applet systems appreciate the security risks of running arbitrary programs on unguarded computers, and the Java and ActiveX communities have taken different approaches to the problem. Java applets run in what is called a *sandbox*. The idea is that the applets' activities are confined to the sandbox, so it cannot do anything harmful. The problem with sandboxes is the tension between a sandbox that is sufficiently restrictive to be safe and one that is open enough for the applet to accomplish something useful. ActiveX controls take a different approach; they have full access to the machine but are digitally signed by the vendor. In this case, the question is not "Is this applet safe?" but rather "Do I trust that XYZ Corporation has made sure it is safe?" The Java community is also developing code-signing technology, so this may be the wave of the future—at least until PC software is no longer subject to virus attacks.

Protocol Attacks

An attacker may occasionally be able to exploit knowledge of the client computer to mount an attack against a network security protocol without actually breaking into the client at all. In 1995, students at the University of California at Berkeley, for example, used knowledge about client computers to mount an attack against the software used for generating cryptographic keys for a secure Web protocol. This permitted them to read messages to and from that particular computer.

Tempest

Tempest is the U.S. government code word for electromagnetic shielding of electronic devices. Most computers radiate electromagnetic energy according to their activities. For example, it is possible, at short and medium range, to pick up and re-create the screen image of a PC based on the radiation from its monitor. Hackers are not likely to launch such an attack, but governments are very good at this sort of thing.

Purposes of Attacks on Client Computers

Once a malevolent piece of code gains access to a desktop computer, what are its intentions?

Annoyance

Some attacks do nothing overtly harmful, but simply display messages on the screen or cause a slowdown. Although not destructive to information, these attacks are sources of great irritation, and users must react as though the attacks were dangerous because they are disruptive and *might* be destructive.

Use of Resources

An attacker may have no particular evil intent against the owner of the compromised machine. Instead, the purpose of the attack may be to accomplish some computation that requires more than the perpetrator's own resources. For example, if the attacker wants to break a cryptosystem by brute force attack, a virus may distribute the computations among hundreds or thousands of unsuspecting machines. Distributed denial-of-service attacks also work this way. Thousands of compromised clients are used to mount attacks on other systems.

Destruction of Information

The viruses that people fear are those that alter or erase information. Having one's hard drive erased is certainly inconvenient and frequently irrecoverable, because many people do not back up their machines.[3] If information is subtly altered, the changes may not even be detected.

Theft of Information

As personal computers are used more frequently for electronic commerce, information of real commercial value, such as account numbers or credit card numbers, may be stored there. This information is a potential target. A virus that steals credentials, sends them out via e-mail, and quietly erases itself may be an effective way to anonymously and remotely gather large quantities of card numbers. Even if the credentials are kept in encrypted files, the virus need only wait around until the next time the file is unlocked. E-mail viruses may not be intended to steal information, but this may be a side effect. Some e-mail viruses mail out copies of any documents they find on the local disk to machines further downstream.

Use of Credentials

One approach to the problem of a virus stealing credentials is to put the important information on a smart card. A private key, for example, may never leave the protected hardware of the card, so it is not subject to theft by a virus. However, a virus might still install itself between the keyboard and screen of the computer and the card, so when the user wants to digitally sign one document, the virus is really arranging for

---

3. There is also a school of thought that erasing everything on a PC and starting over every six months or so is a good way to combat the general accretion of software and files. Still, one would like to make the choice for oneself.

the smart card to sign something else entirely. This sort of problem may be really solved only when at least part of the user interface is inaccessible to viruses, such as a smart card with a built-in display.

Server Security Issues

Server computers generally run applications software or provide sets of services to many different users. Sometimes the users will have the ability to log in to the server, whereas in other situations only the administrators can log in. Server computers generally run multiuser operating systems such as UNIX and the various server versions of Windows.

Methods of Attack on Server Computers

Computer attacks are many and subtle. Sometimes an attack may have a limited objective, such as access to a particular file or application, but more frequently the objective is to gain the ability to install new software or run applications with superuser privileges.

Logging in as an Ordinary User

Often the first step in an attack on a server computer is to obtain a login or shell session as an ordinary authorized user of the computer. There are many ways to do this, such as obtaining or guessing a password, locating an unattended terminal, or taking over an existing communications session.

- Guess a password.

  Use a dictionary of common words and names to guess probable passwords. Telephone the help desk posing as a legitimate user, and have the password reset. Spy on network traffic to catch passwords going by. Use a keyboard sniffer virus to grab passwords.

- Take over an existing session.

  Locate an unattended terminal. Use TCP sequence number attack to hijack a connection.

- Inject commands into an existing session.

  Use improper permissions in the X Window System or on terminal answer-backs to inject commands into an existing session.

- Exploit poorly set security controls.

  Break into a trusted host, or masquerade as one, and use a remote shell protocol that permits login without supplying a password at all.

Once an attacker obtains user privileges, he can explore the system, looking for security weaknesses permitting greater privileges or for security controls that have been set incorrectly. In some cases, user privileges are sufficient. For example, if the log files for a business application are configured with world-read protections, then any ordinary user account will have access to them.

Exploiting Bugs in Applications

Because server computers typically use commodity operating systems, many people have access to the software. Attackers can search for possible weaknesses at their leisure.

- Out-of-range input

  Many applications are not written defensively and do not check their inputs for content or size. For example, if an application uses input buffers of fixed size but does not check the lengths of input data, an attacker can feed a very large message to the application, causing the application memory to be overwritten. If the buffer is allocated on the stack, the attacker can actually overwrite the program return addresses and seize control of the application. If the application has privileges, so does the successful attacker. Even if the attacker cannot get control, the application may crash.

- Failure to check input syntax

  Applications that use interpreted languages such as TCL and Perl, or applications that pass commands for evaluation to other applications, are at risk if they fail to check their inputs carefully. If the attacker can persuade the application to execute an input message as a program or to perform variable substitution on a reply message, then security is at risk.

Exploiting Incorrectly Set Security Controls

Even if server applications are bug free, they can be operated in an insecure manner.

- Incorrect file protections

  Server operating systems have elaborate file protection mechanisms that can easily be misconfigured. If application files are read-accessible to an attacker, valuable information may leak out. If application files or queue directories are writable, it may be possible to trick an application into executing an attacker's instructions with elevated privileges.

- Debugging code left accessible

  If networked applications are installed with debugging code accessible, it may be possible for an attacker to use privileged debugging commands remotely. In some well-publicized incidents, debugging access to mailer software has led to penetration of computers on the Internet.

- Poor default configuration

  Many groups operate server or application software following a default installation. Some installation programs leave the system with an insecure configuration.

Purposes of Attacks on Server Computers

In general, all of the purposes of attacks on client computers also apply to attacks on servers, but these purposes have special significance when applied to servers because a break-in may affect services delivered to many individuals and because the concentration of information in a server may have great economic value.

Access to Information

A break-in of a client computer may reveal a single transaction to an attacker, but a successful break-in of the server may reveal all transactions. For example, if credit card numbers are logged on the server, an attacker may obtain thousands of numbers as the result of a single successful attack. (Preventing this result is one of the design goals of the Secure Electronic Transaction protocol.)

Alteration of Information

Electronic commerce servers may store business records. Destruction or alteration of these records may make it impossible for a business to function, report on taxes, or defend against customer disputes. Alteration of the security configuration can leave a trapdoor for later access by the attacker.

Access to Security Credentials

Servers may store security credentials for many users or for communications with other computer systems. For example, in a network protected by cryptography, the cryptographic keys may be kept on disk. Theft of these keys may compromise the entire network.

Denial of Service

An attack on a server computer may be aimed at denial of service to the entire community. If the server can be made to crash repeatedly, or to become bogged down with unauthorized requests, the system can become unusable.

Achieving Application Security

Achieving computer security is difficult, but some general principles apply.

- Limit access to the system.

  The fewer people with login access to a server, the better. Try not to use an application server for general logins. Make sure that system administrators use good passwords and do not leave logged-in terminals unattended. Consider disallowing network access for system administration.

- Use available security tools.

  There are a variety of system configuration checkers and monitors. These tools can probe a system from the outside for known security weaknesses and can also survey file system protections for suspect usage.

- Protect complex systems with simple ones.

  Most server computer operating systems are too complex to be trusted. Firewalls, which will be discussed shortly, are systems that carefully limit access to the server and that are simple enough to trust. Firewalls may also perform auditing and logging functions.

- Make sure the system is *inside the envelope.*

  Many applications work well in the common case. If the behavior of the server is not understood when disks fill up or when the CPU is overloaded or when too many users are connected, put limits in place that trigger alarms when such unusual operating conditions are encountered.

- Record configuration changes.

  Put procedures in place to maintain records of system configuration and an audit trail of changes.

- Create backups.

  Elementary as it sounds, make sure that server software and application data are backed up regularly. Make sure that the security controls for access to backup tapes are appropriate for the information on the backups.

- Ensure that software is properly installed.

  New installations of software are a leading cause of improperly set security controls. Note that few vendors of application software configure their default settings to provide security.

- Apply security patches.

  Keep up-to-date with announced security patches, and install them expeditiously.

Firewalls

A firewall, as illustrated in Figure 14-2, consists of hardware or software (or both) that isolates a private system or network from a public network. The functions of a firewall are as follows.

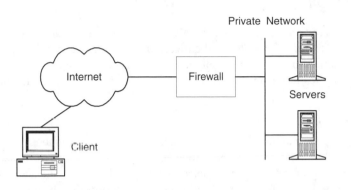

FIGURE 14-2. **Example of an Internet Firewall**

- Packet level filtering

  Firewalls typically include packet-level (network-level) filters that control basic connectivity. Internet Protocol packets, for example, can be accepted or rejected on the basis of source and destination IP addresses, source and destination port numbers, and packet type. These capabilities are used to allow connections from outside the firewall only to particular services on the inside. Another important capability is to reject any packet arriving from the outside that has a source address purporting to come from the inside.

- Application relay

  Firewalls typically implement application protocol relay functions. For example, a relay for the Telnet virtual terminal protocol might permit an outside client to establish a terminal session with an inside host only if the outside user is equipped with a one-time password system such as S/Key or a hardware login token such as SecurID.

- Auditing and logging

  Firewalls create log files of communications activity that are completely independent of the computers on the internal network. These independent audit trails aid containment, because even if an internal system is penetrated, the attacker has no way to erase traces of the attack.

- Concentration of security administration

  If there are multiple server systems inside the firewall, there may be a diffusion of the responsibility for security. The firewall serves as a choke point through which all external communications must pass. As such, it is much easier to manage and operate than multiple independent systems.

Authentication

Authentication is the process of establishing identity as an individual, a function, or a member of a class of individuals. Authentication procedures generally use one or more factors: something you know, something you have, or something you are. A high-security application generally requires at least two factors in the authentication process.

- Something you know

  A password or secret that is known by an individual but not by anyone else. Generally, passwords should not be written down, but arguably this restriction should be relaxed for use on networks. The problem is that people tend to choose poor passwords, so they do not offer much security. Good passwords may be too difficult to remember. Another approach is the use of a pass-phrase consisting of several words.

- Something you have

  A physical key, access card, or passport that is in the physical possession of an individual. In the electronic realm, this may be a hardware token or smart card. Arguably, a complex password or code that is written down is in this category, rather than being "something you know," but traditionally "something you have" also implies that it cannot be copied.

- Something you are

  A fingerprint, retinal pattern, or other so-called biometric that is a physical property of an individual.

Authentication is frequently confused with authorization. One example is an ordinary house key. Possession of the key *authenticates* one as a member of the class of people *authorized* to enter the house. Computer systems generally separate the concepts of authentication and authorization: a known username and password let you log in, but after that your rights are determined by separate *access control lists*.

Passwords

Passwords are frequently used to log in to a computer system or network. The username and password as entered are checked against the password file. If they match, the login is permitted. Passwords can be very secure, but as with most things in security, the devil is in the details.

Choosing Passwords

People tend to choose poor (insecure) passwords, such as words from dictionaries or the name of their spouse. On the other hand, if people do not choose their own passwords, they tend to write them down rather than remember them. In the worst case, passwords wind up on notes stuck to monitor bezels. The usual solution to this problem is to require passwords to be of a specified minimum length, with a mix of letters, numbers, and special characters.

Changing Passwords

In order to preserve security over a long interval, passwords must be changed regularly. Left to themselves, people tend not to do this, or tend to cycle through a small set of different passwords. Some sophistication in the password software is needed in order to enforce regular changes.

Using Passwords at Multiple Sites

When an individual has accounts on multiple computers, or at multiple sites on the Internet, there is a strong tension between using the same password at multiple sites and using different passwords at each site. Using the same password everywhere raises the stakes if the single password is guessed, but using different passwords everywhere makes it very likely that the user will forget one or more of them and be forced to write them down. In either case, having passwords at many different sites compounds the problem of enforcing periodic changes of password.

Password Storage

The password storage system at a password-required site is an obvious security target. The passwords of many individuals are stored in one place, making it a tempting target for attack. The usual way of addressing this problem is to store a hash of each password, rather than storing the passwords in cleartext form, or even encrypted. Because the hash function cannot be reversed, the password cannot be recovered from storage. On the other hand, it is easy to check for a match when a user logs in. In addition to the hash, so-called salt is used as well. Salt is a random number stored with the password file entry that is different for each entry and that is part of the hash computation. Using salt prevents an attacker from computing hashes of many possible passwords and then simply matching against the stored hashes. Such an approach is called a *dictionary attack*.

Default Passwords

There are many, many systems and components that have passwords for administrative or maintenance access, including computer systems, firewalls, and routers. Many of these systems come with default or manufacturers' passwords set, permitting them simply to be plugged in and forgotten. Many of these passwords are never changed and are consequently well known to attackers. A password is useless if not set.

Other Authentication Technologies

Here are some other authentication technologies.

One-Time Passwords

One problem with passwords is that if the password is ever transmitted over an insecure communications channel, the security of the password is suspect. This issue arises, for example, when one logs in to the office computer over a public network or from a customer site. One solution to this problem is to issue each user a set of passwords, each of which can be used only once. Typically the system administrator prints a card for each user, who then crosses out each password after using it. One such system is S/Key, in which a one-way function is used to create a chain of passwords. Each successive password is run through the function to produce the next password. The trick is to use the passwords in reverse order, so that an eavesdropper cannot reproduce the sequence. The central site must store the first password in the sequence and the one most recently used.

Hardware Tokens and Smart Cards

Because the weaknesses of passwords are well known, higher-security applications support the use of hardware devices for authentication. Devices that are restricted to authentication are usually called *tokens*, whereas smart cards can be used for authentication as well as for more general security purposes. Two common types of tokens are made by RSA Security and by Symantec. The RSA Security SecurID card has a window on the front that displays a cryptographically generated random number that changes once a minute. The matching authentication server can duplicate the computation to check the number. The user simply copies the number from the card along with a PIN code into the system. The Symantec Defender card is a small calculator-like device with a numeric keypad and a display. In operation, the system sends the user a challenge code, which is entered into the card along with the user's PIN. The user copies the response code from the card into the system. The server executes the same computation and compares the result.

Smart cards are small cards containing a processor and some memory. These cards may be the size of a credit card, or they may be larger for use with laptop computers, such as PCMCIA cards. Generally, the card memory contains some secret keys for either symmetric or asymmetric cryptography.

Authentication on the Web

The World Wide Web uses a stateless protocol in which each browser request to a server stands alone and does not depend on any context for what has gone before. Therefore, if a Web server wants to authenticate its users, it is necessary to add some

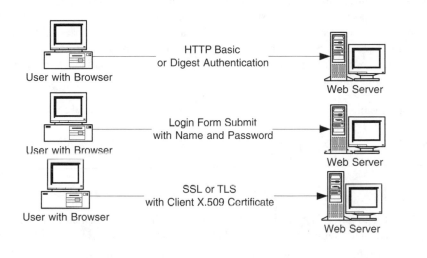

FIGURE 14-3. **Direct Authentication**

kind of authentication to every request as well as to an initial login. In addition, the authentication problem is symmetric: the user wants to know that she is talking to the right server, and the server wants to know that it is talking to the right user.

Client authentication is the process of establishing the user's identity to the satisfaction of the server. We distinguish between systems that authenticate users directly to a commerce server (*direct authentication*) and systems that use third parties as intermediaries (*indirect authentication*).

Direct Authentication

In direct authentication, shown in Figure 14-3, the user authenticates himself directly to the Web server. There are several possible mechanisms for this authentication: basic authentication, digest authentication, login forms, and client certificates.

Basic Authentication

The only authentication mechanism built into HTTP 1.0 is called *basic authentication*. Normally a Web browser making a request to a Web server provides no authentication information. When this is unacceptable to the server, the server responds to the request with an **Unauthorized** code and a realm. The realm is a text string whose purpose is to let the user know which name and password are being requested. Typically the browser will display an authentication pop-up box, with the realm displayed at the top and entry fields for username and password. When the user clicks **OK**, the browser retries the original request, this time supplying the name and password in the HTTP header of the request. The name and password are sent in a coded format that makes them unreadable by eye but trivial to decode with a program. Because the Web is stateless, these credentials must be supplied on every request. Browsers remember which sites require passwords, and supply them automatically on subsequent requests. Some browsers even remember name and password credentials between sessions, so the user need not even remember them (however, they may be available to anyone who uses the same computer).

The main problem with basic authentication is that the password of the user is sent in the clear across the network. This problem can be overcome by using the Secure Sockets Layer (SSL) or Transport Layer Security (TLS), but these protocols introduce a substantial performance penalty when used all the time.

Digest Authentication

Digest authentication is a mechanism for use with HTTP 1.1, defined in IETF RFC-2617. It is a challenge-response protocol in which the server sends the browser a challenge and the browser uses the locally stored password to compute a response. Since the user's password is not sent across the network, digest authentication is much more secure than basic authentication and introduces only a very small performance impact. The digest authentication proposal also includes an optional opaque data field, which the server gives to the browser and the browser hands back to the server. The server can use this field to send an encrypted message to itself, and this message can be used to avoid any database lookups during response validation.

Login Forms

Many Web designers object to basic authentication and digest authentication because those systems give the designers no control over the user experience when someone logs in. Such objections are based partly on their concerns about usability and partly on the simple lack of control and flexibility in the presentation. Both basic authentication and digest authentication are implemented directly by Web browsers, rather than by the HTML Web page delivered by the server. As an alternative, it is possible to use HTML forms to present a login page to users, with a special form field that does not show the password as it is being typed. This approach gives the Web designer nearly total control over the user's experience during the login process.

From a security point of view, however, this method has the same problem as basic authentication: the password is transmitted in cleartext over the network. As with basic authentication, it could be sent using SSL/TLS. An advantage of this method is that the password is sent only once, but then subsequent authenticated requests must use some kind of session mechanism, such as the ones described in the following sections. The combination of a login form with a good session mechanism can be much better than basic authentication, in terms of both the user experience and the security of the resulting system.

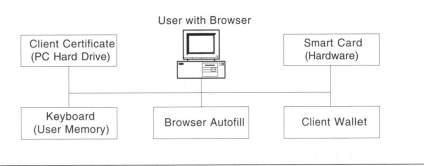

FIGURE 14-4 Credential Storage

Client Certificates

The capability of using public-key certificates for client authentication over the Web first appeared in the S-HTTP protocol in 1994, but this protocol was never widely used. The Secure Sockets Layer (SSL) protocol created by Netscape Communications Corporation introduced the capability of using client certificates in SSL version 2, but such use was not widely deployed until SSL version 3, first supported by Netscape Navigator 3.0 and Microsoft Internet Explorer 3.0. The use of client certificates proceeds in two phases. A client certificate is first created during a conversation with a certificate-issuing server, and thereafter it is available for use with other servers. During certificate creation, the user fills out forms with identification information and creates a public-key pair. The public half of the key, together with the identification, is submitted to the certificate-issuing server, which uses its certificate authority root key to sign the user's public key, creating a certificate. The certificate is returned to the user's browser for storage together with the corresponding private key. Once a client certificate is available, a server wanting to use it for client authentication uses SSL protocol headers to send a request for a certificate to the browser. The browser typically displays a pop-up box allowing the user to select an appropriate certificate from those available and to unlock it with a password. The password protects the private key from other software running on the user's computer. The certificate is transmitted to the server, along with a message signed with the corresponding private key. The certificate creates a connection between the user's identification information and the private key, and the message signed by the private key indicates that the key is indeed in the possession of the user. Together, they let the server know that the user is the individual named in the certificate.

An important problem with these Web authentication techniques is that the end user's PC is usually the weakest link in the security system. Viruses or trapdoors on the PC can easily discover a user's passwords and copy their encryption keys. Hardware devices such as the RSA SecurID provide for one-time passwords. Smart cards keep encryption keys and authentication credentials locked inside protected hardware. These techniques can be very secure, but they are not widely used because of the expense

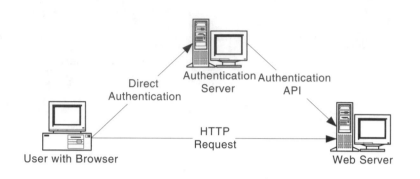

FIGURE 14-5. Indirect Authentication

and the lack of deployed smart card readers on PCs. One area in which hardware solutions may arise first is in wireless, where many new wireless devices include readers for smart cards. Figure 14-4 shows some alternatives for the storage of a user's authentication credentials.

Indirect Authentication

Not all Web authentication occurs directly between the user and the Web server that requires authentication. For indirect authentication, as illustrated in Figure 14-5, the Web server hands off the problem to a remote authentication server. There are several software products that implement third-party authentication, such as those from Netegrity and RSA Security, and there are network service versions, such as Microsoft Passport and the work underway at the Liberty Alliance. The authentication server of a third-party system in turn typically uses one of the direct authentication techniques described above.

Server Authentication

The weakest method of server authentication is to depend on the integrity of the Domain Name System. When the user types *www.xyzcorp.com* into the browser, there is a good chance that the connection will be made to the right server. However, this depends on correct management of many computers, together with constant vigilance by their operators, so stronger methods are desirable.

The most effective means of server authentication available today is the public-key certificate. Secure Web protocols such as SSL permit the server to deliver to the client a public-key certificate signed by a third party—the certification authority (CA). This method requires that the user's browser has the root key for the CA and that SSL/TLS be used for the communications. If the connection succeeds, the user knows that the CA has verified the identity of the server.

In a commercial context this verification may not be adequate, however. Suppose that the user wants to do business with XYZ Corporation, which has an online store. The Web pages for this store may be hosted on a shared computer together with pages from other companies. Consequently, the server certificate may read "Joe's Hosting Service" rather than "XYZ Corporation," which has a good chance of confusing the user. Unfortunately, there is little to be done about this problem.

This problem was handled in the little-used S-HTTP protocol, because every hyperlink in the Web could contain information about the security propertics expected of the destination page. Once the user was satisfied with the initial page, the security properties of subsequent pages would be handled automatically.

Web Sessions

As mentioned earlier, the basic Web protocols are stateless, and each request stands on its own. Consequently, each request must be independently authenticated. This is exactly what happens in basic authentication, in which the user's name and password are passed to the server on each request. The user experience is not bad, because after the first request for name and password from a site, the browser remembers to supply the credentials on subsequent requests. However, the server must independently validate the name and password on every hit. In addition, although the use of a secure protocol such as SSL can overcome the problem of transmitting passwords in the clear, these protocols may not be warranted for all communications, because the content being viewed may not be intrinsically valuable. Digest authentication can solve these problems by making the authentication both secure and lightweight, but it is not widely deployed.

The technique most often used to enable authentication without requiring that all content be encrypted is to create a *session* on top of the basic stateless Web protocols. When the session is entered, the server first authenticates the user. Thereafter, the authentication information is not required on every request, but every request does include information that identifies it as belonging to a particular session. There are two ways to create a Web session today: custom URLs and cookies, as shown in Figure 14-6.

In the custom URL method, the identification of the session is carried in the URL, either as part of the URL query string

    http://www.xyz.com/url/path/name/script.cgi?query&string&with&session_ID

or buried in the URL

    http://www.xyz.com/<sessionId>/url/path/name

FIGURE 14-6. Session Management

The former approach requires that all user interaction be handled by a particular server application, such as a CGI program, that manages the session, and the latter approach requires that the session validation be built into the Web server itself.

In the cookie approach, the session identification information is stored in the browser cookie, so that the browser automatically presents it to the server on every request. This works very well, but there are several problems: not every browser supports cookies, Web proxy servers do not always handle them correctly, and some users may configure their browsers to reject cookies. Even when the mechanism works, if the client communications are not encrypted, the cookie may be stolen by an eavesdropper, who may then use it to gain illegitimate access to the Web site.

For encrypted communications, SSL version 3 and TLS offer an interesting alternative: the client certificate may be requested on the first request to a site. Thereafter, SSL session key caching can be used to reduce the average cost of the authentication by applying it across multiple requests. Both SSL version 3 and TLS offer the added capability of authentication-only connections, which do not encrypt the content or incur the associated performance penalty.

Summary

We have argued that security needs to be a property of the entire system. The essential problem of the security officer is that security has to be strong everywhere, because the attacker needs to find only one weak spot or lapse of operational attention. Security cannot be obtained by use of cryptographic pixie dust alone, although the lack of such technology can leave a system insecure. We advocate a five-step cycle of effort in security: creation of a security policy, addition of security mechanisms and technologies, careful design and operation of the computer and network environment, monitoring and auditing of the operational system, and, finally, evaluation of operations in order to refine the design, implementation, and operation of the system. The security design of the system must also incorporate principles of containment: security problems in one area of the system should be prevented from spreading to other areas.

CHAPTER 15

Payment Systems

Money alone sets all the world in motion.
—Publilius Syrus[1]

The Role of Payment

In many respects, online payment is the foundation of systems for electronic commerce. The ability to take payment distinguishes an electronic commerce system from one that provides only advertising or other communications capabilities. Incorporating payment abilities, however, adds considerable complexity to a system. First, the security of both the payment mechanism and the overall system must be sufficient to protect the system. Second, the system must provide a high degree of integrity for transactions—the system must not lose or inadvertently change a payment transaction.

This chapter considers what happens once the buyer and the seller have agreed on what is being sold and its price. We examine payment systems from several points of view. First, we look at real-world payment systems to understand how we might construct analogous online systems. Second, we describe some of the systems already developed for online payment. Next, we consider how payment for so-called microtransactions might be accomplished. We conclude with a brief discussion of the abstract issue of payment and its role.

---

1. Publilius Syrus (1st century B.C.), *Maxims.*

A Word About Money

Before talking about payment, it is prudent to talk about money. It is convenient to think about two kinds of money: *token* and *notational*. Tokens are like coins or paper money: they have value in and of themselves. In the earliest days of token-based money, the tokens were valued for what they were made of. Today, it is usually the case that token money has value by fiat, because a government has issued the tokens and declared their value.

In contrast, *notational money* refers to something that represents value stored somewhere else. For example, a check has no intrinsic value, but it represents a commitment to transfer money. Moreover, a check cannot be freely transferred around; it is useful only to the party named on it. Payment instruments that extend credit are a variation of notational money. When one uses a credit card, for example, one agrees to pay the designated amount at some point in the future, and the transaction is guaranteed by the financial institution that issued the credit card.[2]

On the Internet, and in the electronic world in general, most systems today use notational money: credit cards, purchase orders (which really represent a promise to pay at some time in the future), and electronic funds transfers. Some newer systems, such as various forms of electronic cash, have not yet gained widespread use, but they are actually uses of token money in electronic form.

Real-World Payment Systems

In many respects, payment online is not very different from payment in the real world. Because we want payment transactions online to have value off the network as well, online payment systems are usually based on existing payment mechanisms. In this section, we review several common payment methods. In particular, we look at the properties that make them attractive for use online or that must be captured in an online analog.

Cash

Cash is perhaps the most familiar and most widely accepted form of payment for face-to-face transactions. For the consumer, it has many important properties.

1. Wide acceptance. Cash is accepted for nearly any transaction (although it is not very common for large ones).

2. Convenience. Cash is easy to use and easy to carry in small quantities.

---

2. Under some circumstances, the bank that issued a credit card may not guarantee the transaction. This is often true for mail-order transactions, where the customer and the card are not physically present.

3. Anonymity. One need not identify oneself to pay in cash.[3]

4. Untraceability. Once cash has been spent, there is no way to trace it back through the chain of those who have possessed it.

5. No buyer transaction costs. The buyer incurs no additional cost for using cash. This makes cash especially useful for small transactions, in which the overhead of a check or credit card would be large compared with the value exchanged. The buyer does have an opportunity cost for holding cash rather than investing the money. Note that a merchant does have some costs for handling cash—transporting it safely to the bank, having it counted by the bank, and so on. Anecdotal reports place these costs at up to 10 percent.

These properties make *online cash* mechanisms attractive for many online transactions, but they also pose some technical challenges in creating such mechanisms. We will discuss some technologies and proposed systems for *electronic cash* systems later.

Credit Cards, Charge Cards, and Debit Cards

Credit cards are very familiar to many consumers, as are various other kinds of charge cards. A credit card, such as one from Visa or MasterCard, operates by extending a buyer credit at the time of purchase, with the actual payment occurring later through a monthly bill. The usual distinction between a *credit card* and a *charge card* is that the balance on a charge card must be paid in full each month, whereas a credit card may carry a balance from month to month, albeit with interest accrued. Cards from Visa and MasterCard are usually credit cards, whereas cards from American Express are usually charge cards. From a merchant's point of view, these cards operate in essentially the same way, and the only difference is whether or not the merchant accepts a particular brand of card. Individual merchants may also have their own store-brand charge or credit cards, for which they handle all of the credit and payment processing.

A related form of payment is a certain class of debit cards that are linked to demand-deposit accounts, such as checking accounts, in banks. These cards usually carry a Visa or MasterCard logo, and they are accepted anywhere that Visa or MasterCard is accepted. Instead of a transaction extending credit, however, the payment is drawn immediately from the linked account. From a merchant's point of view, they operate exactly as credit cards do. This type of card is called an *offline debit card* because the transaction need not be authorized in real time.

By contrast, an *online debit card* requires a real-time authorization using a personal identification number (PIN). Such cards are often ATM cards, and merchants often

---

3. Except for very large transactions, which (in the United States, at least) must be reported to the Internal Revenue Service.

accept them for some kinds of transactions. Like offline debit cards, payment is transferred immediately from the corresponding demand-deposit account.

Merchants pay for the ability to handle credit card transactions. The fees charged vary by the acquiring bank, the size of the merchant, the size of the transaction, the volume of credit card transactions, and the merchant's type of business. For example, a mail-order merchant usually pays more for credit card transactions than a comparable store, because the customer is not present to sign a charge slip. This kind of transaction, known as a *card-not-present* transaction, carries a higher risk that it will not be paid, because the buyer may have stolen the credit card. A typical fee for a retail merchant is 25 cents plus 1.5 percent to 3.0 percent of the total transaction. Mail-order fees can be much higher, ranging from 2.5 percent to 5 percent of the transaction.

Credit cards are very popular for online payment for consumer retail transactions, especially for transactions similar to those performed with credit cards in retail or mail-order businesses off the Net, including ordering of subscriptions to magazines, newsletters, or online information services. Because of the costs associated with credit card transactions, they are inappropriate for individual small transactions. For example, using the rates just given, more than half of the revenue in a $0.50 transaction would go to pay for the credit card transaction. Some approaches to handling small transactions are described in the Micropayments section, which begins on page 312.

Packaging a Payment System

Most consumers think of a credit card as a fairly simple device. We use them for buying things, and later our bank sends a bill. The reality is quite a bit more complex. A credit card is a complex bundle of services.

- Consumer credit

  Most credit cards extend credit to the cardholder. If the cardholder carries a balance from month to month, interest charges accrue. Generally, if the cardholder pays his bill in full each month, no extra charges are made.

- Immediate payment

  Like cash, but unlike checks, credit card transactions result in immediate (overnight) payment to the merchant. This rapid payment can reduce the merchant's requirements for financing inventory.

- Insurance

  Unlike cash, there is no substantial risk of loss to the cardholder. Merely by notifying the card issuer, the card can be disabled, and even without notification, the cardholder's risk is limited.

- Financial clearinghouse

  Credit cards work even when the cardholder's bank is different from the merchant's bank. This simple and perhaps obvious fact makes commerce much easier and is in contrast to, for example, checks. A check drawn on a faraway bank is less likely to be accepted than a local check.

- Global service

  Credit cards handle multiple currencies automatically. The merchant deals in her own local currency, and when the credit card bill arrives, the transactions have all been converted to the cardholder's local currency.

- Record keeping

  Credit cards send periodic statements, which are very useful for reconciling expenses.

- Customer service and dispute resolution

  When a dispute about the quality of a product or nondelivery arises, the cardholder can complain to the card issuer. The merchant's acquiring bank can withhold or reverse payment to the merchant, and this gives the consumer considerable bargaining power to obtain satisfaction.

- Enabling of merchant trust

  To a great degree, consumers can trust merchants who have credit card association logos in their window. The logo means not only that credit card payment is accepted but also that if there is any trouble down the line, the consumer can complain—not to the merchant encountered once in a faraway city, but to his own card-issuing bank.

- Enabling of consumer trust

  To a great degree, merchants can trust consumers who have credit cards. Provided the card is valid and the customer signature matches, the merchant is guaranteed payment. This greatly facilitates commerce.

Credit cards are an expensive means of payment, costing 2 percent to 5 percent of transaction value, but they provide a complex set of services. It is a very interesting thought experiment to disaggregate the credit card and to consider the value of each of the services separately. In addition, when evaluating other payment mechanisms, it is a useful exercise to compare them, feature for feature, against the breadth of services offered by the ubiquitous credit card.

How Credit Card Transactions Work

The steps in a typical credit card transaction are shown in Figure 15-1. After a cardholder gives a credit card to a merchant, the merchant sends an authorization request to the merchant's bank (called an *acquiring bank* or *acquirer*), requesting that the amount of the purchase be reserved against the buyer's credit. The acquirer forwards the request through an interchange network (such as the ones operated by Visa

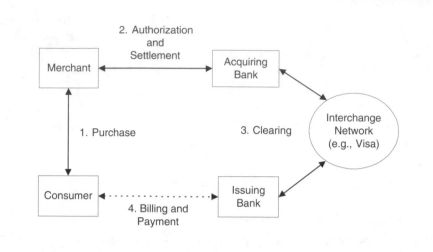

FIGURE 15-1. Credit Card Transaction Flow

and MasterCard) to the bank that issued the buyer's card (called the *issuing bank*). If the credit is available, the issuing bank authorizes the transaction, sending the response back through the network. If not, the issuing bank denies the authorization. The authorization is valid for a specified period of time (three days is common), and it expires at the end of that time unless the transaction has been settled or the authorization renewed.

In most cases, transactions are settled sometime after they are authorized. Authorization responses include codes used for later settlement. Retail store transactions, for example, are typically settled in batches at the end of the day. Mail-order transactions are not settled until the goods are shipped, a requirement usually imposed by the card association rules.

In some cases, it is appropriate to authorize and settle the transaction at the same time. For online systems, this is common for delivery of information products, where the delivery occurs immediately on receipt of payment. Some electronic payment systems combine the final step of payment with the delivery of the information product. Such systems give the buyer greater assurance that the product will be delivered. These systems will be discussed in greater detail later.

In addition to this routine processing of credit card transactions, there are several exceptional situations that must be handled by an online credit card payment system, such as reversing an authorization that is no longer needed, giving credit for a returned item, and applying the appropriate charges when only part of an order can be shipped. In addition, it is very important for vendors of information products to have clear policies for handling customer disputes, because it is much more difficult to return the goods than to return traditional mail-order products.

Computer systems used for processing credit card payments typically connect to computers at acquiring banks for authorization and settlement services. In many cases, the acquirers delegate operation of those computer systems to other organizations, known generically as *card processors*. These companies handle all aspects of the transaction processing and sometimes can act as acquirers themselves. A merchant's banking relationship determines which systems are used for the transaction processing.

As the credit card business evolved, many different communications protocols were created to manage credit card transactions (more than 1,400 of them, by some counts). In addition to standard protocols created by the card associations, many banks created their own to provide enhanced services. Several years ago, the ISO adopted a standard protocol, ISO 8583, for such transactions. ISO 8583 is commonly used for managing card transactions outside the United States, but it is not widely used in the United States. One consequence of a standard emerging from so many different protocols is that the ISO standard has quite a number of optional fields. This variety usually requires specific changes for operation with a given acquirer. To ensure proper operation, acquirers normally require implementations to be certified with a test system before they are put into production use.

Credit card payment is appropriate for a wide range of consumer retail applications. The primary issues are as follows.

1. Privacy of the credit card number and associated information. We describe several methods of providing such security later.

2. Whether or not the transaction values are appropriate for credit card transaction costs. Credit cards are relatively expensive to process, and they may result in chargebacks (with resulting costs to the merchant) if buyers are dissatisfied with their purchases.

3. Whether or not the merchant can create the banking relationship necessary to accept credit cards. Because banks may be reluctant to extend such privileges to new or unfamiliar merchants, it may be difficult for a new business to begin taking credit cards immediately.

Risk Management

There are many aspects of risk management for credit cards; we mention a few here.

- Consumer risk

  In the United States, the Consumer Credit Protection Act limits the liability of the cardholder to $50 in the event his card or card number is used fraudulently. After the cardholder notifies his bank that the card has been stolen, there is no further liability. Frequently, issuing banks do not even charge consumers the $50, on the grounds that it is simply bad public relations. The effect of this law is to place the responsibility for the security of the credit card system on the shoulders of the system designers and operators. Consumers also have substantial recourse in the event of nonperformance by a merchant following a transaction paid for by credit card. The consumer can dispute the charge, and the merchant's bank will retract payment to the merchant until the dispute is settled.

- Merchant risk

  When the cardholder appears in person at the merchant, her card is swiped in an electronic terminal, and the merchant checks the cardholder signature. Generally, if the merchant follows an official protocol for these *card-present transactions*, the merchant's acquiring bank accepts the risk that the card is stolen or fraudulent and guarantees payment to the merchant. On the other hand, when the card is used by mail or telephone, in a card-not-present transaction (also called a *MOTO transaction* for *mail or telephone order*), the merchant is liable in the event of a fraudulent transaction. So far, all Internet transactions are classified as MOTO, although new payment protocols such as SET and 3D Secure may change this. The credit card authorization networks do offer some assistance to the merchant in assessing their risk. One service is the Address Verification Service. The merchant requests the cardholder's billing address from the cardholder, and sends it along with the card authorization request. The purported address is checked against the issuing bank's records, and the response indicates whether there is a match. The merchant can then choose to accept or refuse the transaction. MOTO merchants also build up their own fraud control systems, based on customer history and whatever other information is available.

International Issues

The model of credit card use may be international, but there are regional differences that can affect the design of Internet commerce systems. The following examples illustrate the sorts of issues that arise.

- From and to valid dates

  In the United States, credit cards are usually issued with only an expiration date marked. The expiration date must be entered as part of the authorization request to the card network, so commerce software typically has an order form with fields for card number, card type, and expiration date. In Europe, however, cards are usually issued with both the beginning and the end of the period of validity, and both pieces of information are necessary to authorize a purchase. This means that Internet commerce software for this market must request additional information from the user and route it to the authorization network.

- Bonus payments

  In Japan, it is very common for a substantial portion of annual compensation to be paid to workers in the form of semiannual bonuses. In reaction to this, the retail use of credit cards in Japan has evolved so that the consumer can designate, at the point of sale, that the purchase will be paid for with bonus money. As a consequence, the merchant point-of-sale system has a way of designating a purchase as a bonus payment, and the credit card authorization network passes that information back to the issuing bank. As electronic commerce in Japan grows, Internet commerce software must support this capability as well.

These two examples are relatively minor items whose effects ripple throughout software for Internet commerce. The user interface for the order form needs new fields with new validation routines; the transaction database needs new storage fields for the new capabilities; and the payment processing interfaces need to route additional information to the financial authorization networks. This complexity is difficult to manage, but successful commerce requires getting such details correct.

Checks

Checks are another familiar form of real-world payment. Both consumers and businesses use checks for payment. Consumers use checks for point-of-sale payments as well as for payment of bills. After taking checks as payment during the day, a merchant deposits them in the bank, where they are *cleared* (in the United States) through the Federal Reserve network for the actual funds transfer. Clearing can take several business days, during which the merchant assumes the risk that the customer will not have sufficient funds to cover the check. Because merchants take the risk of nonpayment, they often require substantial identification, such as a driver's license and a credit card, to authenticate the customer. In addition, merchants impose significant penalties for checks that fail to clear. These penalties cover both the merchant's cost in handling the bounced check as well as the fee charged to the merchant by the bank.

Because they involve moving paper, checks are relatively expensive to handle, for merchants and for the banking system. Electronic analogs for checks have been devised, and we discuss them briefly later. In practice, the use of credit cards or debit cards is likely to be far more common in online transactions than electronic checks.

Debit cards are nearly identical to checks from the consumer's point of view, in that the funds are deducted immediately from a demand-deposit account. (Note, however, that with debit cards the funds are deducted from the account immediately, without the "float" that checks provide.)

Electronic Funds Transfer (EFT) and Automated Clearinghouse (ACH)

Electronic funds transfers (EFTs) move money directly between bank accounts, providing same-day or overnight payments. EFTs are commonly used, for example, for large interbank transfers. EFT systems were some of the earliest electronic payment systems, although they have always been on private networks and not on open networks such as the Internet.

EFT transactions move over a variety of networks, such as SWIFT, Fedwire, CHIPS, and Automated Clearinghouse (ACH). The first three of these are primarily used for large transfers, whereas ACH transfers are used for many smaller-valued electronic payments, including payroll direct deposits and preauthorized withdrawals for bill payment, as well as online payments by businesses. For many business-to-business commerce applications, ACH provides a familiar payment method that can be integrated with purchasing over the Internet. ACH transfers are also used by home banking and bill payment applications in cases in which the bank account information for the recipient is known.

Purchase Orders

Strictly speaking, *purchase orders* are not a payment mechanism, but we use this term to refer to a particular kind of transaction between businesses. Transactions between two businesses are typically handled differently from purchases by a consumer. In most cases, the seller extends credit to the buyer, and the seller bills the buyer for the transaction, with an agreement on when the buyer must pay (such as within 30 days or 60 days). A specific purchase is usually tied to a purchase order, which is used by the buyer to track transactions. From the seller's point of view, the purchase order is merely a convenient means of tracking transactions. Final payment is usually done by a check or wire transfer.

How does this translate to the online world? First of all, there must be some means of establishing the business relationship on which credit is extended. The seller typically has a process for verifying the creditworthiness of the buyer, and this process normally extends to online transactions as well. The initial verification is not usually performed in real time, so it may be handled through preexisting channels, or an online registration system may be used to initiate the relationship. Such an online credit application process must capture the information required by the seller's traditional credit application process, which typically includes the name and address of the business, a purchasing contact, and credit reference information. In addition, the online system should gather information, such as a password, used to authenticate authorized buyers from the customer's organization. Of course, the online system should be able to import information about existing relationships so that current customers can purchase online as well, and then should augment the existing information with authentication data used to identify customers for online purchases.

Once the relationship has been established, online purchasing works almost like other online transactions. As part of the order capture process, however, instead of collecting payment information such as a credit card number, the system must collect a purchase order number (or other buyer reference information) as well as authenticate the buyer to ensure that only authorized buyers are making purchases for a particular organization. In addition, the system should be able to check in real time to ensure that the purchase request falls within the available credit extended to the buyer's organization, in case that organization has taken on too much credit or has failed to pay its bills on time. This verification is very similar to the credit check done as part of authorizing a credit card transaction, but it is performed internal to the selling organization. As part of providing good service to customers, the system may also include the ability to handle an emergency request to increase the available credit, with a quick response by the seller that allows the transaction to proceed if appropriate.

Finally, of course, the online purchasing system must be integrated with existing billing and accounts receivable systems so that the appropriate bills and invoices can be generated and tracked. These systems may also be extended to the Internet system to provide up-to-date information for customers about such things as account balances and overdue amounts, as well as the ability to settle outstanding balances using online means of payment such as credit cards or electronic checks.

Affinity Programs

Affinity programs are those that provide some kind of benefit or reward for buying from a particular business or using a particular payment mechanism. Frequent flier miles are one common example, in which buying the product (an airline ticket) provides some points toward a future reward (usually another airline ticket). Many issuers of credit cards provide affinity programs as well, ranging from cash rebates to points good for purchase from a particular catalog, to points good for purchase at a particular store. The goal of these programs, of course, is to increase usage of the payment system or sales at a particular business.

All of these programs can be made part of an Internet commerce strategy as well. There are three primary parts to affinity programs in Internet commerce: collecting and tracking the accumulated *points*, enabling buyers to redeem those points online, and enabling buyers to see their affinity account balances online.

Collecting and tracking the points is usually straightforward. The main issue is integrating the tracking system with the existing system for managing the affinity program. In the case of co-branded credit cards, this is often transparent, because any credit card purchase using that particular card will trigger the addition of affinity points. When points are tied to specific items or specific stores, the accounting must be added to the online transaction system and then integrated with the existing affinity tracking system.

Second, buyers would like to redeem points online. This can be easy or hard, depending on the software selected for the Internet commerce system. In one sense, redeeming points is just another kind of payment, so a system that accommodates multiple payment mechanisms can often be extended easily to handle redemption. Of course, this almost certainly includes the ability to authenticate the buyer to ensure that the legitimate account owner is the one making a purchase. At that point, the main question becomes whether or not items should be priced in a conventional currency, such as dollars, as well as affinity points. Some merchants prefer to avoid pricing items both ways, so that there is no implicit conversion rate between points and currency. Others are content to provide both prices, in effect giving two price tags for an item. Some Internet commerce systems tie the payment mechanism so closely to the catalog, however, that they do not provide the kind of flexibility needed to add redemption systems.

Finally, buyers may want to check their affinity account balances online. Here the Internet system must be tied into the affinity accounting system, along with some kind of authentication to ensure the buyer's identity. As a convenience (or a marketing tool), the online account statement may include links to catalog pages useful for redeeming points, in order to encourage buyers to use them.

One popular way for affinity programs to link to online sales is through gift certificates, which are discussed later. The consumer can view the affinity account online and can request issuance of gift certificates in exchange for points.

The ability to support affinity programs may not seem important at the beginning of an Internet commerce strategy. However, as we have observed, business models and requirements may change significantly over time, and the flexibility to add affinity programs later may be very important in choosing a software system for Internet commerce.

Private-Label Cards

Many businesses, especially retailers such as Sears Roebuck, Home Depot, and Macy's, issue their own credit cards for purchases from their own businesses. In the abstract, such cards behave much like Visa, MasterCard, or other payment cards. In practice, providing such cards as payment instruments for Internet commerce means integrating the Internet system with the card payment system of whatever card is being used. The main technical steps, such as authorization, settlement, credits, and so on, will be processed much as for other credit cards. The flexibility of the Internet commerce system is the key point here, because integrating such payment cards into the system will typically be handled for particular sellers, rather than being part of a general solution.

More recently, many retailers have begun issuing co-branded Visa or MasterCard credit cards, usually with some affinity benefits tied to the cards. These cards, of course, behave just as normal credit cards for purposes of payment processing. They may have some special affinity features for online purchasing, such as special catalogs or online account statements, as we discussed for affinity programs.

Over time, we may also see private-label cards adopting credit card payment protocols such as 3D Secure for their transactions. Such adoption would leverage the infrastructure investment made for those protocols while providing a greater degree of security than would ordinarily be obtained without specialized development.

Money Orders

Money orders are similar to checks, except that payment is guaranteed by a trusted third party, such as the U.S. Postal Service. The primary use of money orders has been to enable mail-order transactions in a way that protected the merchant from the risks of bad checks from remote customers. The customer pays the Postal Service (including a small fee) to issue the money order, which can then be sent to the merchant for redemption with the Postal Service. Money orders are safer than sending cash in the mail, because they can be redeemed only by the entity named on the money order. In the physical world, then, money orders provide three basic capabilities.

1. Insurance against certain kinds of loss (compared with, say, sending cash in the mail).

2. A certain level of privacy and anonymity (less than cash, more than using a credit card directly). Of course, most physical money orders are for mail-order goods, so there is a physical shipping address associated with the order.

3. Matching between buyers and sellers with different payment instruments. If a mail-order merchant does not accept credit cards, for example, a customer can use a credit card to purchase a money order and use the money order to buy goods from that merchant.

In an online money order system, the first capability is not so important, because a properly designed online payment system does not risk losing cash. However, the anonymity property can be stronger, especially for delivering digital goods. Because there is no physical name and address associated with the delivery, the seller cannot tie the transaction to anything more than an IP address on the network. The issuer of the money order has, at most, knowledge of the seller and possibly of the buyer, depending on the actual payment instrument used. Such an issuer may choose to adopt various policies regarding the disclosure of such information. When the issuer can be trusted to follow such policies, both buyers and sellers may have confidence in an appropriate level of privacy for their transactions.

Corporate Purchasing Cards

Many purchases made by businesses are relatively small, such as for office supplies, off-the-shelf software for personal computers, and so on. These purchases often need to be completed quickly and easily, and they commonly require little in the way of approval by others in the organization. In such cases, the corporate overhead of completing a requisition form, creating a purchase order, selecting a vendor, establishing a credit relationship if one does not already exist, receiving an invoice, and paying the bill can be very costly compared with the value of the items being purchased.

One solution to this problem is the *corporate purchasing card*. A corporate purchasing card is essentially like a credit card issued to an individual on behalf of an organization. For the most part, it behaves as a credit card as well, except that most transactions require some additional information about the item being purchased.

This information allows the authorization system to make decisions based on the type of item as well as the availability of credit for the buying organization. For example, one individual may be allowed to buy only basic office supplies, whereas another may be authorized to buy personal computer software as well. As long as everything is in order, the buyer presents the credit card, the transaction is authorized, and the sale is completed.

Effective use of purchasing cards in the online world depends on the ability to capture this extra information about the item being purchased. Without this information, the authorization system cannot make a determination about whether or not the cardholder is permitted to make the purchase. As we have noted before, the flexibility of the payment system and, in this case, its connection to the catalog system, which has the specific item information, are very important in making it possible to use purchasing cards effectively.

Coupons

In general, a *coupon* is an offer to discount a purchase made under specific conditions. Manufacturer's coupons are perhaps the most familiar, offering "50 cents off" or "buy one, get one free." Individual stores may issue their own coupons, and sometimes they accept coupons issued by their competitors. Coupons take many forms, but all are intended to encourage consumers to purchase a particular product. In most cases, coupons are distributed separately from the point of sale of the product, so they help entice customers to visit a store to make a purchase.

Strictly speaking, of course, coupons are not a payment mechanism, but they do share some characteristics with payment. In most cases, we can view coupons as simply altering the final price of a set of goods or services, rather than as paying for them. At that point, any payment mechanism may be used for the purchase.

Before we examine some of the technical ways that coupons can be implemented, let us look at some different kinds of coupons in the physical world. Coupons are typically issued by two kinds of entities: manufacturers and retailers. A coupon from a manufacturer is usually accepted by any retailer selling the product, and the value is reimbursed by the manufacturer. Retailers also issue their own coupons, which are intended for use only at the retailer's stores. In some cases, competitors may also accept the coupons, although the value is (of course) not reimbursed by the issuer. The kinds of discounts that are offered by coupons can vary widely, but here are some of the most common.

- Get a fixed discount.

    The price of an item is discounted by a fixed amount. For example, "50 cents off when you buy product X."

- Get a percentage discount.

  The price of an item is discounted by a percentage. For example, "20 percent off when you buy product Y."

- Buy one, get one free.

  The price of a second item is reduced to zero if another item of the same kind is purchased. This kind of offer has many variations, such as "buy one, get one for 50 percent less" or "buy two, get one free."

- Buy X, get a discount on Y.

  This offer ties two products together, discounting the price of a second kind of product if another kind is purchased.

- After N purchases, the next one is free.

  In this case, the discount is applied after a history of repeated purchases has been established. A common way of doing this is for a consumer to keep a card that is punched for each purchase. When the card is fully punched, the discount can be taken.

Of course, coupons can be constructed in many other ways; the ones just listed are perhaps the most common. The challenge, then, is to translate such coupons into the online world. One way to look at coupons is that they provide a discount rule of the basic form, "If certain conditions have been satisfied, then the total cost of a set of items is changed in a particular way." The fixed-discount case, for example, has the form, "If one item of type X is being purchased, its price is reduced by a fixed amount." A more complicated coupon, offering "buy two, get one free" has the form, "If three items of type X are being purchased, the total price is two times the per-item price."

Although it may seem cumbersome, looking at the discount rules of coupons in this way allows us to write rules for online coupons that can be processed automatically by computer systems. The coupon mechanism can also be very general, which permits the use of different promotional approaches to determine the most effective means of attracting sales.

Gift Certificates

In the real world, a gift certificate is like a check except that it cannot be redeemed for cash but only for a merchandise credit at a particular store. Online, gift certificates work similarly. They are typically represented by strings of letters and digits that can be sent by e-mail or even printed on paper. The buyer wanting to use a gift certificate in partial payment of a purchase merely enters the code on the order form.

Smart Cards

A *smart card* is an object about the size of a plastic credit card that contains a processor, memory, and an interface to the outside world. The term is sometimes used to include PCMCIA devices with similar properties, and the cards that are exactly the size of plastic credit cards are sometimes called *chip cards*. Smart cards are being used for an increasingly large set of applications, including payment. We make a distinction between smart cards and the kind of handheld authentication tokens described in Chapter 14: smart cards provide at least data storage and often some computation based on that data, rather than the (relatively simple) authentication computations used by tokens.

In practice, there is a wide range of smarts on cards. The differences come in the performance and capabilities of the processor, the amounts of RAM and ROM, the speed of the interface to the world, the availability of specialized components for cryptographic operations, and whether or not they can be programmed for different applications. Different applications require different kinds of operations, so it is often important to speak precisely about the application and the kind of card used.

In order to be useful, smart cards require a *reader* of some sort to connect the card with a computer system. There are several different kinds of readers, depending on the technology being used. Chip cards typically have exposed contacts that match up with those in a reader when they are inserted into a slot. This approach is common for smart cards used at retail point-of-sale terminals. Other cards are wireless and use infrared or radio communication to exchange data with the reader. A PCMCIA smart card, of course, uses a standard PCMCIA slot on a laptop or desktop computer. No matter what the mechanism is, however, the site where the card will be used requires a reader. For traditional retail applications, readers are attached to a cash register. For a building-access system, readers are mounted next to doors. For Internet commerce, the computer used by the holder of the smart card must have a reader for the card to be of any use. Over time, it may become common for PCs to be equipped with smart card readers to enable many kinds of authenticated applications, including payment transactions, but at the moment this is a significant barrier to the use of smart cards for Internet commerce.

In the abstract, smart cards provide several capabilities.

- Portable storage

  Because the device is carried around by its owner, it can be used anywhere the owner goes. In particular, it means that the information stored on the card is available wherever the owner takes it, which means that the owner is not chained to a desktop computer in order to use an advanced payment system.

- Secure storage

  A smart card has the potential to provide secure, tamperproof storage for all or part of the information stored on it. This is especially valuable for such things as cryptographic keys or data representing money, as well as for other especially private information.

- Trusted execution environment

  Smart cards are not vulnerable to the viruses and risks of intrusion that plague desktop computers. Because the application runs in this protected environment, it can be given a greater degree of trust.

Some common applications today include the following.

- Prepaid telephone cards

  This application does not require very sophisticated cards, because the main technology used is a set of electrical fuses on a chip that are progressively burned up by the reader. When no more fuses remain, the prepaid value has been consumed and the card is no longer useful.

- Credit and debit cards

  This application is not very common inside the United States, but it is widespread in many other parts of the world. The chip on the card is used to authenticate the card at the retail point of sale, and the cardholder gives a PIN for authentication as well. The smart card provides a greater degree of security than an easily forged piece of plastic with a magnetic stripe.

- Electronic purses

  Several electronic payment systems, such as Mondex and Visa Cash, rely on smart cards as the carriers of value in the system. The goal is to replace cash for small transactions by storing value on a card that can be replenished. Some technologies require that value be transferred only from a card to an authorized vendor, whereas others (such as Mondex) allow card-to-card transfers as well. This latter capability means that users can pay each other for goods or services, just as they can use cash today.

Many other smart card applications are under development, ranging from simple stored-value or authentication systems to sophisticated uses of public-key systems for signing and encrypting documents and payment instructions.

Historically, one of the problems with creating applications for smart cards has been the lack of standard interfaces for communicating with the devices. RSA Laboratories has been leading the development of a standard called PKCS-11, which specifies an API for cryptographic devices such as smart cards. The API, also known as *Cryptoki*, is intended to present a technology-independent view over a wide range of devices.

In a similar vein, the Java Card API is an initiative by Sun Microsystems to use the Java programming language to develop applications for smart cards. The use of a standard programming interface would make it possible for card-based applications to run on many different cards, rather than programming them individually. Many people are also looking for multiapplication cards that may be used in different contexts (for example, different payment systems, medical records, authentication, and so on), rather than requiring people to carry separate cards for different purposes. A common programming interface (Java, in this case) makes it easier to create such multiapplication devices.[4]

Smart cards come to Internet commerce applications in two ways. In the first, the smart card is used on an Internet client to support a standard protocol (such as SSL or SET). In this case, there is no difference from the server's point of view, because the protocol is standard. The client could employ the smart card in many different ways, depending on the security requirements of the application. One use is for the card to authenticate access to encrypted credentials stored on a desktop computer. A second use includes the card in the processing of protocol messages, either by executing the protocol on the card itself or by using the card for cryptographic operations (such as digital signatures) and storing the keys and certificates used for the protocol.

A second way to use smart cards in Internet commerce applications is to develop new protocols that take advantage of the special capabilities of smart cards, particularly for cryptographic operations and key storage. In some cases, the application requirements for the use of cryptographic hardware will also include such hardware at the server as well as the use of smart cards. This approach can be very effective for creating high-security applications, but it increases the overall development costs substantially.

As we have noted, the biggest obstacle to the use of smart cards for Internet commerce is the availability of card readers on computers used for commerce, whether they are in homes or in offices. When the card reader becomes a mass-market device, it will become common to include the use of smart cards in Internet commerce systems. Until then, the use of smart cards in Internet systems is likely to be confined to specialized applications in which the security requirements demand the extra capabilities of smart cards.

Online Credit Card Payment

Credit cards have become the most common means for consumers to pay for goods and services on the Internet. This is not surprising, because many Internet transactions are very similar to mail-order transactions. Consumers are already familiar with

---

4. Carrying one smart card instead of many clearly has some advantages for the person carrying the card. There are two possible problems. First, having multiple applications on a card may tie together different applications that a person wants to keep separate (for example, there is no real need to link a credit card with medical records), so privacy is a concern. The second problem is that plastic cards bearing logos are a form of promotion, and card issuers may be reluctant to give up that promotion in order to join a multiapplication card that displays the logo of a different organization.

credit cards, and the credit card system lowers the risk to the consumer if something goes wrong. From a technical point of view, it is much easier to create a system for processing credit card purchases than to invent a new payment technology. Finally, from a business point of view, many merchants who want to do business online already accept credit cards, so taking advantage of online opportunities does not require establishing a new banking relationship.

Secure Communication

The first credit card transactions on the Internet were not protected against eavesdropping. Early transactions consisted of credit card numbers (and related information) sent by electronic mail, Telnet, or the World Wide Web without encryption for privacy. As electronic commerce systems began to be deployed more widely (primarily on the World Wide Web), system designers took two other approaches: obtaining credit card numbers for customer accounts by telephone rather than over the Internet, and developing encryption systems and security protocols for transmitting the information. Two of the first encryption protocols for the World Wide Web, Secure HTTP and the Secure Sockets Layer (SSL), were developed in part to enable commerce applications.

For many credit card applications, strong cryptography using a protocol such as SSL provides a high degree of communications security. Developing an application is often simplified because the application need not provide additional security or manage a complex protocol. In practice today, almost all consumer Internet commerce transactions are paid for by the consumer typing a credit card number into an HTML form at the store checkout, protected by SSL.

Secure Electronic Transactions (SET)

The Secure Electronic Transactions (SET) protocol was developed jointly by Visa and MasterCard, along with some technology partners, to provide secure credit card transactions over open networks such as the Internet. The protocol includes strong encryption and authentication of all of the parties in a credit card transaction: the buyer (or cardholder), the merchant, and the merchant's bank. Although SET never achieved widespread use, it is interesting to examine it as a system for securing credit card payments.

As described in the Business Description portion of the SET specification, SET was designed with several goals in mind.

1. Provide confidentiality of payment information and enable confidentiality of order information that is transmitted along with the payment information.
2. Ensure integrity for all transmitted data.
3. Provide authentication that a cardholder is a legitimate user of a branded payment card account.

4. Provide authentication that a merchant can accept branded payment card transactions through its relationship with an acquiring financial institution.

5. Ensure the use of the best security practices and system design techniques to protect all legitimate parties of an electronic commerce transaction.

6. Ensure the creation of a protocol that neither is dependent on transport security mechanisms nor prevents their use.

7. Facilitate and encourage interoperability across software and network providers.

In accomplishing these goals, SET also enables the use of the Internet for authorization and settlement of credit card transactions as well as enabling secure communication of payment information from the cardholder to the merchant. As discussed earlier, without SET, a merchant typically connects to an acquiring bank (or other financial processor) using a leased telephone line or dialup connection. SET makes it possible for merchants to use the Internet for such connections, thereby avoiding the extra cost. (Note, however, that there are some disadvantages of this approach as well, which are discussed later.)

At the time SET was designed, the U.S. government strictly regulated the export of cryptographic systems, so SET was carefully constructed to encrypt only financial credentials. Since that time, the U.S. export regulations have been relaxed, so it is less important to limit the use of cryptography. We discuss the export of cryptographic software in more detail in Chapter 13.

A diagram of a SET transaction is shown in Figure 15-2. Before the transaction occurs, the merchant and the consumer must set up for SET transactions by obtaining software and certificates. The merchant interacts with the acquiring bank to obtain a SET merchant certificate. This public-key certificate is signed using the acquiring bank's key, which in turn is signed using the card brand key (Visa or MasterCard, for example). This certificate is used to authenticate the merchant to both the cardholder and the payment gateway during the transaction phase. Similarly, the consumer interacts with his issuing bank to obtain a certificate signed by the issuing bank. The cardholder certificate is optional in the protocol but, if present, is used to authenticate the cardholder to the merchant during the actual transaction.

During the transaction, the following steps occur.

1. The customer interacts with the merchant Web site to select goods for purchase.

2. The merchant sends an order description that wakes up the customer SET wallet.

3. The customer checks the order and transmits a payment request back to the merchant's SET module.

4. The merchant sends the payment request to the payment gateway.

5. The payment gateway validates the merchant and the customer, and obtains an authorization from the customer's issuing bank through an interchange network.

6. The payment gateway sends an order capture token back to the merchant.

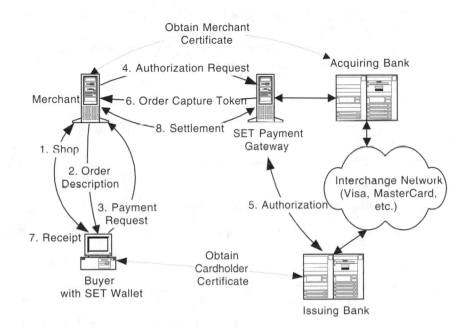

FIGURE 15-2. **Flow of a SET Transaction**

7. The merchant sends a receipt to the customer wallet.

8. Later, the merchant uses the order capture token to settle the transaction.

The protocol definition for SET specifies the message formats, encodings, and cryptographic operations to be used. It does not require a particular method of transport, so SET messages may be carried in HTTP for World Wide Web applications, electronic mail, or any other method. The messages do not need to be exchanged in real time, which permits, for example, effective SET implementation based on electronic mail or other asynchronous systems.

The failure of SET to achieve widespread adoption appears to have resulted from two factors.

1. SET requires buyer software.

   In order for the buyer to compose SET messages and to validate responses, she must install client software—the so-called client wallet. This turns out to be an enormous hurdle to adoption.

2. SET requires expensive merchant software.

In order to use SET, merchants must obtain expensive software and then pay for its integration with their e-commerce system. This didn't work because merchants did not perceive any benefit to them from using SET. Most of the benefits of SET help the banks, not the merchants or buyers.

3D Secure

In response to the lack of adoption and complexity of SET, the card associations have been developing a new system, called *3D Secure*. 3D Secure does not require client software, and the requirements placed on the merchant are substantially reduced relative to SET.

The overall flow of a 3D Secure transaction is shown in Figure 15-3.

1. The end user registers for the 3D Secure program at the Web site of the bank that issued his credit card.

2. The buyer enters his card number into a standard merchant order form.

3. The merchant sends an inquiry over the Internet to the issuing bank to find out whether the customer is registered for 3D Secure.

4. Given an affirmative response, the merchant pops up a daughter window on the customer's screen, which requests the user's 3D Secure password.

5. The password is submitted directly to the issuing bank. The bank validates the customer password, and, if it is correct, formats an authentication message to the merchant.

6. The authentication message, confirming that the user's password is correct, is returned to the merchant via the user's browser.

7. The merchant validates the authentication message using 3D Secure software and, if it is correct, authorizes the transaction through traditional channels to his acquiring bank.

8. The customer receives a receipt for the transaction.

Electronic Cash

Generally speaking, *electronic cash* is a class of technologies that provides an analog of cash represented in electronic form. Electronic cash systems attempt to replicate many of the properties of cash for online transactions: convenience, low (or nonexistent) transaction costs, anonymity, and so on. Although not all electronic cash systems try to satisfy all of these properties, most of them try to enable quick and easy online transactions for small amounts of money.

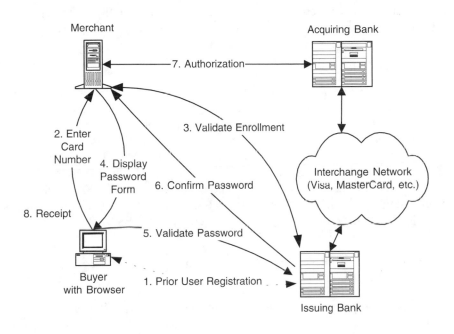

FIGURE 15-3. Flow of a 3D Secure Transaction

Some electronic cash systems require smart cards (plastic cards with processors and memory) for operation; others operate entirely in software (although use of smart card hardware may provide an extra degree of security). When smart cards are used, losing the card means losing the money, just as losing a 20-dollar bill means the money is lost. The card is just like cash, so the story goes, and it should be treated as such. Software systems may provide for backup of the value represented in storage, but losing all copies still means that the value is lost.

Cash Cards

As noted earlier, one of the limitations of traditional credit cards is that they have relatively high transaction costs, and therefore they are not suitable for small transactions. To address this problem, Visa, MasterCard, and others have experimented with *cash cards* that can be used for low-priced items in stores, vending machines, and other venues. The card contains a microprocessor and a few kilobytes of memory. The microprocessor is capable of performing the cryptographic operations needed to debit the card and prevent counterfeiting. Some of these cards can be used only until their original value is consumed; others can be reloaded. So far, these cards have not proved popular in pilot programs, and they remain rare. The communications between the card and a reader is presumed to be a secure channel, so the technology is not suited for transactions on open networks, such as the Internet, at this time.

DigiCash

DigiCash was a company created to market an electronic cash system based on technology developed by David Chaum. Chaum's goals in developing the DigiCash system were to match the properties of cash as closely as possible, particularly anonymity and untraceability. Unlike many other systems, DigiCash does not require a smart card. The result is that DigiCash developed a method for detecting so-called double spending. If the electronic cash is spent only once, all parties remain anonymous. However, if the same electronic coins are deposited at the bank twice, then the identity of the person who copied the money becomes traceable. The company did not find a market for its products, and it ceased operations in 1998.

Micropayments

The term *micropayments* is used to mean many different things. How big a micropayment is usually depends on how big an average or common payment is for the person using the term. Thus, for corporate transactions, a micropayment may be anything less than $100, whereas for a credit card system it may be anything less than $10. In general, we use the word *micropayment* to describe small-valued transactions—say, a few dollars or less. In most cases, micropayments are intended for use with online delivery as well: for example, $0.50 for a magazine article. The term *nanopayment* is sometimes used to describe payments much smaller than micropayments, such as for transactions valued at less than a penny.

Business Models for Micropayments

From a business point of view, the most obvious thing about micropayments is that you really do have to make it up in volume. The arithmetic is simple: if the average transaction size is $0.50, then it takes two million transactions to gross $1 million. Out of that gross come the costs of the computers for handling the transactions and fulfilling the orders, the software for processing the microtransactions, the salaries of the operators to keep them running, power and air-conditioning, and so on. At this stage in the evolution of Internet commerce, micropayment systems do not yet seem to pay for themselves on a large scale.

On a small scale, micropayments may indeed be successful. Consider an individual— not a professional writer—who publishes essays of political commentary on the Web. If 10,000 readers are willing to pay $0.10 per essay, that comes to $1,000 our essayist might not otherwise receive. Even with fairly high costs for operating the micropayment system, the writer may come out ahead financially, as well as gaining from the exposure and visibility generated by the essays. This is a far cry from the financial returns needed to sustain a publishing business, however.

The technology side of micropayments is technically exciting and challenging, as is the vision of the future painted by micropayment proponents. Micropayments may one day be a common form of Internet payments, but it appears for the moment that successful micropayment business models have yet to be developed and deployed.

To date, micropayment systems have not achieved widespread use, although there have been three waves of attempts to build companies around such services since 1994. For the most part, more recent systems are variations on the account-based systems described here and are not technically sophisticated.

Technical Micropayments Systems

There are a variety of technical micropayment systems either under active development or already published. Because this is a rapidly evolving area of technology, the best approach to further research is probably to type *micropayment* into an Internet search engine. Following is a quick survey of some of these systems. Although they are not in widespread use, they represent some of the innovative work that may be incorporated into future payment systems.

MilliCent

MilliCent is a system designed by Mark S. Manasse of DIGITAL Equipment Corporation's Systems Research Center in Palo Alto, California. A view of the entities and relationships in MilliCent are shown in Figure 15-4. MilliCent creates merchant-specific scrip, which is exchangeable only for goods at a particular merchant. Brokers provide a degree of vendor independence by selling scrip on behalf of multiple merchants. MilliCent uses cryptography to protect the system against abuse by end users, such as forgery or double spending of scrip. The other entities in the system have some protections as well. The protections offered by MilliCent are not ironclad, because the system is intended for low-value transactions. The system does not provide transaction audit trails or receipts. The central feature of the design for MilliCent is the exchange of scrip coins for individual Web pages. There is no protection for occasional download failures. The model is similar to that of a vending machine. If an occasional coin is lost, most people will just put in another coin.

NetBill

NetBill is a system developed by Marvin Sirbu and Doug Tygar at Carnegie Mellon University. NetBill provides for both payment and transactional delivery of digital goods. By *transactional* we mean that either payment and delivery of the goods both take place or neither takes place. The system design, shown in Figure 15-5, prevents delivery without payment or payment without delivery.

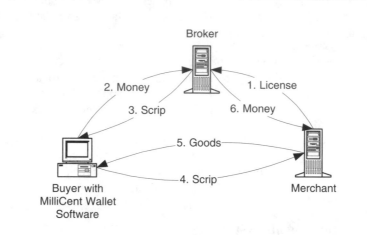

FIGURE 15-4. MilliCent System Design

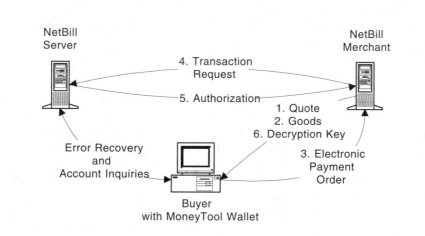

FIGURE 15-5. NetBill System Design

Before any purchases are made, the NetBill customer downloads and installs the MoneyTool wallet application, which works with a Web browser. The customer also uses a traditional payment system such as a credit card to purchase NetBill currency. The customer balance is stored on the NetBill server. For a purchase to be made, the following steps occur.

1. The customer browses the merchant's site and selects a digital good for purchase.

2. The merchant system downloads an encrypted copy of the goods to the customer, along with the price and a timestamp.

3. The buyer's MoneyTool wallet wakes up and composes an electronic payment order (EPO) containing the price, checksum, product ID, and timestamp. The EPO is signed by the customer's cryptographic key and sent to the merchant server.

4. The merchant server sends the EPO, along with the decryption key for the goods, to the NetBill server.

5. The NetBill server validates the EPO, debits the customer account, credits the merchant account, and records the decryption key, all in a transaction. This step ensures the eventual success of the purchase.

6. The NetBill server returns a success message to the merchant, who sends the decryption key to the customer.

7. The customer can now decrypt and view the goods.

Should the customer fail to get the decryption key, or should some other failure occur, the customer can communicate directly with the NetBill server to obtain the key or perhaps learn that the transaction was never recorded (and the money not spent).

For further information on NetBill, see www.netbill.com.

Transaction Aggregation

The business problem to which technical micropayment systems appear to be a solution is the handling of small-valued transactions that cannot justify, for example, a credit card authorization. In some cases, this business problem can also be solved by transaction aggregation. In these schemes, small transactions are grouped together until the total is of a size suitable for handling by a traditional payment system. There are two modes of aggregation: *taxi meter* and *parking meter*.

In a taxi meter, charges accumulate as the taxi moves or waits. The passenger settles the bill at the end of the trip. Taxi meter mode, or *charge-up* transaction aggregation, works the same way: charges accumulate on the account of a customer until a threshold is reached, or until the end of a session or billing period. At that time, the total accumulated amount is settled using a traditional payment system. In this system, the seller extends credit to the buyer, but the sums are small and so not much is at risk. The seller can also simply refuse to do further business with the buyer until the bill is paid. In a variation of the taxi meter scheme, an authorization, or credit reservation, may be made at the beginning of a session, with settlement at the end when the true charges are known.

In a parking meter, a driver parking a vehicle deposits coins in the meter upon parking. The meter then decrements the amount of credit remaining as time is spent. Parking meter mode, or *draw-down* transaction aggregation, works the same way: the buyer prefunds an account with a traditional payment system, and then microtransaction debits are made to the account. In this system, the buyer rather than the seller assumes the risk. Variations include whether or not refunds of partially used credit can be made.

One very interesting difference between these two modes of operation is the allocation of risk and its consequences. Because the buyer takes the risk in parking meter systems, the system can be made available to anonymous customers. In contrast, because the seller takes the risk in taxi meter systems, these systems are typically available only to registered, authenticated buyers.

Transaction aggregation is typically an arrangement between a buyer and a single seller. Technically, a microtransaction aggregation account could be shared by multiple sellers, but whether this is sensible may depend on the system reporting capabilities rather than anything else. Aggregation systems may report only totals or may offer complete transaction detail reporting of the microtransactions themselves. The available degree of reporting is often a function of transaction size. By calculating the equipment and infrastructure costs, the cost of a transaction can be calculated. The data storage necessary to support transaction detail reporting adds significantly to the transaction cost, so detail reporting is sensible only for larger microtransaction amounts. Transaction aggregation micropayments were available in commercial Internet commerce software such as Open Market's Transact as early as 1998.

Peer-to-Peer Payment Systems

As the Internet settled down to credit card payments as the primary payment mechanism for e-commerce, it also became apparent that individuals wanted to be able to pay each other online. This is most visible for auction sites, such as eBay, that promote transactions between individuals, not just businesses. However, individuals can't take credit cards, and there is no widespread alternative on the Internet.

To solve this problem, companies like PayPal, Yahoo, and others have created so-called peer-to-peer payment systems. In these systems, individuals can instruct the service to send payments to anyone with an e-mail address. The individual pays the service with a credit card or direct debit from a bank account. The recipient receives instructions for retrieving the payment, and the service provider collects a small fee.

Peer-to-peer payment systems are increasingly popular, especially for auctions. They are less common for larger-scale Internet commerce operations, but they reflect the continuing innovation in payment systems for the Internet.

Payment in the Abstract

Most of the discussion in this chapter has been about systems for the transfer of money in payment of goods or services. However, much commerce in the real world works in an environment substantially separated from payment.

Business-to-Business Commerce

For example, most business-to-business commerce is conducted as follows.

1. Two businesses establish a commercial relationship. The seller agrees to extend credit to the buyer.
2. The buying organization obtains goods and services from the selling organization.
3. Periodically, a bill is sent from seller to buyer.
4. The buyer pays the bills using a check or other funds transfer.

In this model, payment is a function from one finance department to another and has no direct connection to the actual purchasing. What is really going on here is that many of the real-world and Internet payment systems discussed in this chapter bundle together the functions of authorization and settlement. Credit card systems separate these functions to some degree, but each authorization matches a settlement. In business-to-business commerce, there is no direct connection between authorization and settlement. Let's reinterpret the events.

1. The selling organization makes a decision to extend credit to the buying organization.
2. At the point of purchase, the *requisitioner* must authenticate herself as a representative of the buyer (and sometimes the buying organization must *approve* the purchase through some other internal mechanism). This step is equivalent to credit card authorization.
3. Later, the finance departments reconcile and settle the transactions.

What has happened here is that the buying organization has delegated authority to the requisitioner. In the abstract, this delegation of authority is very much like money.[5]

Information Commerce

Professional users of information, such as lawyers, bankers, and accountants, frequently engage in information commerce, paying for the knowledge and expertise of others, as codified in writing. For example, lawyers use the LexisNexis and Westlaw online services or subscribe to CD-ROM distributions of annotated case law. These information commerce transactions are seldom paid for directly by credit card or cash.

1. A law office sets up a billing relationship with a commercial publisher of case law.
2. On entry to, for example, the online legal information service, an individual lawyer logs in, authenticates himself to the service, and enters an account code. This code will be used for later rebilling of services provided to the lawyer's client.

---

5. Thanks to Dan Geer for explaining the connection between delegation and money.

3. As the lawyer uses the information service, billing events are generated and posted to the law office's account.

4. Periodically, the publisher sends a bill to the law office, and the individual billable items are rebilled, perhaps with a markup, to the clients.

5. The law office pays the publisher.

6. The clients pay the law office.

As in the business-to-business example, the information transaction is not tightly coupled to payment. Instead, authorization and settlement are separated, and there is an initial step of establishing a commercial relationship between the buying and selling organizations. During the transaction itself, an authentication or approval step provides an authorization for the transaction, and the settlement happens later.

Summary

Many people think that the problems of Internet commerce are all associated with payment. This is hardly true, as the other chapters of this book demonstrate, yet payment is an essential component of many commerce systems. There are a tremendous number of payment systems in use around the globe, with various ways of handling the essential issues of authorization and settlement. In addition, different systems are commonly used for business-to-consumer, business-to-business, and information commerce. Payment is an area of ongoing innovation, as our discussion of microtransactions illustrates, and new technologies will continue to emerge. An Internet commerce architecture must therefore be flexible regarding payment technology, yet the designers must understand both the technology and the business issues of managing trust as well as risk.

CHAPTER 16

Shopping Carts and
Order Management

To market, to market, to buy a fat pig,
Home again, home again, jiggety-jig.
—Anonymous[1]

Overview

In the evolution of e-commerce systems, shopping carts and order management are at
the heart of many problems, challenges, and implementation approaches. On the surface, they seem simple, but many subtle (and not-so-subtle) problems arise in trying
to make truly excellent shopping carts for online systems. Like other aspects of e-
commerce systems, the best shopping carts are the ones that do not call attention to
themselves. They work quickly and flawlessly, they don't lose data, and the customer
barely notices the time spent interacting with them.

In this chapter, we look at how shopping carts can and should work, as well as some
different approaches to implementing them. In addition, we go beyond shopping carts
to the problem of managing orders for a customer—that is, what happens when the
customer clicks the **Checkout** button.

---

1. Nursery rhyme *To Market, To Market*.

Shopping Carts

Informally, the shopping cart is the collection of items to be purchased. More accurately, we are considering the creation of a sales order, which in turn is a purchase order that has been accepted by the seller. Web shopping carts, purchase orders, and sales orders are alike in that they contain *header data* and *line-item data*. The header data includes information about the buyer, such as bill-to, sold-to, and ship-to, and the line-item data contains information about the items, such as stock keeping unit (SKU), quantity, price, and requested delivery.

Server-Side Shopping Carts

When the partially completed sales order is stored at the commerce server, it is known as a *server-side shopping cart*, as shown in Figure 16-1. Most Internet commerce systems use server-side shopping carts. The cart is kept in a database or a file, or even in memory, and is indexed by the user ID or some kind of session identifier. Most of the time, a user will have a single cart, but the complexities of the potential process flows through the system sometimes require more. In Open Market's Transact, for example, a user may have up to three carts: a temporary cart created by a catalog server, a session cart containing items selected anonymously, and a user cart containing items selected during a period when the user was authenticated. The various flows eventually merge these three carts before the transaction is complete.

A single transaction engine can be shared by multiple online stores, as illustrated in Figure 16-2. In some cases, a commerce service provider (CSP) operates the engine as a service shared by multiple merchants. Technically, this option is similar to the server-side shopping cart, except that the shopping cart is held in a different server than the catalog. These servers might communicate directly through remote APIs or indirectly through coded URLs activated by the user. This model can also be used by manufacturers or distributors who operate transaction and fulfillment services for their resellers.

Shopping cart items and orders may also be held in a backing system, such as some other kind of enterprise order management system (see Figure 16-3). When the e-commerce system is providing a Web front end for an enterprise resource planning system or customer resource management system, the shopping cart may be stored in the backing system. Two obvious examples are the activation of a previously prepared quote and the use of a previous sales order to form the basis of a new sales order (that is, a reorder).

The final server-side option for shopping carts is to store them in a Web-side system, as shown in Figure 16-4. Often a purchase order is prepared elsewhere and routed to the e-commerce system. Buy-side systems, supply chain systems, portals, and exchanges may prepare complete purchase orders and transmit them to the sell-side

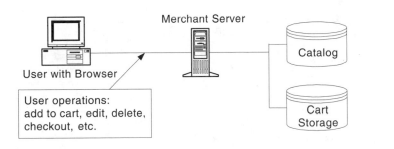

FIGURE 16-1. Cart Managed by Merchant Server

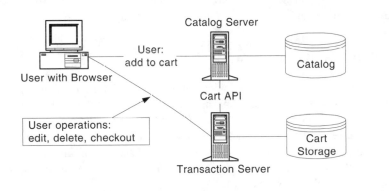

FIGURE 16-2. Cart Managed by Shared Server

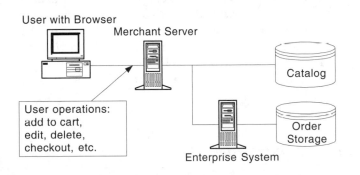

FIGURE 16-3. Cart and Orders Held in Backing System

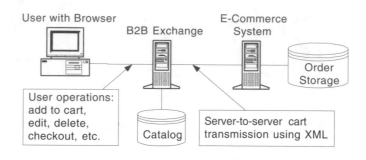

FIGURE 16-4. Server-to-Server Cart Transmission

system. The sell-side system converts the purchase order to a sales order by validating it and accepting it. A negotiation process may be involved.

Client-Side Shopping Carts

Another option, although it is not widely used, is to maintain the shopping cart on the Web client through the use of a Java applet, ActiveX control, or other helper application. The main problem is the extreme difficulty of getting the desired user base to install the helper application correctly or to permit the ActiveX control to operate. In a more limited case, if all the items available for purchase are found on one Web page, then a stateless client applet written in Java or JavaScript can interact with the user to construct a complete purchase order.

Protocol-Based Shopping Carts

One final possibility is that the shopping cart may have no home at all. Some systems maintain the shopping cart as part of the protocol between client and server, sending the cart back and forth as browser cookies or HTML hidden fields. These techniques are fragile—they work or don't work depending on the browser configuration and are not widely used, but they eliminate the need for database I/O on the server to maintain the cart. Interestingly, this application was apparently the original purpose of Netscape's cookies.

Managing Shopping Carts

In this section, we take a more detailed look at what is needed to manage shopping carts and the information in them. In general, this discussion focuses on how to manage server-side shopping carts, but most of the information applies to shopping carts in any form.

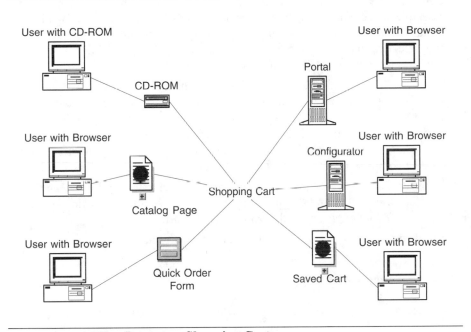

FIGURE 16-5. Adding Items to a Shopping Cart

Item Selection

In this section, we discuss how individual line items are added to the shopping cart. Some examples are shown in Figure 16-5. Some of the methods are as follows.

1. Clicking a Web link. The most common method of adding an item to a shopping cart is to click a URL anchor. This may be the **Buy now** or **Add to cart** button in a catalog, an item link in an affiliate catalog, or even a banner advertisement.

2. On the client. Items may be added to client-side carts directly, by clicking or by a drag-and-drop operation. This can happen either online (with Internet connectivity) or offline, as in a CD-ROM-based catalog.

3. Quick order form. Many sites, particularly industrial catalogs, contain quick order forms in which SKU or part numbers may be directly entered. These numbers are then expanded to complete item identifiers and entered into the shopping cart.

4. Catalog systems. Often a merchant desires to sell a bundle of items with a single click. This may be a package of items with a separate part number (the box and the power cord), or it may be a suggestion ("everything you need for camping").

5. Configurators. Highly complex products often work only when subassemblies are assembled in certain combinations. The process of developing a valid combination is called *configuration*, and, naturally, there are software products such as Calico and Selectica to assist. Configurators prepare lists of subassemblies (items) and can transmit them in batches to the shopping cart.

6. Cross-merchant hand-off. 3COM's Internet Channel Commerce Connectivity specification describes a means of handing off shopping cart contents from one server to another. In 3COM's case, this is done so a product catalog at 3COM can link to any of a number of resellers for purchasing. CNet's product comparison service operates at an earlier point in the chain, merely linking the items in the product comparison to the same item in the reseller's catalog.

7. Items or lists of items may be prepared in a separate application and then transferred in bulk to the shopping cart. In some sense, the originating system is also a "cart" but often a special-purpose, limited cart.

8. Saved shopping cart. A saved shopping cart can be reactivated.

Saved Shopping Carts

Saved carts are useful in many different situations.

1. Saving the cart for an extended period of time while the customer considers the purchase.

2. Saving some items for later purchase.

3. Standard sets of items—for example, "new employee office supplies." Having these sets of items saved makes it more convenient for the buyers to place the order again (which also makes it more likely that they will use the same site again and again, rather than redoing the work elsewhere).

4. Approvals. The requisitioner prepares the cart, but the purchase is made by the approver or by a purchasing agent.

5. Wish lists and gift registries. These applications blur the line between saved carts and custom catalogs, but they frequently provide a method for adding items to a shopping cart, generally with extra information attached. Note that wish lists and gift registries need to be transactional, so that items are removed once purchased.

Purchase Order Information Flow

Processing of purchase orders, once all the items have been assembled in the shopping cart, can be quite complex. This section examines some of the issues and methods for handling them.

Business-to-Consumer Commerce

Although there is no standard for order processing in business-to-consumer (B2C) e-commerce, most vendors of e-commerce systems have implemented a linear process composed of several steps organized as a pipeline. Order processing in Microsoft Commerce Server 2000 is a good and well-documented example. The overall pipeline is divided into two parts: the Plan Pipeline and the Purchase Pipeline, as shown in Figure 16-6.

The Plan Pipeline is responsible for validating the shopping cart and for calculating all charges. The standard Plan Pipeline has 14 stages.

1. Product Information Stage: Obtain product information from database.
2. Merchant Information Stage: Fill in merchant information on order form.
3. Shopper Information Stage: Fill in shopper information on order form.
4. Order Initialization Stage: Assign order ID and initialize order form.
5. Order Check Stage: Verify that order can be processed (typically ensures that the form is not empty).
6. Item Price Stage: Fill in regular prices.
7. Item Adjust Price Stage: Adjust prices for sales or promotions.
8. Order Adjust Price Stage: Fill in total line-item prices.
9. Order Subtotal Stage: Calculate order subtotal.
10. Shipping Stage: Calculate shipping charges for multiple shipments as required.
11. Handling Stage: Calculate handling charges, if any.
12. Tax Stage: Calculate taxes for the United States, Canada, and the European Union.
13. Order Total Stage: Add subtotal, tax, shipping, and handling.
14. Inventory Stage: Verify that items are in stock.

The Purchase Pipeline is responsible for payment and order placement and is often transactional. The standard Purchase Pipeline has three stages.

1. Purchase Check Stage: Verify address and credit card information.
2. Payment Stage: Approve credit card payments.
3. Accept Stage: Create purchase order and initiate order tracking.

Microsoft Commerce Server 2000, like most B2C e-commerce products, is very flexible in its business process. The numbers and purposes of the various pipeline stages are configurable (in the Pipeline Editor) and may contain both compiled and scripted code. Each stage may be composed of several components. Several third parties supply plug-ins for the Microsoft Commerce Server pipelines, and individual installations may also use custom code.

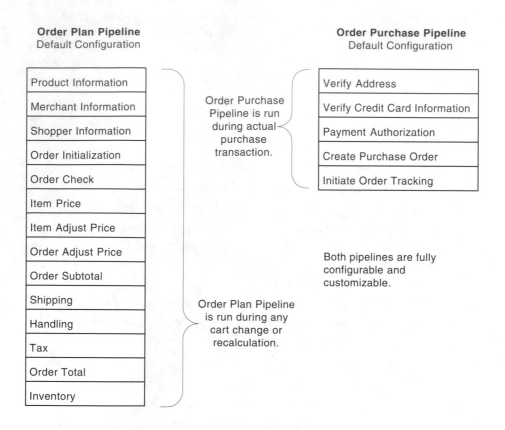

Order Plan Pipeline
Default Configuration

| Product Information |
| Merchant Information |
| Shopper Information |
| Order Initialization |
| Order Check |
| Item Price |
| Item Adjust Price |
| Order Adjust Price |
| Order Subtotal |
| Shipping |
| Handling |
| Tax |
| Order Total |
| Inventory |

Order Purchase Pipeline
Default Configuration

| Verify Address |
| Verify Credit Card Information |
| Payment Authorization |
| Create Purchase Order |
| Initiate Order Tracking |

Order Purchase Pipeline is run during actual purchase transaction.

Both pipelines are fully configurable and customizable.

Order Plan Pipeline is run during any cart change or recalculation.

FIGURE 16-6. **Order Processing Pipelines**

This overall pipeline structure is fairly standard across vendors, but there is no standard way to handle interactions with inventory and fulfillment systems. The usual approach is to provide callout APIs and standard document formats. The most flexible systems then connect to middleware such as IBM MQSeries or Microsoft BizTalk so that professional services can finish the integration.

The dual-pipeline approach to order processing is a consequence of user interface considerations. The first pipeline—the Plan Pipeline in the case of Microsoft Commerce Server—is run many times, typically for every order form page display. Effectively, it is an interactive part of the user experience, and performance is an important consideration. Thus, it performs the following steps.

1. The user changes the shopping cart by adding an item or changing quantities, credit card number, or address, and submits the form.

2. The Plan Pipeline is run to validate and price the order as it stands.

3. Errors and pricing are reported to the customer in a redisplay of the shopping cart.

This process repeats until both the customer and the pipeline are happy with the order.

When the customer attempts to commit the order, the second pipeline is run. Typically this pipeline is run inside a transaction, so that the order is placed if and only if the payment authorization succeeds. Of course, depending on the customer, the system, and the transaction, there may be other conditions to satisfy besides payment. For example, if inventory information is not provided to the customer in real time during the shopping process, an inventory check may cause the transaction to abort at that point.

Within this context, we see that the master copy of the sales order, residing at the Commerce Server, is already assembled by the time either pipeline runs. Before the Plan Pipeline runs, the data may be inconsistent, incomplete, or invalid, but proving this is the purpose of the Plan Pipeline. The planning process iterates, with the user making trial changes to the master data by means of the shopping cart form, until the Plan Pipeline is happy. Note that not all the master data is sent to the user, who gets only a visual representation in HTML. For example, a drop-down box might be provided to select a ship-to address from a predefined list, but not the addresses themselves.

Generally, user communications occur only at the pipeline boundaries, before and after the Plan and the Purchase Pipeline, but there are some interesting exceptions. For example, when the payment system involves SET or a smart card, the payment authorization step, right in the middle of the Purchase Pipeline, and with a transaction open, involves user communication, as the commerce server invokes the e-wallet. Making this work without massive disruption of the Commerce Server's software architecture is difficult.

Order Processing Subsystems

This section discusses the major order processing subsystems, their variations, and their data requirements.

The manner in which data is passed among subsystems and external services is as varied as the software architectures of the vendors. Examples include the use of C++ objects, business documents as data, blackboard systems, Java classes, C libraries, and Enterprise JavaBeans. These various approaches all work well but have different implications for the flexibility, performance, and scalability of commerce solutions. Generally, those architectures with tightly defined data types are more scalable, potentially higher performing, but less flexible.

Order Validation

The starting point for order processing is order validation. This refers to the (usually) local checks of the shopping cart in order to build an internally consistent sales order business document. Most shopping carts are built around HTML forms that are filled in with default values, which can be changed by the buyer. The default values are built from user-specific data and product data, such as quantities. Validation checks may include:

- Checksum test on credit card numbers (so-called mod-10 check).
- Address validity—for example, does the zip code match the city?
- Denied parties list—is the buyer on the Commerce Department's list of terrorists?
- Ship-to—is the ship-to address acceptable?

Many of these tests can be done by local software, but network services are available as well, such as those provided by CyberSource.

Taxes

Sales and use taxes worldwide have incredible levels of complexity. The simplest commerce products have either no tax support or a single tax rate. This is often adequate for a small merchant with a single location. More complex software products have an API into which system integrators can connect tax computation, but they do not include the tax computation software as part of the product. High-end systems typically incorporate versions of third-party tax software, such as that from Taxware and Vertex, or incorporate callouts to service versions of tax software such as those operated by Taxware and CyberSource. Most business-to-business (B2B) systems rely on the tax capabilities of the backing enterprise systems. They may not be real-time capabilities, but the users do not expect them to be.

Tax subsystems typically need ship-to and bill-to information from the buyer, nexus information from the seller, and product information (tax classification) from the shopping cart. The geography is a complex problem. For example, the United States has over 6,000 tax jurisdictions, which do not always follow postal code boundaries. Consequently, correct evaluation of the tax laws requires geocode resolution of the ship-to or bill-to address to a sufficiently fine grain to identify the tax jurisdiction. Product information is also complex, because different tax jurisdictions have different rules about the tax rates that apply to different products. For example, clothing is tax-exempt in Massachusetts.

Outside the United States, many countries use variations of value-added tax (VAT), which has complex rules for transactions that cross national borders. In this area, correct implementation of the tax laws may even have user interface consequences, because the law requires the display of a legal VAT invoice. These complexities tend to break layers of abstraction, add layers of exceptions, and add sneak communication paths to otherwise clean product architectures.

Shipping

Shipping is another area of some complexity. Typically, e-commerce systems employ one of four different models for shipping calculations.

1. Flat rate. The shipping costs are built into the overall cost structure of the business.

2. Shipping models. The merchant can configure shipping price models based on flat rates, weight, or price of goods, and which further vary based on the shipping address (shipping zones) and shipping mode (such as air or ground). These models can usually closely approximate the actual shipping costs.

3. APIs and Web services. Shippers offer price calculation APIs or access to calculations through a Web service. For example, a merchant can make a call to a UPS calculator to determine an appropriate shipping price.

4. Backing system. Backing enterprise systems already calculate shipping charges, so this can be one of the points of integration.

Shipping calculations require a combination of seller information (warehouse locations, pricing models), buyer information (ship-to address, mode), and product information (weight, price).

Most e-commerce systems feature special treatment of shipping charges as part of the order form, but it is an interesting idea to treat such charges as noneditable line items that are computed by the system. This permits, for example, the merchant to offer coupons and discounts that apply to shipping, using the same price adjustment machinery already present.

Inventory

Inventory in e-commerce is problematic. There are no standard APIs. Many e-commerce systems provide no inventory support. Some products, such as Microsoft Commerce Server, provide local database inventory counts, but these counts are not integrated with an enterprise's existing inventory systems. In high-end systems, which are typically highly integrated or built specifically for one organization, inventory information can be provided by enterprise systems or by links to fulfillment houses.

Inventory sometimes requires sold-to customer information, as in the case of releases against purchase orders, and sometimes requires ship-to information, as in the case of warehouse selection. Inventory queries necessarily require product information, such as SKUs and quantities. Available-to-Promise (ATP) systems also require the dates on which goods are required.

Full implementation of inventory management requires transactions, because the buyer's commitment to purchase depends on inventory, and the seller's inventory management depends on the order commitment.

Business-to-Business Commerce

In this section we review two examples of business-to-business purchase order business processes: use of a backing enterprise resource planning (ERP) system and use of the Open Buying on the Internet (OBI) specification.

Backing ERP System

A shopping cart containing a list of items may be created, as was discussed earlier, by a variety of mechanisms: it can be entered by SKU, from a catalog, from an old order or invoice, from a remote system on the Web, or from another source. Once the decision to create the sales order has been made, the processing is split between the e-commerce system and the backing ERP system. Most ERP systems were designed for use by trained, in-house personnel, so some adaptations are necessary when orders from outside the enterprise are processed automatically. Generally the e-commerce system is responsible for authenticating the source of the order and granting the right to place an order, but all further order processing proceeds inside the ERP system.

The interaction of the e-commerce system with the ERP system usually occurs in two parts: order negotiation and order creation. In the order negotiation stage, the ERP system validates the line items, calculates pricing, and produces delivery estimates. The negotiation aspect of this stage occurs when items are rejected, when the size of the order would cause a rejection later (a credit hold, for example), or when delivery terms are inadequate. Once both the purchaser and the ERP system are happy with the order, it is passed to the ERP system for handling. These integration points are illustrated in Figure 16-7. As an example, SAP R/3 has explicit APIs for the steps of order negotiation and order creation—namely the business APIs (BAPIs) `SalesOrder.Simulate` and `SalesOrder.CreateFromData`.

Before the order gets to the ERP system, the e-commerce system is responsible for the customer interface. As discussed earlier, the e-commerce system frequently holds a database of end users authorized to use the system, whereas the ERP system customer master contains information about the purchasing company. The e-commerce system is then able to authenticate individual end users and associate them with one of the enterprise's business partners. The e-commerce system also usually has some level of approval processing, in which end users have restrictions on the kinds of orders they can create, based on dollar or item limits of various kinds or on interfaces to approval processing systems.

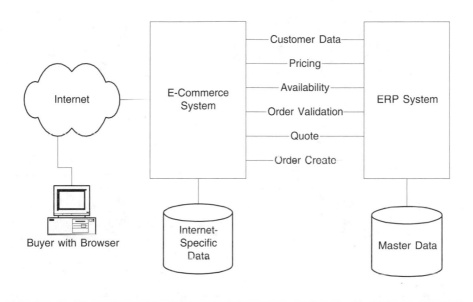

FIGURE 16-7. ERP System Integration

Open Buying on the Internet

The Open Buying on the Internet (OBI) Consortium was formed in October 1996 in an attempt to standardize an open, vendor-neutral mechanism for business-to-business e-commerce. OBI focuses on high-volume, low-dollar transactions in which there is the most to be gained by automation that can reduce per-order overhead costs. The basic idea of OBI is to divide commerce functionality between buying and selling organizations in the way that makes the most sense to both organizations.

The basic elements of OBI are as follows.

- Requisitioners in the buying organization do the shopping, rather than intermediaries in the purchasing department.
- Selling organizations operate online catalogs, because they are best able to keep the catalog information up-to-date.
- Orders are composed at the seller catalog system but routed to the buying organization for approval, because the buying organization is responsible for approval policy and purchasing budgets.
- The approved order is routed to the seller for fulfillment.
- Payments are processed by a third party skilled in such matters.

The OBI order flow is shown in Figure 16-8.

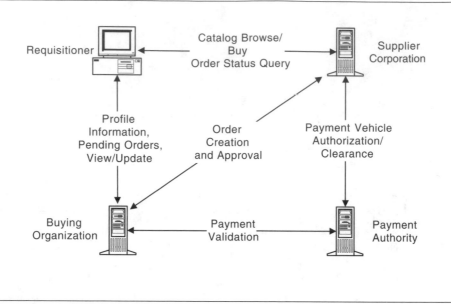

FIGURE 16-8. OBI Order Flowt

The Internet as a Replacement for EDI

Electronic Data Interchange (EDI) refers to the automated transmission of business documents such as purchase orders between enterprises. Many companies are now using document transmission over the Internet as a replacement for the value-added networks (VANs) that used to handle the bulk of EDI data transmission. This is not a straightforward swap, because the Internet itself replaces only communications—it provides none of the value-added services such as buffering, receipts, and reliability. To some extent, these features are now available in various B2B server products, such as iPlanet ECXPert, webMethods B2B Integration Server, and Microsoft BizTalk server. In addition, the VAN operators and new entrants now operate various value-added services over the Internet, to which companies can subscribe.

Shopping Cart Presentation

Presenting a shopping cart to a customer often seems to be a mundane task. However, a poor presentation can lose a sale, whereas a good presentation offers a chance to sell additional products and services. What are some aspects of good presentation of a shopping cart?

First, the presentation should be consistent with the rest of the site. This may seem obvious, but the task is often left as a "simple programming exercise," and the result looks somewhat different from the other pages on the site. This can be particularly true if the shopping cart is stored on another system.

Second, performance is critical. Although performance is almost always a consideration, shopping cart pages typically involve more complex database queries than most dynamic Web pages, and very little of the page generation can be cached. As discussed previously, displaying a shopping cart page can even involve a complex computation of several pipeline stages. To make the interactive display fast enough, the database and pipeline need to be designed to make this kind of operation run quickly, even at the expense of additional complexity.

Third, the shopping cart should provide additional opportunities to offer products and services to customers. The offers may be for related products, accessories, and services, such as extended warranties, or they may simply be offers for popular products and best-sellers. In effect, any page displayed for the user is a chance to continue the interaction and build the relationship with the customer.

Fourth, the shopping cart page is a good place to offer information to the customer. This is particularly true for information of direct interest, such as shipping options, terms, and conditions. Some sites require customers to go through several steps before making such information available, which only frustrates customers who want to know their options before committing to an order.

Finally, bad presentation puts off customers who may simply choose not to buy. From the customer's point of view, it is still an important part of the overall user experience.

Abandoned Shopping Carts

Indeed, the problem of customers who choose not to buy is part of the challenge of "abandoned shopping carts." Many sites (and analysts of various kinds) count the percentage of completed orders and get very concerned if too many shopping carts are used without completing a purchase. From time to time, it's even common to see industry publications wringing their hands over the question of why consumers are abandoning their shopping carts. On the surface, this seems to be a reasonable metric that merits considerable attention. The problem is that many factors contribute to a customer's decision to abandon a cart, and the proper response for a Web site depends on the nature of the problem.

The first and most basic problem with the abandoned shopping cart metric is the assumption that the use of a shopping cart represents an intent to buy. For many people, the shopping cart is often an easy way to keep track of possible purchases, perhaps when comparing prices (or other attributes, such as shipping charges) from different sites. This would be an unusual way to use a physical shopping cart in a physical store, and perhaps the term *shopping cart* is confusing because the analogy breaks down at this point. As an example, consider a customer shopping for a digital camera. To keep track of different choices, based on various models and prices, at four different sellers, the customer creates a shopping cart at each one. In many cases, there is really no other easy, online way to do this. At the end, the customer buys one camera from one site, and the others are all abandoned. Three out of four carts have been left behind, but the initial analysis doesn't tell us much about why the customer went elsewhere.

The other main category of problems regarding abandoned carts is failure of presentation, mostly as discussed above. If a customer can't find some important information, or if the display is slow, or if the system appears to fail in the middle of the transaction, the customer is likely to buy elsewhere.

Summary

For the Internet customer, shopping carts and order management are simply the mechanics of making a transaction work. Therefore, any surprises, failures, or unusual types of behavior are disruptive to the customer's main goal: finishing the transaction quickly and effectively. In this chapter, we have explored some of the various capabilities and approaches used for shopping carts, with a particular eye toward flexible implementation, so the capabilities of the cart can evolve with the overall development of the e-commerce system.

CHAPTER 17　　　　　　 *Transaction Processing*

> Six thousand years ago, the Sumerians invented writing for transaction processing.
>
> —Jim Gray and Andreas Reuter[1]

Transactions and Internet Commerce

This chapter serves two functions: it introduces the technologies of transaction processing as they relate to Internet commerce, and it discusses several issues related to the completeness and integrity of the commerce application, such as backup and disaster recovery.

The purpose of Internet commerce is to facilitate the exchange of payments for goods and services. The purpose of transaction processing, at its most basic, is to ensure that if payment has occurred, then goods are delivered, and to ensure that goods are never delivered to someone who has not paid for them. This is substantially more difficult than it seems.

When commerce is conducted face-to-face, many social and informal mechanisms help perform error recovery. If the change is wrong or goods are not delivered, the individuals involved will usually notice and try again. With information systems, getting the software to work correctly when everything flows smoothly is fairly easy, but getting the software to handle all the potential failures correctly is very hard. Transac-

---

1. Jim Gray and Andreas Reuter, *Transaction Processing: Concepts and Techniques* (Morgan Kaufmann, 1993).

tion processing as a discipline provides a framework for building complex systems so that their behavior is correct, even in the presence of failures.

Overview of Transaction Processing

Functions performed by Internet commerce applications, such as sales and returns, are quite complex. Each function is composed of several other activities. For example, a sale event might include the following activities.

- Debit buyer's account.[2]
- Credit seller's account.
- Record event for business records.
- Transmit order to fulfillment center.
- Issue receipt to buyer.

Transaction systems make sure that all of these activities happen if any one of them does, that the activities of multiple buyers do not interfere with each other, and that records are not lost. From this perspective, transactions have four essential characteristics, known by the acronym *ACID*.

1. Atomicity. In our example, it would be bad if the system debited the buyer without crediting the seller, or if the system charged the buyer without delivering a receipt. In other words, it must not happen that only some steps of the transaction occur. Either all of the steps must be taken, or it must seem to all observers that the transaction never happened at all.

2. Consistency. If the state of the environment is represented by account balances, the presence of receipts, and so forth, it must never happen that the state is inconsistent. For example, accounts must balance both before and after the transaction.

3. Isolation. Because an Internet commerce business transaction takes some period of time, and because there may be multiple transactions underway, it is important that the activities of one buyer do not interfere with those of another buyer. The easiest way to think about this is that even though simultaneous transactions overlap, imagine that they do not overlap, but rather occur in some order or *serialization*—then design the system so that overlapping transactions work as though they were serialized. Figure 17-1 presents an example of this concept.

4. Durability. Once a transaction is complete or committed, it should be impossible for its effects to come undone as the result of a system or component failure. In practice, this means that the results of transactions are reliably recorded on a stable storage medium that is resilient to failure, such as mirrored disk drives.

---

2. From a database point of view, debiting an account is itself a complex operation involving three separate steps: reading the old balance, subtracting the debit, and storing back the new balance.

Consider a single credit transaction, for $10:

- Step 1: Read old account balance (say, $100)
- Step 2: Add credit and old balance ($100 + $10 = $110)
- Step 3: Store updated balance ($110)

Now suppose that two credit transactions are going on at about the same time, one for $10 and one for $20. With no transaction isolation, it might happen that the steps interleave as follows:

- Transaction A, step 1: Read old balance ($100)
- Transaction B, step 1: Read old balance ($100)
- Transaction A, step 2: Add credit and old balance ($100 + $10 = $110)
- Transaction B, step 2: Add credit and old balance ($100 + $20 = $120)
- Transaction A, step 3: Store updated balance ($110)
- Transaction B, step 3: Store updated balance ($120)

At the end, the account has only $120 instead of the correct $130. With transaction isolation, the correct result is the one obtained as if the transactions were serialized, with Transaction A occurring either completely before or completely after Transaction B:

- Transaction A, step 1: Read old balance ($100)
- Transaction A, step 2: Add credit and old balance ($100 + $10 = $110)
- Transaction A, step 3: Store updated balance ($110)
- Transaction B, step 1: Read old balance ($110)
- Transaction B, step 2: Add credit and old balance ($110 + $20 = $130)
- Transaction B, step 3: Store updated balance ($130)

FIGURE 17-1. **Example of Transaction Serialization**

Two-Phase Commit

When a transaction affects multiple resources, perhaps distributed across multiple systems on a network, a technique known as *two-phase commit* is used to ensure that the total transaction is atomic. In this technique, a central transaction coordinator communicates with the various resource managers and orchestrates the transaction.

- Phase 1a—vote

  The transaction coordinator asks each of the resource managers if it can commit the transaction. If they all vote yes, the transaction will commit.

- Phase 1b—record

  The transaction coordinator records in durable storage that the transaction has committed.

- Phase 2a— commit

  The transaction coordinator informs each of the resource managers that the transaction has committed.

- Phase 2b—complete

  The transaction coordinator records in durable storage that it has received acknowledgments from all resource managers. At this point, no extra work will be necessary to recover from a failure.

The point at which this distributed transaction becomes valid, or *committed*, is the point in phase 1b when the transaction coordinator records that the transaction has committed. If any involved system fails before this happens, the transaction aborts and will not be committed anywhere. If any system fails after phase 1b, then the transaction coordinator will orchestrate recovery and eventual commit of the transaction everywhere.

Transaction Processing in Internet Commerce

Let's consider a real example—an Internet commerce system in which the following steps occur.

1. The buyer selects one or several items from a Web-based catalog.
2. The buyer securely enters credit card and shipping information.
3. Product, tax, and shipping charges are computed.
4. The buyer accepts the resulting total amount.
5. A credit card authorization is obtained.
6. An advice of order message is sent to a fulfillment center.
7. The buyer receives a receipt.

The first step is to identify the transaction. Steps 1 and 2 do not need to be "inside the transaction." These steps are the browsing phase and an interactive phase of order completion (entering credit card and shipping information) that may require several attempts to get right. Step 3, in which the order total is computed, does not need to be inside the transaction either, although it is important to disallow any changes in the order that might affect the total (such as adding an additional item to the order). The real transaction consists of steps 4 through 7. From the point that the buyer accepts the order through all activities related to payment and fulfillment, either all steps must be completed successfully or the system must act as though the order had never been accepted.

The transaction may fail for several reasons.

- The seller's computer crashes or there is a power failure.

  From the buyer's perspective, she clicks the **OK to buy** button and nothing happens. She may give up or simply click **OK to buy** again. In either case, she will be unhappy to be charged for goods never received, or to be charged twice for goods received only once.

- The buyer's computer crashes or there is a power failure.

  From the buyer's perspective, he clicks the **OK to buy** button and then the lights go out. When the power comes back, the buyer would like to try again, and be charged exactly once for one set of goods. Because the buyer's computer fails after the seller's computer receives the okay, it is likely that steps 4, 5, and 6 succeed, leaving only step 7. In this case, the commerce system can simply provide a way for the buyer to get a duplicate receipt.

- The credit card authorization fails.

  If the authorization fails, the system should essentially return to step 2, suggesting to the buyer that her card number might have been entered incorrectly and giving her an opportunity to try again.

- The line to the credit card network fails between the time the authorization request is sent and the time the response is received.

  This is a very interesting kind of failure, because the seller's system has no way to tell whether the request message ever got to the credit card network, or whether the reply was lost. It is important that the customer not be charged twice, so the commerce system must employ recovery techniques to figure out whether the authorization succeeded, failed, or never happened.

Integrating External Systems with Transactions

In the preceding section, an example of the communications channel failing during a credit card authorization message was presented. This is an example of a general issue with transaction systems of communicating with devices and systems outside their control. For an outside system to participate in a transaction, the functions of the outside system must be idempotent or testable. *Idempotent* means that if repeated requests for the same action are made, the action will take place only once (or rather, that repeated requests have no additional effect beyond the first). *Testable* means that there is a way for the transaction system to test whether the action has taken place, so as not to make a duplicate request.

In the preceding example of credit card authorization, the card protocols have been designed with a reference number as part of the request. If a duplicate request with a known reference number is received, the credit card system merely returns the previous reply, rather than duplicating the request.

Implementing Transactions

It is not our purpose in this book to explain how to write the code for transaction systems, but some brief examples will be useful.

```
select balance from account where account_id = 12345;
newbalance = balance + 10;
update account set "balance = newbalance" where
account_id = 12345;
commit work;
```

FIGURE 17-2. A Database Transaction in SQL

Database Engines

Most programmers are first exposed to transactions in the context of the Structured
Query Language (SQL) and databases such as Oracle and Microsoft SQL Server. In
these systems, transaction support is provided by the database engine for applications
whose permanent data is stored in the database. The SQL language standard includes
the statements **COMMIT WORK** and **ROLLBACK WORK**, which, respectively,
make all changes permanent or discard all updates since the end of the previous transaction. Consider the example in Figure 17-2, which uses a transaction to protect the
updating of an account balance.

Transaction Processing Monitors

When an application must manage data spread across multiple systems, a transaction
processing (TP) monitor is often used to build the application. TP monitors typically
include many facilities for large-scale applications, such as load balancing and security, but with respect to transaction processing the key benefit they offer is the ability
to coordinate updates to multiple database engines in single transactions. BEA Tuxedo and IBM CICS are widely used TP monitors.

Application Servers

Transaction services are becoming a standard part of application servers. J2EE application servers support the Java Transaction API (JTA), typically through the Java
Transaction Service (JTS). Microsoft systems offer the Microsoft Transaction Service
(MTS). Typically these systems offer the application a standard API with which to
mark transaction boundaries, and translate those boundaries into the proper use of resource managers such as databases and communications managers such as COM and
CORBA.

Application Code

Sometimes transactions must be handled directly by the application—for example,
when a resource used by the application is external. One useful technique for applications programmers to remember is the use of a write-ahead log. Consider the example
from Internet commerce of communicating an order to the fulfillment center when the

> **Write-Ahead Log Algorithm**
>
> 1. Create intentions record `<send order XYZ to fulfillment>`.
> 2. Ensure that the intentions record is written out to disk.
> 3. Complete the sale transaction.
>
> The actual transmission of orders to the fulfillment house is done by the following background job:
>
> 1. Scan for an intentions record not marked *complete* and not locked.
> 2. Lock the record.
> 3. Send it (but the fulfillment center must recognize and ignore duplicates).
> 4. Mark it *complete*.
> 5. Unlock it.
>
> These procedures together provide for transactional acceptance of orders with deferred hand-off to the fulfillment center and error recovery from both system and communications failures.

order is accepted. Communications with the fulfillment center might be slow and you don't want to make the customer wait, or the fulfillment center might be unavailable on weekends, but these should not be reasons to fail to complete the order. Instead, the commerce system can record its intention to communicate with the fulfillment center in a local persistent file, called an *intentions log* or *write-ahead log*, complete the order, and only later push the order out to the fulfillment house. The intentions log also handles communications and system crashes cleanly.

Client Software

In an Internet commerce system, the use of Web browsers or other client software requires special analysis.

- Can unanticipated user events cause unwanted effects?

  As in other systems in which an end user operates the terminal, Internet commerce systems that rely on Web browsers for their user interfaces can expect to receive as input arbitrary sequences of events with arbitrary timing. The user may click any link or button at any time, enter arbitrary information into forms, click the same button over and over again, or simply vanish at any point, only to return hours later. The system must be completely bulletproof against such activities. This problem is much more difficult in Internet commerce than in other systems, because the user terminal—the browser—is a general-purpose device and cannot be easily constrained. In networks of ATMs, for example, the terminal is operated by the end user, but the user's behavior is carefully constrained by the terminal software. While the system is considering a request, for example, all keys but **Cancel** can be locked. On the Internet, the browser works the same way for all applications, and the standard user interface model grants a great deal of power to the user.

- Can unfriendly users generate errors in system behavior?

  Although it sometimes seems as though the desired user population can create the most stressful situations for the system, unfriendly users (or *crackers*) can also cause havoc. Because the system is available to the open network, an unfriendly user can transmit arbitrary bit strings to the system as though they were valid inputs. The system must carefully validate all inputs from any source that is not trusted, and should probably carefully check all inputs, trusted or not. Unfriendly users could even reprogram the user terminal or browser to give it completely different behavior.

Sometimes error recovery is a cost-benefit trade-off. System designers will design the system for the common (correct operation) case and provide rather expensive error-recovery mechanisms. This approach works well when the error cases are unlikely. However, if there is a way for an unfriendly user to force the system to generate errors, or to respond to an apparent error, then even if the system operates correctly, it may perform poorly or invalidate the design assumptions. Again, it is important not to trust any message that could have come from an untrusted party.[3]

Implementing Transaction Processing Systems

Of course, there is more to implementing a business application than ensuring ACID semantics, but a careful analysis of the transactional aspects provides a good basis for system design. In addition, taking this point of view early in the design is much easier than trying to retrofit an existing system to behave better.

Files

It is possible to build a complete transaction processing system on top of an ordinary filesystem. Indeed, in the early days of online transaction processing, systems were built from a TP monitor together with a filesystem. Computer filesystems perform a set of relatively simple operations: create, delete, open, close, read, write, and seek. Filesystems generally provide no assistance in structuring the contents of files and no assistance in managing transactions, except that some operating systems provide basic

---

3. As a particularly egregious example of unwarranted trust, early versions of some Internet commerce systems kept the prices of merchandise in so-called hidden form fields. These fields are not normally visible to the buyer, but an unfriendly user has full access to these fields and could in fact change prices. Sadly, this kind of mistake was still being made in 2002.

facilities to lock and unlock files, protecting them from concurrent access. (Locks are a way of providing isolation semantics at the risk of introducing performance problems and deadlocks.[4]) Nevertheless, files are valuable for several purposes.

- Logs

  Many applications write log files directly to a filesystem. This can be a very high-performance solution, but the required operation—writing a log record to the end of a file—is surprisingly hard to get right. On many filesystems, appending to a file with a single write operation is an atomic operation, but the key word is *single*. A common mistake is using a buffered input/output package to write log files. This appears to work, but the log records can be mangled. A correct implementation makes sure that each write operation contains an integral number of log records. Log files are commonly used for recording application events and errors. For example, most Web servers can be configured to write information about every request to a log file.

- Read-only data

  A filesystem can provide useful storage for read-only data in a transaction system. Filesystems are highly optimized for read-write operations, but other operations, such as locking and unlocking, may not be so fast.

Databases

Fundamentally, databases are a way to store structured information, but they do much more than this. Databases have several important properties.

- Databases support transactions.

  Databases on the market today typically support the Structured Query Language (SQL), which includes all the mechanisms necessary to support transactions. In addition, today's databases are designed to support ACID semantics, which makes it easier to build applications for processing transactions.

- Databases store structured information.

  Online transaction systems work with large numbers of records of many different types. Databases manage all this complexity, leaving the application free to act on the relevant records rather than worry about, for example, storage allocation.

- Databases are self-describing.

  In modern databases, information describing the structure of the database is stored in the database itself. This approach makes it possible to write general-purpose tools that work with information stored in databases without any particular knowledge of the application. For example, general-purpose reporting tools work

---

4. A deadlock occurs when two or more processes are waiting for resources and neither of them can make any progress. For example, suppose two transactions are in progress, and each needs resources A and B. If transaction 1 locks resource A and then attempts to lock resource B, while transaction 2 locks resource B and then attempts to lock resource A, neither transaction can proceed.

this way, making it possible to create new and customized reports without traditional programming.[5]

- Databases permit rapid information retrieval.

    Database managers provide built-in support for searching and selecting particular records from all those stored.

TP Monitors

TP monitors evolved to solve some of the problems of building online transaction processing systems that go beyond data storage and retrieval. A TP monitor is not a replacement for a database, but it provides an additional set of functionality that makes it easier to assemble and operate complex applications.

- Transaction management

    TP monitors provide capabilities for transaction management that at first glance seems to duplicate those of databases. However, TP monitors can coordinate transactions that span multiple databases and that include management of other kinds of resources, such as communications systems or remote applications.

- Application management

    TP monitors provide application management. Registered applications are automatically started whenever the system restarts and are also restarted in the event of crashes. TP monitors also provide facilities for sharing the processing load across multiple systems. These sorts of services are sometimes provided by application servers or Web servers in the Internet context: Open Market's FastCGI can manage applications, as can Microsoft's IIS version 4.0. Simple Web applications implemented as CGI programs may not need management, because they are started anew for each request.

- Terminal and communications management

    Traditional online transaction processing (OLTP) applications depend on networks of hardwired or networked terminals. Message queuing and communications services for such terminals are provided by TP monitors, but these functions are not as relevant for Internet applications, because they are provided by Web servers.

Keeping Business Records

Some of the principal outputs of the transaction processing subsystem of an Internet commerce system are business records of various kinds. Some types of records, such as those for orders and payments, are part of the core operation of the business. Others, such as those containing customer data, create an important information asset of

---

5. Using a good user interface to create a solution to a problem really is programming, it just doesn't seem like it. Good tools work at just the right level of abstraction to match the way the application designer thinks about the problem being solved.

the business   the customer database. Still others, such as tax records, are necessary to satisfy regulatory and legal requirements.

Core Business Records

Some records are essential for managing day-to-day business.

- Orders

  An order is an *offer to buy*, incorporating items, their characteristics, terms and conditions, prices, shipping and billing addresses, and so forth. Each information element is there for a specific purpose. In addition, an order is not created all at once. Instead, an order is built up item by item during an order capture phase, and then missing elements—addresses, tax and shipping charges, and so forth—are added during the order completion phase. When the buyer and seller are both satisfied, the order is completed and becomes a binding agreement.

- Invoices

  An invoice is a record of fulfillment, recording that goods have been shipped or services rendered. Because the buyer now owes the seller money, the invoice is also a bill, but it is not directly coupled to payment. Normally, an invoice is never changed once created, because it represents a statement of historical fact (a product was shipped).

- Payments (receipts)

  A receipt is a record of a payment, usually issued by the seller, but not always (a receipt for a credit would be logically issued by the buyer).

Collateral Business Records

Some records are kept in order to build a long-term information asset.

- Customer database

  Customer names, addresses, buying histories, and preferences help the marketing and sales departments understand their customers better. If the seller's business is distribution rather than production, then maintaining close customer relationships may be the core value of the business. Customer information not only is useful for reports but also is useful online for providing personalized services and customized product catalogs.

- Advertising and tracking

  In Internet commerce, as in no other medium, it is possible to trace how buyers find sellers. The information generated by advertising not only determines who pays whom how much for the ad placement but also works in an active feedback loop to gauge the effectiveness of advertising and to control future efforts. Once a buyer has located a seller, Internet-based systems can track buyer behavior and actions at a very detailed level. This information can refine product presentation and provide opportunities for merchandising.

Government Records

Some records are kept pursuant to external requirements. For example, governments have specific legal requirements for record keeping in support of sales and use taxes. Tax issues for Internet commerce are discussed in Chapter 18.

Record Life Cycle

A typical business record item, such as an order entered by a customer, follows a complex life cycle. Let's follow an order through its life cycle.

- Create

  When a buyer first selects an item for potential purchase, the order is created. This first phase of order building—order capture—can persist for an extended period. During this phase, the order may be a temporary record, perhaps maintained by a Java applet on the buyer's desktop, or it may be a formal database record at the server.

- Store

  During the early life of an order, while the buyer is considering potential items for purchase, it may not be necessary to establish a permanent record. At some point, either because the potential order has reached critical value or merely as a user convenience, the order is stored and given a unique identity. The record may be permanent or may be erased if the order is never completed, but the order identity or reference number is not reused.

- Process

  The order must pass through several stages of processing as part of the normal order flow. For example, shipping charges and taxes are computed and credit authorizations obtained. When the order is finalized, it must be communicated to systems responsible for fulfillment.

- Access

  For some period after the order has been created, it will be in active use. During order processing, the buyer and seller both update the order-in-process, and after finalization, the order is referenced by the customer service subsystem.

- Report

  The order will probably be the object of a variety of reports during its life. Daily sales, open orders, taxable sales, customer billing, and marketing reports all use the order information.

- Archive

  Once the order has completed active processing and a standard span of accessibility for reporting, it is archived. In practice, archival storage may be the same mechanism as system backup, but their purposes are quite different. Backup systems exist in order to recover from hardware or software failures and for disaster recovery, whereas archives represent permanent business records.

- Retrieve

  Occasionally, an order that has been moved offline into archival storage will be needed. For example, suppose records are normally kept online for 60 days, but a customer dispute arises after 90 days. In this case, the records involved must be retrieved from the archives. Retrieval can be a very expensive operation, so the period during which records are kept online must be long enough to make retrieval requests unlikely.

Design Implications of Record Keeping

The record life cycle has several implications for the design of transaction processing systems that create and maintain records. First, let's take a look at the characteristics of the records involved.

Mutable and Immutable Records

Some records, once created, are never changed. Invoices and payment receipts are two examples. These records represent factual records of real events, and therefore are not subject to revision. Such records are called *immutable*. Even when an error is detected later, an immutable record is never revised; instead, a separate *correction record* is created, referencing the first record. In this regard, immutable records are similar to newspapers. Newspapers, once printed, are not changed. In case of error, a correction may be printed in a later edition (but there may be different editions of a particular daily, each with different versions of the same story).

Other records are *mutable* and may be freely changed. For example, during order capture, the items and quantities in the order may change frequently before the order is finalized.

Immutable records permit great simplification of transaction processing systems, because they are never modified. As such, a transaction system does not require complex locking of immutable records to ensure that access to them is consistent. Mutable records require locking, to ensure that while one process is reading the record, another process is not changing it. In addition, copies of immutable records can be made freely; because they are never changed, there is no danger of different copies containing different information.

Failure and Transaction Semantics

Each type of record in an Internet commerce system should be carefully analyzed to establish how it should behave regarding ACID properties. As an example, let's consider the properties that an order should have during the order capture stage, when items are being added or subtracted from the order or when quantities are being changed.

One point of view is that order capture does not need full transaction semantics. Reasoning by analogy with a paper-based order, the order in some sense doesn't even exist until the form is handed to the seller. This analysis might come naturally to a design that implements the order form as a Java applet residing on the buyer's computer. In the normal course of events, the complete order is submitted to the seller, but if the buyer's computer is turned off before the order has been submitted, then the order is lost.

An alternative point of view is that the Internet permits new capabilities by giving even an order-in-process full transactional semantics. For example, if the order is transactional, then the in-process order can accurately reserve against available inventory. If the order is durable, then even a crash of the buyer's computer will not result in a loss of information; the partially completed order will still be there when the buyer comes back online.

Payments, however, require complete transaction semantics. Sellers are unhappy when payments are lost, and buyers are unhappy when payment is made but no goods are delivered.

Access Patterns

The pattern of usage of a type of record is highly relevant to the design of the system intended to support it. A particular record may pass through several of the following types of access patterns during its life cycle.

- Online records

  Some records are used primarily online. For example, during the order completion phase of processing, an order is used primarily online as buyer and seller interactively cooperate to build a complete purchase order.

- Offline records

  Audit records (discussed later) and records for reporting are primarily offline records. Audit records may never be accessed, and reporting is usually done from a copy of the online master records so that the processing and queries associated with reporting cannot disturb the performance of the production system. Offline records certainly must be durable, but because they tend to be immutable, they may have little need for isolation.

- Messages

  A message sent from one system to another is a kind of record, too. This situation arises, for example, when an order leaves the Internet commerce system and enters a traditional fulfillment system. Typically, the hand-off of the order must have transactional semantics—the order must not be lost and must be entered exactly once into the fulfillment system.

Logging

Log records are messages written by an application in sequential order. The name derives from the nautical logbook, which is a record of an ocean voyage. In the computer context, a *log* is any sequentially organized write-once data structure, but for the purposes of this section, messages written to the log are for the benefit of other applications or operations staff and are usually not ever read back by the applications that created them.

Applications write log records for many purposes.

- Error reporting

  Properly written applications should not crash, but when exceptional conditions arise, the application reports the event in the log before proceeding. The purpose of this is to ensure that operations personnel learn that the event has occurred, so they can take corrective action.

- Security events

  Log records report events that do not affect the application's functions but are suspicious, such as malformed input data that is rejected. These events could mean that the remote system creating the data is configured incorrectly or that a hacker is probing for security vulnerabilities in the application.

- Audit records

  Applications write log records to report audit events, such as *sales tax due* or *order created*. These records are useful for review if a problem is later discovered and may be the source of reporting applications.

- Performance measurement

  Log records of system events are usually timestamped so that they can serve as source information about system performance and load—so many transactions per second, each with so much latency.

- User activity reporting

  Logs are used to record raw clickstream data (as Web server logs) or much more complex application-specific user activities, such as searches made in a catalog that are of interest to marketing.

- Application debugging

  It is very common to include code in the application itself to report the flow of control such as procedure entry and exit and to report internal variables during application checkout and debugging. Good programming practice is never to delete such code, but rather to change the level of logging to control the amount of information saved.

There are many kinds of log systems, but most of them decouple the creation of log records from their recording. Log records are structured and contain codes about the part of the system that initiated them, their purpose (debugging versus operational, for example), the severity of the event, timestamps, and free text. The recording part of the log subsystem is able to route different kinds of log events to disk, to network management systems, or to other applications, which might, for example, page personnel if a serious error is reported.

Audits

In normal business terminology, an *audit* is an independent review that verifies that an enterprise's financial records are accurate and that the enterprise has conformed to sound accounting practices. For the purposes of Internet commerce, two other concepts are relevant.

1. Independent verification of design and implementation

   A review is made of the system design and operational practices in order to determine if design objectives have been met. For example, in a security audit, a review is made of every aspect of system design, implementation, and operations to ensure that confidential information is protected and that unauthorized access has not occurred and cannot occur in the future.

2. A record trail of an individual transaction

   The audit trail of a transaction is the collection of records that make it possible to verify that the particular transaction actually occurred in the way it was supposed to have occurred. The audit trail is used for reporting, for customer service inquiries, and for dispute resolutions. It is not part of the main order processing flow.

Summary

Regardless of whether an Internet commerce system is small or large, transaction processing principles cannot be ignored. Even a very simple commerce application consisting of a Web-based order form that appends orders to a file must carefully use file-locking techniques to ensure that nearly simultaneous orders do not cause lost orders or scramble the file. A medium-sized commerce application might use a database management system incorporating transactions, and a very large application might use a TP monitor to route Internet orders into an existing order processing system.

CHAPTER 18

*Integration with
Enterprise Applications*

God is in the details.
> —Popular saying[1]

The Details Behind the Scenes

Internet commerce systems usually do not stand by themselves. They connect with, feed, and are fed by many other software applications in the enterprise, such as enterprise resource planning (ERP), customer relationship management (CRM), and other applications. This chapter does not delve into the inner workings of such applications, but it does address middleware and other technologies that aid in the integration of Internet systems with the rest of the business.

This chapter introduces several commerce issues, such as taxes, logistics, and inventory management, that must be addressed in a complete system for Internet commerce. Internet systems that merely accepting orders may be able to avoid these concerns, but there are few alternatives for systems that must guarantee availability, display accurate prices, and meet legal obligations for payment of taxes.

In practice, these issues simply reflect issues in the real world of business. When a project for Internet commerce grows out of an existing business, such issues can often be solved by integrating the commerce system with existing enterprise systems. But even businesses created solely because of Internet opportunities must manage prob-

---

1. This saying was popular with architect Mies van der Rohe and is often attributed to Gustave Flaubert, but the actual origin is unclear.

lems such as taxes, logistics, and inventory. Indeed, one test of software for Internet commerce is how well it handles these problems.

Enterprise Systems Architecture

Figure 18-1 shows the software systems of a highly integrated enterprise and their interactions with external software systems belonging to partners, customers, and service providers. Highly integrated enterprises use many kinds of software, including the following.

- Enterprise resource planning (ERP)

  ERP systems typically include functionality for running the internal functions of the business in areas such as finance, human resources, manufacturing, and logistics.

- Customer relationship management (CRM)

  CRM systems collectively are those responsible for marketing, sales, and service—every business aspect that touches the customer.

- Data warehouse

  Data warehouse systems are repositories for the business information created by the various other systems in the enterprise. For example, sales data from the ERP system, component cost data from supply chain systems, and customer data from CRM systems may be collected together and used for decision making. Data warehouse systems have arisen for two main reasons. First, the various source systems typically are not designed to retain such information indefinitely. Second, by combining information from disparate systems, new correlations can be discovered.

- Data mining

  Data mining refers to the practice of searching through large volumes of information (typically stored in data warehouses) to answer complex questions and to discover unexpected patterns in data.

- Online analytical processing (OLAP)

  OLAP is closely related to a combination of data warehousing and data mining but has come to be used in those cases in which the data is represented in a multidimensional way to enable fast, interactive queries about the business.

- Supply chain management (SCM)

  Supply chain management goes beyond the functionality of the manufacturing requirements planning modules of ERP systems to fully manage scheduling and acquisition of production material.

- Sales force automation (SFA)

  Sales force automation includes lead tracking, forecasting, compensation, and other activities related to the sales force.

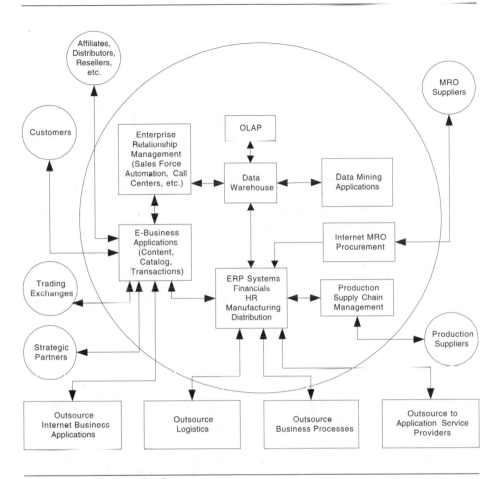

FIGURE 18-1. Enterprise Systems

- Maintenance, repair, and operations (MRO) procurement

  MRO systems are responsible for supplies not needed for product manufacturing. These may include anything from office supplies to plant repair parts. Buy-side Internet commerce systems help to solve these problems.

- E-business

  These are the Internet-based systems this book is about: content management, catalogs, and transaction processing. E-business necessarily overlaps or connects with many other areas of enterprise software.

Integration Pitfalls

Many businesses already have information systems for business management: order processing, manufacturing, accounting, fulfillment, and so forth. It often makes sense for a new Internet commerce system to integrate with the existing information systems wherever possible, rather than running the Internet part of the business completely separately. Integration must be done very carefully, with special attention to the following issues.

- Real-time requirements

  Existing systems may not have the proper real-time requirements for direct connection to an Internet commerce system intended for interactive use. To some extent, these problems can be handled by buffering, queuing, and caching between the Internet system and the existing system.

- Security requirements

  Existing systems may not be designed with appropriate security mechanisms for Internet commerce. For example, most existing systems are designed for use by specifically trained personnel, who work for the system operator. Internet commerce systems frequently need to be directly accessed and operated by untrained end users, who do not work for the system operator.

- Support for required roles

  Existing systems may not be designed with the roles needed by the Internet system. For example, an existing order entry system for a mail- or telephone-order seller would normally be designed for use by an order entry operator, not for use directly by the customer.

- Trust protections

  Existing systems may not be designed to connect directly with systems operated by different organizations. In these cases, special care must be taken to validate all input from "outside."

Middleware

Middleware was developed to solve a variety of problems that arise in the process of integrating several applications. Suppose there are n applications that must work together. The obvious approach is to build pairwise connections between them, but this requires $n(n-1)$ separate integration efforts. When any application is changed, each of that application's links with other applications must be updated. When a new application is added, n integrations with the existing applications must be added. The result of this $O(n^2)$ problem is a management and maintenance nightmare.

Middleware is often portrayed as a "bus" for enterprise information that connects all applications. Each application must communicate only with the middleware, rather than directly with each of the other applications. This converts the $O(n^2)$ problem into an $O(n)$ problem. Furthermore, when an application is added or an existing application is updated, only that application's connection to the middleware must be updated; other applications can continue unchanged. This separation of concerns can greatly reduce the problems of maintenance.

Middleware can also benefit individual applications that are distributed or are intended for use as components of an overall enterprise system. If an application has APIs that are intended for remote use, the application vendor has a choice. On the one hand, the vendor might develop and support the communications machinery and interfaces for many languages and platforms. On the other hand, the vendor might provide a single API with middleware that effectively extends the API to remote applications running on disparate platforms and implemented with different programming languages.

Layers of Middleware

This concept of middleware—common infrastructure that takes care of connecting applications—is fairly compelling. As with other systems we have considered, middleware is now available in multiple layers of functionality.

- Communications layer

    Communications middleware takes care of moving messages between applications. It may take the form of message-oriented, remote procedure call, or publish-subscribe systems (see below). Communications middleware provides libraries and APIs for a variety of languages and platforms.

- Syntax layer

    Once raw communications have been established, the next problem for application integration is message syntax. One system may use ASCII whereas another uses EBCDIC. Monetary amounts may be represented by scaled fixed-point numbers (such as using "10000" to mean "$10.00"). The source message may contain a superset of information required by the target system. Many middleware packages include facilities for handling such syntactic data mapping problems. Some, such as Mercator's Mercator product, specialize in data mapping.

- Semantic layer

    Given communications and syntax, the next problem is semantics, or the meanings of the various application messages. Syntax translation can resolve issues only when the source and destination systems use the same concepts. When concepts differ, or when messages simply do not contain all the information required, then a level of semantic translation and business logic is needed. For example, the source system may deal with customer information as literal names and addresses, whereas the destination system may use customer numbers that refer to an internal customer master database. No level of pure syntax translation can connect these

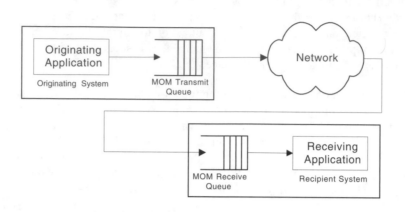

FIGURE 18-2. Message-Oriented Middleware

systems. Instead, some actual business logic must usually be coded for the particular case to take control and, for example, use the customer name and address and look up the corresponding customer ID.

- Business process layer

Finally, even above the level of semantic translation, some middleware systems provide methods to specify, implement, and manage complete business processes, which may involve interactions among several systems with many different message exchanges.

Types of Middleware

There are several fundamental architectures for middleware infrastructure, including message-oriented, remote procedure call (RPC), and publish-subscribe systems.

Message-Oriented Middleware

In message-oriented middleware (MOM), the communication channels are queues, messages may not be delivered immediately, and the recipient of the message does not have to be available at the time the message is sent. Figure 18-2 illustrates a simple MOM system. This model has many good properties, but also some disadvantages: the sender cannot expect an immediate reply, and error indications are delayed. In a way, MOM systems work like e-mail.

The programming model of MOM is simple. The sender composes a message and hands it off to a particular queue in the middleware. The middleware itself is then responsible for routing, storage, and communications, based on its internal configuration. The recipient can choose to be notified when a new message arrives or to poll for

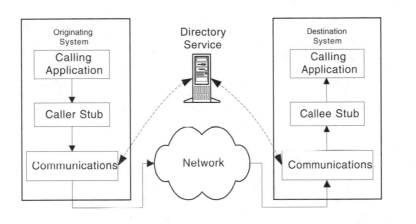

FIGURE 18-3. Remote Procedure Call

new messages. Because the middleware can be configured to save messages in stable storage, it can even substitute for disk files or databases that are used for communications between applications.

IBM's MQSeries is the most widely used message-oriented middleware. Microsoft has added Microsoft Message Queuing (MSMQ) to the Windows platform, and the J2EE specifications include Java Messaging Services (JMS), which provide similar functions.

Remote Procedure Call

Remote procedure call (RPC) services are complementary to message-oriented middleware. Systems based on RPC strive to match the programming model of procedure calls in standard programming languages. The programmer simply writes a procedure call, but the implementation of the procedure is in a remote program, which may be written in a different language and running on a different computer.

The first RPC systems were built in the late 1970s. The most commonly used systems today are the Common Object Request Broker Architecture (CORBA), Microsoft's Distributed Component Object Model (DCOM), and Java's Remote Method Invocation (RMI).

RPC systems start with a description of the interface and its methods. The description can be in a standard language, as in RMI, or it may be in a special interface definition language (IDL), as in CORBA. Tools then compile the interface description to produce *stubs*. The calling program, instead of linking directly to an implementation of the interface, is linked to the calling stub. The calling stub consists of automatically generated code that marshals the procedure arguments into one or more messages and

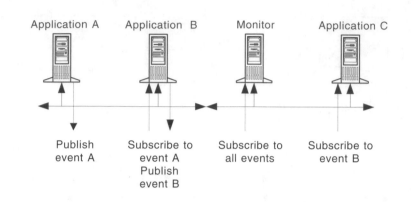

FIGURE 18-4. **Publish-Subscribe Middleware**

sends them to the callee stub. The callee stub, which runs in the destination process, unmarshals the arguments and calls the real implementation of the interface. When the implementation returns, the callee stub marshals any return values and sends them back to the caller stub, which returns to the calling program. This information flow is shown in Figure 18-3.

An additional complication with RPC systems is the problem of binding. Binding establishes the connection between a particular caller and a particular remote implementation. To simplify binding, the callee typically registers with a directory service, and then the caller can bind the interface by looking up the desired callee in the directory.

Publish-Subscribe

Publish-subscribe middleware, shown in Figure 18-4, has a model of communications that is fundamentally different from both MOM and RPC. In the latter two systems, the patterns of communications are defined by the system configuration. In publish-subscribe messaging, all messages are *published* for anyone who is interested, and the applications interested in receiving certain types of messages *subscribe* to them. In order to create a particular message flow, the names of messages must be chosen carefully.

Publish-subscribe systems have the following virtues.

- Communications patterns do not need to be defined in advance.

  It is very easy for new applications to eavesdrop on existing message flows. For example, a data warehouse application may listen to messages exchanged by established applications for order entry and warehouse management.

- System configuration is easy to manage.

  Because messages are automatically routed to systems that require them, based on the names of the events, it is easy to change the physical assignment of applications to systems. Similarly, it is quite easy to manage distributed and replicated applications.

Several companies offer commercial publish-subscribe middleware, including TIBCO, webMethods, and SeeBeyond.

Planning Considerations for Middleware

Although middleware simplifies many of the problems in integrating different applications, there are some important considerations for how it is used. Some common problem areas include naming, security, and external communications.

Naming

We often take for granted the ability of any system to communicate with any other system within the connected LANs of an enterprise. But what happens when one of the applications is suddenly transferred to new hardware as a result of an upgrade or an emergency? The usual approach is to ensure that the applications refer to each other by name rather than by address. A directory is then used to translate the name to the current machine address. Operations personnel can change the addresses behind the application names whenever a change is made. Most middleware packages include the ability to use directory systems, some as simple as the Domain Name System (DNS) and some as richly complex as Lightweight Directory Access Protocol (LDAP), Java Naming Service (JNS), and Microsoft Active Directory. Less appreciated is the need for careful design of the namespace for applications. For example, one should always name applications rather than hardware systems. If two applications that share hardware are ever moved to separate hardware, the conversion will be much easier if each application has its own name.

Security

Within an enterprise, multiple departments must handle information with varying levels of security. Sales forecasts may be restricted to corporate insiders, and design information may be restricted to small departments working with partners. Although middleware facilitates communications among disparate systems, it is also necessary to establish the appropriate security domains for the information carried. This requirement is extended further by the need for communications with groups external to the enterprise. Such security domains require all the machinery of security discussed in Chapters 13 and 14. Applications must authenticate themselves, communications requests must be tested against access controls, and communications must be protected against interception and alteration. Most users of middleware never set up the security machinery that is available, assuming that the bad guys are outside and that corporate firewalls provide adequate protection. Both assumptions are usually wrong, especially as more and more systems are connected to the Internet.

External Communications

The primary goal for middleware systems has been the facilitation of communications internal to an enterprise. As the enterprise becomes more virtual, the need to establish communications links with other enterprises increases. When this occurs, the communications must traverse private communications links or firewalls and the public Internet. Many middleware packages include facilities to route, forward, and proxy messages in order to make these tasks possible, but it is appropriate to make careful inquiries to ensure that a particular package will meet all such requirements.

SAP, for example, offers a program called *saprouter* as part of its suite of communications utilities for its proprietary middleware. This utility can be used to rename and route communications among SAP application components, to encrypt certain communications, and to proxy communications through firewalls.

The fundamental protocol of the Internet, IP, is designed with the ideas that all packets are equal, that any system can communicate with any other, and that considerations of routing should be left to lower layers of the network. This is exactly what is needed most of the time. However, when application-specific communications between two enterprises should traverse a protected link while general communications travel the public Internet, the network becomes difficult to manage. One common approach is to assign special IP addresses for the end applications, with special routing table entries, managed by hand, to control the communications. Unfortunately, such configurations are hard to manage, in part because they diffuse application configuration data among multiple locations. Systems implementing virtual private networks (VPNs) can help, but most of those are intended for use by telecommuting workers rather than by remote applications.

Enterprise Resource Planning Systems

Enterprise resource planning (ERP) systems are large, complex, and expensive. They are also the core information system for many companies. In this section, we describe the relevant points of some of the leading commercial ERP systems.

- SAP R/3

  SAP R/3 is the client-server-based successor to the mainframe R/2. Major R/3 modules include Financial, Sales and Distribution, and Manufacturing. For the most part, SAP R/3 is implemented using the proprietary language ABAP/4. Program modules are stored in a business object repository layered on a relational database and are compiled on demand. R/3 also uses the relational database for both master data (such as customers and products) and business documents (such as orders and invoices). SAP R/3 runs on most major operating system platforms and databases.

- Oracle Applications

  Oracle Applications is an ERP suite that includes Oracle Financials and other modules. Like SAP R/3, Oracle Applications is a client-server system organized around a relational database. Unlike SAP R/3, which can use several different database systems, a variety of databases, Oracle Applications uses many proprietary facilities of Oracle's own database product. Most program modules are coded in Oracle's proprietary language, PL/SQL.

- PeopleSoft

  PeopleSoft's application software business grew from its initial applications in the areas of human resources and employee services into a complete ERP suite. Like the others, PeopleSoft is based on a proprietary language, PeopleTools, that began as a way of customizing user interface screens and connecting them to database records. Recent versions of PeopleSoft applications use a third-party distributed transaction processing monitor/middleware—namely, BEA Tuxedo.

- J.D. Edwards

  The OneWorld application suite from J.D. Edwards is primarily used by midsized enterprises. It is implemented on IBM AS/400 mainframes.

Taxes

Taxes come in many shapes and sizes, depending on the jurisdiction. Indeed, many governments are currently debating what taxes should be applied to Internet transactions and how they should be collected. Although the complexities of tax law are clearly beyond the scope of this book, the following examples illustrate some of the tax-related issues for Internet commerce systems.

Sales Tax in the United States

In the United States, sales tax is owed by purchasers of products to state governments, counties, and localities (cities). In all, there are more than 6,000 rules about sales tax, and they change frequently as governments at all levels change the rules and create new laws. As an additional complication, the tax status of digital goods, called *intangible goods* by tax specialists, is still under active debate.[2]

---

2. One useful discussion of these issues is the article "What Are the Sales Tax Consequences of Retail Marketing on the Internet?" by Scott Walsh, *Journal of Multistate Taxation* (March–April 1997). Available at http://www.taxware.com/news/art_arch/jmst.htm.

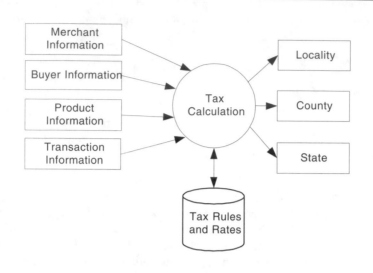

FIGURE 18-5. United States Sales Tax Calculation

Sales tax is frequently viewed by consumers as a simple problem in face-to-face commercial situations. The merchant's cash register calculates the tax due and adds it to the bill. The apparent simplicity results from the fact that almost all the variables in a face-to-face transaction are fixed. For example, the merchant never has to determine if the business is suddenly operating in a different state. In addition, although the buyer nominally owes the tax, the seller is charged with collecting it.

As shown in Figure 18-5, sales tax calculation is a complex function of information about the seller, the buyer, the product, and the transaction.

Seller Information

- Nexus

  Generally, a merchant is responsible for collecting and paying sales tax to a state if the merchant has a commercial presence, or *nexus*, in that state. A *commercial presence* is a legal definition; a store or other substantial facility would certainly qualify, whereas a small sales office might not.

- Point of title passage

  The tax calculation works differently depending on where title for the purchased goods passes from seller to buyer. The usual options are that title passes when the goods are shipped (at the seller's warehouse) or when the goods are delivered (at the buyer's address).

Buyer Information

- Address

  In an electronic transaction, where does the transaction take place? In the case of mail- or telephone-order transactions, the transaction is usually held to take place at the buyer's location. In the case of credit card payment, the buyer's location is usually held to be the same as the billing address of the credit card. This is not perfect, but it is simple and fairly consistent. The buyer's address is then used to determine which jurisdictions may require payment of sales tax. Unfortunately, the jurisdiction cannot be determined simply from a zip code (postal code), because a zip code can span city and county boundaries. Instead, the complete address must be mapped to a *geocode*, which is a geographic location precise enough to determine the tax jurisdiction.

- Tax-exempt status

  Certain nonprofit and educational institutions are not required to pay sales tax, and neither are businesses purchasing items or parts for later resale. In such cases, the purchaser must typically supply a tax-exempt number for the seller's records.

Product Information

- Goods classification

  Not all types of goods and services are taxable in all jurisdictions. For example, in the state of Massachusetts, clothing and cranberries have no sales tax. Clothing is held to be a necessity, and cranberries are a mainstay of the state's agricultural economy. For this reason, individual products must be tagged with a product category code with sufficient precision to allow the sales tax engine to determine the applicable rate, if any.

- Price

  Sales tax is computed as a percentage of item price.

Transaction Information

- Coupons

  Coupons operate in the context of a specific transaction to change the price of an item. The proper computation of sales tax requires such price reductions to be made before tax is calculated.

In order to compute tax, all the necessary source information is fed to a tax rules engine, which produces a total sales tax due for presentation to the customer, and individual tax due amounts to all relevant jurisdictions for inclusion in tax reporting files for the merchant.

Tax computation is such a sufficiently complex issue that companies such as Taxware (www.taxware.com) have come to specialize in this area. They offer tax computation modules and also provide information update services that supply new tax rule databases on a periodic basis.

In very simple situations, small merchants with a commercial presence in just one state may choose to collect sales tax on all transactions, regardless of the actual necessity of doing so. This approach errs on the side of too much tax paid and has a consequent cost to consumers, but it simplifies the life of the merchant.

Canadian Goods and Services Tax

Canadian sales taxes are not as complex as those in the United States. Most provinces collect a federal governmental sales tax, the goods and services tax (GST), at a 7 percent rate plus a provincial sales tax (PST) at a rate that varies from province to province. However, in April 1997, some provinces switched to a new harmonized sales tax (HST), which combines the GST and PST into a single 15 percent tax. As in the United States, tax rates vary for different goods and services.

Special rules apply for goods imported or exported from Canada. As a general rule, whenever taxable goods or services are imported into Canada, GST/PST is incurred. When goods or services are exported from Canada, they are zero-rated, and therefore no GST/PST is incurred. The point of title passage is assumed to be the destination, which is the usual case for retail sales. In other words, if the ship-to address is in Canada, then GST/PST/HST must be computed and displayed to the buyer. The Web site of the Canadian Department of Finance (www.fin.ga.ca) is a good resource.

Value-Added Tax

Many countries in Europe and other parts of the world use a value-added tax (VAT) as a primary source of government revenue. In the case of sales tax, the tax is assessed at the point of consumption, and only the final consumer owes the tax. In contrast, a VAT is assessed anytime goods or services change hands. Resellers pay tax on the goods they buy and are required to collect tax on the goods they sell. In general, these resellers can get a credit for the tax paid on supplies, so the net effect is to tax the *value added* at each stage in the chain.

As usual, the tax rates vary for different kinds of goods and in different jurisdictions. Cross-border rules are particularly complex. The European Union has decided to tax all transactions in the country of origin. This procedure significantly reduces the amount of paperwork for exporting and importing, but it also complicates life for those who are not end users. Resellers in Europe collect tax for all sales, but they must apply separately to each country from which they purchase to obtain refunds of VAT for items resold.

Proper implementation of VAT in an Internet commerce system requires the following steps.

1. Obtain the necessary input information, including location of buyer, goods classification, and merchant VAT profile.

2. Calculate the VAT due for the transaction.

3. Display the necessary legal invoices to the purchaser. Such invoices are necessary if the purchaser is a reseller who will later claim credits or refunds.

4. Prepare the necessary records and audit trails for the merchant for submission to the merchant's VAT taxing authority.

Taxware's WorldTax product automates much of this work, and it handles tax calculations for the European Union as well as Canada and other countries in Europe, Asia, and South America.

Logistics, Shipping, and Handling

Shipping and handling are parts of the overall area of logistics. Once an order has been entered, physical goods must be delivered to the buyer. From the perspective of the buyer, this process appears simple, but it contains surprising complexities of pricing, international shipment, and the automation of handing the order to the shipping company.

Pricing of Shipping and Handling

Shipping costs money. Unless that cost is buried in the seller's overall price structure, it is visible to the consumer. The seller will want the shipping fees to cover the costs, but beyond that, shipping charges can be a marketing tool and a competitive weapon.

Some of the pricing models used in direct marketing, such as catalog sales, are as follows.

- Flat-rate pricing

  For merchants selling a small variety of goods of very similar weight and volume—contact lenses, for example—a flat rate for shipping may be appropriate. The flat rate covers the per-order processing costs of the seller plus the actual shipping charges. For large items, individual item flat-rate charges may apply.

- Weight-based pricing

  For bulk materials, actual shipping charges are usually based on weight. The costs in this model can simply be passed through to the buyer.

- Value-based pricing

  In this pricing model, the shipping charges are based on the total value of the order, either proportionally or stepwise. Such models have the advantage that they are easy for customers to understand. Stepwise pricing also serves a marketing function of encouraging the consumer to add items to the order until it is just below a step boundary, so that they minimize the amortized cost of shipping.

- Distance-based pricing

  Actual shipping charges are sometimes linked to the distance over which the goods must be shipped. This model can combine with any of the previous three to build a model proportional to two different factors, such as value and distance.

International Transport

One likely effect of Internet commerce will be to create many new international businesses. Historically, international commerce has been a province of a few because of its complexity and the difficulties of international sales and marketing. Because the Internet makes international sales easier, many new organizations will have to face the complexities of international transport. Not least among these complexities are customs issues and the difficulty of producing the paperwork necessary for the international shipment of products.

Customs Duties

Customs tariffs and duties vary widely around the world. One step in simplification has been the adoption of the Harmonized Tariff System Classification, which is a standardized numbering system for traded products. The number assigned to each class of product is used by customs officials around the world to determine the duties, taxes, and regulations that apply to the product. A schedule of these classifications is available on the Internet at http://www.census.gov/foreign-trade/www/index.html.

Paperwork

International shipments center around the *commercial invoice*. The commercial invoice identifies the shipping, receiving, and freight companies and describes the contents of a shipment. Its purpose is to consolidate the information needed by customs officials to classify the items shipped in order to assess any taxes and duties required.

Besides the commercial invoice, a wide variety of documents may be necessary for export, shipping, and import. Such documents include the following.

- Bill of lading
- Consular invoice
- Certificate of origin
- Export license
- Insurance certificate
- Shipper's export declaration
- International letter of credit

A full discussion of export documentation is well outside the scope of this book, but for companies based in the United States a good place to start is *A Basic Guide to Exporting*, published by the U.S. Department of Commerce.

Transport and Tracking

There is a large national and international infrastructure for freight and shipping. Companies such as Federal Express, United Parcel Service, Airborne, and DHL provide worldwide services. For large customers, and increasingly for small ones as well, these companies offer automated systems for arranging pickup and shipment of packages. Shipping software creates the appropriate labels, assigns tracking numbers, and schedules pickup and delivery.

Privacy

Several privacy issues arise when logistics are considered. First, is it possible to have an anonymous transaction when physical delivery is needed? Second, what security is offered by package tracking services?

Anonymity

It seems possible that information commerce might be truly anonymous. Payment mechanisms can in principle be anonymous (see Chapter 15), but achieving anonymity in a transaction involving physical delivery of products is more difficult. One approach is to have the delivery company serve as a privacy intermediary between buyer and seller. If the buyer has an account with a delivery company, then the buyer could tell the seller, "Deliver via XYZ shipping to customer 12345." The seller would know what was sold, and the shipper would know to whom it was sold, but neither would have complete information.

A second possibility is *depot delivery*. In depot delivery, the shipper delivers the package to a neighborhood drop-off location such as a grocery store or box company. If the transaction is paid for with electronic cash and the delivery is effectively to "general delivery," then anonymity is possible.

Tracking Numbers

One problem with the current implementation of tracking numbers by shipping companies is that they are not very secure. Frequently, the tracking number is really an account number followed by a sequence number of shipments, together with a simple checksum. Account numbers are easy to obtain—simply buy something from the same company, and check the tracking number. After that, sequence numbers can be guessed fairly easily.

Advanced Logistics

In the early stages of commerce, shipping was fairly simple. One ordered from the factory, and the products were shipped from there to the consumer. This model is a good place to start but does not meet all the requirements for logistics. As examples, we consider the problems of warehouse selection and the virtual corporation.

Warehouse Selection

Large businesses frequently have regional warehouses or warehouses that contain only certain products. In these cases, the products ordered and the ship-to address may influence the choice of fulfillment center. The choice of fulfillment center may in turn affect the calculation of shipping charges. System designers dislike situations in which everything depends on everything, because they make modular design difficult. To simplify such cases, the system may use a standard shipping charge, calculated to match or exceed actual shipping costs. Occasional feedback can be used to adjust the charges.

The Virtual Corporation

The idea of a virtual corporation predates Internet commerce, but the Internet has certainly invigorated it. A virtual corporation might outsource *everything*: product design, manufacturing, distribution, marketing, accounting, and so forth. Many businesses are not completely virtual but depend on partners for substantial components. For example, a distributor of personal computers may manufacture the system unit but obtain monitors from a different manufacturer. If there is no need for a full system test, it makes sense to ship the monitor from one warehouse and the system unit from another warehouse and have the two boxes delivered separately. If this works well, the two boxes will arrive on the same truck at the same time.

Inventory Management

In most commercial transactions, the availability of the product plays a large role in the sale. In face-to-face commerce, the product is on the shelf. In telephone order commerce, the operator usually has access to inventory information. In sophisticated business-to-business commerce, the concept is *available to promise,* wherein the seller's ERP system has such complete visibility into inventory, time in transit, previous commitments, manufacturing capacity, and scheduled arrival of parts that precise commitments for current and future delivery can be made.

Inventory management capabilities will become a standard part of Internet commerce; buyers want to know if they can actually get things they order. If products are not immediately available, buyers will switch to alternatives that are. In some cases, buyers will pay a premium for availability.

For large sellers, the best way to manage inventory is often to integrate the Internet system with the corporate inventory management system. There are two ways to achieve this.

1. Catalog integration

   In this model, the Internet catalog system is updated periodically with information about inventory on hand. The catalog uses this information to mark or simply not display items that are out of stock. Additionally, items that are in short supply are candidates for promotions or sales to clear remaining inventory.

2. Transaction system integration

   In this model, the Internet commerce transaction system is integrated with internal corporate systems. Items on the customer order form are confirmed as available and are reserved against inventory at the point of sale.

Both of these techniques can be used to create a fully integrated system in which items found in the catalog are effectively guaranteed to be available.

The Virtual Warehouse

The just-mentioned techniques can be affordable for large enterprises, but smaller enterprises may not even have computerized inventory systems. One promise of the Internet is that small and medium-sized enterprises can look like larger companies. How can this be achieved in the area of inventory management? One idea is the *virtual warehouse*.

The idea of the virtual warehouse is simple. A small or medium-sized enterprise places a portion of its inventory under the management of the virtual warehouse, which can then make commitments to customers against that allocation. Consider the following sequence of events.

1. A small seller of widgets creates a Web-based catalog. Because the market for widgets depends on immediate gratification of buyers, it is important to ensure availability.

2. Each business day, the seller uses an administrative Web application to grant control of a certain number of widgets, perhaps 50, to the virtual warehouse.

3. When a buyer browses the widget catalog, the catalog system uses a real-time query to the virtual warehouse to obtain the number of widgets on hand. The catalog uses the quantity obtained to control its behavior, selecting regular or promotional pricing.

4. When a buyer selects a widget for purchase, the catalog system obtains a reservation against inventory from the virtual warehouse. The reservation is good for a fixed time, such as 30 minutes. This is similar to the way airline reservations work. The reservation is good for a fixed time, and lapses if the tickets are not paid for before the reservation expires.

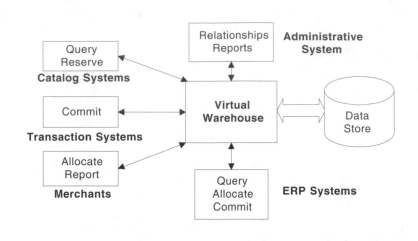

FIGURE 18-6. **The Virtual Warehouse**

5. When the transaction commits before the reservation expires, the Internet commerce transaction system records that fact with the virtual warehouse, confirming the reservation and removing the appropriate widget count from the allocation.

6. During the day, the seller can add or remove inventory from the virtual warehouse, although inventory cannot be removed if held by an active reservation.

In this way, a small enterprise can obtain the benefits of a fully integrated inventory management system without great expense. The virtual warehouse is merely a debit, credit, and reservation system for paper inventory, but the customer is happy because delivery is guaranteed.

The virtual warehouse breaks down only at the margins: if not all inventory is entered in the virtual warehouse, then some customers may not be able to order when in fact supply is available. However, the system never promises delivery to a customer when inventory is *not* available. A logical diagram of the virtual warehouse is shown in Figure 18-6. The virtual warehouse is built around a database that stores items, inventory, and reservations. Around that database are the applications that interact with it on behalf of catalog systems, transaction systems, merchants, ERP systems, and administrators.

Catalog Interfaces

The catalog system can query the inventory status of items in the virtual warehouse and can place temporary reservations against inventory. Queries are used by the catalog software to gauge supply levels in order to select an appropriate presentation in the catalog. The catalog system places a reservation when a buyer selects an item for purchase, such as by putting it into a shopping cart or order form, but the order is not yet confirmed.

Transaction Interfaces

The transaction system, during order processing, checks to see if valid reservations are held for all items being ordered. If they are, then the reservations are confirmed as a component of committing the order. When this happens, the virtual warehouse debits the inventory level.

Merchant Interfaces

Small and medium-sized merchants will interact with the virtual warehouse through Web-based interfaces. The merchant can query inventory levels, generate reports, and, most importantly, allocate new inventory to the warehouse.

Enterprise Resource Planning Interfaces

Large businesses will interact with the virtual warehouse through interfaces with their ERP systems. These systems run the business and have the ability to query, allocate, and commit changes to inventory as a result of external transactions.

Administrative Interfaces

In order to make the virtual warehouse work in a shared-services environment across a public network, administrative utilities are necessary to set up new merchant accounts, control security parameters, and report on activity.

Example: SAP Integration

In this example, we describe a sell-side Internet commerce system integrated with an SAP R/3 Release 4.5B ERP system. Although the SAP software systems include a variety of Internet and Web capabilities, we assume that a non-SAP Internet commerce system has been specified.

Recent versions of SAP R/3 have many externally accessible APIs, including both asynchronous messages (intermediate documents, or *IDOCs*) and synchronous calls (business APIs, or *BAPIs*). The SAP Remote Function Call communications software can be used to permit a remote system to call any function module within SAP, but SAP has also supplied a large number of BAPI calls in an effort to provide standard interfaces that will remain stable across software releases.

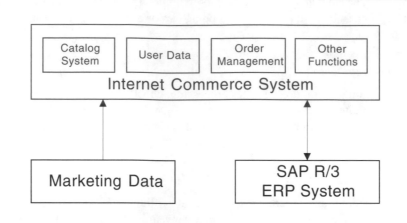

FIGURE 18-7. **Example of Integration with ERP System**

General Scenario

Figure 18-7 shows the general scenario of our integration project. An Internet catalog contains information generated from the ERP system and other marketing data. A user database contains login information for actual users of the system, together with links to the customer master database held by the ERP system. The order management system is responsible for checking pricing and availability of products, for creating new orders in the ERP system, and for reviewing the status of open orders. Finally, other functions, such as checking current account status, may be available.

In order to accomplish these tasks, the following integration touch points are necessary between the Internet commerce system and the ERP system.

- Catalog bulk load

  When the catalog is created, and perhaps at other times, it is necessary to bulk load large quantities of product information into the Internet catalog. Some of this information, such as list pricing, part numbers, and short text descriptions, typically comes from the ERP system, whereas other information, such as graphics, longer descriptions, and specifications, comes from other marketing data. With an SAP ERP system, the information can be obtained by triggering the generation of the MATMAS (material master) IDOC, which is used to convey product information to foreign systems.

- Catalog data update

  During the normal operation of the system, it is necessary to provide incremental updates of the catalog data. The SAP system can be configured such that insert, update, and delete operations in the ERP material master trigger MATMAS IDOCs to update the catalog system.

- Pricing and availability inquiry

  There are many design scenarios for providing pricing and availability information to users of the system. In the current example, we envision the system being used by major customers, who should be provided with accurate contract pricing and product availability information. The information could be provided page by page in the catalog, with the information cached in the catalog, but in this example the order management subsystem provides a personalized purchase order form that accurately reflects customer pricing and product availability. This information can be obtained synchronously from the SAP system by using the `SalesOrder.Simulate` BAPI, which goes through all the steps of order creation except for saving the resulting order.

- Create order

  Once a sales order has been composed, using the catalog, saved shopping carts, or other techniques, it must be entered into the normal flow of order processing. The best method of doing this is to use the SAP `SalesOrder.CreateFromDat1` BAPI.[3]

- Order status inquiry

  Once a sales order is in process, the customer may want to track its progress. Before Dell Computer began using the Internet for sales, customers made about 0.9 inquiries per order. After Dell's Internet system came online, the number of inquiries per order jumped to 14. In the current example, we want to permit customers to query the status of all orders, not just those created via the Internet. For this reason, checking order status becomes a two-step process: first, obtain a list of all open orders using the SAP BAPI `SalesOrder.GetList`, and then retrieve detailed information on each order by using the `SDOrder.GetDetailedList` BAPI. Of course, the first step can be skipped if the customer or the Internet system already has the relevant order number. Many variations are possible, such as uploading order status of all orders from SAP to the Internet commerce system on a daily basis and caching status inquiry results for a time.

- Account status inquiry

  A primary goal of an Internet commerce system is to reduce the number of customer interactions that require mediation by a person. Customers may want to inquire about information other than order status, such as the status of their accounts. This account status inquiry displays the customer's current statement and shows whether payments are due or have been received. In the current example, we use the SAP BAPI `AR.ACC.GetStatement` for this purpose.

- Enrollment and registration

  ERP systems contain customer master records. As is often the case, these records tend to be incomplete or inaccurate for any information that is not actually used

---

3. The `CreateFromDat1` BAPI, an updated version of the `CreateFromData` BAPI, permits entry of such information as credit card information used for a single order.

during the normal course of business. For example, ERP systems tend to contain complete and accurate information for billing and shipping but frequently contain less accurate data about such items as contact information on individuals at customer companies. Consequently, the ERP customer master is probably not a good source of information about the individual requisitioners who are the likely users of an Internet order management system. In the current example, we will use the ERP customer master as master data for partner companies, but we let the Internet system manage user accounts for individuals authorized to access the system on behalf of the partner companies. Furthermore, management of individual entries—changes and deletions—is left to administrators at the partner companies rather than to the seller. To accomplish this design, we use the SAP API to fetch partner information from the customer master, cache that information in the Internet system, and otherwise maintain an independent customer database of Internet users, divided into hierarchical groups by their affiliations with partner companies.

Summary

In order to be successful, Internet commerce must provide complete business solutions. If commerce systems are provided as piece parts that must be assembled by each system operator, they will not achieve much market penetration. Complete solutions must supply implementations of all functionality necessary to complete the online experience or must integrate in real time with external components. In this chapter, we have discussed several subsystems, taxes, shipping, and inventory, which are necessary to build a fully functional system.

CHAPTER 19

Reliable and Scalable Systems

Computer systems can be fast, cheap, or reliable. Choose any two.
—Anonymous

Overview

In the early days of the World Wide Web, most users were not terribly concerned with performance or reliability. Sometimes Web sites were slow, and sometimes they did not respond, but this was to be expected. Besides, many users had slow connections to the network, so they hardly noticed if the server was slow. A popular server might have been overloaded for a while, but then it would recover.

Clearly, the expectations have changed, especially for business Web sites. Sites must be available 24 hours a day, because customers, whether they're on the other side of the world or simply up late, may be there at any time. The systems must be fast enough to satisfy increasingly demanding users, because competitive sites are "just a click away." Customers now have their own high-bandwidth connections, from high-speed corporate networks (if they're in the office) or from their own broadband connections (if they're at home). Moreover, sites must be able to handle high peak loads, because one never knows when a mass of customers may decide that they want whatever is on the site.

Building sites that are fast, reliable, and scalable is probably the most challenging part of creating Internet commerce systems. It is hard enough simply to deliver content in this way, and building transactional capabilities into the system is even more difficult. For many enterprises, creating this kind of site is the most complex case of system engineering and operations they will manage. Unlike many other kinds of enterprise systems, it is nearly impossible to find any time to take a system down for upgrading or maintenance. The users (that is, customers and prospective customers) of the system will not be trained on it, they won't read any documentation, and they'll expect it to work flawlessly at any time of day or night. Furthermore, the use of the system is *a priori* unpredictable, and it isn't related to anything manageable such as the number of employees at a company.

In this chapter, we'll look at some of the basic approaches to building performance, scalability, and reliability into Internet commerce systems. The details will vary depending on the applications in the mix, and some applications don't lend themselves well to these properties. In addition, we'll look at other operational issues, such as backup, disaster recovery, and system upgrades.

Enterprise-Class Concepts

The systems we describe in this chapter are often called *enterprise-class* systems, because companies depend on them to run their businesses. [1] Because the terms that refer to the important characteristics of these systems are used for both technical and marketing purposes, it's helpful to be precise about what we mean.

In this context, *reliability* is a measure of how likely a component is to fail, whether that component is a piece of hardware or a program. This is sometimes measured as *mean time between failures* (MTBF), which expresses the average amount of time that elapses before the component fails. Hardware manufacturers sometimes make available information about the MTBF of, for example, components such as disk drives. A related idea is *mean time to repair* (MTTR), which is a measure of how long it takes to fix something that has broken.

For Web applications, a more important concept is *availability*, which is simply the fraction of the time a service is available for users. For some systems, availability is critical at all times. Other systems can be unavailable on occasion, although the downtime must be scheduled. For example, a system that is offline for maintenance in the middle of the night may be acceptable for office workers. For Internet commerce systems with unpredictable customers, such maintenance may not be possible.

The next important metric is *performance*. System performance can be measured in many ways, but the two most important are usually *latency* and *throughput*. Latency measures how long a user has to wait before something happens—for example, how long it takes to load a product description page from the catalog or how long it takes to add an item to a shopping cart before the next action can be taken. Thus, latency is

---

1. Sometimes the term *carrier-class* is used to imply a higher level of one or more of these properties. It comes from the system requirements for telecommunications carriers, who must operate their services reliably under adverse conditions.

the individual's view of the performance of a system and is the one that really matters to customers. If the latency is too high, customers will just go elsewhere. In contrast, throughput measures how much work a server can do. This is often described in *transactions per second*, although exactly the exact definition of *transaction* depends on what the server is doing, whether it's content delivery or database operations.

The last concept, *scalability,* is harder to measure but is an important property of the system. As the load on a system increases, such as when the number of users increases, how well does the system handle the additional work? Furthermore, how easy is it to add more capacity? The scalability of a system is influenced by its architecture, implementation, and operations.

Reliability

In a large, complex system, the concept of reliability can get rather confusing—in large part because the reliability of the overall system is only loosely related to the reliability of the components used to build it. It is possible to build highly reliable systems out of mostly reliable components, and it is possible to build fragile systems out of very reliable components. For example, the telephone system in the United States is very reliable because of the way the system is engineered, not just because it is built from highly reliable components.

A second source of confusion is the difference between the concepts of hardware reliability and software reliability. Hardware reliability is much easier to understand. In most cases, the hardware stops working, and the failure is more or less apparent (unless it is masked by redundancy). The failure may be signaled by software that isn't getting the right result from the hardware, but (unlike many software bugs) it is uncommon for hardware to silently give the wrong answer. In contrast, software reliability is mostly a question of bugs. A program might crash, or it might report an error, or it might give the wrong answer.

As we shall see, it is usually most important to engineer a system for availability using replicated or multiple components. Because the overall system is designed to tolerate failures of individual components, it isn't always necessary to use highly reliable components. Certainly one shouldn't ignore concerns about reliability, but a reasonably reliable, inexpensive component may be a better choice than a highly reliable but expensive component.

In fact, this idea was part of the original thinking behind RAID storage arrays. Recall that *RAID* is an acronym for *Redundant Array of Inexpensive Disks*. The approach was to build a highly reliable storage system by using less reliable components. With smart engineering and redundant components, it was possible to do this at a relatively low cost. This concept is also the basis for the approaches to building highly available systems that we discuss next.

Percentage Uptime	Downtime per Year
99%	3.7 days
99.9%	8.8 hours
99.99%	53 minutes
99.999%	5 minutes

TABLE 19-1. **Uptime Percentage Compared with Downtime**

Unfortunately, because of the expense of software development, it's difficult to improve the overall availability of a system by building it with redundant software. This approach is used in some very critical applications, such as for the software used in the space shuttle, but it is generally impractical for business applications. Therefore, it's important when buying or developing software to ensure that it meets the reliability goals.

Availability

Availability is often measured by the fraction of time the system is up and running or (put another way) by the amount of time the system is down. In other words, how much of the time is the system available for use? The term *five 9s* is sometimes used to describe systems that are up 99.999% of the time. Table 19-1 compares some uptime percentages with the actual amounts of downtime per year. As you can see, achieving five 9s is quite respectable, as well as quite challenging.

One of the ugly truths about availability metrics is that they do not always count software bugs that cause failures for users. Most of the time, the availability that is being measured is whether or not the system or application is up and running and at least performing basic operations. In this context, a bug that causes the software to miscalculate one out of every ten transactions, for example, does not count as an availability problem.

High-Availability Systems

Internet commerce systems need to be available at the times that customers want to use them. Because Internet commerce systems can attract a worldwide customer base, there is no easy notion of business hours. As a limit, the system may need to be available for use 24 hours a day, 7 days a week.

There are many reasons for a system to be unavailable.

- Regular maintenance

  Systems require periodic attention for making backups, configuration changes, and so on. Typically, configuration changes are tested on a development copy of the system before being rolled into production, so the risk of problems should be low. To the extent that maintenance activities require downtime, the period of unavailability can be scheduled.

- Upgrades

  From time to time, it may be necessary to change major software components for new software releases, new hardware platforms, facility moves, and so on. Such changes will almost always require scheduled downtime unless extraordinary measures are taken.

- Infrastructure failures

  The commerce system typically depends on several systems that are partially or wholly outside one's control: electric power, Internet access service, and other telecommunications services can be disrupted, leading to a loss of service for some or all of the users. Generally, these sources of unavailability can be managed (at a cost) by providing dedicated backup power and backup communications facilities.

- Environmental disasters

  Floods, fires, and other natural or human-made disasters can take a data center out of service regardless of the care taken in hardware and software reliability. The usual approach to these sorts of problems is hot or warm backup data centers, typically geographically distant.

- Software failures

  Software, once installed, doesn't change by itself, but latent problems in software are revealed by changes in the environment. The net effect is that software can stop working. In addition, Internet commerce software is exposed to additional risks; if an essential technology such as an encryption method becomes vulnerable as a result of technical advances, software can become untrustworthy.

- Human error

  Operator errors, configuration mistakes, and the like can bring a system down. In some sense, these factors can be controlled and can be improved by additional training and testing. There are also errors outside one's control. On the Internet, for example, routing errors may be introduced into the network by a different service provider, resulting in a loss of service.

- Hardware failures

  Disks, computers, network routers, and other mechanical and electronic components fail. Although such failures are becoming less common as the basic reliability of electronics improves, the probability of a failure still grows as a function of the number of components in the system.

It is a very good exercise for any system designer or system operator to make a list of every possible source of failure and to explore the consequences of each failure, the appropriate actions to take if it were to occur, and possible ways of preventing the failure or recovering from it more quickly.

Approaches to High Availability

There are two ways to make a system highly available as seen by the end user. The mean time between failures can be made very long, or the mean time to repair can be made very short. In the first case the system doesn't fail, and in the second case it is fixed very quickly.

It is also necessary to consider the real goals of availability. There is an enormous difference, for example, between a system that is available for most of the users most of the time and a system that is available for all of the users all of the time. Finally, what are the transactional requirements? For example, if an application crashes, it is often proper to arrange matters so that the system undoes any partial effects of transactions that were in progress and depends on the end users to try again. On the other hand, this approach doesn't work when transactions are generated by applications that lack the ability to retry.

The two approaches to availability often result in different strategies. Achieving high mean time between failures (MTBF) is often approached through increasing component reliability, whereas achieving short mean time to repair (MTTR) is often approached by making it easy to replace failed components. Often, both strategies are pursued at the same time. RAID systems, for example, achieve high reliability by internally managing failed components. At the system level, however, server computer systems are so complex that their availability is usually improved by having a complete spare system ready to resume service should the primary system fail.

Failover is particularly interesting because replacing a failed component, system, or even data center can also solve problems outside one's own control, such as failures in the infrastructure or environmental disasters. In addition, if multiple systems are online at once anyway, to help with scaling and load balancing, then a failure need only redistribute the load among those systems that are still operational.

Building Highly Available Systems

As suggested in the preceding section, there are essentially two ways to make a system available in the face of failures.

1. Use components that always work.
2. Build redundancy into the system.

The first option is out of our control, because we can only get what's available on the market, and most system components (processors, disks, system units, network components, and so on) will fail at some point. So we will focus on how and where to build redundancy into the system.

The next question about redundancy is how hard it is to keep redundant systems working together. There are three main ways to provide a redundant system, sometimes described as *cold standby*, *warm standby*, and *hot standby*. A cold standby system is essentially keeping spare parts on hand. If there is a failure, the new component is installed and the system is restarted. For some components, this approach is inexpensive, but it usually means that the system is down while repairs are being made. For other components (such as entire computer systems), it is relatively expensive, because one has paid for a machine that is doing no useful work.

In a warm standby system, the backup system is installed and turned on, but it is not actually running any useful applications. If a primary system fails, the warm standby is brought into service in its place. This can be a fairly quick operation, but it takes some time and usually some manual intervention as well.

Finally, a hot standby system is one that is up and running as part of the operational network of systems, but it is not serving customers itself for the application that it is backing up. While it is on standby for one application, it may perform services for another application.

Deciding which approach to use is mostly a function of difficulty and cost. Replicating read-only data is fairly easy, but replicating read-write systems, such as transactional databases, is much harder. Therefore, in the following examples, we take different approaches as we make the system increasingly complex, available, and costly.

Basic Reference Architecture

Figure 19-1 shows a basic Web system using a database, with a dedicated database server. The front-end Web server is responsible for delivering static content and handling requests from Web browsers. The database server receives SQL queries from the Web server for user management, dynamic information (such as pricing, perhaps), and other dynamic data. Although this system is simpler than most real Web operations, it shows the important pieces that we need to tackle in order to make the system more available.

It is easy to see just from Figure 19-1 that the system has several points of failure that put system availability at risk. The Web server, database server, database storage system, and connection to the Internet may each go down, as may the networks connecting the various pieces. In the next few sections, we will replicate various components and explore some of the problems raised by each addition.

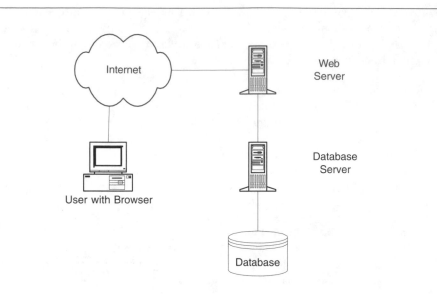

FIGURE 19-1. **Basic Reference Architecture**

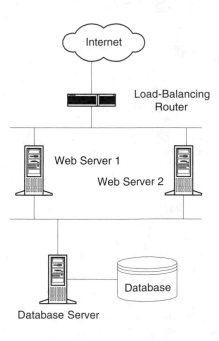

FIGURE 19-2. **Redundant Web Servers**

Redundant Web Servers

The first step is to replicate the Web servers, as shown in Figure 19-2. In our hypothetical design, these are the easiest components to replicate, because they do not
contain state information about transactions in progress. Of course, they do have connections in progress, and any users connected to a server at precisely the time the
server crashes will be affected. However, HTTP connections are typically short-lived,
so the number of users affected is likely to be relatively small. In addition, most users
expect occasional failures on the Web, so they will probably just try to reload the page
in their browsers.

Part of the trick here is also to use a load-balancing IP router. Such a router is able to
forward IP packets to different systems while presenting a single IP address to the
outside world. The router keeps track of open TCP connections as well, so a single
HTTP session goes to just one of the servers. It can detect a server failure and stop
forwarding packets to that system until it is available again. In addition, the router can
spread the load across several Web servers, thereby providing some performance benefits as well.

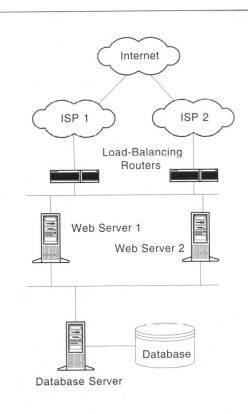

FIGURE 19-3. Redundant Web Servers with Redundant Network Connections

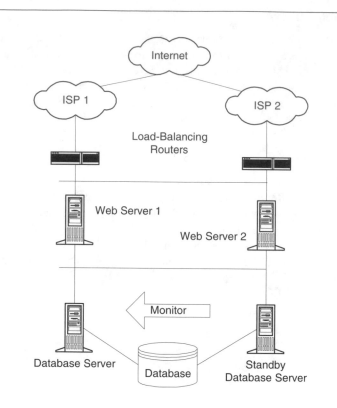

FIGURE 19-4. Standby Database Server

Depending on the application, managing session data may or may not be a problem. If all session data is stored in the database, or in data that comes in the HTTP request (such as cookies and URLs), then there is no problem: any server can handle any incoming request. If the servers store some information themselves, then this scheme will not work, because the state information is not available if the user's next request happens to hit another server.

Finally, the alert reader might have noticed that this system merely replaced one single point of failure—the Web server—with another. A large production system will typically use multiple routers with redundant Internet connections. A simplified form of such a system is shown in Figure 19-3 (and, of course, we expect that the ISPs have their own redundant connections to other service providers on the Internet). Our simplified system also omits many other components that would be common in a real implementation, such as firewalls, other routers, and supporting network servers.

Standby Database Servers

The next step is to augment our replicated Web servers with a standby database server, as shown in Figure 19-4. In this version of the system, the standby database server is turned on and running, but it is not serving any database transactions. Instead, it is monitoring the primary database server to ensure that it is running. If the primary server fails, the standby system will take over the database, and the front-end Web servers will begin using the standby system for database queries.

Why do we take this approach? As noted before, it is much harder to synchronize multiple systems that are trying to read and write the same database. So we simplify the problem by having only one server work on the database at a time. The standby doesn't create any conflicts, because it isn't active. If the primary system fails, the standby system is using the same storage system, so all of the database files and logs are intact on storage. Of course, this requires a database that is robust in the face of crashes, but this is common among serious commercial databases today. This approach also requires a storage system that can be connected to two systems.

Mirrored Storage System

The standby database server strategy leaves one critical single point of failure: the database storage system itself. To eliminate this risk, we introduce a mirrored storage system for the standby database server, as shown in Figure 19-5. As data is written to the primary storage system, it is also copied to the mirrored standby system. If the primary server or the primary storage system fails, the standby system can start operating with all of the data already available to it.

Operational Issues

In practice, the approaches described in this section can be used to build highly available Web systems. Operating such systems is also challenging, because the operators must always be prepared to respond to failures, even in the middle of the night. Depending on the level of redundancy in the system, a single failure may be tolerable, but a second failure (for example) is not. Therefore, it is vitally important to repair a failure as quickly as possible when it occurs, in order to minimize the risk that a second failure will take down the entire system. History records many times when redundant systems failed one after another, and no one noticed until the last one was no longer working.

Replication and Scaling

An electronic commerce system has many dimensions of scaling, which admit different strategies for management.

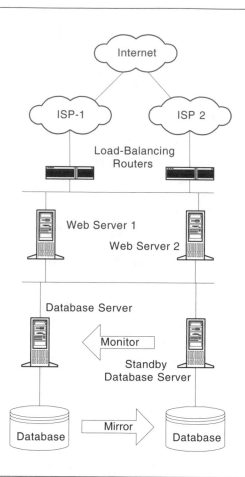

FIGURE 19-5. Mirrored Storage System

- Growth in catalog content

  Catalog or electronic fulfillment content may grow in richness and volume independent of transaction volume. For example, a business delivering digital movies online might have a small transaction followed by delivery of gigabytes of data. This problem is best addressed by replication and duplication of content servers, which can share a common transaction engine.

- Growth in transaction complexity and volume

  Even with a small online catalog, business may boom, leading to a high volume of transactions. If transactions are largely independent of one another, it may be possible to use replicated transaction engines. With complex transactions, however, there may be no substitute for scaling the transaction engine from a single CPU to a multiprocessor to a cluster of systems working from a common database.

- Growth in customer base

  As the customer base grows in size, and covers ever larger geographies, it may be appropriate to replicate servers in geographic areas close to the customers.

Backup and Disaster Recovery

Backup and *disaster recovery* are related. *Backup* refers to the processes that preserve an application's data in the face of hardware failures such as disk crashes. *Disaster recovery* is the broader term that includes the procedures and systems that enable the application to recover not only from hardware failures but also from power losses, earthquakes, and communications failures.

When business applications were primarily batch-oriented, backup and disaster recovery were fairly simple to understand. As transactions occurred, they were written on tapes. Once a day, the transaction tapes were merged with master files on other tapes. Maintaining backups meant saving the old tapes, and in the event of a site disaster, the tapes could be easily run on a similar computer in a different data center.

The situation for online transaction processing is much more complicated, because individual transactions may be occurring on a 24-hour basis, with no downtime to make backups. In addition, availability requirements may be so stringent that the system as a whole cannot stop working as a result of a failure. Instead, failed components must be replaced with spares, without loss of data and with minimal downtime. This sort of reliability can be very expensive.

Because Internet commerce systems enable global operations, even small businesses can have round-the-clock operational requirements for their Internet-based systems.

Summary

Internet commerce is, for many organizations, a mission-critical application. It is also a demanding application, requiring careful design and implementation to create systems that are robust, available, and fast. This chapter has highlighted some of the main architectural questions that must be answered in order to achieve the highest levels of system availability and scalability.

CHAPTER 20

Mobile and Wireless Systems

No matter where you go, there you are.

—Buckaroo Banzai[1]

Overview of Mobile and Wireless Technologies

As we write this book in 2002, one of the noisiest parts of the technology landscape is mobile and wireless technologies. We are bombarded with hype and with devices that claim to revolutionize the way people communicate. Such a revolution shows few signs of taking hold, however. Most mobile phone users in the United States, for example, simply use their phones for voice calls, not data services. Text-messaging systems are quite popular in many other countries of the world, but more advanced services are used only rarely. The pace of technological change in this sector has also been slowed by economic problems.

Although the focus of this book is on Internet commerce, in this chapter we will first step back and take a broader overview of wireless and mobile technologies and then look at how they relate to systems for Internet commerce. Because there are many different kinds of mobile devices with varying capabilities, it is important to have some perspective about those capabilities and how they may be used with Internet commerce systems. The hype around mobile devices is often about mobile commerce (sometimes called m-commerce) and has often focused on the use of Web-enabled

---

1. *The Adventures of Buckaroo Banzai Across the 8th Dimension* (Sherwood Productions, 1984).

mobile phones. By extension, such phones would naturally interact with Internet commerce systems.

A Range of Devices

The first thing one notices in considering mobile devices is that they come in quite a variety with many different characteristics. The main points that they have in common are small size, limited power, limited input/output capabilities, and limited bandwidth (although many are working on technologies to provide greater bandwidth). They range from data-enabled cellular phones (for various kinds of data) to two-way pagers to personal digital assistants (PDAs) with some kind of communications built in or added on. Some devices combine several of these functions in a single package, such as a combination PDA and cellular phone. In a sense, all of them are trying to offer the same value, or at least they are all trying to head in the same direction. The second striking thing about mobile devices is their range of ergonomic values. There are important trade-offs in factors such as battery life, input method, screen size, and overall size. Yet there are few standards for the way they work, ranging from the radio transmission systems that deliver data to the device to the way applications interact with them.

We will now present more detailed descriptions of various mobile and wireless devices. Some (or all) of them may be familiar, and your personal experience with them may be different, but the important points to understand are those that affect how one can use each kind of device in an Internet commerce system.

Wireless PDAs

Wireless PDAs, such as those available from Palm, Handspring, and other vendors, are the devices that come closest to the Web experience, albeit a very limited one. They generally have larger screens, which can actually be used to read e-mail messages or other documents, and they can store significant amounts of data. Most people find the handwriting input system to be clumsy, so they typically do not use them for anything that requires much writing. The battery life of PDAs is now generally quite good, but wireless networking drains power quickly.

One-Way Pagers

Pagers that can receive messages, whether numeric or alphanumeric, are the most common in this category and naturally are the most limited. For our purposes here—the use of the Internet for e-commerce—one-way pagers are not very interesting except for applications in which they can be used effectively for notifications. Auction systems, for example, might notify bidders of new bids or other information via such devices, although the recipients must take some other action, such as using a Web browser, to respond. Other systems might use the pager to add an extra step of confirmation in a payment transaction. In fact, some systems like this have been deployed in Europe using the message capabilities of mobile phones.

In many cases, providers of paging services make it possible to send e-mail to an address that causes the pager to be notified. In such cases, an e-commerce system that can send e-mail notices can already use such pagers, and no other work is needed (except to make sure that the user understands what to do).

Two-Way Pagers

Two-way pagers allow users to respond to messages sent through the paging network. The precise capabilities vary: some pagers allow users to send preset responses (such as *Yes*, *No*, and *Call me*), and some enable them to type messages on a small keyboard. Some have evolved to have limited support for Web interaction as well.

Mobile Phones

Mobile phones are ubiquitous these days, especially among users of e-commerce systems. Some phones have limited capabilities to access the Web, as we discuss in more detail later in this chapter.Voice-only phones can interact only with e-commerce systems that also include voice-response systems. Although there are some specialized applications that use voice interactions effectively, they are not currently part of the mainstream of e-commerce applications.

Smart Phones

Some vendors and mobile telecommunications services also offer so-called smart phones, which typically combine the functions of a mobile phone and a PDA. For our purposes here, they do not make much difference in the system design, because the combination is essentially a convenience for the end user, not a fundamentally different way of interacting with other systems.

Some Detailed Examples

Palm VII

The Palm VII was one of the earliest wireless PDAs to become available. It is just like a Palm organizer, only with a wireless connection. Out of the box, you get several wireless applications, including e-mail (through an account at Palm.Net), stock quotes, news services, driving directions, and others. Many of the applications help with getting information about a specific location: traffic reports,ATM locators, and so on. These applications also demonstrate the value of wireless data on a mobile device: they're important when you're not near your PC (or anyone else's PC).

The Palm VII uses a technology called *Web clipping* that Palm developed to enable application developers to adapt their Web sites and applications for use with the Palm VII. Obviously, the disadvantage is that the extra work has to be done. On the other hand, the resulting applications are well suited to the characteristics of the device. Unfortunately, Palm VII applications can't notify you that anything has changed—no beeps, no vibrations, no automatic checks for e-mail.

Ergonomically, the Palm VII has the same advantages and disadvantages that other Palm organizers have. It's about the same size as the original Palm Pilot, which is a bit large for carrying in a pocket, although this can be done. The screen is of a useful size, and most applications have been well adapted to the smaller screen. One significant limitation is the battery lifetime: the batteries don't last long under intensive wireless use.

EarthLink Wireless: Palm Vx with Novatel Modem

OmniSky was a startup company that provided the infrastructure, packaging, and hardware to adapt the Palm V and Vx for wireless data. EarthLink later acquired the OmniSky technology and subscriber base. The package includes a Minstrel V wireless modem from Novatel, along with software (including software from AvantGo) and the services needed to make it all functional. The package works pretty well. In most respects, it is similar to the Palm VII: it's still basically a Palm device, it works with Web clipping, and it provides e-mail through the service provider (in this case, EarthLink).

There are some interesting differences, however. One is that you can configure the EarthLink system to use up to six Internet mailboxes. This provides access to any POP3 (Post Office Protocol version 3) mailbox available on the public network (although it usually won't reach mailboxes on corporate networks, because it can't go through a security firewall). A second difference is that software provided by AvantGo enables the device to display pages from any Web site. Of course, the pages may or may not be rendered well on the device, but it works well for simple Web sites. The Web clipping applications, like those on the Palm VII, are still better adapted to the characteristics of the device, and the system is able to check for and signal the presence of new e-mail.

Sprint PCS Wireless Web

Unlike the other devices, the protocols used by Sprint PCS have been developed as a proposed set of standards. The protocol of choice for cellular phones and wireless data is the Wireless Application Protocol (WAP). The standards process is still moving along, however, and WAP services are just becoming available in the United States. Because Sprint PCS came to market early, it uses an earlier version of the protocols.

Inside the phone is a mini-browser developed by Phone.com, which was later purchased by Openwave. The phone also includes contact and calendar software, with the ability to synchronize with various PC applications. The mini-browser can interact with specially coded Web sites that use a markup language similar to the Web's HTML, called *Handheld Device Markup Language* (HDML). It also appears that it can use at least some sites coded with the WAP standard Wireless Markup Language (WML). Compared with the Web clipping applications of the Palm VII, they have the same relative properties as traditional PC client-server applications and Web applications. That is, the Web clipping applications are more specialized and elegant in themselves, but you must download code to use them. The mini-browser makes all applications look the same, but you don't need more code. More information about WAP is available from the Open Mobile Alliance (www.openmobilealliance.org).

Getting information into the phone is difficult, however. Telephone keypads simply weren't developed for typing words, and the other buttons for menu selection and navigation are somewhat confusing. Also, it's not possible to add programs to the phone in the way that one can develop new applications (Web clipping or otherwise) for the Palm.

RIM BlackBerry

The RIM BlackBerry is a two-way alphanumeric pager with some PDA-like functions. It has a miniature keyboard, which can be quite effective after some practice. Its value is that it's a very useful pager: the ability to send e-mail from a small device such as a pager is quite handy and can also be discreet in a meeting. Of course, as a pager, it lets you know when there's a new message.

Wireless LAN Technology

You can usually tell when someone is trying to push a technology into the mainstream—in this case, the consumer market: it gets a catchy name. The new name is *Wi-Fi*, but most people still call it by the name the engineers gave it: *802.11b*, the number of the IEEE standard for wireless data networking (sometimes called *wireless LANs*). 802.11b is actually one of a family of wireless networking specifications under the 802.11 umbrella. Some related standards are summarized in Table 20-1.

Perhaps the most dramatic development for 802.11b has been the steep decline in prices since products became widely available in 1999. Wireless LAN hardware has been available from several vendors for a few years now, but it wasn't very common for three reasons: it cost too much, it didn't interoperate, and it was too slow. Of course, these reasons are related—one role of standards is to stimulate competition and, hence, lower prices. In fact, the original 802.11 standard was adopted in 1997 but had a maximum bandwidth of 2 Mbps, far slower than the 10 Mbps or 100 Mbps

802.11b	802.11b is the most common wireless LAN technology, and it is being widely adopted for use at businesses and in homes. It provides bandwidth up to 11 Mbps over a range of several hundred feet. It uses the unlicensed spectrum at 2.4 GHz, as do other common devices such as microwave ovens, cordless telephones, and some baby monitors.
802.11a	Despite the name, 802.11a is a successor technology to 802.11b. It uses a different part of the spectrum (5 GHz), which is not as congested with other devices. It also provides higher bandwidth, at up to 54 Mbps. 802.11a devices became available in 2002.
802.11e	802.11e is a set of changes for all versions of 802.11 to improve the performance of streaming media.
802.11g	802.11g is a set of extensions intended to improve the bandwidth of 802.11b. It will probably deliver bandwidth in the range of 20–54 Mbps. Devices implementing this standard may be available by late 2002, and they will be compatible with existing 802.11b networks.

TABLE 20-1. **Summary of 802.11 Standards**

common in wired LANs. 802.11 systems were also plagued by interoperability problems, which made many organizations leery of deploying this technology.

The market needed something better, and 802.11b has opened up that market. Wireless networks have become increasingly common in office buildings, and their use in the home is growing as well. There are efforts underway to provide wireless LAN access to the Internet in airports, cafes, and other public locations. Some residential areas are also sprouting *community networks* of cooperating homes and apartments with wireless LANs. Indeed, some conferences and meetings, such as those of the Internet Engineering Task Force, are "wired for wireless," with access points scattered around a hotel or conference center. Today these wireless networks are found mostly at more technical events, but it's only a matter of time before they become common at all kinds of events. In fact, much of the networking capacity found at conference venues today was put in over the past decade by the need to service technical events, and that infrastructure is now available to a much wider audience.

Security and the Wireless LAN

Now, suppose you take your laptop with its wireless card and go visit someone else with a wireless net. You turn on the computer, start the software, and find that you're on their network. Some people have even driven around high-tech areas, such as downtown San Francisco, just to see how many wireless networks they could find and join. The results are frightening, at least for companies and individuals who care about who is on their networks. Many networks, including those of banks and other financial institutions, are open to this kind of attack.

Part of the problem is configuration: the network operators didn't change the cryptographic keys used to identify authorized systems to the network. They are also open to let any wireless device obtain a network address and start using the network. Although it is easy to complain that network operators are getting it wrong, the vendors have encouraged this by making the insecure case the easy one, even though it is a configuration that most users do not want.

The 802.11b standard specifies a technique called *Wired Equivalent Privacy* (WEP). WEP uses encryption to protect the data in the air, although most devices use a weak implementation that will not stand up to a determined attacker. Wireless interface cards that do better also cost more, although there is no marginal cost to the manufacturer for the change. There are other subtle problems with the security as well. Effectively, the 802.11b standard creates an open network, and security protocols, such as IPSEC and others, must be layered on to provide any real security for the network. From a network architecture point of view, this isn't necessarily bad, but it is certainly something to be aware of.

The Mobile User Experience

Market observers sometimes talk about the *killer app* for mobile devices of all kinds, and many think there isn't one yet. Actually, we think the killer app for small mobile devices is already clear: person-to-person communication. After all, that is obviously what drove the growth in mobile phones and pagers, and even some data services such as iMode in Japan. For larger mobile devices, such as the Palm, it is possible to provide limited interaction for focused applications, especially those that are useful to people moving around. Such applications include notifications of important news, maps and directions, and information about nearby locations. It is less clear if such devices will ever be commonly used simply to buy books or other items on the Web.

This suggests that there are two kinds of interesting applications for mobile devices: those of particular interest to customers on the move, and those that are useful adjuncts to other e-commerce applications whose main use is on the Web. Obviously, there is a large category of other mobile applications for specific uses, or internal uses within companies and other organizations, but they are outside the scope of this book.

In creating the user experience for mobile devices, we think there are several important rules to consider.

1. Mobile customers have limited time and attention. Although time and attention are not to be wasted on the Web, they are even more critical for mobile applications. The applications should be responsive and quick to use and understand.

2. A small device has limited bandwidth. It can also display only a small amount of data, so it is important to limit how much is downloaded.

3. On a small screen, every pixel is precious, so the information presentation needs to be designed with great care. There is little room for advertising, promotions, or other information not directly focused on what the customer is trying to do. As with rule 1, distractions take away from the customers' ability to accomplish their goals.

4. The experience should be closely integrated with that of the main Web site. If a transaction is made from a mobile device, for example, it should immediately show up on an online statement available through the Web site.

Outsourcing

Before the dot-com market collapsed in 2000, many companies had started to provide wireless data services as application service providers. They would take on the work of delivering a Web site's content to the myriad of different devices available on the market.

In the early stages of this market (which we are still in), this strategy may be a very good one. With so few standards in place, and with such widely varying device characteristics available, it is nearly impossible for an in-house group to develop the infrastructure required to handle such diverse interactions with customer devices. This is particularly true in the consumer market, where one has little influence over what devices customers want to use and where no single device stands out as a market share leader. Using a service provider also makes sense simply to gain access to expertise and avoid a large up-front investment for development. In the early stages, expertise is in short supply, and one can buy it more cheaply through the service provider.

The equation is somewhat different for organizations that control—or at least have great influence over—the devices that are used by the customers of the system. Such control may come because the organization is supplying the devices to customers, as some brokerage houses have done, or because a company is equipping its own employees with devices for access to the corporate network.

Summary

In the e-commerce world, the best ways to use wireless and mobile devices are still in the experimental stages. In 2002, it is too soon to tell how customers will want to use mobile devices to interact with Internet commerce systems, and the technology is still fragmented and changing constantly.

Leading-edge deployments may still want to conduct their own experiments, and it may be appropriate to work with service providers initially to avoid a big investment at the outset. In particular, service providers may be able to provide expertise and support across a broader range of mobile technologies than would be possible in-house.

Regardless of the short-term technology details, the key constraints for the user experience are likely to remain the same for at least the next several years. By focusing on how to deliver value through connections with low bandwidth and low latency, how to use a small display effectively, and how to integrate with the Web experience, mobile applications can build their own bases of loyal customers.

Part Three

Systems for Internet Commerce

CHAPTER 21

Putting It All Together

Three things are to be looked to in a building: that it stand on the right spot; that it be securely founded; that it be successfully executed.

—Johann Wolfgang von Goethe[1]

Building Complete Systems

In Part One of this book, we discussed issues of business, architecture, and implementation. In Part Two, we discussed implementation technologies for various aspects of Internet commerce. In this chapter, we try to assemble the pieces into complete systems. There are many workable ways to build Internet commerce systems; the approaches we describe here are but a few examples.

We will first present an architecture for a federated commerce system. Next, we describe a core system architecture and its requirements, followed by a discussion of how this architecture may be applied to the business models discussed in Chapter 4.

Federated Commerce System

We envision many individual Internet commerce systems as being members of a global federated commerce system, as shown in Figure 21-1. In the federated commerce system, customers may join one or more buyer communities and conduct commerce

1. Johann Wolfgang von Goethe, *Elective Affinities* (1808).

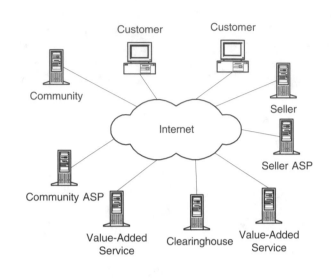

FIGURE 21-1. Federated Commerce System

with any number of sellers. Buyers get the advantages of a single account to remember and unified customer service. Sellers gain the advantages of standardization, ease of use, access to a large aggregation of customers, and easy access to network-based value-added services. In this example, we will abbreviate the generic *federated commerce system* as *FCS*.

The authors first proposed an FCS in a series of memoranda at Open Market in March 1995. In December 1998, Open Market launched an effort called *CommerceTone* to bring a federated commerce environment to the market. The project wasn't finished, but a separate company called CommerceTone was created to deliver some of the envisioned marketing and value-added services.[2]

In March 2001, Microsoft announced its Passport system, which it intended to be the single buyer community for the entire Internet. Passport provides single sign-on for its affiliated Web sites such as the Microsoft Network (MSN) and Hotmail, and also provides a server-side wallet for storage of credit card numbers and other personal information such as bill-to and ship-to addresses. Some of Microsoft's competitors, led by Sun Microsystems, then announced the Liberty Alliance, whose purpose was to create an open, federated single sign-on system, to be followed by some kind of FCS. Microsoft then announced the opening up of Passport to a federated model. At the

---

2. CommerceTone was later acquired by Mercantec.

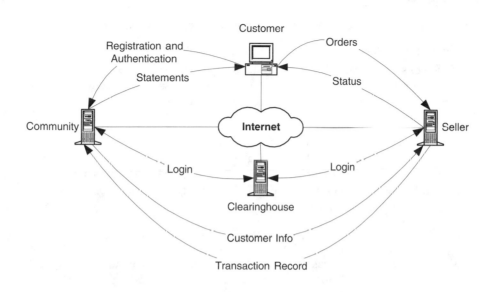

FIGURE 21-2. Federated Commerce System Transaction

time this book is being written, all of these systems are in the early stages of deployment, at best.

Let's follow a typical consumer transaction through its life cycle, with reference to Figure 21-2.

1. Previously, customer Jane joined a buyer community, completing its registration process.
2. Jane connects to the catalog Web site of the seller and selects items for purchase.
3. On the checkout screen, Jane selects **Use my FCS account**.
4. The seller system uses the services of the FCS clearinghouse to locate Jane's home community system (FCS Login).
5. Jane authenticates herself to her own home system.
6. The seller system requests buyer information from the home system, which Jane chooses to release.
7. The seller system completes the transaction and transmits a transaction record to Jane's unified customer statement held on her home system. This could be just a link to the seller's customer service module.
8. Later, Jane can view a unified list of all her FCS transactions and query any of them for status. The status link will take her to the particular seller system for current order status.

Consumer Services

The federated commerce system, if built correctly, has many benefits for consumers.

- Simple purchasing

  If the consumer allows, her home system can release ship-to addresses and payment information to the seller. This allows all participating sites to have a straightforward checkout process with few clicks and no typing.

- Unified statements

  With isolated systems, customer service is problematic because the customer must remember all the sites at which she has made purchases. With federated commerce, the seller always sends a short transaction record to the buyer's home system, to be placed on a unified statement. The unified account statement can also easily be integrated with personal finance software.

- Privacy

  People desire different levels of privacy. Some may choose to join a buyer community that provides cash-back or an affinity program in exchange for revealing additional personal information and accepting advertising. Others may choose to join a high-privacy community, which could go so far as to conceal completely the buyer's true identity from all other sites. In any event, the buyer has the ability to configure her personal privacy policy without the full-time job of studying the policies of every site visited.

- Multiple accounts

  Because there is a single point of control for an account, it is possible to put controls on the use of that account. This might be useful, for example, to allow children to shop online at selected sellers and with preestablished limits on their spending. The parents would have control over the limits on the account, and they would have access to a combined statement summarizing all activity on the family's accounts.

- Multistore gift registry

  Gift registries are typically limited to a single store or chain of stores. In a federated system, it would be straightforward to create gift registries that span multiple stores, providing more choices and easier shopping.

Value-Added Services

Federated commerce, by virtue of standardized APIs and service agreements, makes it straightforward to create value-added services, such as the following.

- Affiliate programs

  The FCS is a natural venue for affiliate programs. Rather than requiring affiliates to join seller programs individually, the affiliate can set up one account and potentially join many programs at once.

- Payment providers

  Payment providers can more easily connect with sellers by virtue of FCS standard interfaces. Standardized service agreements also promote competition.

- Tax calculation

  Domestic and international tax services can easily provide services. Of course, basic Web services do not require a federated system, but standardization of the relevant interfaces makes integration easier. For greater value, tax services could provide filing and payment as well.

- Logistics

  Logistics companies can offer rate calculators, shipping, and package tracking through standard interfaces. By connecting with both the buyer and seller, a logistics company could enhance privacy by concealing the ship-to address from the seller.

The FCS can offer many services, but they all build on three mechanisms.

1. The power of standardized APIs

   The FCS uses a Web services model for communications and integration. This means that interfaces are defined by agreed-on XML data types, and the existence and types of interfaces are defined by XML metadata. The FCS sets standards for the APIs to the network, which helps to ensure that systems provided by different vendors will interoperate.

2. The power of standardized contracts and directories

   Participants in the FCS can take advantage of standard roles. For example, someone can register as an affiliate and agree to the standard affiliate "deal" and then consult listings of sellers who offer that deal and sign up with many of them at once. Similarly, customers of a service who accept a standard deal can select suppliers who offer it. Standardized specifications of agreements such as percentage discounts for quick payment can even be processed automatically.

3. The power of networking

   Metcalfe's Law says that the value of a network increases as the square of the number of participants. Something similar seems to apply to the FCS: the aggregate expense of the network grows linearly with its size, but the savings grow with the number of possible interactions. In addition, the FCS is a boon for service providers, such as logistics companies, that must communicate with both the buyer and the seller. In standalone systems, this contact point is internal and inaccessible, but in the FCS, the contact between buyer and seller is external and easy to hook into.

Who Pays Whom?

As we have learned from the late 1990s, there are many possible business models for Internet services. It is probably easiest to compare parts of the FCS to the credit card system. In the credit card system, whenever a consumer uses a card, most of the money goes to the merchant, but a portion of the payment is split among the merchant's bank, the cardholder's bank, and processing companies. Generally, small fixed fees go to those parties whose role is merely to route transactions, whereas larger, although still small, percentage amounts go to parties who take on the financial risks of fraud, default, and so on. This seems to be a good model for the FCS. Roughly speaking, the network itself, the *clearinghouse*, may qualify for a fixed processing fee, and the buyer's community may qualify for a fixed fee for record keeping, but unless parties take on financial risk, they should not qualify for a fee based on the size of the transaction.

System Functionality

In Chapter 2, we introduced the commerce value chain: attract and keep customers, turn interest into orders, manage orders, and provide customer service. Excellence in managing orders and providing customer service can help attract and keep customers. The more one learns about one's customers (with great attention to privacy), the better one can market to them.

Our implementation approach divides the components of the value chain into the following groups.

- Content servers and applications
- Linking the content to transactions
- Order management, including order processing, payment, fulfillment, and customer service

Walking Through a Transaction

Before we discuss the system architecture and design issues, we'll walk through a transaction.

Before opening for business, a seller creates an online catalog containing the product descriptions, prices, and so forth. The seller also creates a merchant profile, which describes the accepted means of payment and tax and shipping rules, and configures the fulfillment system to route orders.

When the buyer browses the catalog, the purchasing process begins, consisting of the following steps.

1. The buyer locates products of interest in the catalog and clicks the associated offers. This creates items in the buyer's shopping cart.
2. On checkout, the buyer sees the order form, an example of which is shown in Figure 21-3. The screen shown already has some buyer information filled in, as would be the case for a repeat buyer, based on saved member information.

3. The transaction engine calculates sales tax using the buyer's billing address, the seller's tax profile, and the product tax classification code.

4. The transaction engine calculates shipping charges using the buyer's choice of seller-defined shipping methods, together with product price or weight.

5. The buyer clicks **Buy Now**.

6. The transaction engine performs a credit card authorization and address verification check with the seller's choice of card processing network.

7. The transaction is recorded in permanent storage.

8. An advice of order received is routed to the seller.

9. The transaction engine returns a receipt to the customer, which contains a copy of the invoice and a link to a status page for customer service.

10. The seller ships the product and informs the transaction engine of the shipment, using the online order status pages.

11. The transaction engine performs credit card settlement, transferring funds from the buyer to the seller's account.

12. The transaction engine updates the buyer's online statement and optionally sends the buyer an e-mail advising of the order shipment.

Afterward, the buyer's receipt remains active, bringing the buyer to his online statement of activity. Each item is a hypertext link to a status page for the particular transaction.

Digital Goods

If the product purchased is in electronic form, the buyer's receipt is a hypertext link directly to the fulfillment area. Either the receipt carries with it security codes granting access by the buyer to specified areas within the fulfillment site for a specified period of time, or access control for the fulfillment area must be updated.

Subscriptions

If the product purchased is an ongoing subscription to an electronic publication, the transaction engine makes appropriate entries in its subscription database for the purposes of billing and control of access to the fulfillment servers.

When the buyer links to the fulfillment server at a later time, he will be challenged to authenticate himself against the customer database. Then an access control check will be performed against the subscription database. If the subscription is current, the buyer will be granted a ticket good for access to the content areas. Only when the ticket expires, perhaps weekly, will the buyer be required to reauthenticate himself.

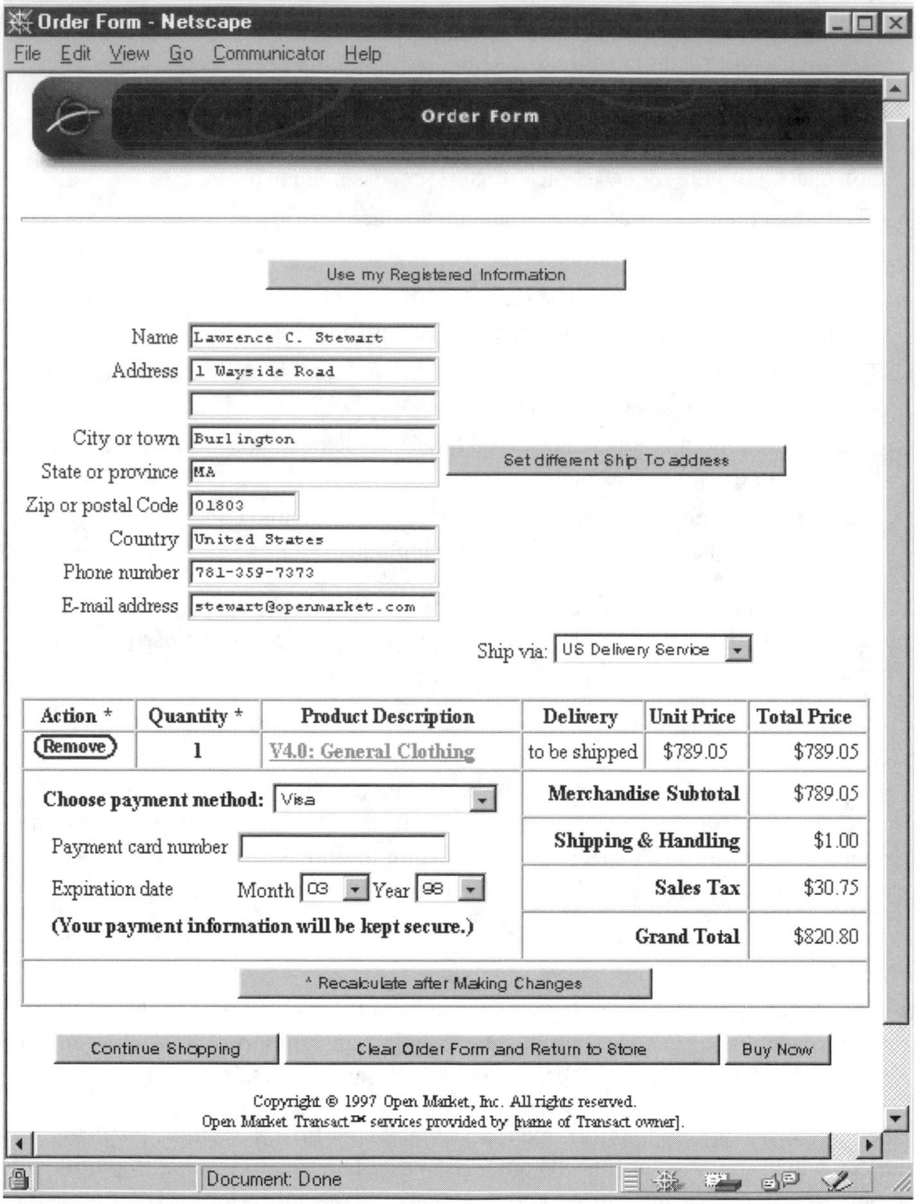

FIGURE 21-3. **Example of Order Form**

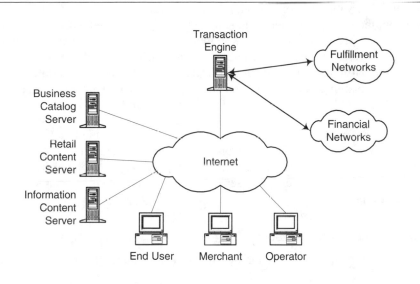

FIGURE 21-4. **Commerce Architecture**

System Architecture

When we introduced various architectures in Chapter 6, we said, "The architecture of a system defines its basic components and important concepts and describes the relationships among them." Figure 21-4 shows a block diagram of a commerce system built from these components. Overall, this is a three-tier architecture with clients using Web browsers connecting over the Internet to content servers of various types. The content servers in turn use shared commerce services. The application is interconnected over the public Internet. Finally, the transaction engine connects to services off the public Internet, such as financial networks and fulfillment systems.

The key architectural ideas are to separate management of content from management of transactions, to support a broad range of applications, to enable scaling of the system, and to accommodate evolution in technology and functionality.

Separating Content from Transactions

When we started thinking through the problems of commerce on the Internet, our first observation was that although we usually think of Web content as being present on a server somewhere on the network, it becomes displayable, rendered text and graphics only on the screen of the end user's Web browser. Consequently, the buyer's decision to buy will be communicated to the rest of the system as a network event, and we do not have to send that event to the same system that generated the page of content.

Our next observation was on the nature of a business transaction. Typically, information about the buyer, the seller, and the product being purchased must be brought together in one place. Buyer information includes items such as means of payment, shipping address, and so forth. Seller information includes items that are not dependent on the particular item sold but that relate to the seller across multiple products, such as payment methods accepted and means of fulfillment. Product information includes items such as description, price, weight, and taxability.

Our key decision was to treat product information as content and to maintain it on a content server, and then to deliver the product information to the transaction server as part of the click-to-buy process, using the standard Web HTTP protocol. This idea enables management of content to be separated from management of transactions, and permits several benefits.

Reduction of Operational Costs

Splitting up content and transaction management can reduce total operational costs.

Content servers have very different operational requirements than transaction servers. Indeed, if content is delivered by e-mail or CD-ROM, there may not be a content server at all.

Placing the transaction and business records in one place minimizes the number of systems that require database management systems and expensive reliability and integrity protections, and minimizes the number of systems that require specialized management and operations skills.

Because many content servers can share the services of a transaction engine, the costs of the transaction engine are amortized over many users. The content server costs are reduced because there is no need for each system to build in all the common costs of transaction handling.

Enabling of Service Providers

Multiple content servers can rely on shared commerce services provided by a transaction engine. This creates a new business—a commerce service provider, which operates a shared transaction system on behalf of multiple content servers. The transaction server can be shared across multiple divisions of a corporate enterprise or as a business in its own right.

Provision of Security Containment

A security systems is as strong as its weakest link. If valuable information is spread around the system, the security properties of the system must be equally strong everywhere. By placing mission-critical business functions and transaction records in a shared transaction server, the security effort can be focused. The efforts of attackers may be concentrated on the transaction system "because that's where the money is," but the vigilance of security mechanisms is concentrated as well.

It is actually easier to secure the transaction engine, which has limited and stylized connections with the outside world, than it is to secure a content server, which must be accessible to content creation and management personnel as well as to customers.

Supporting a Broad Range of Applications

A shared commerce services environment enables a very broad range of commerce applications. At the very simple end of the spectrum, small stores can be prepared with desktop publishing tools and uploaded onto the Net. Offers to sell, encoded in the content, point to a commerce service provider, which manages the resulting orders on a fee basis. There is no need for the content provider to understand or operate a complex transaction system.

In the midrange, dynamic content and rich site-development tools can create a compelling commerce experience for the consumer and provide compelling value for the business user.

At the high end, an enterprise may have multiple divisions with different content systems, sharing transaction services provided by the IT department. The transaction engine may be integrated closely with enterprise financial and logistics systems.

By leveraging a shared infrastructure, small and medium-sized enterprises can access all the services that are available to large enterprises.

Supporting System Scaling

Splitting up content and transaction systems allows them to scale independently. Content systems need to grow according to the type and volume of content, which may be unrelated to the volume of transactions. A dynamic content site delivering pages rich in graphics and multimedia will have greater computing and bandwidth requirements than a content system delivering even a large number of simple pages. On the fulfillment side for digital goods, a single transaction may grant very substantial access rights to fulfillment servers over an extended period.

With the shared services design, content servers can be added to the system as the need for them arises as a result of increased demand for or volume of content. Content servers representing additional businesses may register for commerce services at any time.

The transaction engine also needs to be scalable. We designed it as a set of logical servers backed by a relational database management system. The application logic scales by running the component servers on more powerful hardware or by load sharing. The database scales by running on more powerful hardware and by exploiting the database vendors' parallel and cluster capabilities.

Supporting System Evolution

An architecture is needed when one doesn't know what kinds of problems will arise tomorrow. Internet commerce is changing very rapidly, and so systems installed today will need to add new functionality and exploit new technologies as the industry matures.

Functional Evolution

Separating content and transaction systems permits functions to be added to each system without affecting or requiring upgrades to the other. For example, a new payment method such as purchase orders can be added in one place at the transaction server, making the new functionality immediately available to all affiliated content servers.

A content server employing dynamically generated pages can replace a server using static pages without any change in the transaction machinery.

Technological Evolution

An important part of an architecture is defining interfaces between the parts of the system that remain stable across multiple releases and technological changes. For example, server-side wallets may replace HTML forms and SSL/TLS for credit card payment on the Internet. When wallet support is added to the transaction engine, all the affiliated content servers can take immediate advantage of it without having to upgrade each content system—perhaps using several different content creation and management systems.

Transaction Engine

The best way to think of the transaction engine is as a suite of applications for its different users: buyers, sellers, and operators. This model is shown in Figure 21-5. In more traditional business settings, buyers interact directly with sellers, and both interact directly with operations and support groups. On the Internet, the situation is different because the parties involved are rarely online at the same time. Instead, each group of users interacts with applications that place their retained state in a database where the next group can pick it up and carry on. The database, without loss of generality, can be a set of databases with workflow capabilities.

The transaction engine is organized in this way, with application logic and user interface capabilities for buyers, sellers (merchants), and system operators. It is a rich application; the following sections are not exhaustive but are included here to give

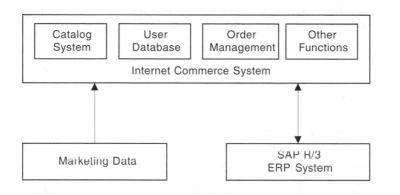

FIGURE 21-5. Transaction Engine Application

readers an appreciation of the kinds of functionalities and APIs that are included. In many implementations, the transaction engine includes the user interface, but in our example, the user interface for the buyers is specifically provided by the content management and catalog systems through transaction engine APIs.

Buyer Applications: User Interface and APIs

The buyer experience is primarily with catalog and other content systems. In the case of high-end content systems, or those with complex marketing and promotions logic, buyer interactions with the transaction engine are indirect, through content server user interfaces supported by application programmer interfaces provided by the transaction engine. In support of simpler catalog systems or of offers made by advertisements, buyers interact directly with transaction engine user interface software.

Buyer Applications with User Interface

- Order capture

  The order capture application appears to be an interactive order form. Buyers populate the order form directly by clicking digital offers and digital coupons, or the seller may prepopulate the order form through an API. The order form provides the facilities for the buyer to adjust item quantities, choose coupons, enter or edit billing and shipping addresses, and select payment and shipping methods. In addition to providing the order form user interface, the order capture subsystem calculates discounts from coupons (including matching coupons against items), validates addresses, and calculates sales tax and shipping charges, leading to an order total. If a consumer payment method such as a credit card is selected, the transaction engine obtains the necessary authorization in real time. The principle is to validate the success of the order to the fullest extent possible while the buyer is online, in order to resolve any problems right away. In the case of digital goods and subscriptions, the buyer experience ends with a receipt, granting immediate access to the appropriate fulfillment server. For physical goods, the buyer obtains a receipt that can be used later for order status and customer service.

- Account registration and management profiles

  There are multiple models of buyers. Walk-in buyers may have no previous relationship with the system. Walk-in buyers must fill out the complete order form, although parts of the process may be automated by buyer software such as an electronic wallet. There are also registered buyers, who have chosen to save an account profile as repeat visitors. Registered buyers get the order form already populated with their stored information, for faster checkout. Registered buyers also have access to account administration applications, for creating and changing user and security profiles and for registering additional means of payment, such as a microtransaction account. Finally, there are buyers whose profiles are held elsewhere by a buyer community that is part of the FCS. These buyers can be handled either as walk-in buyers whose order forms are filled out automatically or as registered buyers, some of whose registration information is held remotely.

- Customer service

  The goal of the customer service applications is customer self-service. For registered buyers, the system provides online statements of all transaction activity. Each item is active and can be clicked through to reach detailed order status information or the catalog page from which the item was originally selected. From the order status screen, the buyer can click through to the package tracking services offered by some logistics companies. The subscription capabilities are also supported by some special customer service applications. For example, if a subscription involves periodic payments and the associated credit card expires or is canceled, the system permits the buyer to substitute a different payment instrument without intervention by the operator.

Buyer APIs

Buyers will not use these APIs themselves. Instead, these are APIs that sellers who have relationships with the transaction engine use in order to implement the buyer experience.

- Commerce objects

  The commerce objects, including offers, coupons, and receipts, constitute the primary API to the transaction engine. These objects are the primary mechanisms through which items for sale, merchandising, and fulfillment of digital goods are handled between content servers and the transaction engine.

- Order injection API

  When a buyer is online, the content server can implement the user interface for the complete buyer experience and then hand off a complete order. In effect, the user interface for the order capture phase of commerce can be remotely located at a content server.

- Customer database API

  As we discussed in Chapter 12, in order to deploy sites with personalized content, a site needs to identify users, track sessions, and build pages according to information stored in a user profile. The transaction engine provides user authentication and session tracking to remotely located content servers through its subscription server and provides remote access to a centrally managed user profile through the customer database API. Individual content servers do not need to store authentication information and do not need to store common profile information, although each content server can extend the profile in a uniform way. Because profile and authentication information is stored in one place, it does not need to be replicated or distributed. A change in the profile made at one content server is immediately available to any other affiliated content server. These services are provided by the SecureLink digital query. When a content server or catalog server participates in the FCS, the customer database API links the content server to whatever buyer community system is the buyer's home system.

Seller Applications and APIs

In order to run an Internet-based business, a seller needs to create content and to configure and manage a wide variety of business rules and services. In our model, catalog content or site content is prepared and managed with a variety of applications and tools, but commerce facilities are centrally managed.

Seller Applications

- Merchant profiles

  In order to run their businesses, the sellers or merchants must configure a variety of business rules. The transaction engine provides a merchant administration application organized as a series of profile screens. The seller configures which payment instruments (such as credit cards) will be accepted from among those offered and, for each payment instrument, how processing is to be handled. For sales tax or value-added tax, the seller provides information on tax jurisdictions and related business rules. For shipping of physical goods, the seller configures an order delivery mechanism and one or more shipper profiles, which provide the business rules for calculating shipping costs displayed to the buyer.

- Order management and fulfillment

  The transaction engine can deliver orders to the seller by online or downloaded report, by fax, by regular or secure e-mail, or by use of the fulfillment API discussed later. The seller has access to tax and transaction statements and reports and can mark orders as *fulfilled* and provide an appropriate e-mail message for the buyer.

- Customer service

    Inevitably, questions and problems arise in handling orders. Our objective is to let buyers resolve their own questions through online customer service but also to provide means for the seller to process returns and credits.

Seller APIs

Most of the seller-oriented APIs were discussed under Buyer APIs because they relate to buyer activities during browsing and purchasing online. The order injection API, however, can also be used in an offline manner.

- Order injection API

    Even when order capture takes place in a medium other than the Internet, there is a benefit in using an Internet commerce system for order management and customer service. The order injection API permits entry of orders originated offline and then applies standard processing and online customer service. This permits both buyers and sellers a unified view of orders.

Operator Applications and APIs

The transaction engine can be operated by a single enterprise on its own behalf, or it can be run by a commerce service provider as a business providing Internet commerce services for other companies. In the first instance the operator applications and APIs are really seller facilities, whereas in the latter instance the operator applications and APIs support central services and policies of the commerce service provider.

Operator Applications

- Configuration

    The transaction engine is designed for great flexibility of installation, business rules, and user interfaces. The operator is responsible for using standard Web tools to create a standard look and feel for the system, even if the customization is only the addition of a name and a logo to the standard templates. The operator must also make a variety of policy decisions about trust, security, payment processing, and privacy. The operator is responsible for installing support for particular payment mechanisms and payment processing systems and configuring them for proper operation.

- Administration

    During normal operation, the transaction engine provides application support for ongoing activation and modification of affiliated content servers and central overrides for payment processing and merchant profiles.

- Reporting and logging

  The transaction engine creates log files for error reporting and audit trails and provides reporting tools for various kinds of system activities and for support of auxiliary activities such as fraud control.

Operator APIs

- Customer database API

  In addition to its use for real-time customer profile access from content servers, the customer database API permits individual or bulk loading of customer information. This makes it possible to Internet-enable existing systems.

- Fulfillment API

  In those cases in which the Internet order management application must directly connect with existing enterprise order management and fulfillment systems, the fulfillment API permits programmatic access to pending orders and dynamic updates of order status on a per-line-item basis.

- Payment API

  The transaction engine contains a variety of built-in Internet-capable payment systems, including credit cards, purchase orders, and microtransactions. However, Internet payment technology is changing rapidly, with debit cards, electronic funds transfer, and electronic checks gaining acceptance and with other, more innovative systems on the horizon. The payment API permits new payment systems and additional implementations of old ones to be added. Catalog content is linked to the transaction engine, which operates as a payment switch,[3] so new payment systems can be added without the necessity of updating any content servers.

System Functionality

The system is designed with groups of functionality for several Internet commerce market segments: business-to-business, business-to-consumer, and information commerce. Many if not most of the differences in required functionality for these markets are addressed by different content systems—catalogs for business-to-business commerce, catalogs and entertainment sites for business-to-consumer commerce, and complex search and retrieval engines for information commerce—but the business rules, payment methods, and common services are also distinct.

---

3. See, for example, "Payment Switches for Open Networks," by D. K. Gifford, L. C. Stewart, A. C. Payne, and G. W. Treese, IEEE COMPCON (March 1995).

Business-to-Business Commerce

- Payment mechanisms

  Most business-to-business (B2B) commerce is not conducted with consumer payment mechanisms such as credit cards. Although procurement cards, the B2B version of credit cards, are undergoing substantial growth, the bulk of B2B commerce is done by one business extending credit to another business, issuing purchase orders, and invoicing, and most payments are made by check or electronic funds transfer. The transaction engine supports purchase orders for order capture, with approval mechanisms for online creation of business relationships.

- Fulfillment

  The fulfillment API provides a way to integrate orders received over the Internet with the order stream from traditional channels.

- Custom catalogs

  Perhaps the most direct and immediate benefit of Internet commerce for B2B applications is the provision of accurate, complete, and timely product information directly to requisitioners in the buying organization. The customer database API provides the catalog access to authentication and profile services to permit the display of contract pricing, customized part numbers, reserved inventory, and other characteristics of business relationships.

Business-to-Consumer Commerce

- Order capture

  The order capture subsystem is designed to be easily used with no training by end consumers. The order form metaphor is familiar to users of paper catalogs, and the system tries hard to validate all input in real time to alert the buyer to any difficulties while she is still online.

- Consumer-oriented payment

  Credit cards are the primary payment mechanism for direct marketing to consumers. They offer substantial convenience and ease of use, and in the United States they provide very strong consumer protections. The transaction engine supports real-time credit card authorization in support of a transparent consumer experience.

- Personalized content and merchandising

  Merchandising and personalization of content are essential for consumer markets in which consumers can choose from a range of suppliers. The transaction engine helps businesses compete on the basis of customer service as well as on price and convenience. Coupons provide a means of merchandising even when the buyer is accessible only by advertising and e-mail. The customer database API permits sites to create personalized experiences for repeat visitors.

- Support for small and medium-sized merchants

  Through seller profiles and the medium of commerce service providers, the transaction engine can offer complex Internet commerce services to small and midsize merchants who cannot afford to own and operate the entire application themselves. Smaller businesses can use Internet hosting services, whereas larger ones keep their catalogs in-house.

Information Commerce

- Business models

  The transaction engine supports business models that are central to information commerce. The essential capability is for authenticated and secure distributed access control to fulfillment servers. An information customer can click an offer for an information product or service and immediately receive the corresponding receipt for access to that service. In the case of ongoing subscriptions to electronic content, the subscription server maintains authentication, access control, and payment information on an ongoing basis.

- Payment models

  In addition to credit cards and purchase orders typical of physical goods, the transaction engine supports microtransactions of either parking meter (prepay) or taxi meter (postpay) styles. These mechanisms permit very lightweight, pay-per-page access to information services.

- Customer service

  In information commerce, or indeed in any business in which item prices are low, it is essential that customer service calls and disputes be held to a minimum. Customer self-service through easy-to-use statements and account administration help to keep customer support costs low.

Case Study: Business-to-Business System

Now let us consider in detail a system for businesses selling primarily to other businesses. A high-level diagram of such a system is shown in Figure 21-6. This system represents a sell-side Internet commerce system for an integrated manufacturing company. The internal operations of the business are managed by a commercial enterprise resource planning (ERP) system, as discussed in Chapter 18. The ERP system will remain responsible for all sales and logistics, including new business obtained over the Internet. In addition, the company wants its Internet users to have access to all of their open orders and quotes, not just to those originally created over the Internet. Consequently, to a substantial degree this B2B system is providing a front end for the existing ERP system, routing and translating existing business documents as well as permitting users to compose new orders using a catalog-oriented Web interface rather than the forms metaphor of the ERP system.

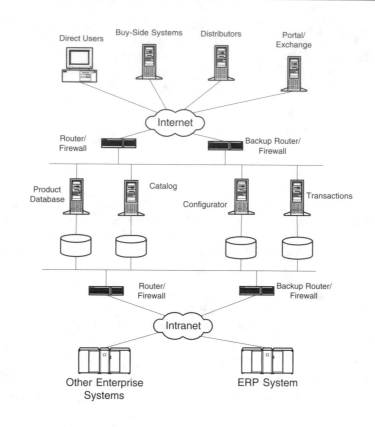

FIGURE 21-6. **Enterprise E-Business Architecture**

The Users

We envision four kinds of users of our sell-side B2B system.

1. Direct users

   Direct users represent not individual consumers but purchasing officers and requisitioners at customer companies who have been approved to create purchase orders against their companies' accounts.

2. Buy-side software

   Buy-side systems such as those envisioned by the Open Buying on the Internet (OBI) Consortium have a complex interaction with sell-side systems, as described in Chapter 6. The requisitioner creates an order, which is then routed to the buy-side system for approval and then returned to the sell-side system for fulfillment.

3. Distributors

Distributors can operate in two modes: they can choose to receive catalog data in XML format for inclusion in their own systems, or they can use the manufacturer's e-commerce system as an application service provider, hosting the distributor catalog, but with the distributor's look and feel. Products may even be drop-shipped directly from the manufacturer rather than ever enter the distributor's inventory.

4. Portals and exchanges

The seller may participate in several portals and exchanges, typically uploading catalog data in XML interchange format and accepting purchase orders in EDI or XML format over the Internet.

Content Systems

In our manufacturing example, we have divided the content systems according to function.

Product Database

The product database is actually not a Web-facing system at all, although it may be used directly to distribute catalog data to portals, exchanges, and distributors. In many companies today, there simply is no central repository of product information. Companies that have relied on print advertising may have no online images and no online descriptions of products, and even their part numbers and pricing information may be locked inside the ERP and may not be immediately available to the Internet. The product database merges and combines all available product information into usable form: SKUs and short descriptions from the ERP system, text from product management and marketing, and images perhaps from the print catalog vendor.

Catalog

The primary client of the product database is the online product catalog, which adds user interface, searching, and navigation to the raw data. When distributors use the manufacturer as a catalog ASP, the catalog system is responsible for hosting the distributors' custom catalogs. The seller may also offer custom catalogs to major customers. These custom catalogs may contain special parts not available to others and may provide direct display of contract pricing.

Configurator

Many manufacturers sell products that must be configured. A good example is a product composed of subassemblies that work only in certain combinations. A *configurator* is a special software application that knows all the complex rules for valid product configuration. A configurator can check a complete configuration for validity, or it may permit end users to configure complex products interactively. In either case, the output of the configurator is a complete bill of materials that can be passed as a unit to the order form.

Transaction System

As we have mentioned, the Internet commerce transaction system for this B2B site is more involved with order creation and routing than with complete order management. Order management is still the focus of the ERP system. One case, however, that will require transactions is when the Internet system must stand in for the ERP system during planned downtimes and periods of unavailability.

Figure 21-7 shows some of the possible options that we envision for order origination and routing. This figure centers around the idea of the shopping cart or order form. The active cart may be loaded from several sources and routed to several destinations. When orders are composed interactively, the processing pipeline of the transaction system actually links out to the ERP systems for customer validation, product pricing, and availability.

Order Sources

The contents of an order can come from many sources.

- Catalog

  Individual line items, or preconfigured assemblies, can be selected from the catalog and entered into an order.

- Quick order form

  Many users of B2B systems are repeat users who know the part numbers by heart. The fastest way to use such a system may be to type the SKUs into a form. The quick order form does this, validates the part numbers, and hands off the line items to the order form.

- Configurator

  Complex products and assemblies may be subject to sophisticated rules specifying valid combinations. A configurator produces a bill of materials (BOM) for a complete, valid configuration. The line items from the BOM are transferred as a unit to the order form.

- Orders and invoices

  Any saved order or invoice may be used as the basis for a new order, by transferring and revalidating the line items.

- Saved shopping carts

  An order that was saved before submittal may be reloaded.

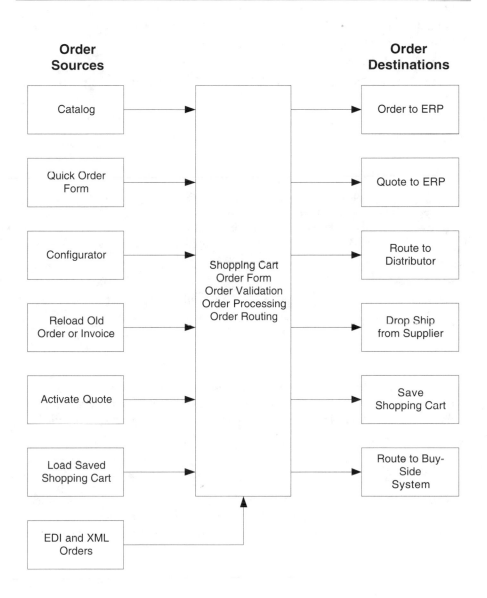

FIGURE 21-7. Enterprise Order Routing

- Quotes

    A quote is an order that is priced and approved by the seller but not yet approved by the buyer. Quotes can be activated but not modified.

- EDI and XML business documents

    Orders can arrive as XML or EDI business documents from portals and exchanges.

Order Destinations

- ERP system

    Orders that are directly processed by the manufacturer are routed to the ERP system for acceptance and processing. Acceptance should be preordained by virtue of the real-time checks done on the order form during processing, but orders that arrive while the ERP system is not available could contain errors. In these cases, the existing ERP error processing or manual intervention would be used.

- Distributors

    The seller or buyer may choose to route some orders to distributors rather than handle them directly. This might be done, for example, when orders are too small or when the manufacturer is consciously choosing not to disintermediate existing channels.

- Suppliers

    Some orders may contain items for which the seller is in fact a distributor for someone else. These orders may be immediately forwarded rather than being routed through the ERP system. This might happen, for example, when a manufacturer of computer systems buys video monitors from a specialized supplier.

- Saved shopping carts

    Some orders may not be submitted at all but rather saved by the buyer for later use.

- Buy-side systems

    As we mentioned in the context of Open Buying on the Internet, after an order is composed by a requisitioner, it may be sent to a buy-side system for approval processing before being reintroduced to the sell-side system, where it is passed to the seller's ERP system.

Case Study: Business-to-Consumer System

Next, let us look at a consumer-oriented system, one that may or may not be part of a federated network. In general, it is able to operate independently, although it may also be integrated with other systems.

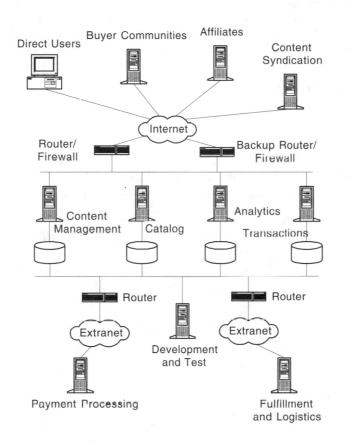

FIGURE 21-8. Consumer System Architecture

Overall System Architecture

The overall architecture of our complete business-to-consumer commerce system is shown in Figure 21-8. Users of the system may be direct users, those whose relationships with the seller are through an affiliate, or those whose relationships are through content syndicated to other systems on the Internet. In each case, the buyer may be associated with a buyer community via the federated commerce system.

The seller's e-commerce system is connected to the Internet using redundant links, firewalls, and routers, in an environment designed for high availability and high reliability. Although not shown in Figure 21-8, the environment is also designed for widely variant loads resulting from holiday shopping and special promotions. As we discussed in Chapter 19, this is typically accomplished by replicating the relevant servers and by using load-balancing routers, or by outsourcing all or part of the site.

The e-commerce system itself has four main components: content management, catalog management, transaction management, and analytics. These systems in turn are supported by development and test systems for validating new features of the site and new versions of software.

Content Systems

We've chosen to separate content management per se from catalog management in this example. This may not be appropriate in all situations, but the ideas that lead one to separation, as discussed in System Architecture, which begins on page 409, have to do with scaling, security, operational requirements, and system evolution. If different parts of the system do not have to integrate tightly and have different requirements along these axes, then it makes sense to run them on separate machines.

Catalog

The catalog system is the primary repository of product information. It may, in fact, be built using a content management system as a foundation. The product information in the catalog comes from multiple sources, including internal enterprise systems for part numbers and pricing, graphic arts systems for product photos, and marketing systems for product descriptions. The catalog system itself provides facilities for product searching and selection, but catalog navigation, look and feel, and display are usually highly customizable for the needs of the organization. Moreover, the catalog system is often responsible for presenting promotions and special offers driven by marketing and the analytics system.

Content management facilities can be used for managing product information, but they are particularly useful for managing the look and feel of the catalog as it evolves—in other words, we are using workflow and other content management facilities to control the catalog's own templates and configuration as much as the catalog content itself. Because of the tight integration required among catalog presentation, promotions, pricing, and the shopping cart, it is likely that the catalog system will provide the user interface for order management even though order processing is provided by the transaction engine.

The catalog system is also the source of product information syndicated to other sites, items for sale through portals, and product information in advertising on other systems.

Content Management

Other than the product catalog itself, all the business Web presence is managed through a content management system. This system provides the general corporate Web presence and the user interface and business logic for commerce but not customer service functions such as repairs and returns processing.

Content

It is now well understood that compelling Web content must undergo continual renewal. Content management systems provide for version management, publishing, workflow, and access control of such content, as well as tools for separating form from content. The same articles can be presented for standard Web browsers or for wireless devices, for example, by using different display templates. Version management permits the consistent release of multiple parts of the site, and publishing permits both periodic release of new content and syndication of content to other systems in the network.

Business Logic

Noncatalog content requires business logic for many purposes, and that logic must be flexible, modifiable, and manageable. This category ranges from fairly straightforward applications such as store locators to perhaps quite highly integrated applications such as returns processing. The business logic must be kept separate from presentation logic and should itself be managed through the content management system, if it has that capability. One implementation is to use a content management system based on the J2EE standards and then to implement business logic components as Enterprise JavaBeans.

Analytics

Many business-to-consumer systems are still electronic analogs of paper catalogs, perhaps with search and navigation added. The trend, however, is to use every scrap of information available about the customers and what they are doing to improve sales and service. The analytics system analyzes customer profiles, transaction records, and clickstreams to generate marketing reports, to gauge the success of promotions, and increasingly to create real-time promotions, special offers, and recommendations targeted at individuals and groups of like-behaving consumers. We've packaged this part of the application separately because analytics systems are specialized and because they have processing requirements that are different from those of the other systems.

Transaction Engine

In this example, we use the same buyer APIs of the transaction engine as in the previous B2B example.

Case Study: Information Commerce

Our system example for information commerce is a newspaper that offers free access to the current issue, subscription-based access to the most recent year, and pay-per-view access to the archives. A diagram of this system is shown in Figure 21-9. This

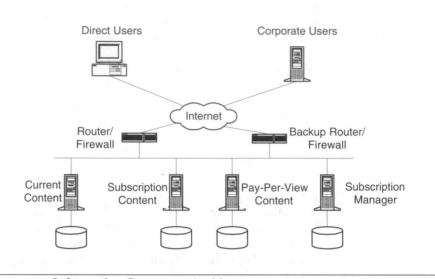

FIGURE 21-9. Information Commerce Architecture

system envisions two classes of customers: direct end users and corporate users. Direct users have purchased their subscriptions individually, and corporate users are members of a group who have collectively purchased access. Note that the information commerce system also requires connections to payment processing networks, but these networks are omitted from the figure.

Content Servers

For clarity of presentation, Figure 21-9 shows separate content servers for the free (current) content, for the subscription content, and for the archives. Technically, these can all be hosted on the same machine, but we have chosen separate systems to exploit the differences in scaling properties. For example, the current issue, offered at no charge, may be freely replicated for availability and performance. The pay-per-view archives, on the other hand, require large storage but relatively lower bandwidth of access.

Subscription Server

The commerce portions of this information commerce system are shown in Figure 21-9 generically as subscription services, but they really include three subsystems.

1. Subscriber database

   The subscriber database provides for registration of users and maintains a database of who should have access to what content on which servers. The subscriber database will be organized hierarchically to support group subscriptions, perhaps with delegation of the administration of group membership. In addition, the subscriber database is responsible for authentication and access control to the servers providing subscription access.

2. Subscription processing

   The subscription processing subsystem manages the payment aspects of subscriptions. Each subscription has various terms and conditions, such as grace and trial periods, installment payments, renewal options, and returns policies. The subscription server performs periodic payment processing as appropriate and provides means for users to replace failed payment instruments with new ones.

3. Transaction processing

   The transaction processing subsystem provides transaction and payment services for the subscription processing subsystem and also provides transaction and microtransaction services for the pay-per-view service. Archived articles may be offered for sale by individual credit card transactions, but microtransactions may make more sense if either the price point is low or the seller wants to offer sales of multiple articles for a single fee or to run a tab, where the customer pays after the fact rather than before.

Summary

In this chapter, we have put together application knowledge and technology and described the architectures of several examples of e-commerce systems. Of course, there are many other approaches to commerce applications, but we hope these examples have provided some insight into ways that ideas about Internet commerce can be turned into real systems. These architectures were designed to provide a foundation for a wide range of commerce applications, and they address many of the problems we have examined in this book.

CHAPTER 22

The Future of Internet Commerce

It's difficult to make predictions, especially about the future.
—Yogi Berra[1]

For all the excitement and hype about Internet commerce over the past few years, the dot-coms and the dot-bombs, we are really just at the beginning of a business revolution. Some businesses will change radically and quickly. For others, the revolution may be less dramatic, but it will happen nonetheless. The choice now is not whether to embrace the Internet, but how to do it and how fast to do it. The customers will demand it, and the competition will stake out the new territory if you do not.

In this chapter, we take a look at some of the predictable changes and trends, as well as the problem of unpredictable or discontinuous changes. Because we expect Internet technologies to continue to evolve rapidly, we discuss some ideas for keeping an Internet commerce system up-to-date. Finally, we return to the strategic imperatives of the Internet.

Accepting that changes will come is the first step. Turning the Internet to your advantage is the next.

---

1. Folklore attributed to Yogi Berra.

Trends

It is always difficult to forecast the future, but we can try to examine some of the forces that will shape it. We are enmeshed in those forces, so they are hard to recognize. Instead, we can look at trends and try to discern historical patterns that may extend into the future.

Hardware Technology Trends

Computing is unlike any other activity in history in its sustained progress. Computer metrics such as processor performance and storage capacity have been undergoing exponential growth for the past 20 years, and the trend is expected to continue for at least another 10 to 20 years. Gordon Moore, one of the founders of Intel, predicted in 1965 that the density of transistors on semiconductor chips would double roughly every 18 months. This prediction has been so accurate that it is called *Moore's Law*. Moore's Law isn't really a law, and staying on the curve has required inspired creativity and enormous capital. As a result, however, we face some nearly certain changes in the Internet environment.

- Computer performance

  We can look forward to 10 or more years of steadily improving performance and declining prices of computer equipment, both personal computers and servers. Between 1982 and 1997, the performance of a $2,000 personal computer increased thousandfold. Between 1997 and 2012, there will probably be another thousandfold improvement. As of early 2002, we are right on track.

- Storage capacity

  In 1985, 5-MB hard drives were common elements of personal computers. Today, 50-GB drives are commonplace—a 10,000-fold improvement. It is more difficult to predict how the next thousandfold improvement in storage will be achieved, but it will happen.

- Communications capability

  In 1985, modems that ran at 1,200 bits per second (bps) were common. In 1997, we had modems operating at 56,000 bps over conventional (albeit high-quality) telephone lines. Today, broadband access by cable or DSL can deliver more than a megabit of bandwidth to a single residence. Internet access by satellite, cable network, and corporate LAN delivers multimegabit performance. It is easy to foresee corporations with gigabit connections to the Internet, and it is certainly plausible to expect individual homes to have multimegabit connections.

- Portable equipment

  Laptops are already approaching the capabilities of desktops, and many people (including the authors of this book) now use portable computers as their primary computing platforms. Smaller *palmtops* have become more common as well.

- Wireless communications

  Wireless data communications will become so common and inexpensive to use that portable devices will be connected to the network at almost all times. Wireless LANs are cheap and common. Wireless wide-area networks are still not cheap, because they piggyback on the cellular networks, but they are nearly ubiquitous.

All of these trends are driven by improvements in hardware of one sort or another, and our conclusions are simply extrapolations based on historical data. Stated simply, they seem almost obvious, but the business implications of these order-of-magnitude changes may be tremendous.

Software Technology Trends

There are many clear trends in software technology as well. These trends include the following.

- Security and authentication

  All of the technological pieces are in place for a global security and authentication infrastructure that should make it possible for businesses and individuals to identify one another and communicate securely over public networks. However, that infrastructure has not yet emerged. Cryptography, smart cards, and digital signatures are all available today, and we expect the necessary supporting systems and environments to be developed and deployed over the next 5 to 10 years. Already there are several efforts toward federated commerce systems. In the meantime, Internet commerce will grow most rapidly in communities of interest, in segments in which some infrastructure exists, and in situations in which offline relationships can be moved online.

- Component software

  The current trend toward object and component software will accelerate. The next steps in this transformation will be software that can assist in its own testing and assembly—extensions of design-time behavior—and a rapid expansion of translation capabilities that can make software objects more adaptable to communications in different formats.

- Business objects

  The great lesson from the slow growth of EDI over the past 20 years is that standard *formats* for data are not enough. What is necessary for interoperability of business messages without costly configuration and development is standardization of *meaning*. In other words, we must move from *syntax* to *semantics*. This shift is well underway with the use of XML to define standard sets of business messages, as well as the development of *business objects* that encapsulate behavior as well as information.

Software Development and Standardization Trends

- Greater interoperability

  The industry trend toward standard, interoperable interfaces between systems will continue. This means that it will be increasingly easier to assemble complete systems using components and packages from multiple vendors.

- More software reuse

  To date, software engineering has been a cottage industry, with hundreds of thousands of skilled workers painfully creating software one line at a time. Mainly through class libraries and other forms of object technology, developers will begin to create new applications by standing on the shoulders of their predecessors rather than by rebuilding every element from scratch.

- Web services and ASPs

  It is now generally recognized that almost any software product can be delivered as a software service over the Internet. Application service providers run what used to be internal enterprise applications, whereas functional modules such as payment, taxes, and logistics are delivered as Web services instead of as software products.

In combination, these effects mean that the rate of change of software will increase. New functionality will take less time to develop. There will be a countervailing effect that the greater complexity of applications will take longer to test, but this effect will be abated by improved understanding of automated testing and software quality assurance. Historically, most bugs are in new code, not in reused components.

Infrastructure Trends

- Commercial environment

  There is very nearly a worldwide common commercial environment for individual consumers—namely, credit cards backed by global brands such as Visa, Master-Card, and American Express. Business-to-business commerce, on the other hand, does not have the same level of service. Services such as those that Dun & Bradstreet offers can help create trading relationships, and electronic funds transfer networks such as ACH can be used for payments. Today, however, these systems are not global, they do not run in real time, and they are not integrated. It seems likely that highly integrated systems specializing in trust and payment for businesses will evolve to support global Internet commerce.

- Government environment

  Today, the government environment is incredibly complex. Taxes, customs, and regulations vary in both space and time, across political boundaries, and as countless regulators and legislators change the rules. It is possible that international unity and concord, driven by commercial demands for a consistent operating environment, will simplify and regularize all the rules, but this seems unlikely. Far more likely is the development of sophisticated, knowledge-intensive software that automates the complexity. As we saw in Chapter 18, once software can fully implement the tax system, its complexity will become more of an irritation than a hindrance to commerce.

- Legal environment

  Today's business environment is the result of centuries of accumulated experience and practice, codified in law and interpreted by the courts. The Internet brings new questions, such as the exact standing of a digital signature or the liability of a certification authority. These questions are currently being tested, jurisdiction by jurisdiction, according to the usual progression of the legal system. Over the long term, however, uniform standards and definitions for commercial practice are essential. At first, these standards will evolve by mapping electronic situations to their closest physical analogies, but occasionally new situations will arise and new precedents will be needed.

Application Trends

In the early days of business computing, enterprises employed staffs of developers and maintained their own business software for applications such as accounting. As the functionality of these applications became standardized, platform vendors began to supply software for applications, and not merely development tools. As the complexity of applications grew, software product companies evolved to deliver packaged application software for business applications. Today, very few companies write their own accounting software.

These trends seem likely to be repeated in Internet commerce. In these early days, enterprises develop their own Internet commerce applications using whatever expertise they have. This period will be followed by one characterized by development tools and applications supplied by software vendors. As the complexity of commerce applications grows, the likely successor stage will be characterized by specialized packaged applications for Internet commerce.

However, there is a countervailing trend that isn't yet clear—namely, that companies will outsource operation of packaged applications to ASPs and that software companies will create Web services rather than product software.

The Internet is growing so rapidly that these phases overlap, and it is easy to point to examples of all these stages coexisting. In developing a strategy for Internet commerce, it is worth considering how your own systems will develop over time and which "build, buy, or rent" decisions are most appropriate for your own company.

Discontinuities

Evolutionary trends can be amazing to contemplate, especially exponential trends, but what about the changes wrought by new ideas? Such changes are potential discontinuities in society and in commerce. It may be fun to invent a slightly better printing press, but what happens when someone creates television?

In software engineering, there is a rule of thumb that every factor of 10 in *quantity* creates a *qualitative* difference. Earlier we suggested that processing power, storage capacity, and communications bandwidth would each improve by a factor of 1,000 over the next 15 years. These changes will create new kinds of experiences, not merely evolutionary changes in current modes of operation. In addition to these sorts of changes, there will be innovations we cannot envision. In the current heady explosion of the Internet, we frequently make the error of thinking that the World Wide Web is the final innovation in networking, and we forget that the Web is only a few years old. Five years from now, the Web may seem like a quaint idea.

Some potentially discontinuous changes seem very plausible, because they have been demonstrated in limited settings. These changes include speech interfaces, natural-language understanding, and virtual reality. Other ideas, such as direct neural control of computers, still seem to be figments of the science-fiction writer's imagination. All we can suggest is that if an idea does not violate physical laws, it will probably be built. One fascinating possibility is the use of nanotechnology to construct physical objects at the other end of a network connection. This will probably not happen by 2005, but within our children's lifetimes it seems entirely possible.

Staying Up-to-Date

The resale value of a new car drops precipitously the moment you drive it off the lot. Even so, a new car can last for years, and in 10 years the new models are not 100 times better. By contrast, the PC you buy today is technologically obsolete by the time you get it installed, and this trend shows no sign of abating.

How do you keep your system up-to-date in this environment? In part, this is the role of architecture in an Internet commerce system. An extensible architecture allows the addition of new components on top of the old ones. A scalable architecture can handle growth smoothly, without disrupting the system for customers. Architecture also provides some guidance on which technology changes make sense and which can be set aside. With this kind of assistance, it becomes much easier to sort through both the hype and the reality of new technologies and new products. Some can contribute to your system; others cannot. In a few years, you may have replaced all the important components of your system, even though the fundamental architecture has not changed much.

Strategic Imperatives

As we suggested in Chapter 3, the Internet introduces two factors into business thinking: the Internet can transform customer relationships, and the Internet can displace traditional sources of business value.

- Transforming customer relationships

  Traditionally, a customer has few points of contact with a business. The Internet allows a complete *outside-in* reengineering of the relationship of a business to its customers, transforming the business from an internal focus to a customer focus.

- Displacing traditional sources of business value

  The Internet transforms business from dealing with physical artifacts to dealing primarily with information. Economies of scale in the physical world are transformed into economies of scope. Distribution becomes an opportunity rather than a constraint. The net effect is to upset the basis of competition.

These factors require nothing less than a fundamental review of business strategy based on a sober assessment of the strength of a business's relationships with its customers and its core value proposition.

Ultimately, customers, not businesses, will determine the fate of Internet commerce. If the Internet is effective for customers, businesses will find ways to deliver value with it. In the process, new businesses will succeed and others will fail. Some existing businesses may negotiate the transition; others will not. We hope that this book will help your business be among the leaders in using the Internet effectively.

Resources and Further Reading

What follows are some resources and readings that we have found useful in our own work on Internet commerce. We have not listed many that deal with particular software packages, because those details change quickly as new versions and new products become available. Rather, we have chosen some that (for the most part) have more lasting relevance to thinking about the design of systems for Internet commerce.

Chapter 1—Introduction

In *Frontiers of Electronic Commerce* (Addison-Wesley 1996), Ravi Kalakota and Andrew B. Whinston examine a wide range of technologies that affect the development and deployment of Internet commerce systems. This book provides an excellent overview for business professionals. Kalakota and Whinston have also written *Electronic Commerce: A Manager's Guide* (Addison-Wesley 1997). David Kosiur's *Understanding Electronic Commerce* (Microsoft Press 1997) is another good overview of what is happening in the Internet commerce market, and it includes some interesting case studies.

Regarding the Internet and the World Wide Web, see *Weaving the Web* by Tim Berners-Lee (HarperCollins 1999). He invented the Web in the first place.

Chapter 2—The Commerce Value Chain

Many of the important legal issues for Internet commerce are discussed in *Law and the Information Superhighway* by Henry H. Perrit Jr. (John Wiley & Sons 1996), as well as in *The Law of Electronic Commerce* by Benjamin Wright (Aspen Law & Business 1995). Note, however, that the law is changing quickly in these areas, although not as fast as the technology. *Code and Other Laws of Cyberspace* by Lawrence Lessig (Basic Books 1999) is about "the relationship between law, cyberspace, and social organization."

Chapter 3—Internet Business Strategy

Kim M. Bayne's *The Internet Marketing Plan* (John Wiley & Sons 1997) and *Marketing on the Internet 2*nd edition, by Jill H. Ellsworth and Matthew V. Ellsworth (John Wiley & Sons 1997) both look at Internet commerce from a marketing point of view, with some high-level descriptions of the technologies used on the Web.

In *The 1:1 Future: Building Relationships One Customer at a Time* (Currency Doubleday 1993), Don Peppers and Martha Rogers examine the business implications of relationships with individual customers. Although this book was published before the Internet came to be used for any significant amount of commerce, the development of Internet commerce only reinforces the central concepts it describes.

net.gain by John Hagel III and Arthur G. Armstrong (Harvard Business School Press 1997) examines the business opportunities offered by the Internet in building virtual communities. *Information Rules* by Carl Shapiro and Hal R. Varian (HBS Press 1999) is "a strategic guide to the network economy." We also note *The Seven Steps to Nirvana: Strategic Insights into eBusiness Transformation* by Mohan Sawhney and Jeff Zabin (McGraw-Hill 2001).

Geoffrey A. Moore has written two classic marketing books about high-technology markets. The first, *Crossing the Chasm* (HarperBusiness 1991), introduces a model of the adoption of new technologies. The second, *Inside the Tornado* (HarperBusiness 1995), is about the market explosion that occurs when new technologies become accessible to mainstream customers.

Chapter 8—The Internet and the World Wide Web

One of the classic introductions to computer networking technologies is *Computer Networks,* 4th edition, by Andrew S. Tanenbaum (Prentice Hall 2002). The book *Interconnections: Bridges, Routers, Switches, and Internetworking Protocols*, 2nd edition, by Radia Perlman (Addison-Wesley 1999) describes many important networking technologies. *Web Protocols and Practice* by Balachander Krishnamurthy and Jennifer Rexford (Addison-Wesley 2001) goes into considerable depth on topics such as caching and traffic measurement.

Richard H. Baker's *Extranets: The Complete Sourcebook* (McGraw-Hill 1997) focuses on creating extranets to link multiple organizations.

An interesting history of the Internet and its predecessor, the ARPANet, can be found in the book *Casting the Net: From ARPAnet to Internet and Beyond* by Peter H. Salus (Addison-Wesley 1995).

For those interested in the details of TCP/IP implementations and how the protocols really work, we recommend *TCP/IP Illustrated, Volume 1: The Protocols* by W. Richard Stevens (Addison-Wesley 1994) and its successors *TCP/IP Illustrated, Volume 2: The Implementation* by Gary R. Wright and W. Richard Stevens (Addison-Wesley 1995), and *TCP/IP Illustrated, Volume 3: TCP for Transactions, HTTP, NNTP, and the UNIX Domain Protocols* by W. Richard Stevens (Addison-Wesley 1996).

For a preview of the changes in IP version 6, see *IPng: Internet Protocol Next Generation,* edited by Scott O. Bradner and Allison Mankin (Addison-Wesley 1996).

Much more information about the Web and its applications can be found in Lincoln Stein's *How to Set Up and Maintaina Web Site,* 2nd edition (Addison-Wesley 1997).

Finally, the Web site of the Internet Engineering Task Force (www.ietf.org) is a good source of information about standards for Internet protocols and provides a view of work in progress for future standards.

Chapter 9—Building Blocks for Internet Commerce

There are many books about Web browsers and servers, as well as about programming environments such as Java, JavaScript, and ActiveX. All of these are changing quickly, and so we suggest seeing what is available about the specific topics of interest when you need the information. The Web sites of the vendors, such as Netscape (www.netscape.com), Sun Microsystems (www.sun.com), IBM (www.ibm.com), and Microsoft (www.microsoft.com) provide a great deal of technical information on their products as well.

For information about J2EE, see *JavaServer Pages*, by Larne Pekowsky (Addison-Wesley 2000) and *Mastering Enterprise JavaBeans,* 2nd edition, by Ed Roman (John Wiley & Sons 2001).

One emerging approach to identifying and finding information online is digital object identifiers, which are described in detail at www.doi.org.

Chapter 10—System Design

For an in-depth discussion of how high-reliability systems are constructed, see *Reliable Computer Systems: Design and Evaluation,* 2nd edition, by Daniel P. Siewiorek and Robert S. Swarz (Digital Press 1992).

Ivar Jacobson's *Object-Oriented Software Engineering: A Use Case Driven Approach* (Addison Wesley 1992) advocates a style in which scenarios for how the software will be used are the basis for design. David Taylor has written an excellent introduction to object technology for managers, *Object Technology: A Manager's Guide,* 2nd edition (Addison-Wesley 1998). Steve McConnell has written some very good books about software development and project management; see *Code Complete* (Microsoft Press

1993), *Rapid Development* (Microsoft Press 1996), and *Software Project Survival Guide* (Microsoft Press 1997).

For programming in the small, *The Practice of Programming* by Brian Kernighan and Rob Pike (Addison-Wesley 1999), *Programming Pearls* by Jon Bentley (Addison-Wesley 2000), and *Extreme Programming Explained* by Kent Beck (Addison-Wesley 2000) are a great place to start.

To see how things can go wrong, see *Software Failure: Management Failure* by Stephen Flowers (John Wiley & Sons 1996).

Chapter 11—XML and Web Services

XML is so popular that there are multiple shelves of books about it in typical technical bookstores, but we recommend Elliotte Rusty Harold and W. Scott Means's *XML in a Nutshell* (O'Reilly 2001) and Michael Kay's *XSLT Programmer's Reference*, 2nd edition (Wrox Press 2001).

Chapter 12—Creating and Managing Content

As with browsers and servers, there is a plethora of books about HTML and its variants. For some topics, the Web itself is the best reference. For example, more information about cascading style sheets can be found at the Web site of the World Wide Web Consortium (www.w3.org).

Adobe's Web site (www.adobe.com) contains information about PDF along with free software for viewing PDF files on various systems.

Martin Nemzow's *Building CyberStores* (McGraw-Hill 1997), focuses on examples and content development for Internet commerce sites.

Programming for the World: A Guide to Internationalization by Sandra Martin O'Donnell (Prentice Hall 1994) predates Internet commerce but is nevertheless a good reference to issues of multiple languages and cultures.

Chapter 13—Cryptography

For a comprehensive discussion of cryptographic algorithms and protocols, there is no better reference than Bruce Schneier's *Applied Cryptography,* 2nd edition (John Wiley & Sons 1997). Richard E. Smith's *Internet Cryptography* (Addison-Wesley 1997) is an accessible discussion of the uses of cryptography for building secure systems on the Internet. Eric Rescorla's *SSL and TLS* (Addison-Wesley 2001) goes into exhaustive detail on the design and implementation of the Web's premier secure protocols. David Kahn's *The Codebreakers: The Story of Secret Writing,* 2nd edition (Macmillan 1997) is a fascinating history of cryptography.

Cracking DES by the Electronic Frontier Foundation (O'Reilly 1998) tells the story of the effort to break the DES cipher by brute force attack.

We also cannot resist the category of crypto-thriller: try Neal Stevenson's *Cryptonomicon* (Avon 1999) and Robert Harris's *Enigma* (Ivy 1996).

Chapter 14—Security

Web Security and Commerce by Simson Garfinkel with Gene Spafford (O'Reilly 1997) is a useful reference on security issues for the World Wide Web. The classic work on firewalls is *Firewalls and Internet Security: Repelling the Wily Hacker* by William R. Cheswick and Steven M. Bellovin (Addison-Wesley 1994). We also recommend *White Hat Security Arsenal* by Aviel D. Rubin (Addison-Wesley 2001).

Building Secure Software by John Viega and Gary McGraw (Addison-Wesley 2001) discusses how to design and build secure systems correctly from the ground up. The particular security issues involved with database systems are described in detail in *Database Security* by Silvana Castano et al. (Addison-Wesley 1995).

Secure Electronic Commerce, 2nd edition, by Warwick Ford and Michael S. Baum (Prentice Hall 2000) focuses on the technical and legal aspects of public-key technology.

Bruce Schneier's *Secrets and Lies: Digital Security in a Networked World* (John Wiley & Sons 2000) is a very accessible discussion of computer security topics.

Chapter 15—Payment Systems

Peter Wayner's *Digital Cash: Commerce on the Net* (Academic Press 1996) discusses many payment systems that have been developed on the Internet, along with the underlying concepts of security and cryptography. At a somewhat higher level, *Digital Money* by Daniel C. Lynch and Leslie Lundquist (John Wiley & Sons 1996) is a useful executive briefing on payment systems for Internet transactions.

Chapter 17—Transaction Processing

C. J. Date's *An Introduction to Database Systems,* 7th edition (Addison-Wesley 2000) is a classic book about database systems from a technical point of view. An authoritative reference on transaction systems is *Transaction Processing: Concepts and Techniques* by Jim Gray and Andreas Reuter (Morgan Kaufmann 1993). *Principles of Transaction Processing* by Philip A. Bernstein and Eric Newcomer (Morgan Kaufmann 1997) is a somewhat more accessible introduction to transaction systems.

Chapter 18—Integration with Enterprise Applications

Regarding databases and their applications, we recommend again *An Introduction to Database Systems* by C. J. Date (Addison-Wesley 2000). *The Data Model Resource Book* series by Len Silverston et al. (Wiley 1997 and 2001) is an excellent compendium of database structures encountered in business applications.

Directly on point is *Enterprise Application Integration* by David S. Linthicum (Addison-Wesley 2000).

For the various ERP systems, we like *Implementing J.D. Edwards One World* by Robert W. Starinsky (Premier 2001), *Oracle Financials Handbook* by David James, Graham H. Seibert, and Joseph Costantino (McGraw-Hill 1999), *Implementing SAP Sales and Distribution* by Glynn Williams (Osborne McGraw-Hill 2000), and *Essential Guide to PeopleSoft Development and Customization* by Tony Delia, Galina Landres, Isidor Rivera, and Prakash Sankaran (Manning 2000).

Chapter 19—Reliable and Scalable Systems

Scaling for E-Business by Daniel A. Menasce and Virgilio A. F. Almeida (Prentice Hall 2000) is an extensive discussion of the technologies, models, performance evaluation, and capacity planning for e-business systems.

Chapter 20—Mobile and Wireless Systems

Programming Applications with the Wireless Application Protocol by Steve Mann (John Wiley & Sons 2000) is a good reference for WAP and the Wireless Markup Language (WML).

Chapter 22—The Future of Internet Commerce

There are many books that look forward to the future of computing, communications, and business. Two in particular that touch on the uses of the Internet for commerce are *What Will Be: How the New World of Information Will Change Our Lives* by Michael Dertouzos (HarperCollins 1997) and *Release 2.0* by Esther Dyson (Broadway Books 1997).

Index

informIT